STUDIES IN FINANCIAL OPTIMIZATION AND RISK MANAGEMENT

FINANCIAL SERVICES: EFFICIENCY AND RISK MANAGEMENT

STUDIES IN FINANCIAL OPTIMIZATION AND RISK MANAGEMENT

CONSTANTIN ZOPOUNIDIS - SERIES EDITOR –

TECHNICAL UNIVERSITY OF CRETE

Studies in Financial Optimization and Risk Management (Series Description)
Prof. Constantin Zopounidis (Editor)
2008. ISBN: xxx

Computational Techniques in Economics and Finance
Constantin Zopounidis (Editor)
2011. ISBN: 978-1-61324-558-3

Financial Services: Efficiency and Risk Management
*Meryem Duygun Fethi, Chrysovalantis Gaganis, Fotios Pasiouras and
Constantin Zopounidis (Editors)*
2012. ISBN: 978-1-62100-560-5

STUDIES IN FINANCIAL OPTIMIZATION AND RISK MANAGEMENT

FINANCIAL SERVICES: EFFICIENCY AND RISK MANAGEMENT

MERYEM DUYGUN FETHI,
CHRYSOVALANTIS GAGANIS,
FOTIOS PASIOURAS AND
CONSTANTIN ZOPOUNIDIS
EDITORS

Nova Science Publishers, Inc.
New York

Copyright © 2012 by Nova Science Publishers, Inc.

All rights reserved. No part of this book may be reproduced, stored in a retrieval system or transmitted in any form or by any means: electronic, electrostatic, magnetic, tape, mechanical photocopying, recording or otherwise without the written permission of the Publisher.

For permission to use material from this book please contact us:
Telephone 631-231-7269; Fax 631-231-8175
Web Site: http://www.novapublishers.com

NOTICE TO THE READER

The Publisher has taken reasonable care in the preparation of this book, but makes no expressed or implied warranty of any kind and assumes no responsibility for any errors or omissions. No liability is assumed for incidental or consequential damages in connection with or arising out of information contained in this book. The Publisher shall not be liable for any special, consequential, or exemplary damages resulting, in whole or in part, from the readers' use of, or reliance upon, this material. Any parts of this book based on government reports are so indicated and copyright is claimed for those parts to the extent applicable to compilations of such works.

Independent verification should be sought for any data, advice or recommendations contained in this book. In addition, no responsibility is assumed by the publisher for any injury and/or damage to persons or property arising from any methods, products, instructions, ideas or otherwise contained in this publication.

This publication is designed to provide accurate and authoritative information with regard to the subject matter covered herein. It is sold with the clear understanding that the Publisher is not engaged in rendering legal or any other professional services. If legal or any other expert assistance is required, the services of a competent person should be sought. FROM A DECLARATION OF PARTICIPANTS JOINTLY ADOPTED BY A COMMITTEE OF THE AMERICAN BAR ASSOCIATION AND A COMMITTEE OF PUBLISHERS.

Additional color graphics may be available in the e-book version of this book.

LIBRARY OF CONGRESS CATALOGING-IN-PUBLICATION DATA

Financial services : efficiency and risk management / editors, Meryem Duygun Fethi ... [et al.].
    p. cm.
 Includes index.
 ISBN 978-1-62100-560-5 (hardcover)
 1. Banks and banking--European Union countries. 2. Bank mergers--European Union countries. 3. Stockholder wealth--European Union countries. I. Fethi, Meryem Duygun.
 HG2974.F5646 2011
 332.1094--dc23

2011035669

Published by Nova Science Publishers, Inc. + New York

CONTENTS

Preface		vii
Chapter 1	Consolidation and Performance in the European Banking Industry: A Survey *Hodian N. Urio and Sailesh Tanna*	1
Chapter 2	Assessing the Adverse Effects of Interbank Funds on Bank Efficiency through Using Semiparametric and Nonparametric Methods *Ahmet Faruk Aysan, Gürdal Ertek and Seçil Öztürk*	41
Chapter 3	One-Stage Approaches and Two-Stage Approaches in Data Envelopment Analysis: How Appropriate Are They for Analyzing Business Process Efficiency? *Anne Dohmen and Matteo Sottocornola*	63
Chapter 4	Measurement of Commercial Banks Performance in EU Countries: A Multi-Criteria Approach *Christos Lemonakis, Ioannis Strikos and Constantin Zopounidis*	93
Chapter 5	Market Crashes and Basel Regulations. The Case of Developed, Emerging and Frontier Stock Markets *Adrián F. Rossignolo*	139
Chapter 6	An Analysis of European Central Counterparty Clearing *Alessandra Tanda*	163

Chapter 7	Do Greek Mutual Funds Investing Abroad Outperform? *Stephanos Papadamou and Konstantina Kiriazi*	**187**
Chapter 8	Accounting Choice Theory: Derivatives Fair Value In Banks In Brazil *Bruna Perlingeiro Iannazzo, Luiz Nelson Guedes de Carvalho, Gerlando Augusto S. Franco de Lima and Iran Siqueira Lima*	**205**
Index		**231**

PREFACE

Over the last decade or so, firms in the financial services industry witnessed fundamental changes in their operating environment, such as deregulation, internationalization, technological innovations, mergers and acquisitions, and more recently a global financial crisis. This book discusses various issues that relate to those changes, while placing particular emphasis on aspects of efficiency and risk management. Topics that are discussed in the book include among others, mergers and acquisitions, liquidity in the interbank market, the evaluation of bank performance with multicriteria decision aid and frontier techniques, value-at-risk modeling, central clearing counterparties, mutual funds, and derivatives and earnings management.

Chapter 1 - This chapter reviews the literature associated with the recent wave of bank mergers and acquisitions in Europe and analyses the evidence with regard to shareholder wealth creation and efficiency. The review provides an understanding of the main motives associated with bank mergers and acquisitions, addresses the main issues driving shareholder wealth creation, discusses the key developments and barriers associated with banking sector consolidation, and highlights the importance of cross-border consolidation in Europe. The literature is reviewed in conjunction with developments in US banking sector consolidation to provide a comparative account of what has occurred over the past twenty years or so.

Chapter 2 - This chapter investigates the relationship between interbank funds and efficiencies for the commercial banks operating in Turkey between 2001 and 2006. Data Envelopment Analysis (DEA) is executed to find the efficiency scores of the banks for each year, and fixed effects panel data regression is carried out, with the efficiency scores being the response variable. It is observed that interbank funds (ratio) has negative effects on bank efficiency, while bank capitalization and loan ratio have positive, and profitability has insignificant effects. This chapter serves as novel evidence that interbank funds can have adverse effects in an emerging market.

Chapter 3 - Data Envelopment Analysis (DEA) is an established method for non-parametric efficiency measurement and it has been widely applied in studying the efficiency of financial institutions. Furthermore, different approaches have been developed to further analyze the results of a DEA in order to get an indication for causes for efficiency or in order to control for environmental factors. This paper will focus on a special application of DEA for the measurement of efficiency of business processes. As an example, a banking back- office process, namely securities settlement and clearing, is analyzed. By using real production data, this paper examines to which degree the commonly applied one-stage and two-stage approaches in DEA are suitable for analyzing the influence of specific categorical variables on business process efficiency. Our findings indicate that both approaches deliver similar results. We also find that different process steps are affected differently by the categorical variable. However, it is shown that existing models of one- and two-stage approaches cannot be applied one-to-one but need to be adjusted for their application on business process level. Furthermore, we conclude that generally the two-stage approach seems to be more appropriate and value-adding to the analysis of the influence of categorical variables on business process efficiency.

Chapter 4 - The European Banking sector has undergone significant changes over the last few years. Taking into account the current legislative framework of the Second Banking Directive for the enhancement of stability in the financial system as well as the new reformed economic environment after the outburst of the 2007 financial crisis in the American banking sector and its contagious effects around the world, the aim of this chapter is to evaluate the recent performance and efficiency of commercial banks operating in the 15 EU countries over the period 2005-2009. The analysis draws upon a multicriteria decision aid approach and a number of bank-specific characteristics collected annually from the consolidated financial statements of a sample of 162 European Commercial banks. This chapter examines the performance of the national banking sectors' in the areas of asset quality, capital structure, cost structure, liquidity and profitability. Then, the multicriteria Promethee methodology is utilized in order to rank the banks according to their performance over a set of multiple criteria, while the ranking result is used to provide a comparative analysis of their strong and weak points for each country separately. The results indicate that, despite the differences observed across the national banking sectors, the adverse macroeconomic and financial markets conditions have severely decreased the accounts of commercial banks in European Union and have negatively affected the majority of their financial indices.

Chapter 5 - Following the subprime crisis of 2007-2008 which uncovered shortfalls in capital levels of most financial institutions, the Basel Committee on Banking Supervision decided to strengthen current regulations contained in Basel II. While maintaining the Internal Models Approach based on VaR, a stressed VaR calculated over highly strung periods is to be added to present directives to compute the new Minimum Capital Requirements. However, as the Basel Committee on Banking Supervision refrained from demanding a particular VaR technique, the adoption of the appropriate specification remains a subject of paramount importance as it determines the financial condition of the firm in the event of abrupt market swings. In this chapter I explore the performance of several models to compute Minimum Capital Requirements in the context of Developed, Emerging and Frontier stock markets within the current Basel II and the future Basel III capital structures. Considering the evidence gathered, two major contributions arise: a) Heavy-tailed distributions –specifically those belonging to the Extreme Value family- emerge as the most accurate technique to model market risks, hence preventing huge capital deficits under Basel II regulations; b) The application of such methods could allow slight modifications to the present mandate and either avoid the stressed VaR factor or at least reduce its weight, thus mitigating its huge impact regarding the enhancement of the capital base. Therefore, I suggest that the inclusion of Extreme Value distributions in VaR models in the respective supervisory accords should reduce the costs associated with the development of accurate schemes and foster healthier financial structures.

Chapter 6 - Central Counterparty Clearing (CCP Clearing) is a process by which a third party interposes itself in every trade, replacing the original counterparties, thereby concentrating and redistributing counterparty risk. The importance of CCP Clearing has been recognised by the literature and by the European regulator. The latter created some Study Groups to investigate the role of these institutions in the context of European market integration, to achieve greater efficiency and to ease cross-border transactions. A very important issue is represented by the costs of services provided by Central Counterparties to traders. In 2006 the major Stock Exchanges, Central Counterparties (CCPs) and Central Securities Depositories (CSDs) voluntary subscribed to the "Code of Conduct for Clearing and Settlement". The aim of the Code was to foster integration and efficiency of European equity markets by improving transparency of price lists, establishing access and interoperability conditions, unbundling services and implementing accounting separation. Starting from the results of the European Commission on trading and post-trading costs the chapter focuses on prices charged by some European CCPs on the regulated equity markets. Part of the literature claims that the form of integration of trading and post-trading services providers can determine the level of prices. Therefore the chapter briefly describes the structures of the institutions operating along the value chain. The analysis of pricing highlights some discrepancies with part of the literature and it also shows how clearing fees have been reduced since the introduction of the Code of Conduct.

Chapter 7 - By investigating Greek Mutual funds investing abroad for the period 2002 to 2008, this chapter tries to shed light on the home bias puzzle from a small country concentrated fund industry. By calculating traditional measures of performance and following rolling regression technique the paper provides evidence that Greek fund managers investing abroad do not outperform the market and do not present any timing skills. In order to achieve better performance than their benchmark they choose to follow different asset allocation as it is implied by our analysis.

Chapter 8 - The purpose is to verify whether there are Earnings Management practices (regarding Accounting Choices) resulting from the impact of accounting for derivatives in Bank institutions available in Brazil under Brazil's Central Bank supervision. One of the innovations presented is that in addition to the use of all Banks on the specified date, which consists of a census, those practices have their focus on Accounting Choice Theory. The approach of the paper is an empirical-analytical one, and its general hypothesis is that there is no Earnings Management for all considered institutions. Additionally, the method considers the panel data analysis and regressions with dummy variables. The classification for the use of these variables includes: size of the Banks; origin; differenced levels of Corporate Governance; and accompaniment by analysts. The data range from 2002 to 2008, for 158 Banks, with 1044 observations. In the models, the evidence points out that it was not possible to identify Earnings Management through Accounting Choices. It means that empirical evidence was not found in the Banks in Brazil, regardless of the size, origin, differenced levels of Corporate Governance and accompaniment by analysts using accounting for derivatives as a tool for Earnings Management.

In: Financial Services: Efficiency and Risk Management
Editors: M. D. Fethi, C. Gaganis et al.

ISBN: 978-1-62100-560-5
© 2012 Nova Science Publishers, Inc.

Chapter 1

CONSOLIDATION AND PERFORMANCE IN THE EUROPEAN BANKING INDUSTRY: A SURVEY

Hodian N. Urio and Sailesh Tanna**
[1] Mount Meru University, Arusha, Tanzania.
[2] Coventry University, UK.

ABSTRACT

This chapter reviews the literature associated with the recent wave of bank mergers and acquisitions in Europe and analyses the evidence with regard to shareholder wealth creation and efficiency. The review provides an understanding of the main motives associated with bank mergers and acquisitions, addresses the main issues driving shareholder wealth creation, discusses the key developments and barriers associated with banking sector consolidation, and highlights the importance of cross-border consolidation in Europe. The literature is reviewed in conjunction with developments in US banking sector consolidation to provide a comparative account of what has occurred over the past twenty years or so.

1. INTRODUCTION

The banking industry throughout the world has experienced considerable changes in the past two decades, owing to factors such as globalization, the spread of information technology, deregulation and the easing of restrictive legislation that previously had left banks without flexibility in the way they have recently conducted their operations across the globe. In the European Union (EU), a wave of bank mergers[1] and acquisitions that began in the 1980s and intensified in the 1990s led to a decline in the number of EU banks from around 9600 to just over 7400 in the period 1997-2003 (ECB, 2004a). This consolidation

---

[*] Email: hodianurio@yahoo.com
[*] Corresponding author, Email: s.tanna@coventry.ac.uk
[1] Throughout this chapter the term merger is used to also mean acquisition, takeover or amalgamation. A wave of such activity is taken to imply consolidation of the industry.

process in the European banking industry resulted in a decrease of almost 23% in the number of banks and has been attributed to technological development, deregulation, launching of the Euro, and enhanced competition (Campa and Hernando, 2006). Most of these mergers occurred among domestic banks which aimed to consolidate their competitive positions within national borders. Other firms in the financial services industry, particularly in the insurance sector, similarly consolidated their positions nationally by engaging in transactions that were mainly domestic. Some merger deals have also taken place amalgamating banks, securities firms and insurance companies to form financial conglomerates (Cabral *et al.*, 2002).

However, bank merger activity declined after 2000 as a result of the slowdown in economic growth and the downward valuation of firms by the stock markets. Mergers in the financial services sector followed almost the same pattern of the consolidation wave, peaking in the late 1990s and then declining after 2000. Between 1997 and 2000, however, the number of merger transactions in the financial services sector rose by more than 47%. As noted above, this period marked a significant change in the economic environment leading up to the launch of the Euro and altered the structure of the financial sector. For instance, Cabral *et al.* (2002) point out that most mergers prior to this time involved small firms which aimed at lowering their costs to improve efficiency. As economic integration deepened among the EU countries, institutions involved in mergers changed focus to pursue market power strategy in order to consolidate their competitive position. Towards the end of the 1990s, banks overtook other financial sector institutions in accounting for most domestic mergers especially in the Euro zone countries.

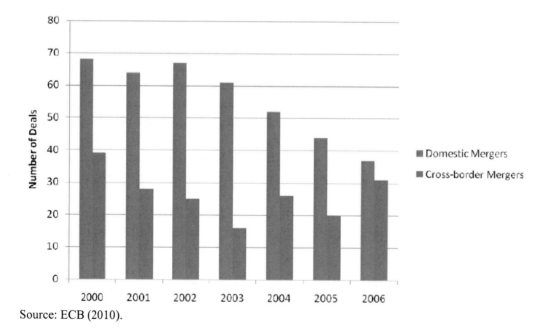

Source: ECB (2010).

Figure 1. EU Bank Mergers: Controlling and Minority Stakes (Numbers).

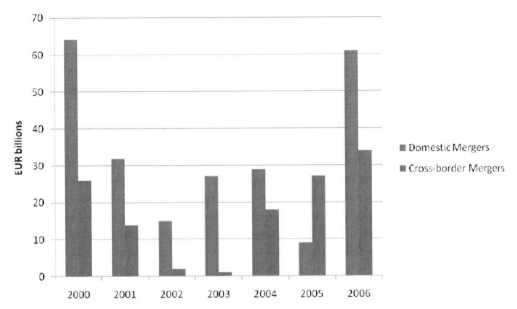

Source: ECB (2010).

Figure 2. EU Bank Mergers: Controlling and Minority Stakes (Values).

Figures 1 and 2, taken from ECB (2010), show the trend in both domestic and cross-border bank mergers by number and value respectively for the EU-27 countries in the period 2000-2006.[2] Cross-border mergers have been far fewer than domestic mergers within Europe and concern about this was raised by the European Central Bank in a report which observes that international mergers in the EU often involved an institution from outside the Union rather than between banks from different countries of the EU (ECB, 2000). In the single European market, banks were expected to establish their presence in a larger geographical region but they focused on consolidating their positions in the domestic market as they faced an increasingly competitive environment (Campa and Hernando, 2006). This meant that cross-border transactions were fewer although this activity has increased more recently (ECB, 2010). In a different report, ECB (2006) documents the number of credit institutions in the EU-25 as having declined from 9,747 in 2001 to 8,684 in 2005, due mostly to domestic mergers which outnumbered cross-border deals.

Increased consolidation of the banking market within national borders is seen by many observers as an attempt by EU countries to create "national champions" before they can compete at the international level. While this may be advantageous for the banks, it is a matter of concern for European policy makers as concentration increases in the banking market. According to ECB (2006), the average five-firm concentration ratio in the EU-25 rose from 33% in 2001 to 45% in 2004. Where concentration has been high and anti-trust issues have been raised, a natural response from European Commission has been to discourage domestic mergers and promote cross-border deals. In reality, domestic mergers that have created large banking institutions have also attracted cross-border bidders seeking to gain market power in the host nation. Typically, bidders find it more efficient to acquire one

---

[2] The figures include all deals with controlling and minority stakes. Cross-border mergers are intra-EU27 deals involving a non-domestic acquirer. Original source: Zephyr Bureau Van Dyjk database.

relatively large bank with a sizeable domestic market share than take over several small banks in order to achieve market power.

Many banks have sought to engage in mergers expecting to gain in efficiency through lower costs and higher profits, enhance their competitive position, cross-sell products upon gaining a larger customer base, and/or diversify risk geographically. Evidence pertaining to the performance aspects of banking consolidation and its impact on shareholder wealth creation is generally wide-ranging and mixed, given the various motives and implications associated with bank mergers. The purpose of this chapter is to review the broad literature on the subject and provide an understanding of the main motives and issues associated with the consolidation process that has been taking place in the banking industry, together with evidence on performance relating to shareholder value and efficiency. While the primary focus is on the EU banking industry, evidence is also drawn from US and international studies which typically serve as benchmark for comparison purposes. Comparison of the EU evidence with that of US seems particularly appropriate owing to the ongoing process of consolidation in the US banking industry and the fact that the majority of bank merger evidence is based on US data. Thus, the review of the literature offers a broader perspective of what has occurred in both the US and European banking markets over the past twenty years or so.

In an attempt to address a broad set of issues discussed in the literature, the rest of this chapter is organised as follows. Section 2 presents an overview of the motives for mergers in the banking industry, distinguishing between internally and externally driven motives as well as providing a perspective from the European Central Bank and the broader literature highlighting efficiency and diversification motives behind bank mergers. Section 3 turns attention to the performance implications and discusses a number of merger success factors associated with value creation for targets and bidders. Section 4 outlines theories that predict shareholder value gains from mergers. Section 5 focuses on key issues that have fostered European bank mergers and the evidence relating to shareholder value creation. Section 6 then looks at broader issues and evidence pertaining to cross-border bank mergers which represent an important part of the banking sector consolidation process in the EU. Section 7 discusses some of the regulatory issues and further developments associated with the process of banking sector consolidation in the EU. Section 8 complements the preceding discussion by providing a comparative account and evaluation of US and EU evidence on shareholder value and efficiency aspects of bank merger performance. Section 9 finally concludes and the two appendices at the end of the chapter provide additional source of information on empirical studies and legislative measures associated with banking sector deregulation in the EU and US.

2. MERGER MOTIVES

Merger motives may be grouped into internally-driven and externally-driven motives, but can also be classified in other ways. The European Central Bank, for example, puts merger motives into four main groups as reported below. Merger motives are also seen as either efficiency-enhancing or resource-pooling in some of the management strategy literature.

2.1. Internally-Driven Motives

Synergy
This is the concept that implies that when two firms combine, the resulting entity acquires a greater value than the sum of its parts and is an argument advanced most often to justify mergers. According to Tourani-Rad and Van Beek (1999), synergy is achieved when the costs of the combined entity are less than the sum of those of the individual firms, and the reduction in costs is attributed to economies of scale and scope, although they also cite gains from reduced management inefficiencies and from reduced risk due to diversification.

Economies of Scale
Banks merge in order to benefit from economies of scale. These occur where one or more of the consolidating banks are operating at less than their optimal level. Economies of scale may be present in any part of the banking business including finance, marketing, management, and operations, and the combined entity benefits from exploitation of these economies. The evidence from studies that have examined economies of scale from bank mergers is generally mixed. Some early studies (Miller and Noulas, 1996; Vander Vennet, 1998) found economies only in small banks, while others (Molyneux *et al.,* 1996; Vander Vennet, 2002) find scale economies even in large European banks. Berger and Mester (1997) find scale economies in large US banks.

Economies of Scope
For institutions in the financial services industry, these occur where the merged entity is able to offer a broader range of financial products using the same assets the former firms owned separately. These are cost-based scope economies. Revenue-based scope economies are realized when, using combined inputs, the same or more financial products than before are now distributed to a larger customer base. Economies of scope are also cited quite frequently as a motive for mergers (Amel *et al.*, 2004).

Market Power
A bank with market power can either raise the price of its products, suffering a loss in sales but not profit, or it can increase its sales by having to lower its price and not affect profit adversely. The bank also has the flexibility to differentiate its products, and by exercising its market power it can act as a barrier to entry, a situation that encourages the incumbent to charge higher prices for its services. This is often a concern for regulators who are always mindful of attempts by two of the largest banks in a market to merge, as the resulting bank would then wield immense market power. Typically, a bank with a small degree of market power may be the target of acquisition by a larger bank, with the purpose of deploying the combined assets more profitably (Moore, 1996).

Inefficient Management
The inefficient management hypothesis suggests that a firm led by an inefficient management will be taken over by another with a management that can run it more efficiently (Berger *et al.*, 2000b). Non-maximization of shareholders' wealth is often cited as the basis for this takeover. Proponents of the hypothesis argue that shareholders, unable to change the management through other means, will seek or agree to a merger by selling off their shares at

a profitable price to facilitate the takeover. A counter argument is that some shareholders expecting better future performance, and therefore greater value for themselves, will seek to extract a high enough price from the bidder in order to compensate them for the future gains they will be foregoing, and this process may render the acquisition ultimately unattractive to the bidder. Results from studies that have investigated the inefficient management hypothesis are mixed (Pasiouras *et al.*, 2011).

In terms of yielding efficiency, there are two specific cases of the inefficient management hypothesis, namely, the *Relative Efficiency Hypothesis* and the *Low Efficiency Hypothesis*. The former proposes that following acquisition of a less efficient target, the bidder can implement value-enhancing changes including removal of the target's management. This view also suggests that the lower the efficiency of the target the greater the potential for post-merger efficiency improvement. The latter proposes improved efficiency for the merged firm if either the target or both the bidder and the target were less efficient than their industry peers. It also suggests that improvement is likely to be greater depending on the gap in inefficiency between either or both the bidder and the target and their peers (Akhavein *et al.*, 1997; Berger *et al.*, 1999).

Diversification of Risk

Banks generally diversify their assets in an attempt to minimize credit and other risks (e.g. interest rate, liquidity, etc) which could have adverse impact on profits. Diversification of risk is also achieved through mergers by expanding geographically and by taking on different products and developing new ones using newly-acquired capability. Diversification is often the main driver of cross-sector conglomerates and cross-border mergers in banking (Berger *et al.*, 2000).

Agency-Related Motives

Most pre-2000 literature especially for the US indicates that bank mergers are value-destroying. This persistent finding led to studies that sought to explain why bank mergers happen when they were not beneficial to shareholders. The prevailing view has been that mergers are motivated by management seeking to enhance their own utility at the expense of shareholders. The existence of agency costs in organizations where ownership is separated from management allows the latter with the opportunity to fix their compensation according to the size of the organization rather than value, which motivates them to engage in mergers even if they are not value creating from the shareholders' perspective. Proponents of this hypothesis believe that management will pursue those goals that enhance their compensation or prestige through empire-building. US studies investigating this hypothesis have shown a positive correlation between firm size and executive compensation. Bliss and Rosen (2001), for example, find merger-related changes correlated to increases in compensation, the latter occurring irrespective of any value creation or efficiency improvements. Rosen (2004) also reports that the likelihood that CEOs will receive higher compensation through acquisitions motivates them to engage in mergers. Hughes *et al.* (2003) find that banks where managements have large ownership stake are casual in choosing merger partners and end up with value destroying acquisitions. Anderson *et al.* (2004) find that post-merger CEO compensation is correlated with anticipated merger gains in shareholder value as measured by announcement day effects. Other compensation packages are structured to take account of post-merger productivity.

A slightly different hypothesis but which also points to managements making decisions in their own interests posits that managers may wish to lead a "quiet life" upon achieving a large size for their firm. This allows them to relax from the pressures of competition by exercising market power to maintain the firm's well-being, and avoid the anxieties of having to improve efficiency and performance (Berger and Hannan, 1998).

In contrast to the pre-2000 US literature, evidence of value-destruction from managerial entrenchment is somewhat less supportive in European banks. The emerging view from early European research that produced less strong evidence of negative merger performance than reported by US studies has been reinforced by more recent evidence (discussed below) that is actually suggestive of positive gains from bank mergers. The results of Corvoisier and Gropp (2002), who examined bank mergers in ten European countries, suggest some evidence of management seeking the "quiet life" as increased banking sector concentration gave rise to less competition in the pricing of demand deposits. On the other hand, in their study of post-merger deposit pricing in Italy, Focarelli and Panetta (2003) report long-term increases in deposit rates especially for more efficient banks, a result which suggests the absence of managerial motives in that market.

Hubris
Sometimes managements are less careful in their decisions, particularly in times of record good performance or when the economic prospects are promising. If opportunities arise for mergers in such periods, managements may blunder due to over-optimism (Roll, 1986) and might therefore engage in mergers that turn out to be value-destroying.

2.2. Externally-Driven Motives

Three major factors are recognized as the external drivers of merger activity in the financial services industry.

Deregulation
Individually, countries have done a lot to liberalize the financial services sector and to remove barriers to greater competition. At the international level, various legislations have been passed in order to increase competition and promote integration in Europe, and to encourage diversification across state borders in the U.S. (Berger *et al.*, 1999; Group of Ten, 2001).

Technological Advances
Changes in technology have affected remarkably the way banks operate, and the speed at which they transact business across the globe, making it easier to engage in mergers. Overall, the impact of technology has been positive, with larger banks having benefited more (Goddard *et al.*, 2001).

Globalization
Globalization has led to increased competition in banking (Goddard *et al.*, 2001). Greater competition has in turn led to consolidation, as institutions sought to increase in size or avoid failure. With a larger size a firm benefits from economies of scale, increases in efficiency and

can therefore compete better. Both deregulation and technological development have helped the globalization process.

2.3. The ECB on Merger Motives

According to the European Central Bank (ECB, 2000), there have been four main motives for mergers in the financial services industry.

Improvement in Efficiency and Profitability
Some analysts believe that a merger automatically results in higher profitability. Although this is mostly the case, it is not always so. Not all mergers succeed in achieving their intended goal in the short period immediately following merger. Even when an efficient institution takes over a less efficient one the combined firm may go through a difficult period for a number of years before it attains the previous efficiency level of the bidder.

Expansion of Product Range and Client Base
This applies more to domestic mergers, with bancassurance transactions offering the typical example. Usually the insurer decides to ensure continued loyalty of existing customers and attraction of new ones by introducing bank products.

Expansion to Other Geographical Locations
For many organizations, acquiring a local business in another country is the only way of establishing business in that market. However, such deals do not always succeed. Different corporate cultures, language barriers, and environmental factors beyond the control of the new organization may lead to failure of the consolidation.

Maximization of Shareholder Value
This is often put forward in the literature as a key motivational factor for consolidation (Berger *et al.* 1999). However, there is also the view that top management are usually concerned with only the major shareholders, most of whom show little interest in the finer details of the deal, and generally avoid involvement in any decision-making.

2.4. Efficiency Enhancement

Although in the literature efficiency is often taken as being embedded in synergy, it is also considered by some as deserving to stand on its own as a motive for merger irrespective of the role of management. It is a value-maximizing motive due to gains that can be realized through cost savings from removal of overlapping operations, streamlining of back-office functions, shedding-off workers, and so on. Generally, efficiency ranks high as a motive for value maximization in bank mergers, considering the potential benefits that can be derived from economies of scale/scope, risk reduction by product/geographical diversification, and taxation. Vander Vennet (1996) finds that efficiency gains can be achieved in both domestic and cross-border mergers where bidder and target are of equal size. However, some studies report that post-merger operating efficiency, profitability, and staff productivity of both bidder and target do not improve significantly relative to non-merging institutions (Berger and Humphrey, 1992; Rhoades, 1993).

2.5. Resource Pooling

Combining special skills and resources by two partners to achieve goals common to both or specific to each one individually is a major motive of strategic alliances (Varadarajan and Cunningham, 1995). Mergers are in fact a tool for expansion and improvement of the resources pool in order to achieve rapid growth or fast-track diversification. For example, where the bidder has an advantage in corporate banking matters, while the targets is well endowed in retail banking and its branch network, then combining these complementary assets is consistent with the desire to promote the universal bank concept. Post-merger challenges at the strategic level include the need to adjust continuously in order to reposition the institution, build the flexibility necessary for developing new products in shortened lead-times, and keep up with the fast pace of technological growth.

3. MERGER SUCCESS: FACTORS EXPLAINING VALUE CREATION

Since it is generally accepted that mergers create value for targets, the focus of many recent studies has been to identify how value is created for bidders. Studies for the EU and the US, the two regions where most investigation has been carried out, have approached the subject with this assumption. Five categories of factors are identified in the literature as having a positive impact on merger value creation in the sense of generating abnormal returns around the date of the announcement of the merger deal.[3] These are considered separately below.[4]

Profitability and Efficiency

Included in this category are the two main cases of the inefficient management hypothesis explained above. The *Relative Efficiency Hypothesis*, which states that efficiency gains (in profit or cost) arise from better management skills of the bidder, can be applied to manage the assets of the less efficient target. The hypothesis suggests that if before acquisition the bidder is more efficient than the target, it can bring the latter's efficiency up to its own level after merger (Berger *et al.*, 2000b). On the other hand, the *Low Efficiency Hypothesis* proposes that the merger event may "wake up" the bidder's management by providing it the "excuse" for carrying out improvements that can lead to higher profitability for the combined institution. These hypotheses have been tested by Pilloff (1996) who finds that post-event improvement in profitability and cost efficiency is positively associated with

---

[3] The abnormal return is the amount by which an actual share price exceeds the share price predicted by an asset-pricing model, and is determined by an event-study methodology.

[4] In addition, agency related factors have been used (mainly in US studies) to explain value destruction or other non-value maximising objectives linked to managerial motives, as noted further below.

the value creation of bank merger transactions. Also, Hawawini and Swary (1990) observe that mergers create value for both bidders and targets when there is a considerable gap in their efficiencies, and that greater value will be created with a larger efficiency gap. As the efficiency gap closes, value creation declines and may approach zero. In fact, some studies find that the higher efficiency of a target has a negative influence on value creation (Houston and Ryngaert, 1994; Madura and Wiant, 1994).

A standard measure of efficiency used in most studies is the Cost to Income Ratio (CIR) which is also sometimes interpreted as a measure of cost efficiency. Another commonly used cost-based accounting measure of efficiency is the Cost to Asset Ratio (CARA), while the most widely used measure of profitability is the Return on Equity (ROE). Frontier and other value-based measures have also been used (Kohers *et al*, 2000; Aggarwal et al, 2006; Fiordelisi, 2008; Chronopoulos *et al*, 2010; Urio, 2011). Irrespective of the measure of performance used, most studies find that lower pre-merger profitability and efficiency of the target (or higher the relative difference in the bidder's favour) improve post-transaction excess returns for the bidder. In their investigation of the poor performance of foreign bank subsidiaries, Peek *et al*. (1999) also find that the target's post-transaction profitability gains are largely influenced by the pre-transaction profitability difference between the target and the bidder, and that cost efficiency gains as measured by CIR are determined largely by the CIR difference between the firms before the transaction.

Relative Size

The asset size of the target relative to that of the bidder is also considered to be a driver of merger success. For the bidder, smaller targets are easier to acquire and value creation is more assured, despite the smaller scale effects (Beitel *et al*., 2004). Hawawini and Swary (1990) find that the bidder's merger success is positively associated with the bidder's relative size vis-a-vis the target. It is therefore generally assumed that for the bidder the merger is likely to be more successful the larger the difference in its size with that of the target.

Bidder's Experience

An experienced bidder is considered to be better at generating post-merger synergies and therefore more likely to create value. Experience in this case is determined on the basis of minority stake in the target, frequency of involvement in cross-border mergers, and other operations in the (host) country. A bidder with prior experience of the target through minority ownership is better able to value the target through superior knowledge of its financial performance, and is in a better bargaining position to avoid overpayment. DeYoung (1997) finds that the experience of the bidder as measured by the frequency of merger involvement has a positive impact on their cumulative abnormal returns (CARs). Similarly, Zollo and Leshchinkskii (2000) observe a significantly positive association between the bidder's experience and its success determined by significantly positive CARs. Beitel *et al*. (2004), measuring experience by frequency of involvement in mergers, also find its effect statistically significant and positive on merger success of European banks. On the other hand, Kaufman (1988) finds that, for those bidders with prior minority interest, the more a bidder's ownership interest increases the less the premium it pays in subsequent acquisitions. Research also shows that turning from minority to majority control leads to successful investment in emerging markets (Chari *et al.*, 2004). The rationale for this is that, where an institution is underperforming, the market rewards the minority owner who by majority acquisition takes the risk of turning that institution around. These and other results by previous studies have led to the hypothesis that having a minority ownership in a target prior to a merger, and therefore particular experience in the target and the country, increases the chances of the bidder realizing positive value creation upon merger announcement.

Target-Country Characteristics

Some studies find that cross-border mergers with targets in developing countries create greater bidder value (Madura and Wiant, 1994; Kiymaz and Mukherjee, 2000) because mergers there appear to be driven more by potential profit opportunities which are greater than in developed markets where competition is higher. In the literature, both Gross Domestic Product (GDP) and the GDP per capita have been used as proxies for profit opportunities (Buch, 2000), although other researchers prefer to use the annual GDP growth rate as it reflects the prospects for future growth and reveals a country's pace of current development.

In a study of the influence of macroeconomic factors on wealth gains from cross-border US mergers, Kiymaz (2004) seeks to explain bidders' significant excess returns using the target country's GDP growth rate. He argues that the target country's high GDP growth rate influences the bidder's excess returns positively as prospects exist for the bidder to gain market share and improve cash flow. On the other hand, as Kiymaz (2004) suggests, it may compel the bidder to pay an unwarranted high premium for the target. An interesting hypothesis that arises from this study is that higher growth potential in the target market, which may be due to the target country being less well developed, will offer higher bidder wealth gains on merger announcement. In the case of EU cross-border mergers with banks from Western Europe taking over other banks or credit institutions in Eastern European countries, Fritsch *et al* (2006) confirm that the GDP growth rate of the target country is a significant driver explaining bidder success.

Regulation in the local market is another factor considered in the literature, as foreign banks typically avoid countries with too much regulation, while merger activity thrives where there is deregulation and privatization. Buch and DeLong (2004) argue that regulations can lower the efficiency of local banks and therefore attract foreign buyers set to improve it. Where previously banks were state-controlled, the extent of market deregulation and liberalization may be seen as representing economic progress and can be used as driver for merger success. This reasoning leads to the hypothesis that a low level of economic freedom or a high level of regulation will be positively associated with bidder's excess returns when bank assets are disposed under privatization. Fritsch *et al* (2006) confirm this finding for bank mergers with targets in CEE countries using an index of economic freedom.

Deal-Specific Factors

A number of deal-specific variables are considered in the literature. The most commonly used is the mode of payment indicating whether the merger is paid for by the bidder in cash or by offer of stock to the shareholders of the target. An offer of stock payment is often interpreted to mean that the bidder's management perceives their firm's stock as overvalued and the target's shareholders will see this as a loss to them. In contrast, the bidder's ability to pay cash may demonstrate its own liquidity and confidence of the benefits anticipated from the merger, and thus interpreted positively by the market. For these reasons, payment in cash is expected to lead to positive excess returns to the bidder on merger announcement.

As many banks were state-owned prior to privatization, some of which were auctioned to the public and others acquired in the 1990s, ownership and method of selling have also been used as deal-specific variables in evaluating the success of mergers in CEE countries (Bonin and Wachtel, 1999; Fritsch *et al*, 2006). Campa and Hernando (2004) find that mergers in government-controlled industries created lower value for bidders than deals in unregulated industries, implying that state-ownership of the target has a negative effect on merger success. One argument, particularly for banks that are auctioned for sale, is that there can be several bidders interested in the deal, and the possibility of overpaying to win the auction renders the process favoring the target rather than the bidder. Also, selling a bank through an auction may suggest that the owners are confident of the superior value of the target, since ordinarily, for a lower quality firm, they would prefer private negotiation. However, investigating privatization in the CEE countries, Bonin and Wachtel (1999) contend that auctioning may expose the target to the possibility of attracting a lower price than it is worth if prospective buyers are too cautious. As arguments over the issue of auctioning are somewhat balanced, there does not seem to be a clear-cut hypothesis on how buying a bank through an auction influences the bidder's excess returns. However, Fritsch *et al* (2006) find that the dummies for auction sale and minority stake in target's shareholding are significant drivers in explaining bidders' success, suggesting that disposal of bank assets by public auction (as opposed to private negotiation) and owning a minority stake before the merger transaction creates value to the bidder.

4. THEORIES OF SHAREHOLDER GAIN IN MERGERS

The preceding section highlights the factors that are used in explaining the impact of mergers on value creation. This section discusses relevant theories that identify the sources of such gains. Lensink and Maslennikova (2008) discuss four categories in which most of the above factors may be grouped.

Theories that Predict Gains for Bidder and Target

Under this category, which encompasses most of the above factors, gains may come through four possible ways: operating synergy, financial economies, enhanced market power, and efficiency improvements. First, with operating synergies, it is assumed that economies of scale and scope exist in the financial services industry. It is assumed further that before the merger, one or both firms involved in the transaction are operating at a level which is inadequate for realizing full economies of scale. Scale economies are also realizable where vertical integration takes place, as activities at different stages of the industry's life cycle become organized under better coordinated supervision. It is possible to achieve economies of scope if the merging institutions make full use of each other's unique specializations. Operating synergies achieved usually by cost cuts have often been cited as the main motive for bank mergers. In the late 1990s for example, US banks saw cost cuts as well as economies of scope as potential sources of merger gains as they considered consolidation (Berger *et al.*, 1999; Hughes *et al.*, 1999).

Second, with financial economies, it is predicted that internal financing becomes available through stronger cash flows of the bidder which render unnecessary any external financing of the target. Also, the combined institution can sustain an increased debt capacity, which can lead to tax savings on any income generated from investments. Additionally, the combined firm may realize economies of scale in issuing securities (Levy and Sarnat, 1970). It is also possible for the combined entity to realize financial synergies through the acquisition of new assets at reduced prices. The assumption here is that a more efficient firm has taken over a less efficient one, and the combined entity has the potential to be highly efficient through bidder's management competence (Copeland *et al.*, 2003).

Third, increased market power arises where, due to competitive pressures, a firm decides to engage in a merger or acquisition to diversify by product or expand geographically. This is likely to lead to substantial gains, although in some cases it could increase costs initially. Hughes *et al.* (1999) cite a diversified product portfolio and promotion of non-traditional financial services as major sources of gains for US bank mergers that took place in the 1990s.

Finally, with regard to efficiency, improvement is expected where a more efficient firm bids for a less efficient one. Value is created through restructuring of operations by the more efficient management. Copeland *et al.* (2003) suggest also that synergies could be achieved through better growth opportunities, leading to a critical size at which economies of scope can be utilized. This view is consistent with the evidence reported by Hughes *et al.* (1999) that economies of scope arising from multiple but related products managed by one firm provided a strong motive for bank mergers in the US in the 1990s. As for improvement in efficiency *per se*, evidence is scant. Houston *et al.* (2001), for example, report that managers engage in mergers expecting to cut costs rather than improve efficiency.

Theories that Predict Gains for the Target at Bidder's Expense

These are based on the *hubris* hypothesis. The suggestion here is that what the target gains the bidder loses so that net gains are zero. Due to *hubris* (or self-confidence), the bidder attaches the target a higher value than the market's evaluation. This leads to an overpayment which translates into a loss for the bidder and a gain for the target.

Theories that Predict Negative Gains

These theories relate to those mergers occasioned by management's self-interest. As agents, managers are expected to act in the best interests of the firm's shareholders. However, in practice this is not always the case. Although with management acting in their own interests the shareholders might also benefit, this gain would be less than it could potentially have been and any loss suffered could have been avoided if the management had acted in the shareholders' interest. A number of US studies have used various proxies of managerial-shareholder conflict as determinants of abnormal shareholder returns to explain not only the negative short term market reaction (value destruction) but also related issues such as how managerial motives is linked to CEO remuneration and other aspects of firm performance (Anderson et al, 2004; Bliss and Rosen, 2001; Cornett et al, 2003; Olson and Pagano, 2005; DeLong and DeYoung, 2007).

Theories that Predict Gains for Conglomerate Mergers

Conglomerate mergers are complex and of a scale that almost ensures a wide variety of gains. For example, management functions are spread over a wider range of activities in the resulting larger and diversified organization. Savings in tax and labour costs may be substantial, although Copeland *et al.* (2003) point out that these may not be the primary motives for such combinations.

5. DEREGULATION AND BANK MERGER PERFORMANCE IN EUROPE

Europe's financial system was for many years different from that of the US where most studies on shareholder gains have been carried out. In the light of the preceding discussion, examining how Europe's financial sector has evolved in the last two decades helps to assess the evidence relating to performance of European bank mergers in comparison with US studies.

Regulatory Changes

As the wave of US bank mergers began to take hold in the 1980s, the banking industry in Europe was subject to regulatory barriers restricting foreign entry and competition (ECB, 1999). Gardener *et al.* (2001) point out that the 1980s ended with the banking sector characterized by low concentration, overcapacity, and operating efficiency below par. Since then most of the protective barriers have been removed with the implementation of measures like the Second Banking Directive (1989), completion of the Single Market (1992), the establishment of economic and monetary union (1999) and the subsequent introduction of the Euro (2002).

As a consequence of these changes, competition increased, profit margins dropped, and banks had to devise measures for improving cost efficiency. Traditional banking has seen a decline and the market-based financial system has been embraced. There has been a trend towards disintermediation and securitization. Financial services traditionally carried out by banks are now increasingly provided by mutual funds, insurance companies and pension funds. With greater competition and disintermediation banks have been taking greater risks by leveraging their capital and transforming loans into marketable securities. This has given rise to products like derivatives and asset-backed securities, increasing the pressure on banks to innovate, improve performance and enhance shareholder value.

Thus, deregulation, disintermediation, increased competition and the drive for new products and services have provided scope for banking sector consolidation allowing banks to increase their size and improve efficiency. As noted earlier, protecting one's domestic market before seeking cross-border expansion became the primary goal for many banks to compete in Europe. It has been suggested that in the 1980s banks sought to expand in size, while in the 1990s the focus was more on gaining a share in the European market (Campa and Hernando, 2006). Hence, product and geographical diversification have been important motives for market expansion apart from banks seeking to preserve domestic market share through horizontal mergers.

Geographical Diversification

Financial deregulation across Europe has provided banks with the opportunity to expand geographically and utilize economies of scope. At the same time, establishment of the Single Market in the EU opened the door for banks previously protected by anti-takeover legislation to be targeted for merger. The *excess demand theory* hypothesizes that when restrictions on cross-border mergers are removed, bidders for a given target will increase, and so will the premium paid for the target (Brewer *et al.*, 2000). On the other hand, as Brewer *et al.* (2000) point out, the *barrier to entry theory* predicts a fall in prices for foreign targets when merger restrictions are removed. The reasoning here is that, while protected, the target may earn excess profits, which then disappear with entry barriers removed. Substitutability increases between target institutions, and this leads to lower merger premiums. Overvaluation becomes less likely, and this may lead the market to respond by recording positive excess returns for bidders.

The evidence in support for geographical diversification, however, is weak. In a study of the US banking industry, Houston and Ryngaert (1994) and DeLong (2001a) find that the market favours intrastate against interstate mergers. They attribute this to the possibility of greater cost savings for banks operating in the same economic environment. Tourani-Rad and Van Beek (1999), analyzing a sample of 17 targets and 56 bidding financial institutions (not just banks) for Europe find that cross-border mergers do not yield returns that are significantly different from domestic ones. Cybo-Ottone and Murgia (2000), studying 54 large European financial deals (including 18 cross-border) find that domestic deals create more shareholder value while cross-border deals reveal positive but insignificant abnormal returns. In an EU-15 study of 98 large mergers between 1985 and 2000, Beitel *et al.* (2004) find that target and bidder returns are not significantly influenced by whether the merger is cross-border or domestic but overall they find abnormal returns higher for domestic mergers, particularly for bidders who are involved in previously less merger activities and when the targets show poor past performance. Campa and Hernando (2004) investigate financial and non-financial mergers over the period 1998-2000 and find that, in the case of cross-border deals, both targets and bidders receive significantly lower cumulative abnormal returns and they report higher value creation from domestic mergers in the more regulated financial industry. In another study, Campa and Hernando (2006), investigating bank and financial institution mergers in the EU-15 over the period 1998-2002, find positive returns for targets and slightly negative for bidders but otherwise no significant variations between cross-border and domestic mergers. Lensink and Maslennikova (2008), analysing value gains to bidders using a sample of 75 banks from 19 European countries over the period 1996-2004, do find positive gains from both domestic and cross-border mergers. They observe that in the decade spanning the mid 1990s to the mid 2000s, the larger Northern European banks from concentrated financial sectors were able to target banks in Southern Europe with greater margins. However, Nnadi and Tanna (2011), using a sample of 62 bank mega-mergers that occurred within the EU during the period 1997-2007, find that cross border mergers are value-destroying while domestic mergers yield relatively better returns, citing that potential downside risks in the bidders' ability to implement restructuring for cost management and profitability on the target banks could explain significantly negative market reaction in cross-border mergers. In general, it appears from the above evidence that shareholder value gains from cross-border mergers are not any higher than domestic mergers although the potential for gains are greater in target markets that are less well developed.

Diversification by Product

The more varied a bank's activities the more types of risk it is exposed to. Perceiving this, the market will expect a risk premium on such bank mergers. DeLong (2001b) reports negative returns for US bank-to-bank mergers but value-creation for diversifying US banks, pointing out that the market evaluates each category of risk differently and expects a higher return from diversifying mergers than from focused mergers. As more non-bank financial institutions engage in traditional banking services the likelihood is that more product market diversification will take place. Market participants (including customers and shareholders) look positively at the availability of multiple services from a single institution. The market in turn will perceive positively any product market diversification, resulting in merger gains.

Some European studies that distinguish between domestic and cross border mergers have also investigated the scope for value gains from product/activity diversification. Cybo-Ottone and Murgia (2000) report statistically significant abnormal returns for both cross product and vertical mergers among European banks for the period 1989-1997. They report that the market views bank to insurance company mergers favorably yielding an abnormal return of 7.03% on average. Lepetit et al (2004) examine value gains from bank mergers between 1991 and 2001 covering 13 European countries and find support for mergers involving cross-product diversification and geographic specialization. Ismail and Davidson (2005) find higher abnormal returns in bank-to-bank compared to cross-product deals, and mixed evidence of abnormal returns in domestic and cross border deals, thus providing weak support for geographical diversification. Similarly, Lensink and Maslennikova (2008) find positive value gains which are significant in diversifying domestic deals, but not in diversifying cross-border deals.

Differences in Merger Performance

Most of the US studies analysing merger gains have observed positive gains for target banks, but negative or statistically insignificant returns for bidders (Berger and Humphrey, 1997; Pilloff and Santomero, 1998; Houston *et al.*, 2001). However, DeLong (2003b) finds non-US bank mergers earn 2% more than their US counterparts while targets earn comparatively 7% less, attributing the difference to the regulatory settings in the two regions.

The universal banking system in Europe meant that banks were able to perform diversification operations which in the US were restricted by law until a decade ago, and the institutional differences between the two banking sectors have been cited as accounting for the varying results. Cybo-Ottone and Murgia (2000), who find significant announcement period excess returns in European bank mergers, examine two important aspects worth mentioning. First, they show that the difference in their results between domestic/cross-border deals is not driven by country-specific effects as their announcement period returns are similar across the countries. Second, their value creating result for domestic deals is attributed to a sub-sample (one-third) of mergers between banks and product diversification of banks into insurance and investment firms. Thus, they argue that more liberal regulations allowing product diversification and the more flexible anti-trust laws in Europe provide banks with the opportunity to achieve economies of scope and improve performance.

Scholtens and de Wit (2001) also compare shareholder wealth effects of bank mergers in Europe to the US. In their sample of 17 European targets and 20 bidders, they find significant positive excess returns for targets, but small though significant returns for bidders. More recently, Hagendorff *et al.* (2008) analyse the value effects of large bank mergers in EU-15 and Switzerland (in relation to US) for the period 1996-2004, and find that bidder returns are significantly more positive than in US, attributing the difference to the existence of lower investor protection economies in Europe.

6. Cross-Border Bank Mergers

Due to their nature and importance to both bidder and target nations, cross-border mergers are often given special attention in the literature as noted from the evidence presented in the last section. This section discusses some of the issues associated with banks expanding their operations abroad and presents evidence that is by nature more international before examining the issues and comparative evidence in Europe and US.

Cross-border mergers in banking are the inherent consequence of the on-going globalization of economic activities. Banks have been expanding their operations abroad for more than a century by opening branches or establishing a subsidiary. The current wave of cross-border financial mergers in Europe can be seen as the alternative and more viable means to acquire greater market share elsewhere in the single market. Empirical evidence shows that banks that expand abroad are generally larger and managed better than those that do not, and come from countries that are more open to international trade with a well developed financial sector. Large banks also tend to follow their clients abroad. Focarelli and Pozzolo (2001), studying bank mergers and shareholdings in OECD countries, find a positive relationship between size and the probability that a bank operates abroad. They also find that highly profitable banks and those whose non-interest income forms a large proportion of their total income are also very likely to have a foreign presence. Tschoegl (2004), investigating subsidiaries of foreign banks in the US, suggests that banks with international operations are usually the larger institutions in their home countries, and going abroad may be the result of lack of further expansion opportunities at home, in addition to antitrust restrictions. Although banks that go abroad are often among the most efficient in their home country, this does not guarantee that they will be equally efficient in the foreign country, compared to their local competitors (Berger *et al.*, 2000b).

Banks, like other firms, are selective in choosing where to expand. Countries with common language and similar legal systems are more likely to engage in cross-border bank mergers than those without (Focarelli and Pozzolo, 2008; Buch and DeLong, 2004). The likelihood of cross-border bank mergers also increase when countries share a currency union (Focarelli and Pozzolo, 2005; Allen and Song, 2005). Similarly, the presence of high quality institutions increases the likelihood of cross-border bank mergers, although firms from a country with institutions of moderate quality find that expanding to a country of a lower institutional environment works to their advantage (Claessens and van Horen, 2007). Studies that examine target countries find that banks prefer to go where competition is low, the environment is bank-friendly, legal institutions are of a high standard, bank activity disclosure requirements are high, and bank supervision is dependable (Focarelli and Pozzolo, 2005; Berger *et al.* 2004). Explicit regulatory barriers aimed to discourage competition also impede cross-border bank mergers (Focarelli and Pozzolo, 2008) and implicit government barriers may also act to restrict entry (Berger, 2007a).

The increased trend in cross-border banking consolidation would not have come about without supportive legislation. In the US, the Riegle-Neal Interstate Banking and Branching Efficiency Act, 1994 allowed banks to operate and acquire banks across state lines, removing restrictions that had been imposed by the McFadden Act of 1927. The Gramm-Leach-Bliley Financial Services Modernization Act, 1999 also removed restrictions to product diversification imposed by the Glass-Steagall Act, 1933, giving banks the freedom to operate as universal banks. In the EU, universal banking was formally enacted into law by completion of the Single Market in 1992. These legislations allowed financial institutions not only to engage in geographical but also product diversification. As a result, there has seen substantial increases in cross-border mergers of financial institutions. Figure 3 compares the transaction values of cross-border bank mergers for both US and EU, showing an increasing trend in both countries over the years leading to 2000. As with domestic bank mergers, cross-border merger activity declined in both regions after 2003 with the global economic slowdown but this trend soon reversed after 2003 and by 2006 the merger activity had not yet peaked.

Considerable research has been undertaken in both US and Europe to study the performance effects of cross-border mergers. Studies that have examined the efficiency implications of such mergers among financial institutions tend to find mixed results. For example, cost efficiency is not found to have improved as a result of financial mergers in either the US (Berger *et al.*, 2000b) or Europe (Vander Vennet, 2002) although evidence is found of slight improvements in profit efficiency and in accounting measures of performance (Vander Vennet, 2002; Elsas *et al.*, 2006).

Studies that examine shareholder value gains in cross-border bank mergers also generally report mixed results. In the US, Cornett *et al.* (2003) find that significant returns accrue to the bidder's shareholders in mergers that are focused both geographically and by product, but not in diversified mergers. DeLong (2003a) reports that the market is found to favour focused rather than diversifying bank mergers. On the other hand, Hendershott et al. (2002) report that cross-border mergers are found to yield statistically significant returns in insurance firms and investment banks but not in commercial banks. US studies that have examined bank-non-bank mergers also find that cross-border and product diversifications are both beneficial (Emmons et al. 2004; Estrella, 2001; Lown et al., 2000). In Europe, as noted above, bank merger studies have similarly found results mixed results, some reporting that domestic bank mergers are more value-creating than cross-border mergers (Cybo-Ottone and Murgia, 2000; Beitel et al., 2004; Goergen and Renneboorg, 2004; Campa and Hernando, 2004, 2006) while others reporting the opposite (Lepetit et al., 2004; Ekkayokkaya et al., 2009).

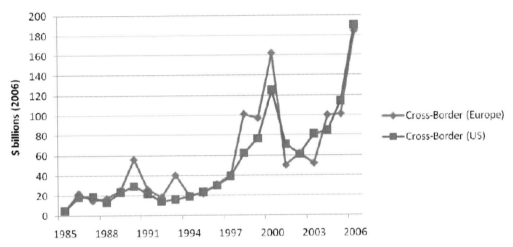

Source: DeYoung et al. (2009).

Figure 3. Cross-border Bank Merger Values for US and Europe.

7. BARRIERS TO EU BANKING SECTOR CONSOLIDATION

As the single market for financial services strengthened in the 1990s with the introduction of the Euro, the expectation was that the universal banking market in the EU would stimulate financial integration and competition, leading to lower costs of financial intermediation. However, as noted earlier, cross-border mergers have generally been far fewer than domestic mergers and this has accounted for the slow pace of financial integration in retail banking. Although it is possible for international banks to expand by branch network in the foreign country, experience shows that *de novo* operations are an expensive and slow way of capturing a new market. Cross-border mergers are therefore seen as the more viable way of strengthening the single market in financial services but regulatory and political barriers have hindered this process of cross-border integration (Hernando et al, 2009). In particular, misuse of supervisory powers and political interference have been identified as two specific barriers to cross-border bank mergers, explaining the preference for domestic over cross-border deals and resulting in some cases to "domestic champions" (European Commission, 2005). In response to this situation, the European Parliament and the Council issued Directive 2007/44/CE, improving procedures and evaluation standards for prudential appraisal of mergers and increases in share ownership. The directive requires, among other things, that upon reaching thresholds of 20%, 30%, and 50% share ownership be notified to the host country supervisor, and clarifies on the timings of the various stages to acquisition, including the conditions for stopping the merger.

The European Commission (2005) also points to another barrier in cross-border mergers being the inability to pay for the deal out of reduced costs, due to limited scope for cost savings out of pre-merger duplicated operations. Government restrictions and institutional barriers have made it hard to realize cost savings through staff layoffs. This experience has led Carbo-Valverde *et al.* (2007) to caution against dependence on scale for enhancing cost efficiency and achieving dominance in the EU market. Such a merger goal may only be achieved with labour market reforms which will allow institutions to reduce their staff costs and better control their input mix.

Some studies report results that are more positive about other aspects of financial integration. For example, Ayuso and Blanco (2001) report that as banking sector consolidation picked up speed in the 1990s, European stock markets moved closer in integration. It has also been observed that there is increasing integration in inter-bank and wholesale banking but not in retail banking. The European Central Bank blames the nature of traditional banking for the slow progress in cross-border expansion of commercial banking (ECB, 2004b). Degryse and Ongena (2004) offer a similar view, and caution that current technologies and regulations are inadequate for removing the obstacles still left before retail banking markets are effectively integrated. Language and distance barriers, brand, reputation, branch networks, and existence of local as opposed to national regulations, are cited by Gual (2004) as contributing to the delay in integration of the retail banking markets. According to Campa and Hernando (2006), lack of integration in the retail markets is reflected in the continued offer of some traditional products by commercial banks in some EU countries. For example, checking accounts contribute more than 50% of retail banking profits in Europe, while in the Anglo-Saxon and Nordic countries traditional products contribute less than 20% of sector profits. In the UK, asset management and related products make up 32% of bank profits, but they account for less than 15% of bank profits in France and Germany. These examples indicate that banking markets function differently across the European Union, and suggests that it may take a long time before the EU market is fully harmonized.

8. US and European Bank Merger Performance

The majority of studies that have examined the merger phenomenon in banking have analyzed 1980s and 1990s data, and most research for these decades investigated the US banking industry. In contrast, European research took time to take off in earnest (with little done on 1980s data) and most studies here have used data on mergers that occurred during 1990s and 2000s.[5] Research done on 1980s and 1990s merger transactions, especially for US deals, reveals that bank mergers are value-destroying (e.g. Siems, 1996; Scott-Frame and Lastrapes, 1998). This has lent credence to the assertion that managements engage in mergers for their own benefits and not that of their shareholders. On the other hand, early European

---

[5] Appendix 1 lists the studies on bank merger performance for the EU, US and other countries, together with a summary of the findings of each study.

studies indicated that mergers were beneficial though no definitive conclusions could be made with limited research done. More recent US research, however, reveals the possibility of efficiency gains from mergers and, similarly, European studies also increasingly find banks mergers to be beneficial (DeYoung *et al*, 2009).

One of the reasons for the difference in the early US and European results is that the two financial systems were fundamentally different for many years until two key legislations were passed in the US. In 1994 the Riegle-Neal Act allowed geographic deregulation so that banks could operate and acquire other banks across state lines. Subsequently, in 1999, the Gramm-Leach-Bliley Act allowed banks to operate the way universal banks had been allowed to operate in Europe for many years before, engaging in commercial banking, insurance, securities, and so on[6]. These two legislative measures have moved the US banking industry much closer to the European model. However, with respect to merger performance there still remains differences, particularly to do with how the combined entity operates after merger. For example, Hagendorff and Keasey (2008) suggest that whereas post-merger European banks focus initially on cost-cutting to improve efficiency, US banks direct most of their effort to enhancing revenue to boost profitability. To support their argument, they find evidence suggesting that the European strategy generates gains, although it takes some years for them to be realized, while the US strategy of revenue enhancement does not show that mergers are beneficial. Increasingly, more studies on 2000s data are finding results that point to positive merger benefits exceeding what was found for studies using 1990s mergers.

While the above evidence reflects the outcome of bank merger studies that typically have used data relating to 1980s and 1990s, there is new interest to look more closely at post-2000 research as recent studies seem to produce results that are supportive of the view that mergers are beneficial (DeYoung *et al.*, 2009). The following discussion reviews merger performance by looking first at the pre-2000 studies before considering how findings of post-2000 studies are changing the general perception on bank merger performance. Most studies have examined the reaction of the stock market to merger announcements as determined by the event study method and post-merger improvements in efficiency as measured by accounting performance ratios or frontier techniques.

Pre-2000 Abnormal Returns

The event study method is used to determine whether a merger announcement leads to a positive reaction by the market as observed in a rise in the share price of the parties to the merger. A rise in the share price above what would have been the price without the merger is said to create an abnormal return and therefore value to the shareholder. In general, a share price is said to represent the net present value of future cash flows from that share; hence the creation of value through an abnormal return.

Most studies that have examined abnormal returns conclude that the 1980s and 1990s mergers led to positive gains for the target shareholders but negative returns for the bidder shareholders (DeLong, 2001a; Pilloff, 1996; Houston and Ryngaert, 1994). In many cases studies that report gains for target shareholders and losses for bidder shareholders report, on

---

[6] Appendix 2 lists additional information on European and U.S. legislative measures on financial sector consolidation.

balance, zero net gains for the combined firm as the two cancel each other. However, some studies report positive gains to both shareholders leading to a positive gain for the combined entity (Houston et al., 2001; Cybo-Ottone Murgia, 2000; Beitel et al, 2004; Brewer et al., 2000).

Post-2000 Studies on Abnormal Returns[7]

Studies examining US evidence continue to find mixed results with regard to shareholder returns from merger announcements. Knapp *et al.* (2005) find negative gains to shareholders and post-merger reductions in profitability, non-interest income and credit quality. On the other hand, Olson and Pagano (2005) report shareholder gains, although they associate these with growth that had started before the merger. Positive gains are also reported by DeLong and DeYoung (2007), which as they point last only for a short while. Penas and Unal (2004) examine and find support for bondholders gain in merger announcements and post-merger decreases in the cost of debt. Hart and Apilado (2002) find that post-1994 US bank mergers after geographic deregulation generated greater returns than mergers before.

In Europe the results are more positive than those of US studies. Even on pre-2000 mergers, Cybo-Ottone and Murgia (2000) and Beitel *et al.* (2004) report positive shareholder returns. Lepetit *et al.* (2004) and Lensink and Maslennikova (2008) examine a range of mergers deals and find positive shareholder returns even for diversifying (bank-non-bank) mergers. Campa and Hernando (2006), one of the few studies to analyze both market reaction and efficiency, investigate 244 European bank mergers over the period 1998-2002 and find announcement period gains for target shareholders but insignificant results for the bidder shareholders. They also find post-merger improvement in efficiency, and in profitability as measured by return on equity. Investigating 98 cross-border mergers involving mostly US and European banks but also some from other economic regions over the period 1985-2005, Schmautzer (2007) finds positive shareholder returns for both the targets and the bidders, with gains being greater for targets. Similarly, Ekkayokkaya *et al.* (2009) report positive shareholder returns on announcement of bank-to-bank mergers, finding that the pre-Euro (1999) returns were larger than those that accrued to post-Euro mergers.

Pre-2000 Studies on Efficiency Gains

Cost efficiency is one of the most thoroughly investigated merger effect as most bidders often suggest that the reason for engaging in a merger is to implement a cost saving strategy that can improve efficiency for the combined firm. Studies[8] that have investigated cost (and also profit efficiency) in the 1980s and 1990s mergers generally find little evidence of efficiency improvements (Group of Ten, 2001; Berger *et al.*, 1999) leading to the consensus view that efficiency gains from these studies were elusive (DeYoung *et al*, 2009).

---

[7] It should be noted that some of the post-2000 studies investigate pre-2000 mergers.
[8] Appendix 1 lists numerous pre-2000 efficiency studies (as well as post-2000 ones) that could not be covered in this review.

Post-2000 Studies on Efficiency Gains[9]

US studies on efficiency show more promising results than the market reaction findings. Investigating bank mergers in the period 1987-2003, Knapp *et al.* (2006) find considerable profit gains that last up to five years after merger. Similarly, Cornett *et al.* (2006) find that revenue efficiency improves in large bank mergers focused by product as well as those focused geographically. In an earlier study that examined 1990s bank mergers, Kwan and Wilcox (2002) find considerable cost savings attributable to those mergers. Overall, following recent findings, the consensus seems to be that US mergers lead to efficiency gains, although further research is warranted for the evidence to be compelling.

In Europe, there is more conviction, as a result of growing evidence, that bank mergers lead to efficiency gains. A number of European studies find post-merger performance gains in efficiency as well as profitability as measured using various ratios over time. Altunbas and Ibanez (2008) find that firms with similar strategies outperform those with different strategies in both efficiency and profitability. A similar result is found by Diaz *et al.* (2004) who report that bank-to-bank mergers perform better than bank-non-bank mergers. Some studies find that cost efficiency gains tend to appear earlier than profit efficiency improvements (Diaz *et al.*, 2004; Campa and Hernando, 2006). In a study of the effects of market power, De Guevara *et al.* (2005) find results to suggest that gains in efficiency arise because market power led marginal costs to fall faster than prices. Huizinga *et al.* (2001) find that both cost and profit efficiency improve after merger but profit efficiency gains are minimal. Ayadi and Pujals (2005) find improvements in both cost and profit efficiency.

Country based studies for Europe also report efficiency improvements in bank mergers. In a study of 61 UK bank mergers, Ashton and Pham (2007) find efficiency improvements, as does Koetter (2005) in a study of German bank mergers that occurred in the 1990s, and De Guevara and Maudos (2007) in an investigation of Spanish bank mergers for the period 1986-2002. In another study of Spanish banks, Carbo and Humphrey (2004) examine 22 mergers for the period 1986-2000 and find improved profitability following a reduction of 0.5% in unit costs and a rise of 4% in returns.

10. CONCLUSION

This chapter has reviewed the motives and evidence relating to performance of bank mergers that are based on the wave of consolidation in banking that began in the 1980s and continued into the 1990s and 2000s with a particular focus on the European Banking industry. Aspects of consolidation that are useful in understanding why mergers of financial institutions occur, including those of cross-border or cross-industry in nature, the efficiency implications and in particular, the impact of mergers on shareholder value creation have been discussed with comparative focus on both EU and US evidence. The review provides an account of key developments and issues that have enabled the bank merger phenomenon along with the emerging importance of cross-border mergers in Europe.

---

[9] It should be noted that among the above post-2000 studies are studies that examine a longer period going back to the 1990s.

A key issue examined in this review is that of shareholder value creation from mergers. The predominant way of investigating shareholder value is by use of event study method which measures the stock market reaction to merger announcement. The review analyses the major factors explaining value creation and the sources of such gains, providing comparative evidence for both EU and the US. Other methods of evaluating performance include comparing efficiency both pre and post merger using frontier techniques, and employing accounting ratios to determine profitability improvements. Some evidence pertaining to these aspects of performance is also examined.

Most pre-2000 studies find evidence that merger expectations with regard to efficiency and shareholder value creation are not realized, and most of this research has examined US banks where evidence of value-destruction is found. These results led to the suggestion that the reason mergers continued despite lack of performance improvements was because they were being undertaken in the interest of the management and not the shareholders. Post-2000 US studies, however, suggest evidence of efficiency improvements, although shareholder value results from studies that examine stock market reaction are roughly evenly split between those which find evidence of gains and those which do not. Studies for bank mergers in Europe, on the other hand, continue to show evidence of shareholder value, efficiency and profitability gains in varying degrees. A possible reason for better results reported in recent research than for those earlier periods may be the existence of better capabilities and scope for improving efficiency, better management skills or simply the employment of improved methods of examining performance by recent studies.

APPENDIX 1: SUMMARY OF BANK MERGER STUDIES

Table 1. Selected Bank Merger Studies (Europe)

Study	Findings
Vander Vennet (1996)	Examining the effects of mergers on the performance of financial institutions, the study finds that domestic mergers between firms of similar size increase the chances of post-merger improvement; in cross-border mergers improvement is observed in cost efficiency. Defensive tactics, management initiative, and growth of firm size, are found to drive most domestic mergers.
Cybo-Ottone, Murgia (2000)	Investigating shareholder wealth, the study finds that mergers between banks and bank acquisition of insurance firms result in positive abnormal returns. Mergers with securities firms and foreign banks generate the opposite results.
Beitel, Schiereck (2001)	This study investigates value creation in intra-sector and cross-sector mergers at domestic and international level. Target banks and the combined firm are found to gain considerably, with only minimal gains for the bidder. However results vary with the period investigated, with bidder banks posting negative abnormal returns mainly after 1998. Cross-border mergers are found to destroy value.
Huizinga, Nellisen, Vander Vennet (2001)	In a study of efficiency, the authors find significant cost efficiency improvement but much less improvement in profit efficiency in banks. They suggest that between banks and consumers, the latter might be the greater beneficiary of bank mergers.
Vander Vennet (2002)	Focusing on cross-border transactions, the study finds that takeover of a poorly performing bank by a very efficient bidder eliminates the inefficiencies, more through improved revenue than cost efficiencies.

Berger (2003)	Targeting cross-border and cross-sector mergers, this study looks at the impact on bank efficiency of the single European market. The study finds diseconomies of scope arising from post-merger organizational challenges, while suggesting potential for revenue enhancements through diversification, installation of one-stop shopping, and improvement in branding.
Altunbas, Marques Ibanez (2008)	Interested in strategic focus, the study examines similarities in banks engaged in mergers. One major finding is that the more the similarities in cross-border mergers the more the financial returns. Also, domestic mergers tend to be costly where the partners are strongly dissimilar.
Beitel, Schiereck, Wahrenburg (2004)	The study examines stock market reaction to merger announcements, and finds that stock markets favour intra-sector mergers where also the banks operate in the same geographical area. Banks inexperienced in mergers create greater value than those with prior experience. The study suggests that the market is more interested in particular managerial goals than in creation of shareholder value.
Cummins, Weiss (2004)	With its focus on value creation in insurance firms, the study finds abnormal returns generally positive for targets and negative for bidders in domestic mergers. Cross-border mergers also are positive for targets, but value-neutral for bidders. These results suggest that international mergers are beneficial.
Goergen, Renneboog (2004)	Investigating abnormal returns, the study finds high value creation for targets but near zero values for bidders. Hostile takeovers generate even higher abnormal returns for targets and even less values for bidders. UK mergers record better results than those in other European countries. Also, cash transactions generate higher values than those settled in stocks or mixed payments. The study found that the relative size of partners in a merger or their past performances did not affect their ability to create value. Domestic mergers were found to create more value than cross-border mergers. Targets in the UK, Austria, Switzerland and Germany generated more value than those in other countries. Managerial motivation, synergy creation, and agency problems were found to drive the majority of European bank mergers.
Diaz, Ollala, Azofra (2004)	Analyzing intra and inter-sector mergers, finds improvement in bidder long-term profitability, especially among bank mergers. Also, bidders record the least improvement in inter-sector mergers.
Lepetit, Patry, Rous (2004)	Examining value creation, the study finds large benefits for the targets, in both domestic and cross-border mergers. Bank- insurance mergers generate lower returns than bank-bank combinations
Ayadi, Pujals (2005)	The study investigates profitability and efficiency in both domestic and cross-border mergers. Cost efficiencies are realized in both the target and the bidder. Revenue diversification leads to profitability improvement in both domestic and cross-border mergers.
Campa, Hernando (2006)	A study investigating value creation, it finds that merger announcements generate value for target shareholders, with little effect on those of the bidder. A year after merger, abnormal returns are about zero. In general, targets have below average performance in their sector before merger. Two years after merger, targets are found to have improved significantly in efficiency.
Fritsch, Gleisner, Hoshauzer (2007)	Focusing on firms in Central and Eastern Europe targeted mainly by bidders from Western Europe, the study fails to find any significant effects of target characteristics on the bidder's share price. Rather, bidder banks' abnormal returns seem to be driven by the target country's GDP growth rate, regulatory regime, the extent of economic freedom, and deal-specific dummies.

Table 1. Continued

Study	Findings
Lorenz, Schiereck (2007)	The research compares mergers that fail to materialize after announcement with those which are concluded. The bidder experiences negative returns, while the target banks' share price gains considerably.
Beccalli, Frantz (2009)	Considering European bidders with bank targets from all over the world, the study examines how a merger impacts several performance indicators. The study reports that the combined bank's ROE may decline, and cash flow creation may suffer. And improvement in cost efficiency is not achieved until after five to six years.
Fiordelisi (2008)	The study examines efficiency and, using an EVA model, estimates value creation in mergers in UK, Germany, France and Italy. Efficiency is found to increase slightly in bidders over a five-year period, but it declines in targets. More value creation is found in mergers than in acquisitions.
Ekkayokkaya, Holmes, Paudyal (2009)	This study looks at shareholder value creation following EMU and the easing of barriers to cross-border mergers. The authors report a decrease in shareholder returns, attributing this to the increased competition that ensued among market players.

Table 2. Selected Bank Merger Studies (US)

Study	Findings
Berger, Humphrey (1994)	Investigating efficiency, the study does not find clear evidence of whether mergers improve efficiency or not, observing improvement in some mergers and decline in efficiency in others. The study suggests the potential for small firms to realize efficiency, as well as scale and scope economies.
Rhoades (1994)	The study considers performance in bank mergers and fails to find significant improvement therein. However, using the event study technique the author observes that mergers create value for target bank shareholders.
Peristiani (1997)	Examining post-merger performance, the study finds that the new bank does not improve on the bidder's pre-merger efficiency, although profitability increases and economies of scale are realized. Post-merger performance is found to be dependent on how well the management succeeds in using the bank's assets for quality improvement.
Siems (1996)	Using mega-mergers this study finds positive returns for targets and negative for bidders. The market is seen to react positively on mergers, expecting them to result in improved cost efficiency, but not leading to increased market power.
Study	Findings
Akhavein, Berger, Humphrey (1997)	Examining efficiency in mega-mergers, the study reports significant improvement in target profit efficiency, attributing it to change of strategy from investing in securities to doing so in market loans.
Berger (1998)	Investigating efficiency, this study reports benefits for banks whose pre-merger efficiency levels were considerably low. No benefits are observed for those firms that had above average efficiency levels pre-merger. Efficiency gains are attributed to a shift in investment strategy towards more customer loans and diversification of risk.
Boyd, Graham (1998)	Focusing on small banks, this study reports cost reduction and improved efficiency for involved banks post-merger.
Rhoades (1998)	Nine different cases are reviewed to examine the impact of bank mergers on efficiency. Improvement in efficiency is found in medium-sized banks. Cost

	efficiency improvement is rarely observed, although cost cutting is a common feature after merger. IT integration and operational challenges pose challenges that make it difficult to realize efficiency improvements earlier envisaged.
Scott-Frame, Lastrapes (1998)	This is a study of shareholder wealth. It reports that target shareholders gained at the expense of the bidder owners upon merger. It also observes that bidder banks can improve their benefits by engaging in interstate rather than intrastate mergers and a method of payment that involves goodwill and its amortization.
Berger, Demsetz, Strahan (1999)	This is a review of 250 studies. Mergers in financial institutions are found to lead to greater market power, improved payment systems, better bank services for small and medium enterprises, diversification of risk, and improved profitability. With increased systemic risk, costs increase for the country's financial system, while the regulatory authorities create more safety tools.
Hadlock, Houston, Ryngaert (1999)	The study examines bank performance, its governance at corporate level, and management incentives. Findings show that a bank's likelihood of becoming a merger target is related to the proportion of equity that its managers hold. The less the shares they hold the greater the probability that the bank will be targeted for merger.
Kwan, Laderman (1999)	Value creation and performance are examined in this study. Shareholder returns are insignificant, as well as profit efficiency. This is irrespective of the high levels of efficiency in some banks pre-merger.
Berger, De Young (2000)	This is a study on cross-border and geographical expansion. Efficiency is found to be unaffected by expansion, with highly efficient banks maintaining their pre-event efficiency levels.
Brewer, Jackson, Jagtiani, Nguyen (2000)	This study examines shareholder value creation. Premium offered in the price for the target is found to depend on the level of the bank's capitalization and its profitability. Returns to the target are linked to its size and its share of the local market. Value gains are found to be considerably lower in large-to-large bank mergers than in mergers of different size banks.
Kane (2000)	Analysing mega-mergers, this study shows that large bank bidders gain in value when the targets are large in size and located in the same country. Such bidders seem to benefit from their "too big to fail" status which apparently the markets recognize.
Zollo, Leshchinskii (2000)	This is a study of post-merger performance in banking. To improve performance both in the short-term and the long-term, partner banks must succeed in integrating their systems. The greater the degree of integration the more assured the banks will be of improved long-term performance.
Bliss, Rosen (2001)	In this study the relationship between mergers and managers' compensation is examined. Salary levels are found to be positively associated with mergers. In particular, CEO compensation is linked to size implying that as mergers lead to a larger size they also give rise to greater compensation. This is in spite of any fall in the bidder price which sometimes happens upon merger. Managers whose compensation is by stock options usually have less incentive to engage in mergers.
DeLong (2001a)	This study seeks to demonstrate that markets favour mergers where the partners focus their operations on limited sources of revenue streams and restrict their geographical coverage. Greater long-term efficiency is achieved where the bidder is not so efficient initially and the method of payment for the transaction is not solely in cash.
DeLong (2001b)	In this study, a cluster of mergers with a geographical and activity focus are shown to gain greater value, while unfocused mergers destroy value. The study also finds that value creation upon merger announcement increases in relative size of target to bidder.

Table 2. Continued

Study	Findings
Hart, Apilado, (2002)	This study examines bank merger returns with a focus on the period before and that after The Riegle-Neal Interstate Banking and Branching Act, 1994. Targets are found to gain more value than bidders both before and after the Act. The combined entity also shows potential for creating value. Overall, mergers are found to create greater returns after than before the Act.
DeLong(2003a)	The purpose of this study is to analyse long-term performance of mergers with market expectations. Due to the difficulty of predicting merger outcomes, market expectations are usually not realized. Sources and magnitudes of revenue typically impact negatively on long-term performance.
Anderson, Becher, Campbell (2004)	The study analyses CEO compensation post-merger, and finds that increases are linked to the higher productivity that is realized after merger, and not to the increased size of the institution as found by other studies.
Pilloff (2004)	This is a comprehensive study of the acquisition likelihood characteristics of US bank mergers, finding that mergers mostly involved small banks operating in proximity of the larger bidder banks. As expected, there was more merger activity in urban than in rural markets. Most targets operate in only one state and the bidder usually has at least one office in that state.
Hannan, Pilloff (2005)	This study examines the effect of capital adequacy requirements (Basel II) on bank mergers. Banks involved in merger activity are found to be those which meet the regulatory capital requirements. Often they have capital exceeding those requirements, which motivates them to engage in mergers.
Mayer, Sommer, Sweeny, Walker (2005)	This is a study of three mergers undertaken by the same bank. Only one of those mergers creates value, and this is due to the substantial number of shares held in the target by its managers and employees.
Al Sharkas, Hassan, Lawrence (2008)	Analysing post-merger performance, this study finds post-merger improvement in both operating efficiency and allocative efficiency. The combined bank operates at a lower cost than a non-merged bank as a result of access to better technology, and realizes cost savings that accrue from a better mix of production inputs.

Table 3. Selected Bank Merger Studies (International)

Study	Findings
Becher (2000)	The study examines shareholder value creation, finding that targets earn 20%, bidders break even, and the combined institution generates 3%.
Berger (2000)	The study compares the US and Europe on integration processes, finding considerable potential for efficiency gains, although in practice they are realized in only a few cases. Revenue efficiency is found to be more easier to achieve than cost efficiency, the main driver being risk diversification.
Berger, De Young, Genay, Udell (2000b)	Reviewing many bank studies, the study finds that domestic banks are more profit efficient than foreign banks. It also finds that in general US banks are more efficient than other countries' banks in a foreign country.

Focarelli, Pozzolo (2000)	This study investigates the causes of bank foreign expansion in OECD countries. The major finding is that the decision to go abroad is largely linked to the presence in the target country of international investors with foreign country experience, and a head office in a country where the banking sector is efficient.
Floreani, Rigamonti (2001)	Investigating mergers in the insurance industry, the study finds high bidder shareholder returns, particularly in European-non-European firm mergers. The authors also report that the higher the value of the transaction the greater the returns to bidder institutions.
Focarelli, Pozzolo (2001)	The research examines why cross-border expansion is not as common in banks as it is in other sectors. Information asymmetries are found to be one of the reasons, as well as regulatory restrictions. Size of the banks is not a factor in the decision to expand abroad. Presence of international investors in the target country encourages cross-border growth.
Houston, James, Ryngaert, (2001)	This is a long-term merger study that compares performance with management and analysts' expectations, as well as market predictions from their initial reactions. The study finds that mergers that took place in the second half of the 1990s generated cost efficiencies expected by managements.
DeLong (2003b)	Comparing the US and the rest of the world in analysing market reactions to merger announcements, the study finds that non-US bidders earn more returns than American counterparts. However, US targets earn more than rest of the world targets.
Amel, Barnes, Panetta, Salleo (2004)	Examining banks, insurance firms, and asset management institutions, the study finds mergers are beneficial to small companies, but scale economies are low and managerial efficiencies minimal.
Buch, DeLong (2004)	This international study of cross-border mergers finds that information asymmetry and, to a lesser extent, regulatory hurdles are major obstacles to cross-border expansion.
Scholten, De Wit (2004)	This study considers shareholder value creation upon merger announcement for two samples, one American and the other European. In both samples, bidders suffer negative returns. Target banks earn positive returns in both cases but European targets earn less than their US counterparts. Differences between bidder and target returns in Europe are smaller than in the US.
Buch, Delong (2008)	The study investigates efficiency and risk in cross-border mergers and what factors drive them. Foreign banks are found to be more efficient than local ones, and systemic risk is observed, though low. There is no clear-cut conclusion on what the drivers of cross-border mergers are.
Focarelli, Pozzolo (2008)	This study analyses cross-border mergers in banks and insurance firms. Both institutions tend to pursue a 'follow the client' strategy, with the insurance firms also more concerned than banks in risk diversification. Barriers to foreign expansion affect banks more than they do insurance firms.
Williams, Liao (2008)	Considering shareholder wealth, this study focuses on emerging markets. Like in most studies, target shareholders are found to earn positive returns while bidders suffer negative returns. Value is found to be linked to the target country's economic conditions, profit performance of the target, and the method of settlement used in the transaction.

Source: Adapted from Bottiglia *et al.* (2010).

APPENDIX 2: EUROPEAN AND US LEGISLATION

Table 4. Legislation Impacting on the EU Banking and Financial Sectors

1977	*First Banking Directive*: Removed obstacles to the provision of services and establishment of branches across the borders of EU member states, harmonized rules for bank licensing and established EU-wide supervisory arrangements.
1988	*Basel Capital Adequacy Regulation (Basle 1)*. Minimum Capital Adequacy requirements for banks (8% ratio). Capital definitions: Tier 1 (Equity); Tier 2 (near equity). Risk-weightings based on credit risk for bank business.
1988	*Directive on Liberalization of Capital Flows*. Free cross-border capital flows, with safeguards for countries having balance of payments problems.
1989	*Second Banking Directive*. Single EU banking license. Principles of home country (home regulators have ultimate supervisory authority for the foreign activity of their banks) and mutual recognition (EU bank regulators recognise the equivalence of their regulations). Passed in conjunction with the Own Funds and Solvency Directives, incorporating capital adequacy requirements similar to Basel 1 into EU law.
1992	*Large Exposure Directive*. Bank should not commit more than 25% of their own funds to a single investment. Total resources allocated to a single investment should not exceed 800%of own funds.
1993	*Investment Services Directive*. Legislative framework for investment firms and securities markets, providing for a single passport for investment services.
1994	*Directive on Deposit Guarantee Schemes*. Minimum guaranteed investor protection in the event of bank failure.
1999	*Financial Services Action Plan (FSAP)*. Legislative framework for the Single Market in Financial Services.
2000	*Consolidated Borrowing Directive*. Consolidation of previous banking regulation.
2000	*Directive on e-money*. Access by non-credit institutions to the business of e-money issuance. Harmonized rules/standards relating to payments by mobile telephone, transport cards, and Basle payment facilities.
2001	*Directive on the Reorganization and Winding-Up of Credit Institutions*. Recognition throughout the EU of reorganization measures/winding-up proceedings by the home state of a EU credit institution.
2001	*Regulation on the European Company Statute*. Standard rules for company formation throughout the EU.
2002	*Financial Conglomerates Directive*. Supervision framework for a group of financial entities engaged in cross-border activities (banking, insurance, securities).
2004	*New EU Takeover Directive*. Common framework for cross-border takeover bids.
2005-2010	*White Paper on Financial Services Policy*. Plan to implement outstanding FSAP measures, consolidation/convergence of financial services regulation and supervision.
2007	*Markets in Financial Instruments Directive*.
2007	*Capital Requirements Directives* (i.e. the Directives 2006/48/EC and 2006/49/EC) implement the "*International Convergence of Capital Measurement and Capital Standards*" (labeled as Basel II) for credit institutions and investment firms set by Basel Committee on Banking Supervision from 2008.

Source: Goddard *et al.* (2007) with authors' updates.

Table 5. Major Legislative and Regulatory Changes
Affecting US Banking Consolidation

Year	Description
1980	*Depository Institutions Deregulation and Monetary Control Act (DIDMCA)*. Raised federal deposit insurance coverage limit from $40,000 to $100,000. Allowed depositories to offer negotiable order of withdrawal (NOW) accounts nationwide. Eliminated usury ceilings. Imposed uniform reserve requirements on all depository institutions and gave them access to Federal Reserve services.
1982	*Garn-St. Germain Act*. Permitted money market deposit accounts. Permitted banks to purchase failing banks and thrifts across state lines. Expanded thrift lending powers.
1987	*Competitive Equality in Banking Act* (CEBA). Allocated $10.8 billion in additional funding to the Federal Savings Loan Insurance Corporation (FSLIC). Authorized forbearance program for farm banks. Reaffirmed that the "full faith and credit" of the US Department of the Treasury (Treasury) stood behind federal deposit insurance.
1987	Board of Governors of the Federal Reserve System (Federal Reserve) authorized limited underwriting activities for Bankers Trust, J. P. Morgan, and Citicorp with a 5 percent revenue limit on Section 20 ineligible securities activities.
1989	*Financial Institutions Reform, Recovery, and Enforcement Act* (FIRREA). Provided $50 billion in taxpayer funds to resolve failed thrifts. Replaced Federal Home Loan Bank Board with the Office of Thrift Supervision to charter, regulate and supervise thrifts. Restructured federal deposit insurance for thrifts and raised premiums. Re-imposed restrictions on thrift lending activities. Directed the Treasury to study deposit insurance reform.
1989	Federal Reserve expanded Section 20 underwriting permissibility to corporate debt and equity securities, subject to revenue limit.
1989	Federal Reserve raised limit on revenue from 20 eligible securities activities from 5 percent to 10 percent.
1991	*Federal Deposit Insurance Corporation Improvement Act* (FDICIA). Directed the Federal Deposit Insurance Corporation (FDIC) to develop and implement risk-based deposit insurance pricing. Required "prompt corrective action" of poorly capitalized banks and thrifts and restricted "too big to fail". Directed the FDIC to resolve failed banks and thrifts in the least costly way to the deposit insurance funds.
1993	Court ruling in *Independent Insurance Agents of America v. Ludwig* allowed national banks to sell insurance from small towns.
1994	*Riegle-Neal Interstate Bank and Branching Efficiency Act* (Riegle-Neal).Permitted banks and bank holding companies (BHCs) to purchase banks or establish subsidiary banks in any state nationwide. Permitted national banks to open branches or convert subsidiary banks into branches across state lines.
1995	Court ruling in Nationsbank v. Valic allowed to sell annuities.
1996	Court ruling in *Barnett Bank v. Nelson* overturned *states'* restrictions on bank insurance sales.
1996	Federal Reserve announced the elimination of many firewalls between bank and nonbank subsidiaries within BHCs.
1996	Federal Reserve raised limit on revenue from Section 20 eligible securities activities from 10 to 25%.
1997	Federal Reserve eliminated many of the remaining firewalls between banks and nonbank subsidiaries within BHCs.

Table 5. Continued)

Year	Description
1999	*Gramm-Leach-Bliley Financial Modernization Act* (BLG). Authorised financial holding companies (FHCs) to engage in a full range of financial services such as commercial banking, insurance, securities and merchant banking. Gave the Federal Reserve, in consultation with the Treasury, discretion to authorize new financial activities for FHCs. Gave the Federal Reserve discretion to authorize new complementary activities for FHCs. Established the Federal Reserve as the "umbrella" regulator of FHCs. Provided low-cost credit to community banks. Reformed the Community Reinvestment Act. Eliminated the ability of commercial firms to acquire or charter a single thrift in a unitary thrift holding company.
2001	Federal Reserve issued revisions to Regulation K. Expanded permissible activities abroad for US banking organizations. Reduced regulatory burden for US banks operating abroad and streamlined the application and notice process for foreign banks operating in the Unite States. Allowed banks to invest up to 20 percent of capital and surplus in Edge Corporations. Liberalized provisions regarding the qualification of foreign organizations for exemptions from the nonbanking prohibitions of Section 4 of the Bank Holding Companies Act. Implemented provisions of Riegle-Neal that affect foreign banks.

Source: Jones and Critchfield (2005).

REFERENCES

Aggarwal, R., Akhigbe, A., and McNulty, J. E. (2006) 'Are differences between acquiring bank profit efficiency priced in financial markets?' *Journal of Financial Services Research.* 30 (3), 265-286.

Akhavein, J. D., Berger, A. N., and Humphrey, D. B. (1997) 'The effects of megamergers on efficiency and prices: Evidence from a bank profit function'. *Review of Industrial Organization.* 12 (1), 95–139.

Allen, F. and Song, W. L. (2005) 'Financial integration and EMU'. *European Financial Management* 11 (1), 7-24.

Al-Sharkas, A. A., Hassan, M. K., and Lawrence, S. (2008) 'The impact of mergers and acquisitions on the efficiency of the US banking industry: Further evidence'. *Journal of Business Finance and Accounting.* 35 (1-2), 50–70.

Altunbas, Y. and Marques Ibanez, D. (2008) 'Mergers and acquisitions and bank performance in Europe: The role of strategic similarities'. *Journal of Economics and Business.* 60 (3), 204–222.

Amel, D., Barnes, C., Panetta, F., and Salleo, C. (2004) 'Consolidation and efficiency in the financial sector: a review of the international evidence'. *Journal of Banking and Finance.* 28 (10), 2493–2519.

Anderson, C., Becher, D., and Campbell, T. (2004) 'Bank mergers, the market for bank CEOs, and managerial incentives'. *Journal of Financial Intermediation.* 13 (1), 6–27.

Ashton, J. K. and Pham, K. (2007) 'Efficiency and price effects of horizontal bank mergers'. available from http://papers.ssrn.com/sol3/papers.cfm [January 5, 2011].

Ayadi, R. and Pujals, G. (2005) 'Banking mergers and acquisitions in the EU: Overview, Assessment and Prospects'. available from http://www.suerf.org [January 5, 2011].

Ayuso, J. and Blanco, R. (2001) 'Has financial market integration increased during the nineties?' *Journal of International Financial Markets, Institutions and Money.* 11 (3-4), 265-287.

Baradwaj, B. G., Fraser, D. R., and Furtado, E. P. H. (1990) 'Hostile bank takeover offers: analysis and implications'. *Journal of Banking and Finance.* 14 (6), 1229-1242.

Beccalli, E. and Frantz, P. (2009) 'M&A Operations and performance in banking'. *Journal of Financial Services Research.* 36 (2-3), 203-226.

Becher, D. A. (2000) 'The valuation effects of bank mergers'. *Journal of Corporate Finance.* 6 (2), 189-214.

Beitel, P. and Schiereck, D. (2001) 'Value creation at the ongoing consolidation of the European banking market'. Institute for Mergers and Acquisitions, Working Paper No. 05-01.

Beitel, P., Schiereck, D., and Wahrenburg, M. (2004) 'Explaining M&As Success in European Banks'. *European Financial Management.* 10 (1), 109-139.

Berger, A. N., and Humphrey, D. B. (1992) 'Megamergers in banking and the use of cost efficiency as an antitrust defense'. *Antitrust Bulletin.* 37 (3), 541–600.

Berger, A. N. and Humphrey, D. B. (1994) 'Bank scale economies, mergers, concentration, and efficiency: The US experience'. Financial Institutions Center, The Wharton School, University of Pennsylvania, Working Paper No. 94-25.

Berger, A. N. and Mester, L. J. (1997) 'Inside the Black Box: What explains the differences in the efficiencies of financial institutions?' *Journal of Banking and Finance.* 21 (7), 895-947.

Berger, A. N. and Humphrey, D. B. (1997) 'Efficiency of financial institutions: International survey and directions for future research'. *European Journal of Operational Research.* 98 (2), 175-212.

Berger A. N. (1998) 'The efficiency effects of bank mergers and acquisitions: a preliminary look at the 1990s data'. in *Bank Mergers and Acquisitions. eds.* Amihud Y., and Miller, G. Boston: Kluwer.

Berger, A. N. and Hannan, T. H. (1998) 'The efficiency cost of market power in the banking industry: a test of the 'quiet life' and related hypotheses'. *Review of Economics and Statistics.* 80 (3), 454–465.

Berger, A. N., Demsetz, R. S., and Strahan, P. E., (1999) 'The consolidation of the financial services industry: Causes, consequences, and implications for the future'. *Journal of Banking and Finance.* 23 (2–4), 135–194.

Berger, A. N. (2000) 'The integration of the financial services industries: where are the efficiencies?' *North American Actuarial Journal.* 4 (3), 25-52.

Berger, A. N., Cummins, D. J., Weiss, M.A., and Zi, H. (2000a) 'Conglomeration versus strategic focus: Evidence from the insurance industry'. Board of Governors of the Federal Reserve System.

Berger, A. N., DeYoung, R., Genay, H., and Udell, G. F. (2000b) 'Globalization of financial institutions: evidence from cross-border banking performance'. Brookings-Wharton Papers on Financial Services, 23–120.

Berger, A. N. and DeYoung, R. (2000) 'The financial performance of cross-regional commercial banks in the U.S.: Some clues regarding the eventual structure of a consolidating industry'. Board of Governors of the Federal Reserve System.

Berger, A. N. (2003) 'The efficiency effects of a single market for financial services in Europe'. *European Journal of Operational Research.* 150 (3), 466-481.

Berger, A. N., Buch, C. M., DeLong, G. L., and DeYoung, R. (2004) 'Exporting financial institutions management via foreign direct investment mergers and acquisitions'. *Journal of International Money and Finance.* 23(3), 333–366.

Berger, A. N., Bonime, S. D., Goldberg, L. G., and White, L. J. (2004) 'The dynamics of market entry: the effects of mergers and acquisitions on entry in the banking industry'. *Journal of Business.* 77 (4), 797–834.

Berger, A. N. (2007) 'Obstacles to a global banking system: 'Old Europe' versus 'New Europe''. *Journal of Banking and Finance.* 31 (7), 1955–1973.

Bliss, R. T. and Rosen, R. J. (2001) 'CEO compensation and bank mergers'. *Journal of Financial Economics.* 61 (1), 107–138.

Bonin, J. P. and Wachtel, P. (1999) 'Lessons from Bank Privatization in Central Europe'. available from http://deepblue.lib.umich.edu/bitstream/2027.42/39631/3/wp245 [January 5, 2011].

Bottiglia, R., Gualandri, E., and Mazzocco, G. N. (eds.) (2010) *Consolidation in the European Financial Industry.* Eastbourne: Palgrave.

Boyd, J. H. and Graham, S. L. (1998) 'Consolidation in US banking: implications for efficiency and risk' in Amihud, Y. and Miller, G. (eds.) *Bank Mergers and Acquisitions.* London: Kluwer Academic Publishers.

Brewer, E., Jackson, W., Jagtiani, J. and Nguyen, T. (2000) 'The Price of Bank Mergers in the 1990s'. Federal Bank of Chicago, *Economic Perspectives*, March, 2–23. available from www.chicagofed.org [January 5, 2011].

Buch, C. M. (2000) 'Why Do Banks Go Abroad? Evidence from German Data', *Financial Markets, Institutions and Instruments.* 9 (1), 33-67.

Buch, C. M., and DeLong, G. L. (2004) 'Cross-border Bank Mergers: What Lures the Rare Animal?' *Journal of Banking and Finance.* 28 (9), 2077-2102.

Buch, C. and DeLong, G. L. (2008) 'Banking globalization: international consolidation and mergers in banking'. available from http://ideas.repec.org/p/iaw/iawdip [January 5, 2011].

Cabral, I., Dierick, F., and Vesala, J. (2002) 'Banking Integration in the euro area'. ECB Occasional Paper No. 6.

Campa, J. M. and Hernando, I. (2004) 'Shareholder value creation in European M&As'. *European Financial Management.* 10(1), 47-81.

Campa J. M. and Hernando, I. (2006) 'M&A performance in the European financial industry'. *Journal of Banking and Finance.* 30 (12), 3367–3392.

Carbo-Valverde, S. and Humphrey, D. B. (2004) 'Predicted and actual costs from individual bank mergers'. *Journal of Economics and Business.* 56 (2), 137–157.

Carbo-Valverde, S., Humphrey, D., and Del Paso, R. L. (2007) 'Do cross-country differences in bank efficiency support a policy of "national champions"?' *Journal of Banking and Finance.* 31 (7), 2173-2188.

Chari, A., Oumet, P., and Tesar, L. L. (2004) 'Cross border mergers and acquisitions in Emerging Markets: The stock market valuation of corporate control'. available from http://papers.ssrn.com/sol3/papers.cfm [January 5, 2011].

Chronopoulos, D. K., Girardone, C., and Nankervis, J. C. (2010) 'Post-merger bank efficiency and stock market reaction: the case of the US versus Europe'. in *New Issues in*

Financial Institutions Management. ed. by Fiordelisi, F., Molyneux, P., and Previati, D. Eastbourne: Palgrave Macmillan.

Claessens, S. and van Horen, N. (2007) 'Location Decisions of Foreign Banks and Competitive Advantage'. *World Bank Policy Research Working Paper*. No. 4113.

Copeland, T. E., Weston, J. F. and Shastri, K. (2003) *Financial Theory and Corporate Policy*. 4th edn. New York: Pearson Education.

Cornett, M. M., Hovakimian, G., Palia D., and Tehranian H. (2003) 'The impact of the manager-shareholder conflict on acquiring bank returns'. *Journal of Banking and Finance*. 27 (1), 103–131.

Cornett, M. M., McNutt, J. J., and Tehranian, H. (2006) 'Performance changes around bank mergers: revenue enhancements versus cost reductions'. *Journal of Money, Credit and Banking* 38 (4), 1013–1050.

Corvoisier, S. and Gropp, R. (2002) 'Bank concentration and retail interest rates'. *Journal of Banking and Finance*. 26 (11), 2155-2189.

Cummins, J. D. and Weiss M. A. (2004) 'Consolidation in the European insurance industry: Do mergers and acquisitions create value for shareholders?' Wharton Financial Institution Center Working Paper 04-02, University of Pennsylvania.

Cybo-Ottone, A. and Murgia, M. (2000) 'Mergers and shareholder wealth in European banking'. *Journal of Banking and Finance* 24 (6), 831–859.

Degryse, H. A., Masschelein, N., and Mitchell, J. (2006) 'Staying, dropping, or switching: the impacts of bank mergers on SMEs'. Tilburg Law and Economics Center (TILEC) Discussion Paper No. 2006-034, December. available from http://papers.ssrn.com/sol3/papers.cfm [January 5, 2011].

Degryse, H. A. and Ongena, S. (2004) 'The impact of technology and regulation on the geographical scope of banking', *Oxford Review of Economic Policy*. 20 (4), 571-590.

De Guevara, J. F., Maudos, J., and Perez, F. (2005) 'Market power in the European banking sector'. *Journal of Financial Services Research*. 27 (2), 109–137.

De Guevara, J. F. and Maudos, J. (2007) 'Explanatory factors of market power in the banking system'. *The Manchester School*. 75 (3), 275–296.

DeLong, G. L. (2001a) 'Focusing versus diversifying mergers: analysis of market reaction and long-term performance'. available from http://papers.ssrn.com/sol3/papers.cfm [January 5, 2011].

DeLong, G. L. (2001b) 'Stockholder gains from focusing versus diversifying bank mergers'. *Journal of Financial Economics*. 59 (2), 221–252.

DeLong, G. L. (2003a) 'Does Long-term Performance of Mergers Match Market Expectations? Evidence from the US Banking Industry'. *Financial Management*. 32 (2), 5–25.

DeLong, G. L. (2003b) 'The announcement effects of US versus non-US bank mergers: do they differ?' *The Journal of Financial Research*. 26 (4), 487-500.

DeLong, G. L. and DeYoung, R. (2007) 'Learning by observing: Information spillovers in the execution and valuation of commercial bank M&As'. *Journal of Finance*. 62 (1), 181–216.

DeYoung, R. (1997) 'Bank mergers, X-efficiency, and the market for corporate control'. *Managerial Finance*. 23 (1), 32–47.

DeYoung, R., Evanoff, D. D., and Molyneux, P. (2009) 'Mergers and Acquisitions of Financial Institutions: A Review of the Post-2000 Literature'. *Journal of Financial Services Research.* 36 (2-3), 87-110.

Diaz, B., Olalla, M., and Azorfa, S. (2004) 'Bank acquisitions and performance: evidence from a panel of European credit entities'. *Journal of Economics and Business.* 56 (5), 377–404.

Ekkayokkaya, M., Holmes, P., and Paudyal, K. (2009) 'The Euro and the changing face of European banking: evidence from mergers and acquisitions'. *European Financial Management.* 15 (2), 451–476.

Elsas, R., Hackethal, A. and Holzhauser, M. (2006) 'The anatomy of bank diversification'. available from http://papers.ssrn.com/sol3/papers.cfm [January 5, 2011].

Emmons, W. R., Gilbert, R. A., and Yeager, T. Y. (2004) 'Reducing the risk at small community banks: is it size or geographic diversification that matters?' *Journal of Financial Services Research.* 25 (2-3), 259–281.

Estrella, A. (2001) 'Mixing and matching: Prospective financial sector mergers and market valuation'. *Journal of Banking and Finance.* 25 (12), 2367–2392.

European Central Bank (ECB) (2000) 'Mergers and acquisitions involving the EU banking industry – facts and implications'. ECB, Frankfurt

European Central Bank (ECB) (2004a) 'Report on EU Banking Structure'. ECB, Frankfurt, November.

European Central Bank (ECB) (2004b) 'Research Network on Capital Markets and Financial Integration in Europe'. ECB, Frankfurt, December.

European Central Bank (ECB) (2010) 'EU Banking Structures'. ECB, Frankfurt, September.

European Central Bank (ECB) (2006) 'EU Banking Structures'. ECB, Frankfurt, October.

European Commission (2005), '*Cross-border Consolidation in the EU Financial Sector'.* available from http://ec.europa.eu/internal_market/finances/docs/cross-sector/mergers/cross-border-consolidation_en [January 5, 2011].

Fiordelisi, F. (2008) 'Efficiency and shareholder return in banking'. *International Journal of Banking, Accounting and Finance.* 1 (2), 114-132.

Floreani, A. and Rigamonti, S. (2001) 'Mergers and shareholders' wealth in the insurance industry'. available from http://papers.ssrn.com/sol3/papers.cfm [January 5, 2011].

Focarelli, D. and Pozollo, A. F. (2000) 'The determinants of cross-border shareholdings: an analysis with bank-level data from OECD countries'. available from http://ideas.repec.org/p/bdi/wp/temi [January 5, 2011].

Focarelli, D. and Pozzolo, A. F. (2001) 'The patterns of cross-border bank mergers and shareholdings in OECD countries'. *Journal of Banking and Finance.* 25 (12), 2305–2337.

Focarelli, D., Panetta, F., and Salleo, C. (2002) 'Why do banks merge?' *Journal of Money, Credit and Banking.* 34 (4), 1047–1066.

Focarelli, D. and Panetta, F. (2003) 'Are mergers beneficial to consumers? Evidence from the market for bank deposits'. *American Economic Review.* 93 (4), 1152–1172.

Focarelli, D. and Pozzolo, A. F. (2005) 'Where do banks expand abroad? An empirical analysis'. *Journal of Business.* 78(6) 2435-2463.

Focarelli, D. and Pozollo, A. F. (2008) 'Cross-border M&As in the financial sector: is banking different from insurance?' *Journal of Banking & Finance.* 32 (1), 15-29.

Fritsch, M., Gleisner, F., and Holzhauser, M. (2006) 'Bank M&A in Central and Eastern Europe' available from http://papers.ssrn.com/sol3/papers.cfm [January 5, 2011].

Gardener, E. P. M., Molyneux, P. and Moore, B. (2001) 'The Impact of the Single Market Programme on EU banking'. *The Service Industries Journal.* 21 (2), 47-70.

Goddard, J., Molyneux, P., and Wilson, J. O. S. (2001) *European Banking: Efficiency, Technology and Growth.* Chichester: John Wiley & Sons.

Goddard, J., Molyneux P., Wilson, J. O. S., and Tavakoli, M. (2007) 'European Banking: An Overview'. *Journal of Banking and Finance.* 31 (7), 1911-1935.

Goergen, M. and Renneboorg, L. (2004) 'Shareholder wealth effects of European domestic and cross-border takeover bids'. *European Financial Management.* 10 (1), 9-45.

Group of Ten, (2001), *Report on Consolidation in the Financial Sector.* available from http://www.imf.org/external/np/g10/2001/01/eng [January 5, 2011].

Gual, J. (2004) 'The integration of EU banking markets'. Centre for Economic Policy Research, London. Discussion Paper Series No. 4212.

Hadlock, C., Houston, J. and Ryngaert, M. (1999) 'The role of managerial incentives in bank acquisition'. *Journal of Banking and Finance.* 23 (2-4), 221-249.

Hagendorff, J., Collins, M., and Keasey, K. (2008) 'Investor Protection and the Value Effects of Bank Merger Announcements in Europe and the US'. *Journal of Banking and Finance.* 32 (7), 1333-1348.

Hagendorff, J. and Keasey, K. (2009) 'Post-merger strategy and performance: evidence from the US and European banking industries'. *Accounting and Finance.* 49 (4), 725-751.

Hannan, T. H. and Pilloff, S. J. (2005) 'Will the proposed application of Basel II in the United States encourage increased bank merger activity? Evidence from past merger activity'. Federal Reserve Board of Governors. Finance and Economics Discussion Series No. 13.

Hart, J. R. and Apilado, V. P. (2002) 'Inexperienced banks and interstate mergers'. *Journal of Economics & Business.* 54 (3) 313-330.

Hawawini, G. A. and Swary, I. (1990) *Mergers and Acquisitions in the US Banking Industry: Evidence from the Capital Markets*, New York: Elsevier Science Publishers.

Hendershott, R. J., Lee, D. E., and Tompkins, J. G. (2002) 'Winners and losers as financial service providers converge: evidence from the Financial Modernization Act of 1999'. *Financial Review.* 37 (1), 53–72.

Hernando, I., Nieto, M. J., and Wall, L. D. (2009) 'Determinants of domestic and cross-border bank acquisitions in the European Union'. *Journal of Banking and Finance.* 33 (6), 1022-1032.

Houston, J. H. and Ryngaert, M. D. (1994) 'The overall gains from large bank mergers'. *Journal of Banking and Finance.* 18 (6), 1155-1176.

Houston, J. H., James, C. M. and Ryngaert, M. D. (2001) 'Where do merger gains come from? Bank mergers from the perspective of insiders and outsiders'. *Journal of Financial Economics.* 60 (2-3), 285-331.

Hughes, J. P., Lang, W., Mester, L. J., and Moon C. G. (1999) 'The Dollars and Sense of Bank Consolidation'. *Journal of Banking and Finance.* 23 (2–4), 291–324.

Hughes, J., Lang, W., Mester, L., Moon, C. G., and Pagano, M. (2003) 'Do bankers sacrifice value to build empires? Managerial incentives, industry consolidation, and financial performance'. *Journal of Banking and Finance.* 27 (3), 417–447.

Huizinga, H. P., Nelissen, J. H. M., and Vander Vennet, R. (2001) 'Efficiency effects of bank mergers and acquisitions in Europe', Ghent University. Working Paper No. 106.

Ismail, A. and Davidson, I. (2005) 'Further analysis of mergers and shareholder wealth effects in European banking'. *Applied Financial Economics.* 15 (1), 13-30.

Jones, K. D. and Critchfield, T. (2005) 'Consolidation in the US Banking Industry: Is the "Long Strange Trip" About to End?' *FDIC Banking Review.* 17 (4), 31-61.

Kane, E. (2000) 'Incentives for Banking Megamergers: What Motives Might Regulators Infer from Event-study Evidence?' *Journal of Money, Credit and Banking* 32 (3), 671-701.

Kaufman, D. J. (1988) 'Factors affecting the magnitude of premiums paid to target-firm shareholders in corporate acquisitions'. *The Financial Review.* 23 (4), 465-482.

Kiymaz, H. and Mukherjee, T. K. (2000) 'The impact of country diversification on wealth effects in cross-border mergers'. *The Financial Review.* 35 (2), 37-58.

Kiymaz, H. (2004) 'Cross-border acquisitions of US financial institutions: Impact of macroeconomic factors'. *Journal of Banking and Finance..* 28 (6), 1413-1439.

Knapp, M., Gart, A., and Becher, D. (2005) 'Post-merger performance of bank-holding companies 1987–1998'. *Financial Review.* 40 (4), 549–574.

Knapp, M., Gart, A., and Chaudhry, M. (2006) 'The impact of mean reversion of bank profitability on post-merger performance in the banking industry'. *Journal of Banking and Finance.* 30 (12), 3503–3517.

Koetter, M. (2005) 'Evaluating the German bank merger wave'. available from http://papers.ssrn.com/sol3/papers.cfm [January 5, 2011].

Kohers, T., Huang, M. and Kohers, N. (2000), 'Market perceptions of efficiency in bank holding company mergers: The roles of the DEA and SFA models in capturing merger potential'. *Review of Financial Economics.* 9 (2), 101-120.

Kwan, S. H. and Laderman, E. S. (1999) 'On the portfolio effects of financial convergence – a review of the literature'. Federal Reserve Bank of San Francisco, *Economic Review* 2, 18-31.

Kwan, S. H. and Wilcox, J. A. (2002) 'Hidden Cost Reductions in Bank Mergers: Accounting for More Productive Banks'. *Research in Finance.* 19, 109-124.

Lensink, R., and Maslennikova, I. (2008) 'Value Performance of European Bank Acquisitions'. *Applied Financial Economics.* 18 (3), 185-198.

Lepetit, L., Patry, S., and Rous, P. (2004) 'Diversification versus specialization: an event study of M&As in the European banking industry'. *Applied Financial Economics.* 14 (9), 663–669.

Levy, H. and Sarnat, M. (1970) 'Diversification, Portfolio Analysis and the Uneasy Case for Conglomerate Mergers'. *Journal of Finance.* 25 (4), 795-802.

Lorenz, J. T. and Schiereck, D. (2007) 'Completed versus canceled banking M&A transactions in Europe'. Working Paper available at http://affi2007.u-bordeaux4.fr/Actes [January 5, 2011]

Lown, C. S., Osler, C. L., Strahan, P. E., and Sufi, A. (2000) 'The changing landscape of the financial service industry: what lies ahead?' Federal Reserve Bank New York, *Economic Policy Review.* 6(4), 39–54.

Madura, J. and Wiant, K. J. (1994) 'Long-term valuation effects of bank acquisitions' *Journal of Banking and Finance.* 18 (6), 1135-1154.

Mayer-Sommer, A. P., Sweeney, S. and Walker, D. A. (2005) 'Effect of bank acquisition on shareholder returns'. *Bank Accounting & Finance.* 18 (4), 11-16.

Miller, S. M. and Noulas, A. G. (1996), 'The technical efficiency of large bank production', *Journal of Banking and Finance.* 20 (3), 495-509.

Molyneux, P., Altunbas, Y., and Gardener, E. (1996) *Efficiency in European Banking.* Chichester: John Wiley & Sons.

Moore, R. R. (1996) 'Banking's merger fervor: Survival of the fittest?' Federal Reserve Bank of Dallas. *Financial Industry Studies*, December, 9-15.

Nnadi, M. and Tanna, S. (2011) 'Analysis of Cross-border and Domestic Mega-M&As of European Commercial Banks', forthcoming *Managerial Finance.*

Olson, G. T. and Pagano, M. S. (2005) 'A new application of sustainable growth: a multi-dimensional framework for evaluating the long run performance of bank mergers'. *Journal of Business, Finance and Accounting.* 32 (9-10), 1995–2036.

Pasiouras, F., Tanna, S., and Gaganis C. (2011) 'What drives acquisitions in the EU banking industry? The role of bank regulation and supervision framework, bank specific and market specific factors'. *Financial Markets, Institutions and Instruments*, 2 (2), 2011, p. 29-77.

Peek, J., Rosenberg, E. S., and Kasirye, F. (1999) 'The Poor Performance of Foreign Bank Subsidiaries: Were the Problems Acquired or Created?' *Journal of Banking and Finance.* 23 (2-4), 579-604.

Penas, M. and Unal, H. (2004) 'Gains in bank mergers: Evidence from the bond market'. *Journal of Financial Economics.* 74 (1), 149–179.

Peristiani, S. (1997) 'Do Mergers Improve the X-Efficiency and Scale Economies of U.S. Banks? Evidence from the 1980s'. *Journal of Money, Credit, and Banking.* 29 (3), 326–337.

Pilloff, S. J. (2004) 'Bank merger activity in the United States 1994-2003'. Board of Governors of the Federal Reserve System, Staff Study 176, May.

Pilloff, S. J. (1996) 'Performance changes and shareholder wealth creation associated with mergers of publicly traded banking institutions'. *Journal of Money, Credit, and Banking.* 28 (3), 59–78.

Pilloff, S. and Santomero, A. M. (1998) 'The value effect of bank mergers and acquisitions'. in *Bank Mergers and Acquisitions.* ed. by Amihud, Y., and Miller, G. Boston: Kluwer Academic Publishers.

Rhoades, S. A. (1993) 'The Efficiency Effects of (in-market) horizontal bank mergers'. *Journal of Banking and Finance.* 17 (2-3), 411-422.

Rhoades, S. A., (1994) 'A summary of merger performance studies in banking, 1980-93, and an assessment of the operating performance and event study methodologies'. Federal Reserve Board. Staff Study No. 167.

Rhoades, S. A. (1998) 'The efficiency effects of bank mergers: an overview of case studies of nine mergers'. *Journal of Banking and Finance.* 22 (3), 273–291.

Roll, R. (1986) 'The Hubris Hypothesis of Corporate Takeovers'. *Journal of Business.* 59 (2), 197-216.

Rosen, R. J. (2004) 'Betcha can't acquire just one: merger programs and compensation'. Federal Reserve Bank of Chicago. Working Paper No. 2004-22.

Scholten, B. and De Wit, R. (2004) 'Announcement effects of bank mergers in Europe and US'. *Research in International Business and Finance.* 18 (2), 217-228.

Schmautzer, D. (2006) "Cross-border bank mergers: Who gains and why?" Working Paper. available from http://papers.ssrn.com/sol3/papers.cfm [January 5, 2011].

Scott-Frame, W. and Lastrapes W.D. (1998) 'Abnormal returns in the acquisition market: the case of bank holding companies 1990-1993'. *Journal of Financial Services Research.* 14 (2), 145-163.

Siems, T. F. (1996), 'Bank mergers and shareholder wealth: evidence from 1995's megamerger deals'. Federal Reserve Bank of Dallas. *Financial Industry Studies*, August.

Tourani-Rad, A. T. and Van Beek, L. (1999) 'Market Valuation of European Mergers'. *European Management Journal.* 17 (5), 532-540.

Tschoegl, A. E. (2004) 'Who owns the major US subsidiaries of foreign banks? A note.' available from http://fic.wharton.upenn.edu/fic/papers/03 [January 5, 2011].

Urio, H. N. (2011) 'The impact of Mergers and Acquisitions on Bank Efficiency in Europe', unpublished PhD Thesis, Coventry University.

Vander Vennet, R. (1996) 'The effect of mergers and acquisition on the efficiency and profitability of EC credit institutions'. *Journal of Banking and Finance.* 20 (9), 1531-1558.

Vander Vennet, R. (2002) 'Cross-border mergers in European banking and bank efficiency'. available from http://www.ecri.be/new/system/files [January 5, 2011].

Vander Vennet, R. (1998) 'Cost and profit dynamics in financial conglomerates and universal banks in Europe'. available from http://papers.ssrn.com/sol3/papers.cfm [January 5, 2011].

Vander Vennet, R. (2002) 'Cost and profit efficiency of financial conglomerates and universal banks in Europe'. *Journal of Money, Credit and Banking.* 34 (1), 254-282.

Varadarajan, P. R. and Cunningham, M. H. (1995) 'Strategic alliances: A synthesis of conceptual foundations'. *Journal of the Academy of Marketing Science.* 23 (4), 282-296.

Williams, J. and Liao, A. (2008) 'The search for value: cross-border M&A in emerging market'. *Comparative Economic Studies.* 50 (2), 274-296.

Zollo, M. and Leshchinkskii, D. (2000) 'Can firms learn to acquire? Do markets notice?' available from http://knowledge.wharton.upenn.edu. [January 5, 2011].

In: Financial Services: Efficiency and Risk Management
Editors: M. D. Fethi, C. Gaganis et al.

ISBN: 978-1-62100-560-5
© 2012 Nova Science Publishers, Inc.

Chapter 2

ASSESSING THE ADVERSE EFFECTS OF INTERBANK FUNDS ON BANK EFFICIENCY THROUGH USING SEMIPARAMETRIC AND NONPARAMETRIC METHODS

Ahmet Faruk Aysan[1], Gürdal Ertek[2]* and Seçil Öztürk[3]**

[1] Bogazici University, Department of Economics,
Bebek, 34342, Istanbul, Turkey.
[2] Sabancı University, Faculty of Engineering and Natural Sciences,
Orhanlı, Tuzla, 34956, Istanbul, Turkey.
[3] Bogazici University, Department of Economics,
Bebek, 34342, Istanbul, Turkey.

ABSTRACT

This chapter investigates the relationship between interbank funds and efficiencies for the commercial banks operating in Turkey between 2001 and 2006. Data Envelopment Analysis (DEA) is executed to find the efficiency scores of the banks for each year, and fixed effects panel data regression is carried out, with the efficiency scores being the response variable. It is observed that interbank funds (ratio) has negative effects on bank efficiency, while bank capitalization and loan ratio have positive, and profitability has insignificant effects. This chapter serves as novel evidence that interbank funds can have adverse effects in an emerging market.

JEL Classification Codes: C14 (Semiparametric and Nonparametric Methods), C67 (Input–Output Models), G21 (Banks; Other Depository Institutions; Micro Finance Institutions; Mortgages)

Keywords: Turkish Banking Sector; Interbank Funds; Data Envelopment Analysis; Efficiency; Panel Regression; Cluster Analysis, Two Step Procedure

---

* ahmet.aysan@boun.edu.tr
* ertekg@sabanciuniv.edu
* secil.ozturk@boun.edu.tr

1. Introduction

The aim of this chapter is to assess the effects of interbank fundson the efficiency of banks. Together with investment securities, interbank funds are among the major components of other earning assets, which constitute one of the outputs used commonly in measuring the banks' efficiency. This chapter has two steps in analyzing the role of interbank funds on efficiency. First, the efficiency scores are calculated with a non-parametric method, namely through Data Envelopment Analysis (DEA). Then, the efficiency scores obtained in the first stage are regressed on the potential determinants of bank efficiency frequently suggested in the literature. In addition to the existing determinants of efficiency, this chapter particularly focuses on the role of interbank funds in explaining the efficiency scores. The regression specifications have also other independent variables, such as the profitability ratio, number of branches, and loan ratio, which are shown to have a relationship with the efficiency of a bank in the existing studies.

The reason why this chapter focused particularly on this component of other earning assets is attributable to the developments in Turkish banking sector, especially following the crises in 1994 and 2001. Banking industry in Turkey was strictly regulated before 1980. The government had restrictions on the foreign exchange reserves, interest rates paid by banks to depositors, market entry and even on the number of branches. Although this closed system appeared to provide a safe environment for the banks in the financial sector, it hindered the financial system to develop through competition and innovation. After 1980 a financial liberalization program was initiated in which limitations on foreign exchange reserves and market entries from abroad were removed. Accompanied with these regulations, by the establishment of Interbank Money Market in 1986, domestic banks also started to open new branches abroad and became able to borrow and lend among themselves. However, the financial system was still subject to government interventions, which eventually resulted in a financial crisis in 1994. These government interventions to the domestic debt market caused the system to be more prone to liquidity risk because of increased maturity mismatches between assets and liabilities. In the restructuring period of the crisis, monetary policies mainly aimed at shifting domestic borrowing from the Central Bank of Turkey to commercial banks. Starting from 1996, public debt was financed through short term government bonds and treasury bills with high interest rates. The main motivation of commercial banks in purchasing the government securities was to be immune to the credit risk while receiving high profits. However, this way of financing the public debt increased the vulnerability of the financial sector and together with other factors like currency risks and maturity mismatches, ultimately drove the Turkish economy into more severe crises[10] (Özatay and Sak, 2002; Turhan, 2008).

Interbank money market is a useful intermediary between banks when they have liquidity shortages. Figure 1 shows the change in the amount of interbank funds in Turkey between 2001 and 2006. For each period, the averages of the amount of interbank funds are taken. The initial observations point out that except 2001, interbank funds have an increasing trend and this fact confirms the increasing importance of interbank funds in the recent years. In Figure 2, the real change in interbank funds is represented by its growth rate and the results confirm that interbank funds level shows an increasing trend from 2001 to 2006. Hence, we

---

[10] Also see Al and Aysan (2006), Aysan and Ceyhan (2008-b), Aysan and Ceyhan (2008-c).

investigate whether this increase in the volume of interbank funds has an effect on efficiencies of banks in Turkey. The main problem with interbank money market is the volatility of its overnight rates. This volatility was attempted to be reduced in 1996 and 1997 to maintain the financial stability. However the consequences were not as expected.

In 2001, the government abandoned the strict monetary policy pursued and shifted to the floating exchange rate regime. The monetary policy before the crisis aimed at reducing the inflation and interest rates. Nevertheless, in November of 2000 an economic volatility shook this stable environment while the political tension erupted. The stabilization program adopted suffered from lack of credibility issue. In only one day, 7.5 billion dollar was drawn from Central Bank of Turkey and the overnight interest rates rose up to 7500 percent. The financial crisis also accounts for the decline in the interbank funds in 2001 since the overnight interest rates showed a dramatic hike.

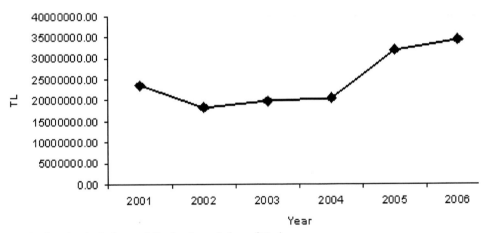

Source: Authors' calculation and Banks Association of Turkey.

Figure 1. Change in Interbank Funds between 2001 and 2006.

The 2001 economic crisis caused especially small and medium scale businesses around Turkey to be shut down and many people to lose their jobs. After the crisis, banks changed the way they report their balance sheets and started to use inflationary accounting. Due to this change, balance sheet items before 2001 are not consistent with those after 2001. In addition, political and macroeconomic environment is more stable since then. Hence taking pre- and post-2001 periods together may bias the efficiency scores, as the conditions changed dramatically. Due to this reason, this chapter only focuses on the post-crisis period.

As the system became free from government interventions and open to the global financial system, a more competitive environment was achieved. Previously, it was sufficient for banks to establish a good reputation for keeping their existing clients or reaching potential ones. However, after the liberalization efforts they need to offer more branches and become more technologically developed to compete with their rivals and survive in the market. Another major change was the improvements in how the banks operate. The main source of revenue for banks comes from loans, since banks invest the sizable fractions of the deposits collected in loans to the individuals and firms. Alternative ways of utilizing deposits are through government and other securities transactions and interbank funds. Hence, banks operating in Turkey shifted some of their resources from the traditional way of banking to these alternatives.

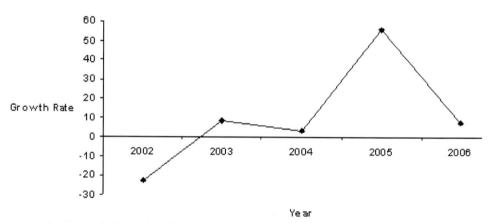

Source: Authors' calculation and Banks Association of Turkey.

Figure 2. Change in Growth Rate of Interbank Funds between 2001 and 2006.

In modeling the efficiency and choosing the set of inputs and outputs, this chapter relies essentially on Stavarek (2003) and Isik and Hassan (2002). Similar to Isik and Hassan (2002), the chapter improves Stavarek (2003) by incorporating off-balance sheet items and other earning assets into analysis. Other earning assets are critical in measuring the efficiency of banking in Turkey since its components play a considerable role in the banking operations in Turkey. The establishment of Interbank Money Market for Turkish Lira in 1986 enables banks to fund each other so that they can meet their liquidity needs in the short term. Hence interbank funds emerge also an alternative way of investing the available deposits. Another alternative to extending the loans as mentioned before is dealing with investment securities, that is, giving loan especially to the government or to other institutions through buying their issued papers. Off-balance sheet items need to be included among the list of outputs since their ignorance results in miscalculation of the efficiency scores.

This is the second study that investigates the effects of interbank funds on efficiency within a DEA framework, and the first study that combines DEA, panel regression, cluster analysis and data visualization in critical investigation of the banking sector in given country. The analysis of the sector during post-crises period, covering 2001-2006 is also novel.

The organization of this chapter is as follows. A selective review of the literature is presented in the following section. In section 3, the methodology used, namely Data Envelopment Analysis (DEA), is briefly explained. In section 4, the data set and the empirical setting are described and the reasons behind the selection of the variables in the two stages of the empirical model are given. In section 5, nonparametric estimation results are presented and analyzed with the regression specifications. In section 6, a cluster analysis of the banks in Turkey for the year 2006 is carried out based on the results of earlier sections. The results of the cluster analysis are also visually presented in this section, to provide comparisons between clusters. Conclusions are relegated to the final section.

2. LITERATURE REVIEW

The first group of studies related to this chapter present the historical development of the Turkish banking sector. Akin et al. (2009) provides a detailed history of the Turkish banking sector between 1980-2004. Steinherr et al. (2004) focus on the period between 1990-2004, including a discussion on the efficiency and competitiveness of the sector. Ozkan-Gunay and Tektas (2006) investigate the sector between the years 1990-2001 and observes sector-wide decline in efficiency. Evren (2007) analyzes the post-crises period, investigating the impact of post-crisis consolidation trend in the sector on the number of bank branches, i.e., availability of banking service. A very extensive cross-industry study on Turkey by the leading management consulting firm McKinsey (2003) shows that the banking sector as a whole has a labor productivity at only 42 percent of US levels. The study mentions macroeconomic instability and the distorting effect of high real interest rates as contributors to the low productivity.

Fethi and Pasiouras (2010) present a comprehensive review of 196 papers which employ operations research (OR) and artificial intelligence (AI) methodologies for evaluating bank performance. 151 of the reviewed papers use DEA or related techniques for estimating bank efficiencies. Since the authors list most of the papers on the topic, the applications of DEA for benchmarking financial institutions in a rich variety of countries is not detailed here, and the reader is referred to the mentioned review paper. Instead, as a second group of the papers in literature, the studies focusing on the Turkish banking sector will be presented.

Isik and Hassan (2002) examine the impact of bank size, corporate control and governance, holding affiliation, international presence, and ownership on the cost and profit efficiency of Turkish banks between 1988 and 1996. The authors compare cost efficiency with profit efficiency for the case of Turkish banks, and reveal that profit efficiency can be high regardless of cost efficiency, pointing out to an imperfect market with profit opportunities for all types and sizes of banks. The DEA model in this chapter is the same as in Isik and Hassan (2002), except that here, short term loans and long term loans are considered within a single output, total loans, and personnel expenses are taken as an input, rather than the number of employees. Additionally, the time frame considered in Isik and Hassan (2002) is 1988-1896, the pre-crises period, whereas the time frame considered here is 2001-2006, the post-crises period.

Isik and Hassan (2003-a) employ a DEA-type Malmquist index and examines the change in efficiency of Turkish banks during the 1981-2000 period, during which the sector was regulated. Their study reveals that all forms of banks have significantly increased their productivity after the deregulation, mostly due to improved resource management practices, rather than improved scales. Isik and Hassan (2003-b) investigates the impact of the 1994 crisis, observing a significant decrease in efficiencies during the crisis, affecting foreign banks and small banks the most, and public banks the least. Again using a DEA-type Malmquist Index, Alpay and Hassan (2006) compare the efficiencies of the Interest Free Financial Institutions (IFFIs) in Turkey with the conventional banks in the period 1990-2000.

The authors conclude that are IFFIs have higher cost efficiency (47.5% versus 26.6%) and revenue efficiency (75.3% versus 42.9%). Isik (2008) compares the performance of de novo banks (banks that have joined the banking system after deregulation) against the performance of established banks.

Hauner (2005) is the only study found that investigates the impact of interbank funds (deposits) on efficiency. Hauner (2005) covers German and Austrian banks in the period 1995-1999 and concludes that "more cost-efficient banks draw a larger part of their funds from interbank deposits and securitized liabilities". The authors employ the ratio of interbank funds to total assets, whereas this chapter investigates the ratio of interbank funds only to other earning assets.

Benchmarking studies mentioned so far all adopted DEA-type models. On the other hand, Secme et al. (2009) evaluate five leading banks according to two methodologies for multi-criteria decision making, namely fuzzy Analytic Hierarchy Process (AHP) and Technique for Order Performance by Similarity to Ideal Solution (TOPSIS). The authors incorporate measures of both financial and non-financial performance into their analysis.

Two artificial intelligence methods, also recognized as data mining methods, that deal with the grouping of a set of entities are cluster analysis (clustering) and classification (Han et al., 2005). Cluster analysis enables reduction of dimensionality by reducing a set of observations into clusters (groups) without any prior knowledge of any class information. Classification, on the other hand, aims at predicting the class of observations, given a subset of the entities whose class values are known, namely the training set. Cluster analysis has been applied in this chapter, since the main goal is to discover possible hidden structures in the considered data set, without any prior class information. Now, the literature that applies cluster analysis in the analysis of banking sector will be summarized.

Cluster analysis has been employed to reveal the strategic categories (clusters) among Spanish savings banks between 1998 and 2002 (Prior and Surroca, 2007), Polish banks between 1997-2004 (Hałac and Żochowski, 2006), and banks in California, USA between 1979–1988 (Li, 2008). The methodology has also been applied in investigating the stability of Czech banks between 1995 and 2005 (Černohorská et al, 2007) and the behavioural patterns of Russian banks between 1999-2007 (Aleskerov et al., 2008). Brown and Glennon (2000) is the study with the largest sample: ~11300 banks in the USA are clustered for the years 1990 and 1991 and the cost structures are compared across the clusters. Meanwhile, cluster analysis has been applied by Ho and Wu (2006) to reduce the number of financial indicators in benchmarking three major banks in Australia.

Lin (2006) differs from other studies that incorporate cluster analysis, in that clustering is based on the reference set of each inefficient bank, obtained from a DEA model, with the cluster centers being the efficient banks. Marín et al. (2008) is the only study that was encountered in literature that computes the efficiencies based on DEA, and then clusters banks, and finally compares the efficiencies and other characteristics across the clusters. This study encompasses DEA, factor analysis, cluster analysis, and bootstrapping in its analysis of 82 banks in Spain. This chapter follows the same approach of combining DEA and cluster analysis as Marín et al. (2008), and further presents the results of cluster analysis through data visualization, enabling the derivation of insights into the profiles of the identified clusters.

3. METHODOLOGY

The chapter has two phases in terms of the methodology used. In the first step, efficiency scores are estimated with and without other earning assets in the output set where the nonparametric technique of Data Envelopment Analysis (DEA) is used. DEA measures the relative efficiencies of a set of entities, namely decision making units (DMUs), as compared to each other. An efficient DMU, a DMU with an efficiency score of 1, is not necessarily efficient compared to the universal set of entities, but is efficient only when compared with the group of entities selected for the model. Input oriented BCC (Banker, Charnes, Cooper, 1984) model is selected from various types of DEA models, because it can handle negative values in the output set, which is the case for this chapter's data set. Aforementioned negative values exist in the data set of net interest income which is one of the outputs used for the estimation of efficiency scores in DEA. Net interest income of the banks represents the difference between interest revenues and interest expenses. When the amount of interest expense is greater than that of interest revenue, negative values of net interest incomes emerge in the data. That is why for some banks in certain years we have negative values in the data set of net interest income and hence we use BCC version of DEA.

The difference of BCC from other DEA models is that it assumes variable returns to scale, which means that its production frontier is piecewise linear and concave. Figure 3 illustrates the variable returns to scale nature of BCC model.

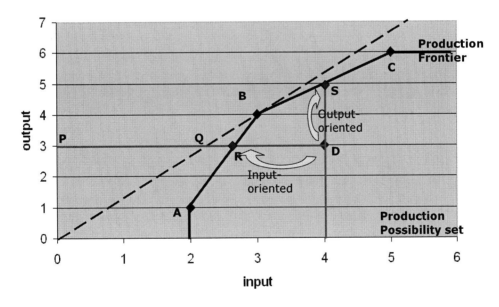

Figure 3. Efficiency Frontier for the BCC model, illustrated for a hypothetical model with one input.

In Figure 3, there are four decision making units (A, B, C and D) and three of them (A, B, and C) are efficient since they are enveloping the inefficient one (D) with the polyline connecting them. R and S are the projections of decision making unit D on the efficient frontier. R is the input-oriented projection while S is the output-oriented one. The uppermost

DMUs are the most efficient ones because the output/input ratio is maximized and hence productivities are maximized at these points. The productivity of an inefficient DMU such as D is given by the ratio PR/PD. The reference set for D is composed of B and C, which means in order to be efficient, D should set these two DMUs as benchmark. The critical issue here is the shape of the efficient frontier. It is not linear, since it is not exhibiting constant returns to scale at all points; rather it is a concave curve where it has increasing returns to scale in the first solid line segment, followed by decreasing returns to scale in the second part and at the intersection of two, there is constant returns to scale.

The model was first proposed by Banker, Charnes and Cooper (1984). The mathematical model for the input-oriented BCC Model (Cooper et al., 2006) is given below and is solved for each DMU to compute its efficiency:

$$(BCC) \max \ \theta_B \tag{1}$$

$$, \qquad , \qquad ,$$

where $[X]=(x_j)$ is the matrix of input variables and $[Y]=(y_j)$ is the output matrix of variables, λ is a column vector and e is the raw vector of 1's. θ_B is the input oriented efficiency score for the DMU that the model attempts to find out.

In order for a DMU to be efficient, there are two conditions that should be satisfied:

    I. $\theta_{B}=1$
    II.   There should not be input excesses and output shortfalls

According to the methodological framework of Fethi and Pasiouras (in press), this chapter measures *technical efficiency* (as opposed to cost and/or profit efficiency), assumes *variable returns to scale* (as opposed to constant returns to scale), builds an *input-oriented DEA* model (as opposed to an output-oriented model), follows the *intermediation approach* for the selection of inputs and outputs (perceives banks as financial intermediaries between savers and investors), accounts for environmental variables using a *two-stage approach* with traditional DEA in the first stage and regression in the second stage. The methodological setup of this chapter is in accordance with its goals, and the conventional practice in literature: For example, Berger and Humphrey (1997) suggest the intermediary approach when benchmarking financial institutions as a whole, while they suggest the alternative production approach for benchmarking branches of a single institution. On the other hand, the studies reviewed in Fethi and Pasiouras (2010) by far employ an input-oriented model, assuming that managers have higher control over inputs compared to outputs.

In this chapter, after obtaining efficiency scores using DEA, a fixed effects panel regression[11] is run in the second stage of the empirical analysis. The dependent variable is the

---

[11] Before applying fixed effects panel regression, variables were checked for autocorrelation. The result of the test show that there exist no autocorrelation hence we continued with the Hausman test to compare fixed effects versus random effects regressions. According to the result of the test, there is no significant difference between two models in terms of consistency of the estimates. Therefore, we are indifferent between two models. In the literature using this two-step procedure fixed effects panel regression is used, so we provide the results of this analysis. In the appendix, the results of random effects regression will be presented as well.

efficiency scores with and without other earning assets obtained in the first step, such that the effects of different variables on efficiency and their significance can be observed. The set up for the fixed effects panel analysis is:

$$Y_{it} = \alpha + \beta X_{it} + \varepsilon_{it} \qquad (2)$$

$$\varepsilon_{it} = u_i + v_{it} \qquad (3)$$

$$i=1,..., N \text{ and } t=1,...,T$$

where Y_{it} stands for the efficiency scores, α is the constant for the regression model, X_{it} is the matrix of independent variables and ε_{it} is the random error in the regression. u_i represents the individual-specific, time-invariant effects, which are assumed to be fixed over time for each bank in this model.

This two step empirical methodology emerges to be widely used in recent studies[12]. For example, a similar study was conducted by Arestis et al. (2006) where they assessed the relationship between financial deepening and efficiency in some non-OECD countries. The authors have used a two-step procedure: After measuring the efficiency scores, they regressed them on several variables representing financial deepening. The rationale behind using this two-step procedure was explained by Arestis et al. (2006) as to prevent any measurement error that may exist in the DEA since it is a non-parametric method for efficiency calculation. Additionally, this procedure deepens the analysis by presenting effects of other variables on efficiency scores as well as the variable of concern.

4. DATA AND EMPIRICAL SETTING

In this chapter, the decision making units (DMUs) of the DEA model are the commercial banks operating in Turkey, including those owned by the Turkish state and foreign entities within the years 2001 through 2006. The data for inputs and outputs are obtained from the Banks Association of Turkey. The variables used in the data set are as follows:

Inputs:
I.   Personnel expenses: Represents the cost of labor, covering wages and all associated expenses
II. Fixed assets: Stands for the cost of capital
III. Total deposits: The sum of demand and time deposits from customers and interbank deposits

Outputs:
I.   Net interest income: The difference between interest income and interest expenses
II. Off balance sheet items: Guarantees and warranties (letters of guarantee, bank acceptance, letters of credit, guaranteed pre-financing, endorsements and others),

---

[12] Also see Aysan and Ceyhan (2007), Aysan and Ceyhan (2008-a) for studies that analyze the Turkish banking sector using the same two-stage approach.

commitments, foreign exchange and interest rate transactions as well as other off-balance sheet activities

III. Total loans: The net value of loans to customers and other financial institutions

IV. Other earning assets: Interbank funds (sold) and investment securities (treasury and other securities)

In the literature, different studies use different models where almost all variables change due to the approach applied. Since there exist no universally accepted set of inputs and outputs, it is crucial to explain why these variables are selected for DEA analysis. The reason why personnel expenses and fixed assets are chosen as inputs is obvious. Without necessary equipment, building and human resource it is not possible for a bank to operate. Therefore, their existence and functioning are vital in determining the efficiency of a bank.

Total deposits are included as well because money collected by banks from their customers is used for investments in the form of instruments like loans, securities or interbank funds. The banks operate as if they convert these inputs, like time and effort of personnel, equipment and deposits from customers into outputs like the loans to firms, to individuals, to government through treasury bills or to other banks. Hence, the loans and other earning assets are also taken as outputs.

The net interest income is the output of a bank where interest expenses and interest income are the inputs. The literature on efficiencies on banking supports the idea that off balance sheet items need to be included in the measurement in addition to balance sheet items. According to Clark and Siems (2002), excluding off balance sheet items leads to an underestimation of the efficiency scores, given that non-traditional ways of banking like the letters of credit, futures or forwards are not taken into account otherwise. Hence by considering off balance sheet items in the output set, we do not ignore banks' asset management activities. DEA is conducted with and without other earning assets to see the difference between these two efficiency scores. The computations are conducted using the DEA-Solver software (Cooper et al., 2006).

The results of DEA are presented in the Appendix where average efficiencies for all banks over the selected time frame are given (see Table A.1). The most obvious outcome in Table A.1 is that the exclusion of other earning assets in the outputs decreases the efficiency scores. There are fifteen banks that are efficient in all periods. Only one of them, Ziraat Bankası, is a state bank. Hence other state banks may take Ziraat Bankası as a benchmark to enhance their efficiency scores. Six banks out of fifteen efficient banks are foreign banks. This result shows that foreign banks have not performed systematically better as compared to their domestic counterparts. Based on the average efficiency scores, one can also conclude that more efficient banks usually come from the groups of private banks and foreign banks. This finding supports the idea that these groups of banks have invested more to improve their technology and used their resources more productively in the post crisis period. In the last column of Table A.1, percentage differences between the efficiency scores of including the other earning assets and excluding them are presented as well. The efficiency scores of Toprakbank and Turkishbank display an extreme difference (194 percent and 100 percent) between these two different calculations. Other than these two banks, the percentage differences are always positive and are at most 20 percent.

Figure 4 shows the average efficiency scores of all banks for the years 2001-2006. The time series above in Figure 4 shows the scores with the other earning assets included, whereas the time series below shows the scores with the other earning assets excluded. There is an increasing trend in both series implying that the commercial banks in Turkey improved their productivities in the restructuring period. However, excluding other earning assets in the output set causes efficiency scores to be underestimated.

Having included the other earning assets in the computations, we obtain the efficiencies for every bank over the selected years. Figure 5 shows the improvements in the efficiencies for all the 48 banks that existed for at least one year through 2001-2006, plotted using Miner3D software[13]. In the figure, *Year* is mapped to the X axis, *DMUs* are mapped to the Y axis, and *efficiency scores* are linearly mapped to colors of the glyphs (data points). The light colors denote higher efficiency scores. The darkest colors denote that the bank did not exist in that year. For example, the bank WLG existed in 2001, but did not exist through 2002-2006.

In the second part of the analysis, the efficiency scores are regressed on the following independent variables: interbank funds, bank capitalization, loan ratio, total assets/number of employees, return on assets (ROA), number of branches, and foreign/domestic and state/private dummies.

The critical variable that this chapter aims to evaluate the effect of interbank funds/OEA ratio as the critical variable and its ratio in the other earning assets is included in the regression specifications. The effect of interbank funds on the efficiency is expected to be negative because high investment in interbank market is an indicator for inefficiency, confirming that the bank could not invest in more profitable assets or loans with greater returns than the interbank funds (Adenso-Diaz and Gascón, 1997). The loans are expected to yield higher returns for the banks. However, the interbank loans tend to offer lower interest rate returns and hence provide less profit opportunities for the banks.

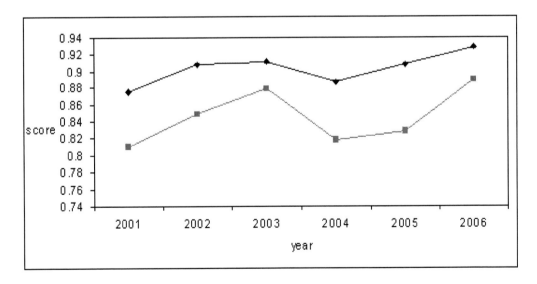

Source: Authors' calculation and Banks Association of Turkey.

Figure 4. Efficiency Scores between 2001 and 2006.

---

[13] See the webpage of the program for details: www.miner3d.com

The loan ratio and bank capitalization are expected to have positive impact on efficiencies. The loan to asset ratio indicates how much loan an asset can generate. Therefore, an increase in this ratio implies that the bank uses its assets more efficiently. The bank capitalization is gauged as the ratio of equity to total assets. As this share increases, the amount of assets transferred into equity increases. Since equity is a vital source for the survival of the bank and its operations, it is expected to have a positive relationship with efficiency. Moreover, it is expected that when the owners of the banks put more capital (equity) into their banks, the banks are expected to run more efficiently while alleviating the moral hazard problem.

The total asset to number of employees is another indicator showing the performance of an employee in asset generating activities and it is tested in (Isik and Hassan, 2002). For the period of 1988 and 1996, Isik and Hassan (2002) demonstrated its relationship with the efficiency. Hence we attempt to figure out if this relationship exists in recent years as well. If the relationship still remains, it is expected to be positive because per employee asset needs to be higher for the more efficient banks. Among profitability ratios, Return on Assets (ROA) is taken and it is the net income over total assets. As a bank performs better, it becomes more profitable through managing its assets more successfully and increasing its income. Hence there needs to be a positive relationship with ROA and efficiency scores.

The number of branches denotes the accessibility of the banks to the existing and potential customers and directly affects the amount of deposits. Thus this variable is expected to have a positive relationship with the efficiency scores. The effects of state/private and foreign/domestic dummies on the efficiency scores are ambiguous. There are mixed evidence on the effects of different ownership structure on efficiency. However, the private commercial banks and the foreign banks in general tend to be more efficient than the state banks (Isik and Hassan, 2002).

The correlation matrix is presented in Table 3. Even though the bank capitalization and loan ratio have positive impacts on efficiency, they are negatively correlated with each other. Hence, an attempt to increase efficiency through increasing one of them is likely to cause the other variable to worsen. The same result is also valid for the assets/employee ratio since it is negatively correlated with both the bank capitalization and loan ratio while all of them have positive relationship with efficiency. Interbank to other earning assets ratio is weakly related with bank capitalization, while their correlations with efficiency are adversely related. The negative correlations between interbank/other earning assets and loan ratio are as expected since the banks have fewer assets to use for the interbank funds as the loan ratio increases.

5. EMPIRICAL RESULTS

The main contribution of this chapter is to analyze how the efficiency scores are affected by the increasing volume of interbank funds. The results of the analysis are evaluated in two parts given that the dependent variable is either the efficiency scores with other earning assets or without it.

In Table 4, the results of the regression on the efficiency with two dependent variables are presented. The coefficients and t-values (in the parenthesis) are presented in the table.

Table 1. Number of Efficient Decision Making Units

Year	Total number of banks	Number of efficient banks with OEA	Number of efficient banks without OEA
2001	42	28	23
2002	36	20	18
2003	36	25	23
2004	33	16	11
2005	33	18	15
2006	32	21	19

Source: Authors' calculation and Banks Association of Turkey.

Table 2. Descriptive Statistics

Variables	Num. of Observations	Mean	Std Dev	Min	Max
Interbank/Other Earning Assets	212	0.463	0.543	0.001	6.978
Efficiency with Other Earning Assets	212	0.902	0.164	0.150	1.000
Efficiency without Other Earning Assets	212	0.845	0.209	0.138	1.000
Bank Capitalization	212	0.175	0.168	-0.353	0.850
Loan Ratio	212	0.296	0.187	0.000	0.733
Asset/Employee	212	2508	1994	90	16879
Return on Asset	212	-0.008	0.099	-0.641	0.322
Number of Branches	212	149	268	0	1504

Source: Authors' calculation and Banks Association of Turkey.

Table 3. Correlation Matrix

	Interbank	Efficiency with OEA	Efficiency w/o OEA	Bank Capital.	Loan Ratio	Asset / Employee	ROA	No of Branches
Interbank	1.000							
Efficiency with OEA	-0.236	1.000						
Efficiency w/o OEA	-0.197	0.822	1.000					
Capitalization	0.093	0.054	0.160	1.000				
Loan Ratio	-0.174	0.124	0.244	-0.379	1.000			
Asset/ Employee	0.070	0.210	0.135	-0.028	-0.214	1.000		
ROA	-0.035	0.171	0.160	0.070	0.105	0.228	1.000	
No of Branches	-0.205	0.171	0.183	-0.171	0.059	-0.033	0.105	1.000

Source: Authors' calculation and Banks Association of Turkey.

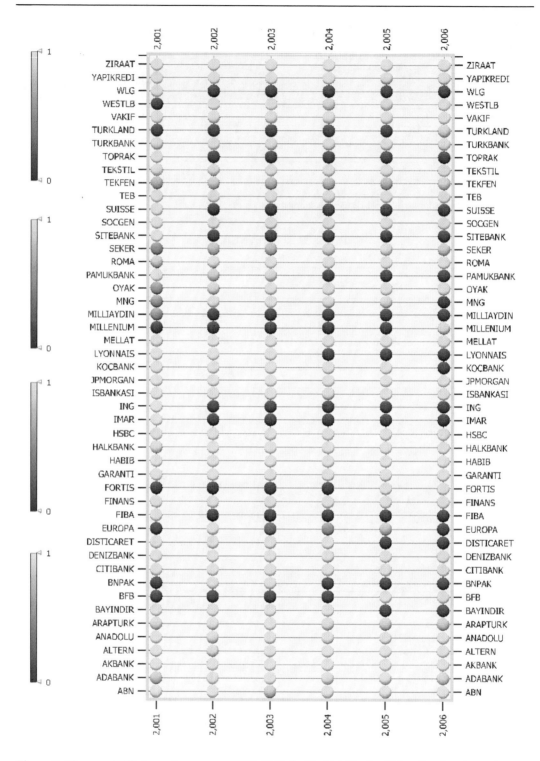

Figure 5. Change of Efficiency Scores over 2001-2006 for Turkish Banks (Other Earning Assets is included in the DEA model).

Table 4. Fixed Effects Panel Regressions

Independent Variables	Dependent variable	Dependent variable
	Efficiency with	*Efficiency without*
	Other Earning Assets	*Other Earning Assets*
Interbank/OEA	**-0.068**	**-0.049**
	(-4.44)*	**(-2.47)**
Bank Capitalization	**0.251**	**0.457**
	(2.89)*	**(4.01)***
Loan Ratio	**0.239**	**0.432**
	(3.69)*	**(5.16)***
Assets/Employees	**0.00001**	0.00001
	(1.74)*	(0.61)
Return on Assets	0.015	-0.149
	(0.14)	(-1.09)
Number of Branches	-0.00002	-0.00002
	(-0.12)	(-0.29)
Foreign/Domestic	-0.022	-0.007
	(-0.28)	(-0.07)
Constant	**0.804**	**0.656**
	(19.48)*	**(12.31)***
R-square	0.736	0.729
Number of Observations	212	212

In the first fixed effect panel regression specification, the explanatory variables are regressed on the efficiency scores with other earning assets included as output. The interbank/other earning asset is significant and affects the efficiency scores adversely, as expected. The loan ratio and bank capitalization are significant in explaining efficiencies and they have a positive relationship with efficiency. This supports the view that when the banks turn their assets into more lucrative investments, their efficiency scores improve. Interestingly, the ROA and asset/employee ratio are not significant in explaining the dependent variable. Finally, number of branches and foreign domestic dummies are not significant, either.

In the second panel, the dependent variable stands for the efficiency scores without the other earning assets. The aim of this second regression specification is to uncover whether the other earning assets drastically alter the main findings. The results are not much different from the findings of the previous regression. The interbank funds, the bank capitalization and loan ratio are still significant. The interbank funds variable has a negative relationship with efficiency while the bank capitalization and loan ratio are positively correlated with the efficiency scores. Similar to earlier results, other variables are found to be insignificant in explaining the banks' efficiencies.

This chapter's findings regarding the effects of interbank funds contradict with the results of Hauner (2005), where interbank funds are found to have positive effects with a significance level of 1%. There can be several reasons for the contradictory results: Firstly, the environmental settings are not the same: Hauner (2005) investigates the banks in Germany and Austria, where we investigate the banks in Turkey. It is only expected that the banking sector in these two different settings are different. Secondly, the time frames are different: Hauner (2005) considers the period 1995-1999, whereas we consider the period 2001-2006. Thirdly, Hauner (2005) considers the ratio of interbank funds to total assets as a factor, whereas we consider the ratio to only other earning assets. One future research area is to investigate the causes of the varying results, and also collect evidence from other countries and time frames.

6. CLUSTER ANALYSIS

In section 5, the variables interbank funds, banks capitalization and loan ratio were determined to be highly significant in determining the average efficiency scores over the years 2001-2006. In this section, a cluster analysis is carried out for the year 2006 using the above three factors, and the efficiency scores for 2006 computed with and without OEA, totaling to five variables. Then the results of the cluster analysis are combined with two additional status variables, State/Private and Foreign/Domestic.

Figure 6 shows the results of cluster analysis, which was carried out using the k-means clustering algorithm (Han et al., 2005) implemented within Miner3D software. K-means partitions a set of observations into k distinct clusters such that similar observations can be identified. In this case, the observations are the banks, and the clustering is performed using the five variables mentioned above. Table A.1 lists the clusters that each of the banks that exist in 2006 belong to.

ClusterNo	AVG(2006_Interbank/OEA)	AVG(2006_BankCapitalization)	AVG(2006_LoanRatio)
1	0.19	0.10	0.55
2	0.67	0.15	0.63
3	0.62	0.13	0.35
4	0.45	0.12	0.57
5	0.67	0.12	0.12
6	0.13	0.17	0.39
7	0.11	0.12	0.33
8	0.93	0.83	0.00
9	0.73	0.59	0.01
AVG(Column	0.44690625	0.17871875	0.4091875

ClusterNo	AVG(2006_Eff_Excluding)	AVG(2006_Eff_Including)	PercOfForeign	PercOfPrivate	NoOfBanks
1	0.97	0.99	0.17	0.83	6
2	1.00	1.00	0.71	1.00	7
3	0.56	0.92	0.00	1.00	2
4	0.67	0.70	0.00	0.33	3
5	1.00	1.00	1.00	1.00	4
6	0.61	0.63	0.50	1.00	2
7	0.93	0.98	0.20	0.40	5
8	0.68	0.68	0.00	1.00	1
9	1.00	1.00	0.50	0.50	2
AVG(Column	0.88984375	0.92809375	0.34	0.79	

Figure 6. Results of Cluster Analysis for the Year 2006.

Banks in clusters 1 and 2 (first two rows in Figure 6) exhibit similar characteristics as can be seen from similar bar levels under each column. These are also the two clusters with the most elements (last column), and are almost all efficient in both DEA models (with and without OEA). These two clusters mainly differ from each other with respect to their interbank/OEA values, as can be seen from the large difference in the bars under the column AVG(2006_Interbank/OEA). After combining data on the ownership status of banks, it is also observed that these two clusters differ significantly with respect to their Foreign/Domestic ownership. 71 percent of the banks in cluster 2 are foreign, whereas only 17 percent of banks in cluster 1 are foreign. Thus a careful analysis of clustering results revealed that among efficient banks that operate similarly (low bank capitalization, high loan ratio); domestic banks have low interbank/OEA values, whereas foreign banks have high interbank/OEA values.

Two clusters are composed of a small percentage of private banks: Cluster 4, which is composed of three banks, contains two state banks and one private bank (hence the percentage of private value of 33 percent). Cluster 7 is composed of five banks, three of them state banks, and two of them private banks (hence the percentage of private value of 40 percent). Even though these two clusters are characterized by the felt presence of state banks, their average efficiency scores differ significantly: average efficiency for cluster 4 is 0.70 in the second DEA model, whereas average efficiency for cluster 7 is 0.98. A curious investigation of the values under other tables reveals differences that can explain this significant difference. The banks in cluster 4 have a high average value of 0.45 for interbank/OEA for 2006, whereas banks in cluster 7 have a low average value of 0.11. The values under the bank capitalization column are the same. However, the values under average loan ratio column also differ significantly (0.57 vs. 0.33). The interbank/OEA values and loan ratios were proven to have negative effect on efficiency scores by the panel regression in section 5. Thus, it is reasonable that cluster 7 has a higher average efficiency compared to cluster 4.

7. CONCLUSION

Starting from the beginning of 1980s, the banking sector in Turkey was liberalized through the new banking laws and the establishments of regulatory financial agencies. The traditional way of banking where loans are the main output of the banking operations started to change in this process. Banks began to lend other banks through Interbank Money Market and to give loans to the government through treasury bills. Therefore, this chapter aims to find out the developments in the interbank funds and its effect on the bank efficiencies for the periods 2001-2006. Turkish economy suffered from major financial crises in 2000 and 2001. In the post-crisis episode, the banking sector in Turkey has better performed its intermediatory role between borrowers and lenders. Hence, the focus is on post-crisis period to find out the effects of increasing volume of interbank funds in recent years.

After conducting Data Envelopment Analysis (DEA) to find efficiency scores, fixed effects panel regressions are carried out to uncover the role of certain selected factors on the efficiencies of the banks in Turkey. Besides showing the statistically significant factors that affect efficiency including the interbank funds, a historical summary of efficiencies of banks operating in Turkey and the results of a cluster analysis for the year 2006 are visually presented, accompanied with newly discovered insights.

The effect of interbank funds stands to be negative and statistically significant. This result supports the idea that the higher amount of investment in the interbank funds is an indicator of inefficiency. The bank capitalization and loan ratio are other significant variables and they are positively correlated with efficiency. The profitability and efficiency are not significantly associated to each other, confirming the earlier findings of Abbasoğlu et al., (2007). The asset/employee ratio, measuring the amount of asset an employee can create, and the number of branches are found to be insignificant in affecting efficiency. Finally, foreign/domestic dummy is found to be insignificant as well. Overall, this chapter uncovers the adverse effects of the interbank funds on the efficiencies while the loan ratio enhances the efficiency scores. Hence, the empirical findings of this chapter confirms the argument for an emerging market economy that the bank efficiency is enhanced through extending relatively longer term loans as opposed to extending shorter term loans to other banks.

8. APPENDIX

Table A.1. Average Efficiency Scores of DMUs

DMU Abbreviation	DMU Full Name	Cluster No (in 2006)	Excluding OEA	Including OEA	Perc. Change in Efficiency
ABN	ABN Amro Bank	7	0.7	0.84	0.20
ADABANK	Adabank	8	0.74	0.78	0.05
AKBANK	Akbank	1	1	1	0
ALTERN	Alternatifbank	2	0.94	0.95	0.01
ANADOLU	Anadolubank	3	0.76	0.93	0.22
ARAPTURK	Arap Türk Bankası	6	0.68	0.77	0.13
ROMA	Banca di Roma	2	0.86	0.9	0.05
EUROPA	Bank Europa		0.49	0.5	0.02
MELLAT	Bank Mellat	2	0.89	0.98	0.10
BAYINDIR	Bayındırbank		1	1	0
BFB	Birleşik Fon Bankası	9	1	1	0
BNPAK	Bnp-Ak Dresdner Bank		0.9	0.92	0.02
CITIBANK	Citibank	5	0.99	1	0.01
LYONNAIS	Credit Lyonnais Turkey		1	1	0
SUISSE	Credit Suisse First Boston		1	1	0
DENIZBANK	Denizbank	2	0.89	0.97	0.09
DISTICARET	Dış Ticaret		0.88	0.98	0.11

	Bankası				
FIBA	*Fibabank*		1	1	0
FINANS	*Finansbank*	2	1	1	0
FORTIS	*Fortisbank*	1	0.89	0.99	0.11
DMU Abbreviation	*DMU Full Name*	Cluster No (in 2006)	Exclu-ding OEA	Inclu-ding OEA	Perc. Change in Efficiency
GARANTI	*Garanti Bankası*	1	1	1	0
HABIB	*Habib Bank*	5	1	1	0
HALKBANK	*Halkbank*	7	0.8	0.95	0.19
HSBC	*HSBC*	2	1	1	0
ING	*ING Bank*		1	1	0
IMAR	*İmarbank*		1	1	0
ISBANKASI	*İşbankası*	7	0.94	0.97	0.03
JPMORGAN	*JPMorgan Chase Bank*	9	0.95	1	0.05
KOCBANK	*Koçbank*		0.99	1	0.01
MILLENIUM	*Millenium Bank*	4	0.75	0.75	0
MILLIAYDIN	Milli Aydın Bankası		0.31	0.36	0.16
MNG	MNG Bank		0.71	0.75	0.06
OYAK	Oyakbank	1	0.81	0.82	0.01
PAMUKBANK	Pamukbank		0.68	0.78	0.15
SITEBANK	Sitebank		1	1	0
SOCGEN	Societe Generale	5	0.89	1	0.12
SEKER	Şekerbank	6	0.55	0.59	0.07
TEB	TEB	1	0.97	0.97	0
TEKFEN	Tekfenbank	4	0.49	0.56	0.14
TEKSTIL	Tekstilbank	2	0.86	0.87	0.01
TOPRAK	Toprakbank		0.34	1	1.94
TURKBANK	Turkish Bank	3	0.43	0.86	1.00
TURKLAND	Turkland Bank	4	0.66	0.68	0.03
VAKIF	Vakıfbank	1	0.76	0.87	0.14
WESTLB	West LB AG	5	0.88	0.89	0.01
WLG	Westdeutsche Landesbank		1	1	0
YAPIKREDI	Yapı Kredi Bankası	7	0.93	0.95	0.02
ZIRAAT	Ziraat Bankası	7	1	1	0

Source: Authors' calculations.

Table A.2. Random Effects Panel Regressions

Independent Variables	Dependent variable	Dependent variable
	Efficiency with	*Efficiency without*
	Other Earning Assets	*Other Earning Assets*
Interbank/Other Earning Assets	-0.070	-0.052
	(-4.80)***	(-2.72)**
Bank Capitalization	0.229	0.470
	(3.22)***	(5.30)***
Independent Variables	Dependent variable	Dependent variable
Loan Ratio	0.199	0.396
	(3.46)***	(5.44)***
Assets/Employees	0.00001	0.00001
	(2.26)*	(1.47)
Return on Assets	0.009	-0.069
	(0.09)	(-0.58)
Number of Branches	-0.00004	-0.00009
	(-0.76)	(-1.23)
Foreign/Domestic	0.022	0.044
	(0.57)	(0.95)
Constant	0.804	0.612
	(20.23)***	(12.82)***
R-square	0.736	0.729
Number of Observations	212	212

* Indicates significance at the 10% level, ** indicates significance at the 5% level, *** indicates significance at the 1% level.

REFERENCES

Abbasoglu, O.F., Aysan, A.F., Gunes, A., 2007. Concentration, competition, efficiency and profitability of the Turkish banking sector in the post-crises period. *The Banks and Bank Systems* 2, 106-115.

Adenso-Diaz, B., Gascon, F., 1997. Linking and weighting efficiency estimates with stock performance in banking firms. The Wharton Financial Institutions Center.

Akin, G. G., Aysan, A. F., Kara, G. I. and Yıldıran, L., 2009, Transformation of the Turkish Financial Sector in the Aftermath of the 2001 Crisis, Turkish Economy in the Post-Crisis Era: the New Phase of Neo-Liberal Restructuring and Integration to the Global Economy, Z. Onis, and F. Senses (eds.) Routledge, pp. 73-100.

Al, H., Aysan. A.F., 2006. Assessing the preconditions in establishing an independent regulatory and supervisory agency in globalized financial markets: The case of Turkey. *International Journal of Applied Business and Economic Research* 4, 125–146.

Aleskerov, F., Belousova, V., Serdyuk, M., Solodkov, V., 2008. Dynamic analysis of the behavioural patterns of the largest commercial banks in the Russian federation. Working Paper No. 12/2008, International Centre For Economic Research, State University – Higher School of Economics, Moscow, Russia.

Alpay, S., Hassan, M.K., 2006. A comparative efficiency analysis of interest free financial institutions and conventional banks: A case study on Turkey. ERF 13th Annual Conference.

Arestis, P., Chortareas, G., Desli, E., 2006. Technical efficiency and financial deepening in the non-OECD economies. *International Review of Applied Economics* 20, 353–373.

Arestis, P., Chortareas, G., Desli, E., 2006. Financial development and productive efficiency in OECD countries: An explanatory analysis. *The Manchester School* 74, 417–440

Aysan, A.F., Ceyhan, S.P., 2008-a. What determines the banking sector performance in globalized financial markets? The case of Turkey. *Physica A: Statistical Mechanics and its Applications* 387, 1593-1602.

Aysan, A.F., Ceyhan, S.P., 2008-b. Globalization of Turkey's banking sector: Determinants of foreign bank penetration in Turkey. *The International Research Journal of Finance and Economics* 15, 90-102.

Aysan, A.F., Ceyhan, S.P. 2008-c. Structural change and efficiency of banking in Turkey: Does the ownership matter?. *Topics in Middle Eastern and North African Economies*, MEEA Online Journal 10.

Aysan, A.F., Ceyhan, S.P., 2007. Why do foreign banks invest in Turkey?. *Asian and African Journal of Economics and Econometrics* 7, 65-80.

Banker, R.D., Charnes, A., Cooper, W.W., 1984. Some models for estimating technical and scale inefficiencies in data envelopment analysis. *Management Science* 30, 1078–1092.

Berger, A.N., Humphrey, D.B., 1997. Efficiency of financial institutions: International survey and directions for future research. *European Journal of Operational Research* 98, 175–212.

Brown, J.A., Glennon, D., 2000. Cost structures of banks grouped by strategic conduct. *Applied Economics* 32, 1591-1605.

Černohorská, L., Černohorský, J. Teplý, P. 2007. The banking stability in the Czech Republic based on discriminant and cluster analysis. *Anadolu University Journal of Social Sciences* 7, 85-96.

Clark, J.A., Siems, T.F. 2002. X-efficiency in banking: looking beyond the balance sheet. Journal of Money, *Credit and Banking* 34, 987–1013.

Cooper, W.W., Seiford, L.M., Tone, K., 2006. Introduction to Data Envelopment Analysis and Its Uses. Springer Science Business Media.

Fethi, M., Pasiouras, F., 2010. Assessing bank efficiency and performance with operational research and artificial intelligence techniques: A survey. *European Journal of Operational Research* 204, 189-198.

Hałaj, G., Żochowski, D., 2006. Strategic groups in Polish banking sector and financial stability. Working paper. Accessed on November 2009, retrievable from http://mpra.ub.uni-muenchen.de/326/

Han, J., Kamber, M.. Pei, J., 2005. Data Mining: Concepts and Techniques. Morgan Kaufmann.

Hauner, D., 2005. Explaining efficiency differences among large German and Austrian banks. *Applied Economics* 37, 969–980.

Ho, C-T., Wu, Y.S., 2006. Benchmarking performance indicators for banks. *Benchmarking: An International Journal* 13, 1463-5771.

Isık, I., Hassan, M.K., 2002. Technical, scale and allocative efficiencies of Turkish banking industry. *Journal of Banking and Finance* 26, 719–766.

Isık, I., Hassan, M.K., 2003-a. Financial deregulation and total factor productivity change: An empirical study of Turkish commercial banks. *Journal of Banking and Finance 26, 719–766.*

Isık, I., Hassan, M.K., 2003-b. Financial disruption and bank productivity: The 1994 experience of Turkish banks. *The Quarterly Review of Economics and Finance* 43, 291–320.

Isik, I., 2008. Productivity, technology and efficiency of de novo banks: A counter evidence from Turkey. *Journal of Multinational Financial Management* 18, 427–442.

Li, J., 2008. Asymmetric interactions between foreign and domestic banks: Effects on market entry. *Strategic Management Journal* 29, 873–893.

Lin, L-J., 2006. Identifying strategic groups with the data envelopment analysis method: Taking Taiwan banking industry as an example. M.Sc. Thesis, Graduate School of Industrial Engineering and Management. Accessed on November 2009, retrievable from http://ethesys.isu.edu.tw/ETD-db/ETD-search/view_etd?URN=etd-0820107-080851

Marín, S., Gómez, J., Gómez, J.C., 2008. Eficiencia técnica en el sistema bancario español. Dimensión y rentabilidad. El Trimestre Económico 75, 1017-1042.

McKinsey Global Institute, 2003. "Overview" (Section 1) and "Retail Banking" (Chapter 3), in Turkey: Making the Productivity and Growth Breakthrough, MGI Report, February 2003. Accessed on November 2009, retrievable from http://www.mckinsey.com/knowledge/mgi/turkey/perspective.asp

Ozatay, F., Sak, G., 2002. The 2000–2001 Financial crisis in Turkey. Brookings Trade Forum 2002. Currency Crises Washington D.C.

Ozkan-Gunay, E.N., Tektas, A., 2006. Efficiency analysis of the Turkish banking sector in precrisis and crisis period: A DEA approach. *Contemporary Economic Policy* 24, 418–431.

Prior, D., Surroca, J., 2007. Cognitive strategic groups and long-run efficiency evaluation: The case of spanish savings banks. Working Paper 07-10, Departamento de Economía de la Empresa, Universidad Carlos III de Madrid, Spain.

Seçme, N.Y., Bayrakdaroğlu, A., Kahraman, C., 2009. Fuzzy performance evaluation in Turkish banking sector using analytic hierarchy process and TOPSIS. *Expert Systems with Applications* 36, 11699–11709.

Stavárek, D., 2003. Banking efficiency in Visegrad countries before joining the European Union. Workshop on Efficiency of Financial Institutions and European Integration, Technical University Lisbon, Portugal.

Steinherr, A., Tukel, A., Ucer, M., 2004. The Turkish banking sector: Challenges and outlook in transition to EU membership. *Bruges European Economic Policy Briefings.*

Turhan, I., 2008. Why did it work this time? A comparative analysis of transformation of Turkish economy after 2002. *Asian African Economics and Econometrics* 8, 255-280.

In: Financial Services: Efficiency and Risk Management
Editors: M. D. Fethi, C. Gaganis et al.

ISBN: 978-1-62100-560-5
© 2012 Nova Science Publishers, Inc.

Chapter 3

ONE-STAGE APPROACHES AND TWO-STAGE APPROACHES IN DATA ENVELOPMENT ANALYSIS: HOW APPROPRIATE ARE THEY FOR ANALYZING BUSINESS PROCESS EFFICIENCY?

Anne Dohmen[*] and Matteo Sottocornola[*]
Frankfurt School of Finance & Management.

ABSTRACT

Data Envelopment Analysis (DEA) is an established method for non-parametric efficiency measurement and it has been widely applied in studying the efficiency of financial institutions. Furthermore, different approaches have been developed to further analyze the results of a DEA in order to get an indication for causes for efficiency or in order to control for environmental factors. This paper will focus on a special application of DEA for the measurement of efficiency of business processes. As an example, a banking back- office process, namely securities settlement and clearing, is analyzed. By using real production data, this paper examines to which degree the commonly applied one-stage and two-stage approaches in DEA are suitable for analyzing the influence of specific categorical variables on business process efficiency. Our findings indicate that both approaches deliver similar results. We also find that different process steps are affected differently by the categorical variable. However, it is shown that existing models of one- and two-stage approaches cannot be applied one-to-one but need to be adjusted for their application on business process level. Furthermore, we conclude that generally the two-stage approach seems to be more appropriate and value-adding to the analysis of the influence of categorical variables on business process efficiency.

Keywords: Data Envelopment Analysis (DEA), Efficiency, Process Measurement, Efficiency Drivers

---

[*] Email: a.dohmen@fs.de
[*] Email: m.sottocornola@fs-students.de

1. INTRODUCTION

Market conditions, price levels, and service production capability in terms of productivity and efficiency are the main determinants of banks' profitability (Varmaz, 2006). Since ongoing changes in exogenous factors lead to decreasing interest margins and fees, banks, in order to maintain a satisfying level of profitability, are forced to focus on an increase in their efficiency (Rose and Hudgins, 2004; Varmaz, 2006). In academic research, techniques to measure efficiency can be separated into two main groups – parametric and non-parametric methods (Lovell, 1993). A survey of studies on the efficiency in the financial services sector shows that the usage of methods from either one of these groups is rather balanced (Berger and Humphrey, 1997). Data Envelopment Analysis (DEA) has been found to represent the most commonly used non-parametric method for measuring the efficiency in banking (Cinca et al., 2001). Within this context, most measurements are pursued on an organizational level, and only very few studies can be found that apply DEA to a business process level (Frei and Harker, 1999).

Using business processes as a starting point for measuring the efficiency of banks implies several advantages. Since the delivery of financial services of banks is pursued in their business processes, these serve as a key element for evaluating service capability or performance (Kueng et al., 2001). Within this context, business processes are the basis of enterprises' productivity and efficiency (Hammer and Champy, 1993). Following this, Burger and Moormann (2010) demonstrated how DEA can be used for measuring efficiency of business processes. As an extension of their findings, this paper deals with the question how the influence of categorical variables on the measured efficiency of business processes can be quantified and analyzed. So far, either DEA-based one-stage approaches or two-stage approaches have been commonly used for including categorical variables in the efficiency analysis. This paper analyzes to what extent these approaches are suitable for measuring the impact of categorical variables on business process efficiency.

To address this research question, we analyze the securities settlement and clearing process of one of the largest European banks, relying on an actual production dataset. We measure its efficiency with DEA and further apply a one-stage approach and a two-stage approach to the same dataset. A comparison of the results in light of the formulated hypotheses will give an indication (a) of the influence of categorical variables on the efficiency of the securities settlement and clearing process and (b) of strengths and weaknesses of applying either a one-stage approach or a two-stage approach for analyzing business process efficiency.

The remainder of this paper is structured as follows. Section 2 gives a comprehensive overview on related work. Section 3 describes the securities settlement and clearing process to be analyzed in the context of this paper. Section 4 describes the hypotheses and methodology. In section 5, the results are presented, and a comparison of both approaches is provided in section 6. Section 7 offers concluding remarks.

2. RELATED WORK

2.1. Using Data Envelopment Analysis for Measuring Business Process Efficiency

As a non-parametric method, DEA determines the efficiency of the objects of analysis (called Decision Making Units, DMU) via an empirically based best practice frontier. The distance from the best practice frontier determines the level of inefficiency for each DMU (Charnes et al., 1978). DEA is especially appropriate for analyzing input-output relationships in cases where the production function is unknown and cannot be approximated beforehand (Cooper et al., 2004).

Efficiency analysis in banking has a long tradition (e.g. Casu and Molyneux, 2001; Goddard et al. 2001; Berger and Humphrey, 1997). Usually applied on an organizational or branch level, only few studies can be found that focus on applying frontier analysis to a process level (e.g. Frei and Harker, 1999) where some suffer from methodological constraints (Seol et al., 2007). Having identified this lack of research, Burger and Moormann (2010) propose a DEA-based method for measuring intrinsic process efficiency. In their approach, called "Benchmarking of Transactions," single transactions (the objects or process instances passing through the process) serve as DMUs in a Data Envelopment Analysis. Applying this method yields an empirical production function of best practice transactions. As a result, an average efficiency score for the process can be calculated from the DEA efficiency scores for each transaction. This suggests that the average efficiency of a large dataset of transactions from the same process gives an indication of the efficiency of this process. In addition, the Benchmarking of Transactions approach overcomes previous drawbacks of efficiency measurement techniques in business process management, which are based on simple metrics (Neely et al., 1997). Instead, it allows a quantitative measurement of process efficiency from the perspective of production theory. We conclude that Benchmarking of Transactions is the appropriate starting point for analyzing process efficiency in our context.

2.2. Categorical Variables in DEA Models

Efficiency can be influenced by endogenous as well as exogenous qualitative factors (Cook et al., 1993). As a consequence, these factors are often quantified to accommodate the DEA structure. In many instances, however, this quantification is superficial, particularly if the data are simply an ordinal ranking of DMUs (Cook et al., 1996).

Usually, many exogenous inputs are represented as discrete values, but, likewise, internal and controllable factors can also be quantifiable only in discrete terms. This leads to problems with the traditional DEA approach in which a composite DMU as a convex combination of other DMUs' inputs and outputs is created for determining relative technical inefficiency. This convexity assumption leads to the consideration that the marginal productivity of input factors is equal and constant for all DMUs. Hence, any categorical variable that introduces discontinuity elements in the function is not manageable with traditional models without relaxing this constraint (Banker and Morey, 1986a).

So far, different approaches have been developed to deal with categorical variables in DEA. *One-stage approaches* and *two-stage approaches* are widely used in the context of efficiency analysis.

2.2.1. One-Stage Approaches

Following a one-stage approach, categorical variables are included directly in the DEA in order to account for environmental factors influencing the efficiency of DMUs. With these approaches, the production frontier is adjusted according to the group of DMUs that are faced with common environmental factors (see, e.g., Banker and Morey, 1986a; McCarty and Yasiawarng, 1993; Olesen and Petersen, 2009). A one-stage approach consists of applying one single (but adjusted) DEA model. Outstanding strengths of the one-stage approaches are the conceptual simplicity of its application and the robust and consistent results in terms of discriminating power between DMUs that compose the peer groups (Cooper et al., 2007).

The evolution of one-stage approaches is based on the pioneering work of Banker and Morey (1986a). One example of including categorical variables in a CCR model (Charnes et al., 1978) concerns the introduction of ordinal inputs and/or outputs. An example for this procedure can be found in Cook et al. (1993). In this study, the implementation efficiency in new technology adoption in terms of the installation of types of robotics systems in different industrial plants was analyzed. Categorical input variables such as system complexity, urgency, and previous experiences were considered. Moreover, management satisfaction was further introduced as an output.

In this study, the CCR model was modified by introducing a one-dimensional vector for each DMU defined as follows (Banker and Morey, 1986a):

$$\delta_{kl} = \quad 1 \text{ if DMU } k \text{ is ranked in the } l\text{th position,}$$
$$0 \text{ if otherwise}$$

The modified CCR model is:

$$\max \mu Y_0$$

Subject to:

$$vX_0 + W\delta_0 = 1$$
$$\mu Y_k - W\delta_k \leq 0 \text{ for all K}$$
$$\mu_r \geq \varepsilon \text{ for all r}$$
$$v_i \geq \varepsilon \text{ for all i}$$
$$W \in \Psi \tag{1}$$

Where $W = (w_1, w_2, w_3, \ldots, w_l)$ and Ψ is the permissible set of worth vectors[14].

The pioneering approach by Banker and Morey (1986a) is only applicable if the environmental variables can be unambiguously ordered according to their strength of influence on efficiency. In their approach, the reference set of a DMU are all those DMUs that are faced with the same or weaker environmental influences. Furthermore, this approach requires the direction of influence upon efficiency to be known *a priori*.

---

[14] For a comprehensive discussion on the appropriate structures of the permissible set for Ψ see Cook et a. (1993).

In a further evolution, the constraint of the single ordinal input was adapted to deal with a mix of both ordinal and cardinal qualitative and quantitative inputs and outputs (Cook et al., 1996). The model was applied to the prioritization of research and development (R&D) initiatives in a major public utility corporation with a large R&D department that had to rank projects in a budget-constrained environment. The following vectors were added:

$\gamma_{rl} = 1$ if DMU n is ranked in the l position of the r ordinal output
$$0 \text{ otherwise}$$

and

$\delta_{il} = 1$ if DMU n is ranked in the l position of the i ordinal input
$$0 \text{ otherwise}$$

The modified model is:

$$\max \mu Y_0 + \Sigma_{ORD} W_r^1 \gamma_r(0)$$

Subject to:
$$vX_0 + \Sigma_{ORD} W_r^2 \delta_r(0) = 1$$
$$\mu Y_0 + \Sigma_{ORD1} W_r^1 \gamma_r(n) - vX_n - \Sigma_{ORD2} W_i^2 \delta_i(n) \leq 0$$
$$\mu_r \geq \varepsilon \ r \varepsilon CARD_1$$
$$v_i \geq \varepsilon \ i \varepsilon CARD_2$$
$$\{W_r^1 W_i^2\} \in \Psi \tag{2}$$

Where ORD 1 and ORD2 represent the sets of ordinal outputs and inputs; $CARD_1$ and $CARD_2$ represent the sets of numerical outputs and inputs respectively. Ψ represents the set of allowable worth vectors[15].

The introduction of categorical variables or, more precisely, treating a variable as a discrete variable rather than as a continuous one, and the consequent modification of the linear programming system leads to some special characteristics. Firstly, since constraints become more stringent, DMUs that were efficient in the first case slightly increase their efficiency. On the other hand, the efficiency value of inefficient DMUs is not increased. This improves the credibility of the model. Secondly, sometimes the introduction of categorical variables leads to a reduction of the discriminating power of the model (Banker and Morey, 1986b). The main limitation is the difficulty to *jointly* include inputs and outputs of different nature such as continuous ones and discrete ones. In these cases, the one-stage structure forces to combine continuous and discrete inputs and outputs in the same level. Thus some models, as the one presented by Kamakura (1988), are not capable of identifying inefficiencies that result from the continuous input-output variables but only inefficiencies stemming from changes in the discrete values. The combination of both types of variables in one objective function leads to difficulties in interpretation, because the magnitudes of the continuous variable are affected by the units they are measured in. This is not the case when discrete variables (binary in the specific model) are used (Russeau and Semple, 1993).

---

[15] For a comprehensive discussion on the appropriate structures of the permissible set for Ψ see Cook et al. (1996)

Another approach that can be assigned to one-stage approaches concerns the comparison of efficiency between two systems, also called the *Systems Model* (Cooper et al., 2007). This model is appropriate if some DMUs use another transformation process of inputs to outputs compared to a group of other DMUs. As a consequence, the general convexity assumption in DEA holds only within the same group of DMUs (the same system) but not between these systems. To account for this situation, Cooper et al. (2007) present a mixed integer LP program that includes a binary variable for allocating each DMU to the respective system. This allocation has to be defined *a priori*. One drawback of this model is that only discrete categorical variables can be utilized and that only one categorical variable can be analyzed at once.

2.2.2. Two-Stage Approaches

In two-stage approaches, a DEA analysis and additional statistical tests are applied. Generally, in the second step, a set of factors is included as independent variables in a regression model in order to explain the variation in efficiency scores obtained by DEA in the first stage (see, e.g., Sexton et al., 1989; McCarty and Yasiawarng, 1993). The evolution of two-stage approaches basically goes back to a pioneering work by Timmer (1971), in which he compares approaches to explain determinants of technical efficiency of U.S. agriculture by Ordinary Least Squares (OLS) and Analysis of Covariance (AC). Several adjustments of two-stage approaches are very commonly used in academic literature (see Simar and Wilson, 2007 for an overview, even though the same authors emphasize methodological weaknesses of these approaches). Due to its intuitive applicability, this approach has turned out to be often used in academia (Steinmann, 2002). Some essential works in the development of two-stage approaches are described in the following.

McCarty and Yasiawarng (1993) use a two-stage DEA-based model for assessing the technical efficiency of U.S. public schools. They address the problem that DEA efficiency scores are "truncated from below at one" (p.276), i.e., they are bounded to values between 0 and 1, so that an OLS regression will not yield unbiased und consistent estimators. As a consequence, they apply a tobit model, which takes into account censored observations, e.g., within a certain interval. Finally, they calculate the "pure" technical efficiency of the schools by subtracting the estimated parameters of the tobit regression from the efficiency scores calculated by the DEA in the first step. Similar to this, Dusansky and Wilson (1995) apply a tobit regression model to assess the effect of different exogenous factors having an effect on technical efficiency.

Fried et al. (1993) apply a two-stage regression based model for evaluating the performance of US credit unions. Their analysis is based on a FDH (Free Disposable Hull) approach for calculating the radial efficiency of credit unions in the first stage. As a second step, they utilize two different regression models. First, in a logistic regression, the dependent variable is expressed as a credit union being dominated and radially inefficient or as being undominated and radially efficient. This variable is regressed on a set of uncontrollable factors. The second model tries to explain the variation in efficiency with the inclusion of slack. In their approach, the authors improve previous two-stage approaches which suffered from the fact that slacks were not considered. The results they obtain are very similar between both models; however, they loosely conclude a strong preference for the second model which includes non-radial elements, namely the slack.

Bhattacharryya et al. (1997) criticize the prevalent two-stage approaches, which use Limited Dependent Variable Models like tobit and logit models, for possibly not being able to explain the complete variation in the efficiency scores, i.e., that the regression residuals still incorporate unexplained variation. As a proposed answer to this problem they apply a stochastic frontier regression model which distinguishes the variation in efficiency scores on the basis of a systematic component, including possible explanatory exogenous factors, and a random component.

Lovell (1993) summarizes some cautionary notes that should be taken into account when applying two-stage approaches. First, he states that "efficiency scores are bounded, either by zero and one or below by one" (p. 53). This indicates that including efficiency scores as the dependent variable in a simple OLS would lead to distorted results. The choice of an appropriate, limited dependent variable regression, like a tobit model, generally solves this problem, as in McCarty and Yasiawarng (1993). Second, he emphasizes the fact that one has to be cautious in the choice of input variables in the first stage and explanatory variables in the second step. Potential factors have to be chosen a priori, and, thus, results also rely on the choice of right variables. Furthermore, he points out that "explanatory variables influence the efficiency with which inputs generate outputs; they do not influence the transformation process itself" (p.53f.), and that a correlation between input variables and explanatory variables can be problematic if an econometric approach for estimating technical efficiency is used in the first stage.

Besides the common one-stage and two-stage approaches, new methodologies have been developed in recent years, and they are based on combinations of DEA with other methods, for example, with Neural Networks (Emrouznejad and Shale, 2009), Decision Trees (Seol et al., 2007), or Cluster Analysis (Po et al., 2009), and Data Mining (Dohmen and Moormann, 2010). For the scope of this paper, the analysis is limited to the classical one-stage and two-stage approaches.

As a conclusion, based on the review of current literature on one- and two-stage approaches, it seems that a state-of-the-art method for any of these approaches does not exist. This indicates that the appropriate model has to be defined on a case-by-case basis, depending on the context of analysis and the hypotheses formulated.

3. THE SECURITIES SETTLEMENT AND CLEARING PROCESS

In this paper, the settlement and clearing process of a large German bank is analyzed for its efficiency. We use actual production data for this purpose and we take the complete process chain (*end-to-end*) into account. The securities settlement and clearing process covers all activities necessary for executing the purchases and sales of securities. The processing lifecycle can be basically broken down into five steps, namely (a) trade capture, (2) transaction enrichment, (3) validation, (4) internal booking, and (5) clearing and settlement. Figure 1 shows a depiction of the securities settlement and clearing process to be analyzed in this paper.

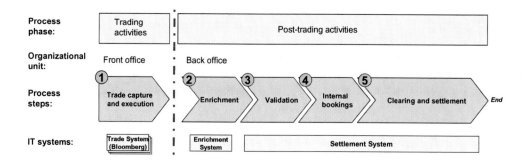

Figure 1. The securities settlement and clearing process.

A transaction in the context of this paper is considered to be the case or process instances for the securities settlement and clearing process. According to van der Aalst et al. (2007, p. 713), "the case (also named process instance) is the "thing" which is being handled, e.g., a customer order, a job application, an insurance claim, a building permit, etc.." This indicates that a transaction (TX) of the securities settlement and clearing process has to pass all the relevant process steps before it has been fully processed. A trader captures a transaction in the front office system. The transaction sometimes needs to be enriched with missing static data in order to prepare the settlement and clearing. Afterwards, the transaction is validated against the counterparty. After successful validation, the internal bookings start. Finally, the clearing and settlement takes place where the respective payments and securities are exchanged.

Many different tasks need to be performed in order to process a single securities transaction. From a regulatory perspective, there is a mandatory separation of duties between front office and back office. In addition to the trader who captures the transaction in the front office, various back office related roles are involved in the processing. Despite standardization of the process, substantial performance differences in the clearing and settlement of these transactions can be observed in reality (Burger et al., 2009; Buger and Moormann, 2010). Several different IT systems and many people are involved in the process execution. The processing of a transaction further depends on information from and validation of external parties, like the trade counterparty and the Central Securities Depository (CSD). As a consequence, processing times of transactions can vary substantially.

Burger et al. (2009) and Burger and Moormann (2010) show in two different case studies that this process incorporates a high variation in process performance and that the total cycle time ranges from one day up to more than 50 days. The reasons for this high variation can be manifold. The analysis of our paper builds directly upon the case study of Burger et al. (2009) and utilizes the same dataset. The subsequent step is to analyze the influence of categorical variables on this high variation in process performance.

3.1. Data and Transaction Categories

3.1.1. Dataset

The case study of this paper analyzes the complete process chain of the securities settlement and clearing process of a large European bank. The analysis covers the process steps (1) trade capture to (5) final clearing and settlement of securities transactions. The sample consists of 11,869 transactions that occurred in May 2008. All securities transactions are homogenous with respect to the security type (bonds), time horizon, and processing route.

The dataset was provided by a major German bank. The dataset consists of timestamps for specific process steps of each transaction as well as a list of the transactions' characteristics from which the categories have been formed. The timestamps available for the securities settlement and clearing processes are depicted in Figure 2. For an introduction to securities operations in general please refer to Simmons (2001).

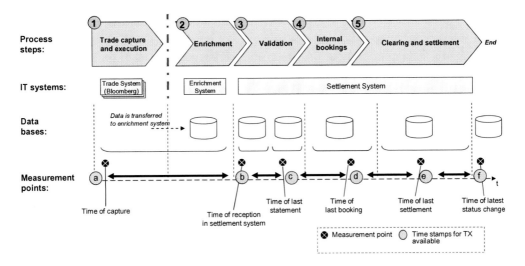

Figure 2. Steps of the securities settlement and clearing process and available timestamps.

The measurement point (a) represents the point in time when the trader captures the trade in the front office system - the starting point of the securities settlement and clearing process. Measurement point (b) incorporates the point in time when the transaction has been recognized to enter the settlement system. Here, the process step of validation starts. The transaction can be regarded to be handled during validation until measurement point (c), the time of the last statement. This is when the transaction has been finally classified as "matched" for the trade agreement, i.e., all relevant validation documents and information have been exchanged between the bank and the counterparty. A trade can, for example, not be agreed upon if a counterparty does not confirm the trade nor if there are discrepancies between the bank's and the counterparty's information about the trade value or the amount of securities to be traded (Simmons, 2001). After validation, the internal bookings occur until measurement point (d), time of last booking. At this point in time, it is assumed that the booking is finalized. Measurement point (e) represents the time of last settlement, i.e., the point in time the transaction is considered to be finally settled. Before this, settlement can still fail if, e.g., there are non-matching settlement instructions, insufficient securities at the depository, or insufficient cash collateral or credit lines to cover the trade (Simmons, 2001). Generally, the process step of clearing is situated between internal bookings and final settlement, for example, if the trades are cleared by a central counterparty, such as Clearstream (Simmons, 2001). Measurement point (f) is the final timestamp when a transaction is located in the settlement system. After point (f), the transaction is fully cleared and settled and the process ends. The time difference between (e) and (f) can occur due to any activities that have to be performed after settlement and before the value date, i.e., the physical exchange of securities and money.

The dataset provided by the bank has some limitations. First and foremost, no timestamp is available for the starting point of the process step enrichment. In order to prevent a distortion of the results, only trades that did not need manual intervention during enrichment are taken into account for this analysis. This means that for the dataset at hand only those transactions are included that show a fully automatic processing time from (a) to (b). This is one of the main limitations of our analysis, since the step of enrichment is generally regarded to be the most inefficient one. Nevertheless, for all process steps following enrichment, different transaction types are assumed to require different processing times. This analysis allows to assess the applicability of one-stage and two-stage approaches for business process efficiency analysis with the dataset at hand. An analysis of the efficiency of the process step enrichment can be found in Burger and Moormann (2010).

3.1.2. Variables

As a prerequisite for the upcoming analysis the following assumptions are made:

- Each transaction is defined as a DMU in the Data Envelopment Analysis.
- Each transaction included covers all process steps from (1) trade capture to (5) clearing and settlement and is automatically processed from measurement point (a) to (b).
- Input factors: We use the transactions' cycle times for each process step as input variables. The processing time for transactions might be different between different process steps and also show variation within a certain process step. This means that the transaction with the shortest *total* cycle time might be very efficient in one process step but less efficient in another process step. Using the cycle time for each process step as different input variables enables to account for variations in process execution on a process step level.
- We utilize an input-oriented model, and our dataset is composed only of fully processed transactions.
- Within the available attributes of the dataset, we choose the most relevant categorical variables which are expected to have an influence on process efficiency. The categories defined for analysis are described in the following paragraph.

Table 1 shows the summary statistics of the input variables. Cycle time 1 is calculated as the difference subtracting timestamp (a) from timestamp (b), cycle time 2 by subtracting timestamp (b) from timestamp (c) and so forth. It is noteworthy that the step (e)-(d), i.e., settlement, is the process step that takes on average the longest processing time in comparison to the other steps. For the DEA, the input variables are used in an indexed form, where the 100% value is the maximum value of the respective variable.

Table 1. Summary statistics of input variables

	Cycle Time 1 (Automatic)	Cycle Time 2	Cycle Time 3	Cycle Time 4	Cycle Time 5
Minimum	00:01:00	01:01:04	00:00:01	00:00:01	00:03:00
Maximum	00:02:08	45:23:57	48:09:35	03:08:44	03:00:59
Mean	00:01:01	01:09:06	00:55:00	02:19:48	00:13:36
Median	00:01:00	01:07:43	00:01:00	02:06:09	00:10:38
St.dev.	00:00:04	01:04:44	01:19:05	02:16:37	00:09:14

Format: [dd:hh:mm], dd=days, hh=hours, mm=minutes.

3.2. Transaction Categories

Figure 3 shows the proportion of dataset's transactions that were classified in each category.

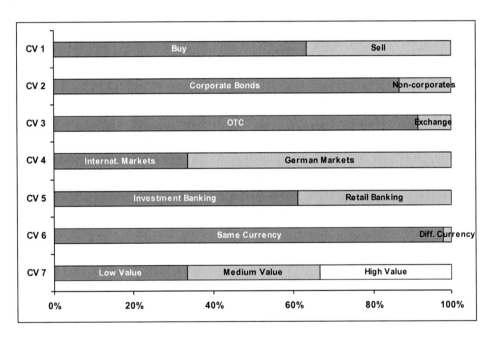

Figure 3. Proportion of transactions per categorical variable [CV=Categorical Variable].

The following categorical variables have been formed.

- Buy/Sell *(Categorical Variable 1)*: There are processed transactions that represent a trade of either buying or selling of securities from the trader's perspective.
- Corporate Bonds/Non-corporate Bonds *(Categorical Variable 2)*: The dataset is divided into transactions of corporate bonds and treasury bills.
- Exchange/Over-the-counter (OTC) *(Categorical Variable 3)*: The trades initiating the processing were performed on a bond exchange or at over-the-counter markets.

- International Markets/German Market *(Categorical Variable 4)*: The trades captured were either traded in international markets or German markets.
- Investment Banking/Retail Banking *(Categorical Variable 5)*: Transactions were initiated either by the investment banking department or the retail banking department of the bank.
- Trading Currency = Booking Currency/Trading Currency ≠ Booking Currency (Categorical Variable 6): For some transactions the trading currency is the same as the booking currency. For the remaining transactions the currencies differ.
- High Value/Medium Value/Low Value *(Categorical Variable 7)*: The value of the underlying trade differs between the transactions. Thus, a classification of the transactions into the top, middle and bottom 33% in value of the underlying trade was conducted.

4. HYPOTHESES AND METHODOLOGY

4.1. Hypotheses

Generally, process performance comprises the factors time, cost, and quality (Neely et al., 1997). From an efficiency perspective, the optimal mix of inputs and outputs is sought and, with regard to the current challenges for European banks, a minimization of inputs utilized for a given output is required in order to decrease costs. Dealing with the securities settlement and clearing process, cycle time has to be considered as the main measure of efficiency. Process costs are in this case very closely connected with cycle time. In the process under analysis, it can be expected that some transactions, according to the category they have been assigned to, need a longer processing time than others. From the practical experience with the tasks of back office operations, seven hypotheses about the influences on categorical variables on efficiency are derived.

First, the buy/sell category consists of securities that are either bought or sold by the trader. It can be expected that the time for processing a buy or a sell order is similar. As a consequence, the following hypothesis is formed:

H_1: *There is no difference in the processing efficiency of transactions between the buy and sell categories.*

Second, the dataset is divided into transactions of corporate bonds and non-corporate bonds (e.g. treasury bills). It can be expected that non-corporate bonds are processed in a shorter time, since the number of different available treasury bills is smaller compared to the number of corporate bonds because of the significant amount of different corporations. The second hypothesis is thus:

H_2: *Transactions that incorporate trades of corporate bonds are determinants of the transactions' processing inefficiency measured.*

Third, for the category exchange/over-the-counter, it can be expected that transactions originated in the over-the-counter market need more time in back office processing. Usually, the trade of bonds over the counter incorporates more specific trades than if traded on an exchange. A reason for this is that for very specific bonds the liquidity at an official exchange is not high enough so that a direct trading partner is searched via OTC (e.g., direct phone call of the broker to a trade candidate). The more specific and less liquid the bonds are, the higher is the probability that transaction-specific activities have to be pursued during the back office processing. The validation with a counterparty gained over the counter might be more time-consuming as well, since for these trades the probability is higher that a counterparty is not connected to the bank's or the market's automatic trade matching system (e.g., TRAX) but will instead send a confirmation via fax or e-mail. This leads us to the formulation of the following hypothesis.

H_3: Transactions that incorporate trades at the over-the-counter-market are determinants of the process inefficiency measured.

Fourth, in general, a bank is more often involved in national trades than in international ones. This indicates that the counterparties might be frequent trading partners, and, thus, validation and settlement will run more smoothly. For instance, during the process step of validation, the trade has to be validated by the counterparty. For most trades at German markets (and at least within the European Union), there are IT functions available that enable an automatic matching of the counterparties and ease communication (e.g., TRAX, S.W.I.F.T.). For trades at international markets (especially outside the European Union), this is not always given, and the probability of a non-electronic validation of the counterparty and missing or wrongly sent data is higher. Via S.W.I.F.T., for example, most settlement instructions are sent and can be matched and confirmed automatically. If a counterparty does not use S.W.I.F.T., such information might be sent by fax or e-mail. As a consequence, the following hypothesis is formed:

H_4: Transactions that incorporate trades at international markets are determinants of the process inefficiency measured.

Fifth, the dataset is split into trades that are originated by either the investment banking or the retail banking department of the bank. It is not absolutely clear what kind of difference in the influence on efficiency can be expected. However, potentially detected differences between both initiating departments would be interesting results and would lead to further investigations into the reasons for such a result. So far, we have formulated the following hypothesis for this category:

H_5: There is no difference in the processing efficiency of transactions between the investment banking and retail banking categories.

Sixth, it is more likely that transactions for which the trading currency and the booking currency are the same require less processing time compared to transactions where they differ. This difference is expected to be especially strong for the process step 4 (internal booking). This leads to the following two hypotheses:

H_6: Transactions that do not incorporate the same currency for the trade and the booking are determinants of the inefficiency measured.

H_{6a}: The difference in processing efficiency between bonds traded and booked in the same currency versus a different currency is especially strong for the process step 4 (internal booking).

Seventh, the dataset was divided into three categories according to the value of the underlying trade. From an operational risk perspective, high value trades should be processed with more care in order to avoid mistakes, which can have very costly consequences for the bank. The formulation of a hypothesis is not straight-forward in this case, since a longer processing time cannot be directly explained as conducting a more careful review and in turn lower operational risk. However, analyzing differences in processing time between different value trades would be an interesting endeavor that should be elaborated further. This leads us to the following hypothesis:

H_7: Transactions that incorporate high value trades are determinants of the process inefficiency measured.

4.2. Methodology

In order to derive a conclusion about the applicability of one-stage and two-stage approaches for analyzing business processes, we examine all hypotheses using both a one-stage and a two-stage approach.

4.2.1. Methodology for One-Stage Approach

Two relevant CCR-based one-stage DEA models exist for context of our analysis (Cooper et al., 2007): The CAT Model (Categorical Variables Model) and the SYS Model (Systems Model).

The main conceptual difference between the two listed models lies in the fact that for the CAT model the integer values attributed to the categorical variable have to follow a hierarchical ranking (Cooper et al., 2007). This constraint is relaxed in the SYS model, which deals with efficiency differences between groups of DMUs without any hierarchical ranking of them (Cooper et al. 2007). We cannot derive a hierarchical order for each of our defined categories (e.g., buy versus sell) and hence we allocate the DMUs to different systems according to each categorical variable. For each categorical variable, we perform the following SYS model (exemplified for systems A and B; z is the binary variable for allocating the DMU to the respective system):

$$\min \theta$$

$$
\text{subject to: } \theta x_0 \geq X_A \lambda_A + X_B \lambda_B
$$
$$
y_0 \leq Y_A \lambda_A + Y_B \lambda_B
$$
$$
Lz_A \leq e\lambda_A \leq Uz_B
$$
$$
Lz_B \leq e\lambda_B \leq Uz_B
$$
$$
z_{A} + z_B = 1
$$
$$
\lambda_A \geq 0, \lambda_B \geq 0
$$
$$
z_A, z_B = \{0,1\} \tag{3}
$$

Applying this model, we can evaluate not only the efficiency of each DMU but we can also compare the two systems by taking into account the average efficiency score.

4.2.2. Methodology for the Two-stage Approach

In order to conduct the two-stage approach, an input-oriented CCR-model is applied first (Charnes et al., 1978), and, in this model, each transaction is treated as a DMU. Following a purely input-oriented perspective on process performance, the outputs are normalized according to Dyson et al. (2001) and are set to the integer value of 1. This can be interpreted as the transaction has being fully processed. Denoted in its dual model (envelopment form), for each transaction (DMU) *i* the following linear program is applied:

$$\min_{\theta,\lambda} \; \theta$$

subject to
$$\theta x_i - X\lambda \geq 0$$
$$Y\lambda \geq y_i$$
$$\lambda \geq 0 \tag{4}$$

where θ is a scalar and X and Y are the input- and output vectors, respectively.

For the second step, two alternative tobit regression models are built. First, a tobit regression based on the following equation is performed:

$$EFF_i = \beta_0 + \beta_1 TIME_i + \beta_2 BUY_i + \beta_3 CORP_i + \beta_4 OTC_i + \beta_5 INT_i + \beta_6 IB_i$$
$$+ \beta_7 ECURR_i + \beta_8 HV_i + \beta_9 MV_i + \varepsilon_i \tag{5}$$

where EFF_i is the efficiency score for each transaction i calculated in the previous step, $TIME_i$ is the total cycle time (sum of all process steps) for each transaction i, and $\sum_{j=2}^{9} \beta_j \{BUY_i,...,MV_i\}$ are dummy variables allocating the transactions to the categories defined in section 3.

Including the input variables used for measuring the DEA efficiency scores in the first stage as an independent variable in the second step is an unusual approach. Within this context, e.g., McCarty and Yasiawarng (1993, p. 285ff.) even write:

> "...the two-stage approach can be problematic when there is strong correlation between the first-stage inputs and the second-stage independent variables. If these variables were strongly correlated, then the claim that the two stages incorporate fundamentally different types of inputs, controllable and uncontrollable, becomes untenable. In this case, DEA scores computed in the first stage are likely to be biased in the sense that they would actually reflect effects of both categories of inputs."

However, it should be noted that we utilize the two-stage approach in a fundamentally different context and for answering a fairly different research question. We intentionally *assume* that the DEA efficiency scores reflect effects of the input variables (i.e., cycle times) and the categories (difference in cycle times according to the respective category). Furthermore, we do not *per se* divide input factors and categorical variables in controllable and *un*controllable factors. Instead, we pursue a different intention. In order to analyze the efficiency of a business process, it is of interest to investigate if and to what extent differences in processing efficiency and the influence of input factors on overall process efficiency exist between the defined categories of transactions. Hence, the aim is to explain if and to what extent the relationship between cycle time and efficiency differs between categories, i.e., the dummy variables. Thus, e.g., the coefficient of the variable BUY should be interpreted as the additional magnitude the cycle time has for BUY-transactions, *ceteris paribus*, on the transactions' efficiencies. The problem of correlation between the input variables and the explanatory variables, as reported by Lovell (1993), is mainly a problem in cases of an econometric estimation of technical efficiency in the first stage, if the parameter estimation to determine technical efficiency is based on similar variables that seek to explain these results. Since in our case we use a non-parametric approach in the first stage, this biasing problem should be reduced.

The dummy coefficients give the intercept differences of the regression line between the different categories. This means that differences in the influence on efficiency between the categories is analyzed whereas the regression slope stays constant.

Our second regression model aims at capturing the influence of cycle time on efficiency for each process step and to further control for differences between categories. For this purpose, the cycle times of the five process steps and all dummy variables are included in the regression. In addition, the analysis focuses on the question whether there are direct effects of categorical variables on specific process steps. For this purpose, variables capturing the interaction for each category with each cycle time per process step are formed. The interaction variables are interpreted as differences in the regression slope according to the defined categories. This leads us to the following regression model:

$$EFF_i = \beta_0 + \sum_{j=1}^{5} \beta_j \{CYCTIME1_i;...CYCTIME5_i\} + \sum_{j=6}^{11} \beta_j \{BUY_i;...;MV_i\}$$

$$+ \sum_{j=12}^{52} \beta_j [\{BUY_i;...;MV_i\} * \{CYCTIME1_i;...;CYCTIME5_i\}] + \varepsilon_i \qquad (6)$$

where EFF_i is the efficiency score for each transaction calculated in the previous step, $TIME_i$ is the total cycle time (sum of all process steps) for each transaction i., and $\sum_{j=2}^{9} \beta_j \{BUY_i,...,MV_i\}$ are dummy variables indicating the defined categories, CYCTIME1 is the cycle time of process step 1, CYCTIME2 of step 2 and so forth.

5. RESULTS

5.1. Results for One-Stage Approach

In the one-stage approach, only one categorical variable can be tested at once. As a consequence, a separate SYS-DEA-model is applied for each hypothesis. All calculations were performed using DEA Solver Pro 6.0k. The results are summarized in the following paragraphs.

5.1.1. Categorical Variable 1: «Buy» vs. «Sell»

Table 2 summarizes the results for the categorical variable about "buy"- versus "sell"- transactions.

We wrongly assumed that any differences occur between BUY and SELL-transactions. The outcome shows a slightly higher efficiency in the BUY-transactions (avg. 0.6108) compared to SELL-transactions (avg. 0.5777). However, the efficient frontier for both systems consists of both BUY and SELL-transactions. The least efficient transaction overall is from the BUY-group.

Table 2. Results one-stage approach "Buy" vs. "Sell"

	Total	System 1 (Buy)	System 2 (Sell)
No. of DMUs	11869	7533	4336
Average	0.5987	0.6108	0.5777
SD	0.1509	0.1338	0.1747
Maximum	1.0000	1.0000	1.0000
Minimum	0.2062	0.2062	0.2065
No. of DMUs with inappropriate Data	0		
No. of efficient DMUs	75		
No. of inefficient DMUs	11794		
No. of over iteration DMUs	0		

5.1.2. Categorical Variable 2: «Corporate Bonds» vs. «Non-corporate Bonds»

Table 3 shows the results of the second categorical variable applied.

Table 3. Results one-stage approach "Corporate Bonds" vs. "Non-corporate Bonds"

	Total	System 1 (Corporates)	System 2 (Non-corporates)
No. of DMUs	11869	10282	1587
Average	0.5914	0.5986	0.5451
SD	0.1487	0.1480	0.1448
Maximum	1.0000	1.0000	1.0000
Minimum	0.2018	0.2018	0.2221
No. of DMUs with inappropriate Data	0		
No. of efficient DMUs	66		
No. of inefficient DMUs	11803		
No. of over iteration DMUs	0		

The results of the corporate bonds versus the non-corporate bonds transaction category show a higher efficiency score for corporate bonds (avg. 0.5986) compared to non-corporate bonds (avg. 0.5451). This result contradicts the expectations. However, differences between the groups are only small.

5.1.3. Categorical Variable 3: «Over-the-Counter» vs. «Exchange»

Table 4 shows the results of the third categorical variable.

Table 4. Results one-stage approach "OTC" vs. "Exchange"

	Total	System 1 (OTC)	System 2 (Exchange)
No. of DMUs	11869	1009	10860
Average	0.6657	0.5164	0.6795
SD	0.1695	0.1408	0.1652
Maximum	1.0000	1.0000	1.0000
Minimum	0.2221	0.2259	0.2221
No. of DMUs with inappropriate Data	0		
No. of efficient DMUs	84		
No. of inefficient DMUs	11785		
No. of over iteration DMUs	0		

The results indicate a higher efficiency for transactions initiated by trades at an exchange compared to OTC-transactions, a result that had been expected. Unfortunately, the results may be biased by the unbalanced distribution of the population between the two segments (91.5% of the transactions belong to the exchange group).

5.1.4. Categorical Variable 4: «German Markets» vs. «International Markets»

Table 5 shows the results of the fourth categorical variable.

Table 5. Results one-stage approach "German Markets" vs. "International Markets"

	Total	System 1 (German Markets)	System 2 (International Markets)
No. of DMUs	11869	7880	3989
Average	0.5937	0.6009	0.5796
SD	0.1487	0.1525	0.1399
Maximum	1.0000	1.0000	1.0000
Minimum	0.2018	0.2221	0.2018
No. of DMUs with inappropriate Data	0		
No. of efficient DMUs	68		
No. of inefficient DMUs	11801		
No. of over iteration DMUs	0		

The results confirm the higher complexity of the transactions initiated by trades on international markets as assumed in H_4. The average efficiency score for the domestic markets category is higher (avg. 0.6009) than the average of the international markets category (avg. 0.5796).

Table 6. Results one-stage approach "Investment Banking" vs. "Retail Banking"

	Total	System 1 (Investment Banking)	System 2 (Retail Banking)
No. of DMUs	11869	7260	4609
Average	0.5965	0.5727	0.6341
SD	0.1512	0.1590	0.1294
Maximum	1.0000	1.0000	1.0000
Minimum	0.2049	0.2049	0.2229
No. of DMUs with inappropriate Data	0		
No. of efficient DMUs	75		
No. of inefficient DMUs	11794		
No. of over iteration DMUs	0		

5.1.5. Categorical Variable 5: «Investment Banking» vs. «Retail Banking»

Table 6 shows the results of the fifth categorical variable.

H_5 assumed no differences in efficiency between transactions operated by retail or investment banking. Nevertheless, trades initiated by the retail department seem to be more efficient in settlement and clearing compared to those initiated by the investment banking department (avg. 0.6341 vs. avg. 0.5727). The difference between the average efficiency scores of the two clusters is high compared to the other categorical variables. Furthermore, the higher efficiency of retail transactions is also confirmed by the lower standard deviation of the efficiency score and by the presence of the minimum efficient transaction in the investment banking segment.

Table 7. Results one-stage approach "Equal Currency" vs. "Different Currency"

	Total	System (Equal Currencies)	System 2 (Different Currencies)
No. of DMUs	11869	11628	241
Average	0.5936	0.5944	0.5538
SD	0.1488	0.1483	0.1663
Maximum	1.0000	1.0000	1.0000
Minimum	0.2027	0.2027	0.2259
No. of DMUs with inappropriate Data	0		
No. of efficient DMUs	67		
No. of inefficient DMUs	11802		
No. of over iteration DMUs	0		

5.1.6. Categorical Variable 6: «Trading Currency = Booking Currency» vs. «Trading Currency ≠ Booking Currency»

Table 7 shows the results of the sixth categorical variable. The segmentation according to the correspondence of trading and booking currency seems to confirm the expected lower efficiency of the transaction where the two currencies are different (avg. 0.5944 vs. avg. 0.5538). Despite the small difference in the average efficiency, we can state that transactions with unequal currencies seem to involve partly more complex handling because of the higher standard deviation reported. Unfortunately, the segmentation according to the categorical variable led to unbalanced groups (98.0% vs. 2.0%).

5.1.7. Categorical Variable 7: «Low Value» vs. «Medium Value» vs. «High Value»

Table 8 shows the results of the seventh categorical.

Table 8. Results one-stage approach "Value"-categories

	Total	System 1 (Low)	System 2 (Mid)	System 3 (High)
No. of DMUs	11869	3956	3957	3956
Average	0.6069	0.6318	0.6109	0.5782
SD	0.1506	0.1493	0.1442	0.1533
Maximum	1.0000	1.0000	1.0000	1.0000
Minimum	0.2097	0.2221	0.2579	0.2097
No. of DMUs with inappropriate Data	0			
No. of efficient DMUs	78			
No. of inefficient DMUs	11791			
No. of over iteration DMUs	0			

The results cannot reject H_7. Indeed, high-value transactions present a lower average efficiency (avg. 0.5782) in comparison with the mid-value transactions (avg. 0.6109) and smallest transactions. (avg.0.6318). Both the minimum efficiency value and of the highest standard deviation are located in System 3.

5.2. Results Two-Stage Approach

As the first step, the efficiency scores were calculated using a CCR-input-oriented DEA model (constant returns on scale). All calculations were performed using DEA Solver Pro 6.0k. Table 9 shows the summary results.

The results show an average efficiency score of 0.5912 and 62 reference transactions that have been classified as being fully efficient. It should be noted that $CYCTIME_1$ has been excluded from the analysis since not enough variation in the data could be found.

The following table shows the results for the second step, i.e., the tobit regression following equation (5). All regressions were performed using STATA 10.1.

Table 9. Results CCR DEA-model

No. of DMUs	No. of efficient DMUs	Average Efficiency Scores	St.dev. Efficiency Scores	Maximum Efficiency Score	Minimum Efficiency Score
11869	62	0.59	0.149	1	0.20

Table 10. Summary results of regression (5)

Variable	Coefficient		
TIME	-1.279***		TIME=total cycle time
BUY	0.034***		BUY = bonds buy-side
CORP	0.026***		CORP = corporate bonds
OTC	0.070***		OTC = bonds traded at over-the-counter markets
INTERN	-0.012**		INTERN = international trades
IB	-0.007*		IB = investment banking trades
ECURR	0.005		ECURR = currency of trade = currency of booking
MV	-0.017***		MV = medium value of underlying trade
HV	-0.029***		HV = high value of underlying trade
_cons	0.575***		
/sigma	0.134		
*** signifcant at 1%, ** significant at 5%, *significant at 10%			
Obs. Summary		1	left-censored observation at effsc<=0.020180415
		11802	uncensored observations
		66	right-censored observations at effsc>=1

The coefficients of the dummy variables have to be interpreted as changes in the intercept according to each category, indicating a *general* difference in the relationship between all process steps and the efficiency scores. The coefficient of TIME can be interpreted as the magnitude of the total cycle time on the efficiency scores. It should be noted again at this point that TIME is purposely included as a dependent variable in the regression, even though there is an obvious dependency between the dependent variable and total cycle time. However, the question to be answered is to what extent the influence of cycle time on the efficiency score differs between the defined categories. As a consequence, this procedure is regarded to be appropriate in our case.

From the eight dummy variables included, five are found to be significant at 1%, INTERN is found to be significant at 5%, IB is found to be significant at 10%, and ECURR is found not to be significant.

The coefficient of the BUY-category is found to be significant and positive. This could mean that, on average, BUY-transactions need less time compared to SELL-transactions. It indicates that with the same time invested a higher efficiency in comparison to all other transactions is reached for the processing of BUY-transactions. In order to highlight this effect, their efficiency scores could be adjusted (increased) in order to reflect the special characteristics of the BUY-group and to be comparable to the scores of the SELL-category. Finally, H_1 has to be rejected since a significant difference in the influence of time on the efficiency score for BUY-transactions compared to SELL-transactions was found.

For OTC-transactions, a positive and significant coefficient is found. This result contradicts the expectations formulated in the H_2. Thus, H_2 has to be rejected for the results of this dataset. It indicates that OTC-transactions, on average, require less processing time and that their calculated efficiency score has to be refined upwards in order to be comparable to Exchange-transactions. For international transactions, investment banking transactions, high-value and medium value transactions, negative coefficients are found, significant at 5%, 10%, and 5%, respectively. These results indicate a more negative relationship between time and the efficiency scores on average, compared to the respective base dummies. This was expected for international trades, high-value and medium-value transactions, as reflected in the formulation of hypotheses H_3 and H_7, respectively. For H_4 (investment banking vs. retail banking), we could not formulate a valid hypothesis beforehand, but the results suggest that investment banking transactions are associated with a lower efficiency score, i.e., on average, they require a longer processing time. This leads us to a rejection of H_5 but only at a significance level of 10%. The dummy variable ECURR is found to have a non-significant coefficient. Thus, based on these results, there seems to be no difference between transactions where the trading currency and the booking currency are the same versus where they are different, and H_6 has to be rejected.

A second regression is conducted following equation (6). Due to the exclusion of CYCTIME1 in the first step, this variable is excluded from the regression as well. Table 11 shows a summary of the results.

CYCLETIME3 shows a very high negative magnitude. This means that especially step 3 is a major determinant of the efficiency score. This can be intuitively understood, since CYCTIME3 showed the highest average processing time compared to the other process steps. Interesting to notice is the positive coefficient sign of CYCTIME2. This would mean that the cycle time of process step 2 is positively associated with efficiency. This could be explained by the fact that this process step seems to have a less severe impact on the overall efficiency compared to the other process steps.

The BUY dummy variable now shows a negative sign. This happens because we now control for differences in the slope of the relationship between cycle time and efficiency, according to each process step. The interaction variables predict steeper slopes for the interaction of BUY with process step 2 (validation), step 4 (settlement), and step 5 (final activities). A steeper slope of the negative relationship between CYCLETIME4 and efficiency indicates that an increase in CYCLETIME4 is associated with a higher *decrease* in efficiency for BUY-transactions compared to SELL-transactions. This means for process steps 4 and 5 that the negative relationship between time and efficiency is stronger for BUY-transactions compared to SELL-transactions. For the negative association between cycle time of process step 3 and efficiency, a flatter slope has been found for BUY-transactions, indicating that this relationship is weaker than for SELL-transactions. The results can be interpreted as follows. Generally, the relationship between time and efficiency is less for BUY-transactions (i.e., they need more processing time), reflected by the downward shift of the regression intercept by -0.076, the coefficient of the BUY-dummy. However, the relationship between time and efficiency also differs between the process steps, reflected in the differences in regression slopes, i.e., the coefficients of the interaction variables. When now controlling for differences in slopes, which are in most cases much steeper, it becomes apparent why in the previous regression results BUY has been found to have a positive coefficient. *On average*, a positive difference to SELL could be found, when not controlling for slope differences.

Some more striking results of this regression should be further noticed. For the interaction variable OTC*CYCTIME3, a very high positive and significant coefficient value is found. This means that especially for the process step of booking, the influence of time on efficiency is much stronger for OTC-transactions than for Exchange-transactions. The influence of time on efficiency is stronger for international trades for the process steps in clearing and settlement (process steps 4 and 5). This can be intuitively understood since international trades might require more interaction with the counterparty, the depository of the respective country, and thus entail more process activities until the trade is finally settled. It is also reasonable to assume that the physical exchange of securities and money (also if done electronically, like in most cases) requires more activities than for German trades, as for most German trades a Central Securities Depository comes into play. When looking at the interaction variables of the ECURR-category, it is interesting to notice that there is a stronger influence on efficiency for all process steps *except* for CYCTIME3, which is the process step of booking. Thus, H_{6a} has to be strongly rejected here. For the value-categories, the influence is similar for both dummies and, strikingly, it is strongest for the process step of booking. At this point, there could be an extra check of all relevant information before the trade is finally booked. It should be noticed that during the settlement and clearing process the so called four-eye-principle is used at several points. This means that a second person has to check changes in the transaction's data and to actively release the transaction for further processing. This can consume a substantial amount of processing time. A positive significant coefficient is also found for the interaction of both MV and HV with CYCLETIME2 (validation). This makes sense, since for high value trades the control might be much higher. One can certainly assume that *under no circumstances* will transactions be forwarded to the booking step if not all information is matched exactly with the counterparty, whereas for low value trades less care might be taken.

Generally, the results of this regression are similar to those obtained in the one-stage approach and the general model of the two-stage approach (regression (5)), but they facilitate a more detailed analysis and interpretation by taking into account the direct impact of the categorical variables on the different process steps.

Table 11. Summary results of regression (6)

Variable	Coefficient	
CYCLETIME2	1.587727***	CYCTIME2= cycle time process step 2
CYCLETIME3	-9505.616***	CYCTIME3= cycle time process step 3
CYCLETIME4	-0.2914924*	CYCTIME4= cycle time process step 4
CYCLETIME5	-0.2105938***	CYCTIME5= cycle time process step 5
BUY	-0.075702***	BUY = bonds buy-side
CORP	0.0320132***	CORP = corporate bonds
OTC	0.1873035***	OTC = bonds traded at OTC-markets
INTERN	-0.1519714***	INTERN = international trades
IB	0.1061308***	IB = investment banking trades
ECURR	-0.1004578***	ECURR = currency of trade = currency of booking

Table 11. Continued

Variable	Coefficient
MV	-0.0222253***
HV	-0.0504457***
BUY*CYCLETIME2	0.209314**
BUY*CYCLETIME3	-0.7353816***
BUY*CYCLETIME4	1.365117***
BUY*CYCLETIME5	0.0927221***
CORP*CYCLETIME2	-0.0173397
CORP*CYCLETIME3	-0.1225071
CORP*CYCLETIME4	0.0058061
CORP*CYCLETIME5	-0.0933288***
OTC*CYCLETIME2	-1.507988***
OTC*CYCLETIME3	9312.837***
OTC*CYCLETIME4	-3.144825***
OTC*CYCLETIME5	-0.692299***
INTERN*CYCLETIME2	0.7756763***
INTERN*CYCLETIME3	-0.686681***
INTERN*CYCLETIME4	2.470394***
INTERN*CYCLETIME5	0.1517285***
IB*CYCLETIME2	-1.161069***
IB*CYCLETIME3	0.21404
IB*CYCLETIME4	-1.782907***
IB*CYCLETIME5	0.1038928**
ECURR*CYCLETIME2	4.837031***
ECURR*CYCLETIME3	1.336015
ECURR*CYCLETIME4	1.772312***
ECURR*CYCLETIME5	0.0963108***
MV*CYCLETIME2	0.0431978
MV*CYCLETIME3	193.4186***
MV*CYCLETIME4	0.4310571***
MV*CYCLETIME5	-0.0296486
Variable	Coefficient
HV*CYCLETIME2	0.785315***
HV*CYCLETIME3	192.7433***
HV*CYCLETIME4	0.720026***
HV*CYCLETIME5	-0.0225903
_cons	0.6737669***
/sigma	0.1093332

MV = medium value of underlying trade

HV = high value of underlying trade

*** signifcant at 1%, ** significant at 5%, *significant at 10%

Obs. Summary			
		1	left-censored observation at effsc<=0.020180415
		11802	uncensored observations
		66	right-censored observations at effsc>=1

6. COMPARISON OF BOTH APPROACHES FOR THEIR APPLICABILITY TO BUSINESS PROCESS ANALYSIS

A striking difference between one-stage and two-stage approaches lies in the treatment of DMUs that are efficient by default, i.e., which use a unique combination of inputs and outputs, so that it is not comparable to other DMUs (McCarty and Yasiawarng, 1993). In the one-stage approach, such a DMU will turn out to be efficient but it is only compared to itself for assessing the efficiency scores. In these cases, a two-stage approach will be better suited to assessing the efficiency, since, in the second step, the DMUs' efficiency, after accounting for influencing factors, is assessed in absolute and not in relative terms. The same authors find that the one-stage model showed slightly fewer DMUs with positive slack and positive surplus. The disadvantage of the two-stage approach of the non-inclusion of potential slacks is also reported by Fried et al. (1999) and Fried et al. (2002). These are general strengths and weaknesses of the one-stage and two-stage approaches.

In our case, we are particularly interested in the applicability of these approaches to analyzing business process efficiency. In order to receive some first insights into this research question, we have analyzed several hypotheses by applying both approaches. Generally, quite similar results have been found as Table 12 summarizes.

Table 12. Summary results of one-stage and two-stage approach

	One-step approach	Two-step approach	
		General Model	*Interaction Model*
H1	BUY more efficient	BUY positive influence on efficiency	BUY sign. stronger influence on efficiency for s2, s4, s5; sign. weaker for s3
H2	CORP more efficient	CORP positive influence on efficiency	CORP sign. weaker influence on efficiency for s5
H3	OTC less efficient	OTC positive influence on efficiency	OTC sign. stronger influence on efficiency for s3; weaker for s2, s4, s5
H4	INTERN less efficient	INTERN negative influence on efficiency	INTERN sign. stronger influence on efficiency for s2, s4, s5; weaker for s3
H5	IB less efficient	IB negative influence on efficiency	IB sign. weaker influence on efficiency for s2, s4; stronger for s5
H6	ECURR more efficient	no significant difference	ECURR sign. stronger influence on efficiency for s2, s4, s5
H7	MV and HV less efficient	MV and HV negative influence on efficiency	MV and HV sign. stronger influence on efficiency for s3, s4
s2=CYCTIME2, s3=CYCTIME3, s4=CYCTIME4, s5=CYCTIME5			

However, it has become obvious that already existing models for both the one-stage and the two-stage approaches cannot be applied one-to-one when analyzing business process efficiency. Adjustments to existing models have been described within the context of this paper, and, in a comparison of both approaches, we have derived the following conclusions. First, the one-stage approach only allows including one categorical variable at once. In cases which involve many different transaction characteristics that are considered to have an impact on process efficiency, this approach will become too extensive. Furthermore, since only one variable is tested at once, dependencies between the categorical variables cannot be captured by the one-stage approach. However, this approach, following the Systems Model by Cooper et al. (2007), can be quickly applied for one or few categorical variables and yields results that can be easily interpreted. It can help in obtaining a first glance at the effect of certain categorical variables on process efficiency.

The two-stage approach has been adjusted for this analysis by including the input variables as dependent variables besides a set of dummy variables representing the categorical variables. The major advantage of this approach is that all categorical variables can be tested at once, so that dependencies between them are controlled for. It facilitates interpreting the results in terms of a ceteris-paribus-analysis. However, our research has shown that further adjustments of the regression model, e.g., by including interaction variables, can change results significantly. It thus seems to be important not only to take intercept differences but also slope differences in the regression line into account. Furthermore, it seems to be valuable to split the process into different process steps in order to obtain more detailed results. Especially for the interpretation of the interaction variables it adds substantial value to be able to distinguish between process steps, since categorical variables can influence process efficiency differently from step to step. It is a trade-off to decide on the granularity of the process steps to be included. The more detailed the process steps are, the more variables and interaction variables have to be included. On the other hand, a more generic definition of the process steps may yield less valuable results. A major drawback of both approaches is that the categorical variables have to be defined beforehand. As a consequence, only those variables can be captured that are expected to have an influence on process efficiency. This, however, will not always be straight-forward to determine and it might also prevent the identification of other crucial inefficiency determinants.

7. CONCLUSION

This paper investigates the applicability of one-stage- and two-stage approaches in DEA for analyzing process efficiency. We found that both approaches have their own strengths and weaknesses but that overall the two-stage approach seems to be more appropriate for analyzing business process efficiency. This paper adds to current research because of the following major aspects: (a) it shows the applicability of existing DEA approaches in a new context, thus reviving the discussion about strengths and weaknesses of one-stage- and two-stage approaches; (b) the results of the analysis provide first indications concerning the determinants of the inefficiency in securities settlement and clearing; and (c) it enlarges the research within the field of both efficiency analysis and business process management.

However, the results we present in this paper suffer from some limitations as well. First, the dataset did not reveal information about the process step enrichment which is generally considered to be a major determinant of inefficiency in securities settlement and clearing. It is definitely worthwhile to conduct further research with a different dataset and to include this process step as well. Second, some categorical variables were based on an unbalanced amount of transactions for each category. The robustness of results could be improved when performing the analysis with more balanced groups again. Third, the analysis was based on the data from one bank for a time horizon of one month. The results would gain in significance if the same analysis were conducted with different datasets again. Finally, only time was considered to be an important input variable. The analysis should be expanded to incorporate more different input variables. Furthermore, it would be interesting to include both continuous and discrete variables as potential determinants of process inefficiency.

Overall, it can be concluded that the research on finding methods for analyzing the determinants of process inefficiency is a worthwhile topic that deserves further attention. Within this context, concepts from traditional efficiency analysis, like DEA for example, seem to add substantial value. More research on the applicability of other concepts from this research discipline to business process management would therefore be desirable.

REFERENCES

Banker, R.D., Charnes, A., Cooper, W.W. (1984): Some models for estimating technical and scale efficiencies in data envelopment analysis, *Management Science* 30(9): 1078-1092.

Banker, R.D., Morey, R.C. (1986a): The use of Categorical Variables in Data Envelopment Analysis, *Management Science* 32(12): 1613-1627.

Banker, R.D., Morey, R.C. (1986b): Efficiency analysis for exogenously fixed inputs and outputs, *Operation Research* 34(4): 513-521.

Berger, A.N., Hancock, D., Humphrey, D.B. (1993): Bank Efficiency Derived from the Profit Function, *Journal of Banking and Finance* 17: 317-48.

Berger, A.N., Humphrey, D.B. (1997): Efficiency of Financial Institutions: International Survey and Directions for Future Research, *European Journal of Operational Research* 98(2): 175-212.

Bhattacharyya, A., Lovell, C.A.K., Sahay, P. (1997): The impact of liberalization on the productive efficiency of Indian commercial banks, *European Journal of Operational Research* 98(1997): 332-345.

Burger, A., Dohmen, A., Moormann, J. (2009): Efficiency Measurement on a Process Level Using Data Envelopment Analysis: *An Application to Securities Settlement and Clearing, Proceedings of the 22nd Australasian Banking and Finance Conference,* 16.-18.12.2009, Sydney, Australia.

Burger, A., Moormann, J. (2008): Productivity in banks: myths & truths of the cost income ratio, *Banks and Bank Systems* 3(4): 92-101.

Burger, A., Moormann, J. (2010): Performance Analysis on Process Level: Benchmarking of Transactions in Banking, *International Journal of Banking, Accounting and Finance, forthcoming.*

Casu, B., Molyneux, P. (2001): Efficiency in European Banking, in: Goddard, A., Molyneux, P., Wilson, J.O.S. (eds.): European Banking: Efficiency, Technology and Growth, Chichester, John Wiley & Sons: 99-140.

Caves, R.E., Barton, D.R. (1990): Efficiency in U.S. manufacturing industries, MIT Press, Cambridge/Mass.

Charnes, A., Cooper, W.W., Rhodes, E. (1978): Measuring the efficiency of decision making units, *European Journal of Operational Research* 2(4): 429-444.

Charnes, A., Cooper, W.W., Rhodes, E. (1981): Data Envelopment Analysis: Approach for Evaluating Program and Managerial Efficiency - with an Application to the Program Follow Through Experiment in U.S. Public School Education, Management Science 27(6): 668-697.

Cinca, C.S., Molinero, C.M., García, F.C. (2002): Behind DEA Efficiency in Financial Institutions. Discussion Papers in Accounting and Finance, University of Southampton.

Cooper, W.W., Seiford, L.M., Zhu, J. (2004): Data Envelopment Analysis: History, Models and Interpretations, in: Cooper, W.W., Seiford, L.M., Zhu, J. (eds.): Handbook on Data Envelopment Analysis, Boston, Kluwer Academic: 1-39.

Cooper, W.W., Seiford, L.M., Tone, K. (2007): Data Envelopment Analysis: A Comprehensive Text with Models, Applications, References and DEA-Solver Software, Boston, Kluwer Academic.

Cook, W.D., Kress, M., Seiford, L.M. (1993): On the use of Ordinal Data in Data Envelopment Analysis, *Journal of the Operational Research Society* 44: 133-140.

Cook, W.D., Kress, M., Seiford, L.M. (1996): Data Envelopment Analysis in the Presence of Both Quantitative and Qualitative Factors, *Journal of the Operational Research Society* 47: 945-953.

Dohmen, A., Moormann, J. (2010): Identifying Drivers of Inefficiency in Business Processes: A DEA and Data Mining Perspective, to be published.

Dusansky, R., Wilson, P.W. (1995): On the relative efficiency of alternative modes of producing a public sector output: The case of the developmentally disabled, *European Journal of Operational Research* 80: 608-618.

Dyson, R.G., Allen, R., Camaho, A.S., Podinovski, V.V., Sarrico, C.S., Shale, E.A. (2001): Pitfalls and protocols in DEA, *European Journal of Operational Research* 132(2001): 245-259.

Ekkayokkaya, M., Holmes, P., Paudyal, K. (2009): The Euro and the Changing Face of European Banking: Evidence from Mergers and Acquisitions, *European Financial Management* 15: 451-476.

Emrouznejad, A., Shale, E. (2009): A combined neural network and DEA for measuring efficiency of large scale datasets, *Computers & Industrial Engineering* 56: 249-254.

Frei, F.X., Harker, P.T. (1999): Measuring the Efficiency of Service Delivery Processes: An Application to Retail Banking, *Journal of Service Research* 1(4): 300-312.

Fried, H.O., Lovell, C.A.K., Eeckaut, P.V. (1993): Evaluating the performance of US credit unions, *Journal of Banking and Finance* 17: 251-265.

Fried, H.O., Schmidt, S.S., Yaisawarng, S. (1999): Incorporating the operating environment into a nonparametric measure of technical efficiency, *Journal of Productivity Analysis* 12 (1999): 249–267.

Fried, H.O., Lovell, C.A.K., Schmidt, S.S., Yasiawarng, S. (2002): Accouting for Environmental Effects and Statistical Noise in Data Envelopment Analysis, *Journal of Productivity Analysis* 17: 157-174.

Goddard, J.A., Molyneux, P., Wilson, J.O.S. (2001): European Banking. Efficiency, Technology and Growth, Chichester, John Wiley & Sons.

Golany, B., Roll, Y. (1989): An Application Procedure for DEA, Omega 17(3): 237-250.

Hammer, M., Champy, J. (1993): Reengineering the Corporation – A manifesto for Business Revolution, Collins Business Essential.

Kamakura, W.A. (1988): A note on "the use of categorical variable in data envelopment analysis", *Management Science* 34(10): 1273-1276.

Kueng, P., Meier, A., Wettstein, T. (2001): Performance Measurement Systems must be engineered, *Communications of AIS* 7(1): 1-27.

Lovell, C.A.K. (1993): Production Frontiers and Productive Efficiency, in: Fried, H.O., Lovell, C.A.K., Schmidt, S.S. (eds.): The Measurement of Productive Efficiency, Techniques and Applications, New York Oxford. Oxford University Press: 3-67.

McCarty, T.A., Yasiawarng, S. (1993): Technical Efficiency in New Jersey School Districts, in: Fried, H.O.; Lovell, C.A.K.; Schmidt, S.S. (eds.): The Measurement of Productive Efficiency. Techniques and Applications, New York Oxford, Oxford University Press: 271-287.

Neely, A., Richards, H., Mills, J., Platts, K., Bourne, M. (1997): Designing performance measures: a structured approach, *International Journal of Operations & Production Management* 17(11): 1131-1152.

Olesen, O.B., Petersen, N.C. (2009): Target and technical efficiency in DEA: Controlling for environmental characteristics, *Journal of Productivity Analysis* 32: 27-40.

Paradi, J.C., Vela, S., Yang, Z. (2004): Assessing Bank and Bank Branch Performance: Modelling Considerations and Approaches, in: Cooper, W.W., Seiford, L.M., Zhu, J. (eds.): Handbook on Data Envelopment Analysis, Boston, Kluwer Academic: 349-400.

Po, R.-W., Guh, Y.-Y., Yang, M.-S. (2009): A new clustering approach using data envelopment analysis, *European Journal of Operational Research* 199: 276-284.

Schmiedel, H., Malkamäki, M., Tarkka, J. (2006): Economies of scale and technological development in securities depository and settlement systems, *Journal of Banking and Finance* 30: 1738-1806.

Seol, H., Choi, J., Park, G., Park, Y. (2007): A framework for benchmarking service process using data envelopment analysis and decision tree, *Expert Systems with Applications* 32(2): 432-440.

Sexton, T.R., Leiken, A.M., Nolan, M.S., Less, S., Hogan, A., Silkman, R.H. (1989): Evaluating Managerial Efficiency of Veterans Administration Medical Centers Using Data Envelopment Analysis, *Medical Care* 27(12): 1175-1188.

Simar, L., Wilson, P.W. (2007): Estimation and inference in two-stage, semi-parametric models of production processes, *Journal of Econometrics* 136(1): 31-64.

Simmons, M. (2001): Securities Operations: A Guide to Trade and Position Management, Chichester, John Wiley & Sons.

Soteriou, A. Zenios, S.A. (1999): Operations, Quality, and Profitability in the Provision of Banking Services, *Management Science* 45(9): 1221-1238.

Steinmann, L. (2002): Konsitenzprobleme der Data Envelopment Analysis in der empirischen Forschung, PhD-Thesis, Faculty of Economics, University of Zurich.

Timmer, C. P. (1971): Using a Probabilistic Frontier Production Function to Measure Technical Efficiency. *Journal of Political Economy,* 79(4):776–94.

Rose P.S., Hudgins S.C. (2004): Bank Management & Financial Services, 6th Edition, Irwin: McGraw-Hill.

Russeau, J.J., Semple, J.H. (1993): Notes: Categorical Outputs in Data Envelopment Analysis, *Management Science* 39(3): 384-386.

Van der Aalst, W.M.P., Reijers, H.A., Weijters, A.J.M.M., van Dongen, B.F., Alves de Medeiros, A.K., Song, M., Verbeek, H.M.W. (2007): Business process mining: an industrial application, *Information Systems* 32: 713-732.

Varmaz, A. (2006): Rentabilität im Bankensektor, Wiesbaden, Deutscher Universitäts-Verlag.

In: Financial Services: Efficiency and Risk Management
Editors: M. D. Fethi, C. Gaganis et al.

ISBN: 978-1-62100-560-5
© 2012 Nova Science Publishers, Inc.

Chapter 4

MEASUREMENT OF COMMERCIAL BANKS PERFORMANCE IN EU COUNTRIES: A MULTI-CRITERIA APPROACH

Christos Lemonakis[1], Ioannis Strikos[2]* and Constantin Zopounidis[3]**

[1] PhD Candidate, Department of Production Engineering and Management, Technical University of Crete, 73100 Chania, Greece.
[2] MSc in Business Economics, Finance and Banking, Department of Economics, University of Portsmouth, Portland Street, PO1 3D3 Portsmouth, UK.
[3] Prof. at the Department of Production Engineering and Management, Technical University of Crete, Financial Engineering Laboratory, 73100 Chania, Greece

ABSTRACT

The European Banking sector has undergone significant changes over the last few years. Taking into account the current legislative framework of the Second Banking Directive for the enhancement of stability in the financial system as well as the new reformed economic environment after the outburst of the 2007 financial crisis in the American banking sector and its contagious effects around the world, the aim of this chapter is to evaluate the recent performance and efficiency of commercial banks operating in the 15 EU countries over the period 2005-2009. The analysis draws upon a multicriteria decision aid approach and a number of bank-specific characteristics collected annually from the consolidated financial statements of a sample of 162 European Commercial banks.

This chapter examines the performance of the national banking sectors' in the areas of asset quality, capital structure, cost structure, liquidity and profitability. Then, the

---

* culemon2004@yahoo.gr
* avsecon@hotmail.com
* kostas@dpem.tuc.gr

multicriteria Promethee methodology is utilized in order to rank the banks according to their performance over a set of multiple criteria, while the ranking result is used to provide a comparative analysis of their strong and weak points for each country separately.

The results indicate that, despite the differences observed across the national banking sectors, the adverse macroeconomic and financial markets conditions have severely decreased the accounts of commercial banks in European Union and have negatively affected the majority of their financial indices.

Keywords: European Commercial Banks, Financial Ratio Analysis, Multicriteria Decision Aid Methodology, Performance, Ranking

INTRODUCTION

The banking system is considered of high importance for any country's economic growth, financial stability, as well as money transmission and liquidity, facilitating the development of other businesses and increasing the competition between them. Undoubtedly, in nowadays the European banking industry has fundamentally been transformed due to deregulation, technological change, and the opening of the financial markets. According to Molyneux and Wilson (2007), the developments in information technology allowed for the exploitation of scale and scope economies and at the same time the establishment of Euro in the Union as a commonly accepted currency caused shift changes in the banking sector. Furthermore, the First and especially the Second European Banking Directive (Basel Committee on Banking Supervision, 2003; 2005) defined the basic operating rules within a Single European Financial Market System and provided banking institutions with equal opportunities, allowing them to operate freely in foreign markets within the integrated banking sector in the Union that were previously regarded as inaccessible.

However, as Pasiouras and Kosmidou (2007) have pointed out, the same factors have also resulted in a more intense competition within the Union's banking sector, significantly affecting its profitability. Not only banks had to offer their products and services in lower prices, but also the income generated from international transactions concerned with the conversion of currencies has been largely eliminated. What is more, non-financial firms have been allowed to enter the market and make available similar financial products and services, placing even greater pressure on the already existing financial institutions. In view of the enlarged European market, many banks reacted by increasing their size in order to compete more efficiently, resulting in an extended level of integration through acquisitions and mergers. Unavoidably, all these swift changes have significantly affected financial instructions' performance since they created new challenges for banks to reduce their operating costs, protect themselves from risk exposures, increase management efficiency and find new ways of generating additional income by switching to non interest income activities.

Economic literature has given significant attention to the issue of efficiency within the banking industry. Nonetheless, due to the intangible nature of their products and services, financial institutions' efficiency and competitiveness has special measurement problems. The majority of past studies have concentrated on a variety of methods including output measurement and alternative cost efficiency techniques, which have been used widely by academic researchers to evaluate the performance of the banking industry. For instance, Murray and White (1983) attempted to investigate through a translog cost function, the degree to which scope and scale economies were present for the Canadian credit unions. Gilligann et al. (1984) utilized the same technique for the US banks, but Hunter et al. (1990) were based on an intermediation approach and a multi-cost production function to chapter the efficiency of US banks. In his chapter, Revell (1980) examined the US commercial banks' performance with interest margins, while normal correlation analysis was applied by Arshadi and Lawrence (1987). On the other hand, Miller and Noulas (1996) who provided strong evidence for the advantage that the large banks have over the smaller one, investigated the issue in terms of technical efficiency.

In 2008, Kosmidou and Zopounidis (2008) in their work, recognizing the complex nature of the banking sector, attempted to examine the issue of performance and efficiency for the Greek commercial and cooperative banks over the period 2003-2004 by implementing a multicriteria approach which allows for the simultaneous consideration of multiple criteria in accessing banking performance. In their chapter, commercial banks were found to increase their customer base and their accounts, improve their financial indices and hedge the financial risks, enhancing their competitiveness and profits for the examined period.

Based on the earlier studies of Pasiouras and Kosmidou (2007) and Kosmidou and Zopounidis (2008), this chapter aims to extend their previous work and proceed in the evaluation of commercial banks' performance operating in 15 European Union countries during the period 2005-2009. Using a multicriteria decision aid model, this is the first chapter that attempts to utilize this technique in analyzing the performance of a massive number of banking institutions (162 in total) operating in the 15 EU countries in the context of the integrated European banking market and especially in view of the new vulnerable and reformed economic environment after the global financial crisis of 2007. Therefore, it is of high importance to examine whether there is any evidence of significant impact on the efficiency of the overall European banking system or whether there are still countries where the banking sector proved to be well protected and less vulnerable to the incidents followed after the bursting of financial crisis, the collapse of large financial institutions, the rescue of banks by national governments and the downturn in stock markets around the world. This is accomplished by ranking the selected banks according to their performance. The ranking result is then used to provide a comparative analysis of the strong and weak points of commercial banks for each country separately.

KEY ELEMENTS OF THE EUROPEAN BANKING SECTOR AND THE CRISIS ENVIRONMENT

The European banking systems have underpinned significant changes over the last two decades. Table 1 summarizes some key structural indicators for the banking sectors of the EU-15. It is remarkable that since 1985, there has been a gradually decrease in the total number of credit institutions operating in the 15 European countries from 12,473 to 6,961 in 2009. However, in spite of the fact that the number of banks decreased, the total size of branch networks increased by 42,600 units during the same period. It should be noted here that in the majority of the EU-15 countries (11 out of 15) the number of branches either remained relatively stable or increased. On the other hand, Belgium, Denmark, Netherlands, and especially the UK, have experienced a considerable reduction in the figures of their branch networks.

In the meantime, the data show that the number of employees has also increased, reaching in total 2.8 million in 2009, an increase of around 24.06%. Nevertheless, there were noteworthy differences between the countries, with Austria, Ireland, Italy, Portugal and Sweden experiencing small employment growth, in contrast to that of Greece, Luxembourg, Netherlands, Spain, Germany and (to a greater extent) of the UK, where the change was significant. There were also countries where the number of employees actually decreased, as it was the case in Belgium, Denmark and Finland. As far as the total assets are concerned, the reported data indicate a severe increase between 1985 and 2009, which in nominal terms surpassed the 600 per cent on average for the five largest European Union countries, namely those of the UK, Germany, France, Italy, and Spain. As a final point, the figures in the last column in table 1 which show the five-firm concentration ratio for total assets (CR5) do not imply the existence of a specific trend in banking sector concentration. The CR5 seems to have increased in some countries but the opposite holds for some others between the same periods. As Maudos and Fernandez de Guevara (2004) have pointed out, the increased concentration in non-traditional banking services may have compensated the propensity towards deconcentration in conventional credit activity.

Definitely, all the above trends support the view that not only did those countries characterized by large banking sectors have undergone more widespread consolidation, but also that it was mainly mergers and acquisitions (M&A) that have largely driven the consolidation process and not the restructuring of the branch network. M&A activity witnessed a noticeable boost in 1991, the same year when the Treaty on European Union was signed, and retained its high levels up to 2004. Initially, the major participants in most M&A deals were basically small-sized local financial institutions, while the involvement of larger banks in such activities did not take place until the beginning of the new millennium. Nowadays a large number of European Banks belongs to wider groups of entities, known as financial conglomerates, whose major business is concerned with offering no less than two of the primary financial services (i.e. banking, insurance and securities). The financial groups that managed to arrange banking and insurance services have experienced significant growth even beyond the local market within they operate. According to the ECB article for the "Consolidation and Diversification in the Euro Area Banking Sector (2005)", during the period 1985-2004 a considerable number of such type of bank-insurance groups came into sight as a result of a series of large M&A deals between domestic European banks and insurance companies.

It is widely accepted today that the three forces of deregulation, technological change, and the opening of the financial markets have been key contributors to the development process of European Banking. Nevertheless, there is a debate over the achieved degree of integration in the European banking industry. In fact, since 1977 a sequence of regulatory measures has been developed in order to facilitate the integration of European financial institutions. These legislative changes, reviewed in Table 2, and more specifically the two Banking Directives, have targeted mainly in the deregulation and liberalization of European markets in order to increase the competition among credit institutions. Meanwhile, the creation of Economic and Monetary Union (EMU) not only has it led many financial institutions to become international, enhancing their geographical diversification, but also contributed to the transparency and unity of banking practices. However, despite the incessant efforts by European regulatory authorities towards the creation of a Single European Financial Market System [Hartmann et al. (2003), Baele et al. (2004), Cappiello et al. (2006)], there is a number of analysts [Berger et al. (2001), Buch and Heinrich (2002), Berger et al. (2003)] who pretend that the divergences in the existing fiscal and legal systems, as well as the culture, language and economic conditions across the European countries are still considerable impediments to the integration process.

Table 1. Structural indicators for EU15 banking sectors

Country	Number of banks				Number of branches			
	1985	1995	2005	2009	1985	1995	2005	2009
Austria	1406,0	1041,0	818,0	790,0	-	-	4300,0	4167,0
Belgium	120,0	143,0	100,0	104,0	8207,0	7668,0	4564,0	4316,0
Denmark	259,0	202,0	197,0	164,0	3411,0	2215,0	2122,0	1996,0
Finland	498,0	381,0	363,0	349,0	-	1612,0	1616,0	1538,0
France	1952,0	1469,0	854,0	712,0	25782,0	26606,0	27075,0	38479,0
Germany	4739,0	3785,0	2089,0	1948,0	39925,0	44012,0	44044,0	39411,0
Greece	41,0	53,0	62,0	66,0	1815,0	2417,0	3543,0	4078,0
Ireland	42,0	56,0	78,0	498,0	-	808,0	910,0	1228,0
Italy	1101,0	970,0	792,0	801,0	13033,0	20839,0	31504,0	34035,0
Luxembourg	177,0	220,0	155,0	147,0	120,0	224,0	246,0	229,0
Netherlands	178,0	102,0	401,0	295,0	6868,0	6729,0	3748,0	3137,0
Portugal	226,0	233,0	186,0	166,0	1494,0	3401,0	5422,0	6430,0
Spain	364,0	506,0	348,0	352,0	32503,0	36405,0	41979,0	44431,0
Sweden	598,0	249,0	200,0	180,0	-	-	2003,0	2147,0
UK	772,0	564,0	394,0	389,0	22224,0	17522,0	13130,0	12360,0
EU15	12473,0	9974,0	7037,0	6961,0	155382,0	170458,0	186206,0	197982,0

Table 1. Continued

Country	Employees ('000s)				Total Assets (billion euros)				Concentration (CR5)			
	1985	1995	2005	2009	1985	1995	2005	2009	1985	1995	2005	2009
Austria	-	-	75,3	77,2	-	-	721,2	1036,6	-	39,0	45,0	37,2
Belgium	71,0	77,0	69,5	66,0	285,9	589,4	1055,3	1155,5	48,0	54,0	85,3	77,1
Denmark	52,0	47,0	47,6	50,1	96,3	125,5	746,6	1104,5	61,0	72,0	66,3	64,0
Finland	-	31,0	23,6	24,9	-	-	234,5	387,6	-	70,6	82,9	82,6
France	449,0	408,0	442,2	492,4	1348,8	2513,7	5073,4	7155,5	46,0	41,3	51,9	47,2
Germany	591,0	724,0	705,0	685,6	1495,1	3584,1	6826,6	7424,0	-	16,7	21,6	25,0
Greece	27,0	54,0	61,3	65,7	69,2	94,0	281,1	490,1	80,6	75,7	65,6	69,2
Ireland	-	-	37,7	38,2	21,0	45,8	941,9	1323,6	47,5	44,4	47,8	58,8
Italy	319,0	337,0	335,7	322,6	546,8	1070,5	2509,4	3692,0	-	32,4	26,8	34,0
Luxembourg	10,0	19,0	23,2	26,4	169,8	445,5	792,4	797,5	26,8	21,2	30,7	27,8
Netherlands	92,0	111,0	120,2	110,0	226,7	250,0	1697,8	2217,0	72,9	76,1	84,5	85,0
Portugal	59,0	60,0	54,0	62,2	38,0	116,3	360,2	520,2	61,0	74,0	68,8	70,1
Spain	244,0	249,0	252,8	267,4	311,3	696,3	2152,8	3433,3	35,1	47,3	42,0	43,3
Sweden	-	-	44,9	49,1	-	-	659,3	934,5	-	86,5	57,3	60,7
UK	350,0	383,0	534,5	471,1	1293,6	1999,5	5897,7	9421,0	-	28,3	36,3	40,8
EU15	2264,0	2500,0	2827,6	2808,7	5902,5	11530,6	29950,1	41092,9	478,9	779,5	812,8	822,8

Sources: ECB (2005a), ECB (2010).

Table 2. Review of European directives on banking/financial markets

Year	Description
1977	First Banking Directive. With this directive any firm making loans and accepting deposits was defined as a credit instituion.
1988	Basel Capital Adequacy Regulation (Basle 1). It defined the minimum capital adequacy requirements for banks with Tier 1 and Tier 2 ratios.
1988	Directive on deregulation of Capital Flows. Cross-border capital movements in EMS countries have been liberalized.
1989	Second Banking Directive. Credit institutions can offer their financial services anywhere within the EU state through the single banking market. No additional autorization is required from the host country. Introduction of the Principles of equal treatment and home country regulations alongside with the incorporation of new capital adequacy requirements.
1992	Large Exposures Directive. The proportion of a bank's own funds to equity capital for a single investment is limited to 25%. The total exposure to a single investment should not be greater tham eight times of its won funds.
1993	Investment Services Directive. The application of the Second Banking Directive rules to investment firms.
1994	Deposit Guarantee Directive. The establisment of a minimum deposit insurance fund in the event of a bamk failure.
1999	Financial Services Action Plan (FSAP). Legislation framework for the achievement of a single financial market.
2000	Directive on e-money. EU rules on electronic money. Access provided to new companies fostering real and effective competition between all market participants.
2001	Directive on the Reorganisation and Winding-Up of Credit Institutions. Home country supervisors have the autority to close an institution
2001	Regulation on the European Company Statute. Legislation framework for the formation of a "European company"
2002	Financial Conglomerates Directive. Supervisory framework for financial concglomerates across the EU.
2004	New EU Takeover Directive. A framework of common laws for takeovers in the EU to ensure an adequate level of protection for minority shareholders across the EU in public offers.
2005-2010	White paper on Financial Services Policy. The consolidation of the progress achieved the elimination of remaining barriers and the improvement of legislation and controls are the leitmotifs of the White Paper for the period 2005-2010
2006-2008	Capital Requirements Directive (Basle 2). Aims in greater stability in the financial system throught a "three pillars" concept: (1) new minimum capital requirements (addressing risk), (2) supervisory review, giving regulators much improved tools over those available to them under Basel 1 , and (3) market discipline

Source: ECB (2005b, Table 2).

Technological advances had also a great impact in the structural change of the banking sector, mainly through a series of innovations in delivery systems and in information management that lead to a significant cost reduction positively affecting the performance and profitability of banks. Among the most important innovations are the internal banking systems, automated teller machines (ATMs), electronic funds transfer at the point of sale (EFTPOS), telephone banking, and more recently e-money and internet banking (Humphrey et al., 2006). All these technological developments have dramatically reformed the financial services industry allowing new "players" to enter the market (i.e. brokerages, online banks and other utility companies) and provide consumers with comparable financial services within and across countries (Claessens et al., 2002).

Last but not least, the macroeconomic environment has been a crucial driving force in the consolidation process of credit institutions as well. The favorable economic conditions and the prosperous interest rate setting during the 1990's have given financial institutions the opportunity to increase their profits and use the reserves to expand their operations and finance the acquisition of less powerful rivals. On the contrary, the slowdown in M&A activity that was observed during the period 2001-2003 was due to the general economic downturn caused by the incidents of September 11, 2001 and the stock market downturn of 2002.

It is true that Economic integration within and across countries, deregulation, advances in telecommunications, and the growth of the Internet and other telecommunication technologies have severely changed the structure and nature of European financial services, greatly benefiting the credit institutions that operate in member countries. Nonetheless, all these developments have also posed several challenges to European banks significantly affecting their performance due to the increased levels of competition generated from the expansion of foreign banks in many European countries (Lensink and Hermes, 2004). What is more, the same financial products and services that were previously offered only by banks are now accessible through a large number of non-financial entities, including telecommunication and utility companies that offer payment and other services, placing additional pressure on traditional financial institutions to further reduce their operating costs, protect themselves from risk exposures, increase management efficiency and find new ways of generating additional income by switching to off balance sheet business and bancassurance activities. It is noteworthy that the non-interest income as a percentage of total income was 40% in 2003, an increase of more than 11.5% since 1992. Moreover, Laeven and Levine (2007) reported that in the case of large banking institutions non-interest income activities represented almost 50% of their total income. As Morttinen et al. (2005) have pointed out, this pattern may have contributed to the stabilization of profitability which is crucial for banks to survive, grow and prosper in a continuous changing economic environment.

In addition to the above difficulties, we have recently entered in a world historical situation where the current crisis is approaching the dimensions of the worldwide crisis and subsequent depression of 1929–1938. Initially appeared as a structural crisis and one of overcapacity in the car industry and as a real-estate crisis in the US, Great Britain, Ireland, and Spain, the first world economic crisis of the 21st century started to intrude on the financial sector at the turn of 2006 to 2007. Local mortgage banks went into the red through massive write-downs and in June 2007 the American investment bank Bear Stearns had to liquidate two of its hedge funds, in the first incident of this kind. Because these suffering American mortgage credits had largely been packed into non-transparent credit derivatives which were sold on into the whole world, the drop in their price and the connected massive increase in risk premiums led to a global chain reaction which overlapped with the mortgage crises in Great Britain, Ireland and Spain. The subprime crisis reached its first peak in the summer of 2007. Its global character became immediately clear when the first action in support of banks threatened with collapse was taken at the periphery of events, while all the banks' troubles originated in the Anglo-Saxon crisis centers, as in the case of the illiquidity of Düsseldorf Internationale Kreditbank (IKB) or Sächsische Landesbank (SachsenLB), but also in that of the massive write-downs and trading losses of the Swiss 'universal bank' UBS. Since summer 2007, the mortgage crisis has become a world-wide financial crisis, encroaching on the entire banking system by September 2008. The British mortgage lender Northern Rock collapsed in March 2008. Subsequently, after the initial German rescue missions of the previous year, the UK also undertook state intervention on a massive scale for the first time (Northern Rock received a comprehensive guarantee of state support).

The shock waves still continue unabated, as is evident in the massive write-downs and operating losses of practically all globally acting banks. Government guarantees for increasingly outsourced toxic assets, public injections of capital to refill equity as well as an increasing number of state shareholdings in financial sector capital are rescue measures which have been launched in practically all metropolitan countries and which will most likely continue to be part of government agendas. Since summer 2007 governments have been trying to keep the money and capital markets going by means of coordinated interest rate cuts by Central Banks, along with supply of liquidity to the collapsed interbank markets and the absorption of troubled securities and debt instruments into the regulated public sphere. As the most recent data show, it has not yet been possible to halt the worldwide drying up of credit and the flight of asset owners from financial funds to the 'safe havens' of 'hard' currencies and state bonds. The reason for this is simple: the losses on mortgage chapter and credit derivatives are followed by increasingly foul credit card leasing, and department store credit debts, whose extent is as yet largely unknown but which has already led to the de facto breakdown of Citigroup, once the largest US commercial bank. An end to the global financial and credit crisis is not in sight, and this occurs in a situation where it worsens the structural and industrial sector crisis which started parallel to it, spreading like slow fire to affect all parts of the world economic system.

EMPIRICAL STUDIES ON BANKING PERFORMANCE

The constantly changing environment in which banks conduct their business has largely attracted the attention of many academic researchers and policymakers. Over the years, a quite reasonable number of studies have examined the profitability and performance of the banking systems using relevant approaches and methodologies. Molyneux and Thorton (1992) by estimating a simple linear equation attempted to analyze the factors influencing the profitability of banks in numerous European countries. In their chapter, bank concentration, nominal interest rates, and the government ownership were found to have a positive impact on return on equity measure. Ten years later Abreu and Mendes (2001) tried to provide new evidence on the issue considering both bank-specific explanatory variables and external factors, such as financial structure variables as well as regulatory and macroeconomic indicators. The results indicated that net interest margins were positively affected by operating costs, equity to assets and loan to assets ratios, while a negative correlation was recorded for banks' market shares. As far as the macroeconomic factors are concerned, their findings implied a close positive association between inflation and bank performance, while the opposite held for unemployment rate. The chapter of Staikouras and Wood (2003) on the European banking sector concluded that return on assets are negatively correlated with loans to assets ratio and the proportion of loan loss provisions. In addition, there seemed to exist a positive association between a bank's equity and a bank's performance, while among the three macroeconomic factors examined, the same conclusion was evident only for the level of interest rates. Similarly, by using cross sectional and dynamic panel estimations, Goddard et al. (2004) analyzed the performance of a sample of banks operating in 5 major European countries namely those of UK, Germany, France, Italy, Spain and Denmark. The authors highlighted the importance of capital-assets ratio relationship and non interest income activities for a bank's performance, as well as the weak size–profitability relationship. Moreover, the results indicated that banks' profitability was remarkably stable during the examined period, despite the intense competition in European financial markets.

There is also an extensive empirical work regarding the degree to which scale and scope economies are present in the banking sector, an issue closely related to its efficiency. However, the conclusions drawn from the different published chapters are rather mixed. Gilligan et al. (1984) tested for scope economies using a traditional translog cost function. Their chapter supported the hypothesis of economies of scope across the balance sheet of banks, but no evidence was indicated for the presence of scale economies. Lawrence (1989) tested for cost complementarities by utilizing a generalized functional form in a multiproduct production function. For the purposes of his analysis, a variety of output measures has been considered (i.e. deposits, investments, loans) along with a range of factor inputs (i.e. interest costs, computer rental costs, wages). Nonetheless, the results suggested that cost complementarities were present only in cross-product terms. On the other hand, an intermediation approach and multi cost production function was used by Hunter et al. (1990) to analyse bank production. In contrast to Lawrence (1989) chapter, the authors could not find evidence to support his earlier findings for economies of scope. Shaffer and David (1991) also utilized a translog cost function with and without hedonic terms to examine the question of cost advantages for very large multinational banks operating in U.S. In the absence of hedonic terms they found evidence of scale economies, while in the translog equation with the hedonic terms included, scale was reduced from the level of without hedonic terms.

Humphrey (1992), in an attempt to provide further evidence on the issue, used alternative measures of output to test for the presence of scale economies for US banks and concluded that the flow measure was not as accurate as the stock measure of output. His analysis was grounded on the evaluation of a cost function as well as the implementation of a non-parametric growth accounting procedure and the results suggested that there are slight diseconomies of scale for large US banks but slight economies of scale for smaller US banks. Four years later, Altunbas and Molyneux (1996), published a work for the cost structure in Germany, Italy, France, and Spain using an intermediation approach. Their chapter provided little support of the idea that cost advantages and increased business size could be vital for a banking institution to generate income in a broadly defined market under a single European financial system.

A common belief among empirical researchers is that the benefits that can be gained on average cost savings by taking advantage of the potential opportunities for economies of scale are less than those that can be generated by eliminating operational inefficiencies. On average, most studies have reported scores for operational inefficiency that range between 20% and 30%. In other words, this means that the best-practice bank has a cost saving which is 30% lower than the corresponding cost of the average bank and the latter can achieve this lower cost by imitating the tactics of the cost efficient bank. On the other hand, in those studies that have supported the existence of increasing returns to scale, the advantage gained in cost reduction tends to be smaller with increases in scale. For instance, the expected reduction on average cost would be less than 5% even if a bank manages to double its size (100% increase in scale). As far as the improvements in cost efficiency that can be achieved through the realization of economies of scope, the empirical results are rather ambiguous.

The literature on the issue of financial institutions' operational efficiency has been further enriched by the implementation of the profit function in the measurement of bank performance (Berger and Mester, 1997). In contrast to a standard cost function in which the bank aims to maximize its cost saving in producing the exogenous defined outputs given the inputs cost, both output and cost are considered decision variables directly determined by credit institutions.

In the most recent years, numerous academic chapters have also focused in frontier analysis for the evaluation of financial institutions' efficiency. Rangan et al. (1988; 1990) used the non-parametric Data Envelope Approach (DEA), to measure the efficiency of a sample of banks operating in US. They analyzed both scale and technical inefficiency and bank output was measured with intermediation approach. Their chapter showed the efficiency score of 0.7 implying 30% wastage of the inputs actually used, all due to technical inefficiency. It was also indicated a positive relation of technical efficiency with bank size. Unlike Rangan et al. (1988; 1990), Field (1990), who applied the same methodology for UK building societies, found the majority of these societies - over 80% - lacking the ability to perform effectively mainly due to scale inefficiencies and concluded that size was negatively related with overall technical efficiency.

Berger and Humphrey (1997) fully reviewed in their chapter a large number of early academic researches - over 120 - that dealt with financial institutions efficiency and applied either non-parametric [i.e. Free Disposal Hull (FDH), DEA] or parametric frontier approaches, like the Stochastic Frontier Approach (SFA), Thick Frontier Approach (TFA) and Distribution Free Approach (DFA), examining a wide range of institutions operating in 21 countries at several time periods. They reported that the majority of these studies focused mainly on cost rather than profit efficiency, while some later studies, specifically those of Berger and Humphrey (1997) and Berger and Mester, (1997) have considered both types of efficiency. Furthermore, risk variables were also included in the studies of Berg et al. (1992), McAllister and McManus (1993), Mester (1996), Berger and DeYoung (1997) and Rao (2005). What remains a fact from the above chapters is that efficiency standings vary relying on which methodology and measure of output is applied. However, as Berger and Humphrey (1997) have pointed out, fairly stable efficiency estimates can be obtained over time once the researcher chooses to use a specific frontier approach and output measure.

Although the relevant studies for US banking sector are considerably more compared to that of Europe, during the last two decades there is a sufficient number of studies concerned with the issue of bank efficiency in EU countries including those of Dietsch and Weil (1998), Altunbas et al. (2001), Bikker (2002), Cavallo and Rossi (2002), Maudos et al. (2002), Casu and Molyneux (2003), Schure et al. (2004) and Staikouras et al. (2008). There are also some earlier works, referring to those of Berg et al. (1993), Lang and Welzel (1996), Pastor et al. (1997), Lozano-Vivas (1997), Dietsch and Lozano-Vivas (2000), but these studies has focused mainly either on a fraction of selected markets or individual countries.

Similar techniques to those described above have also been applied by other studies that dealt with the efficiency differences of local and foreign banks. The major finding in the studies of Mahajan et al. (1996), Hasan and Hunter (1996), and Chang et al. (1998) was that local US banks have a significant advantage in terms of efficiency compared to foreign banks operating in US and more profitable as well according to Seth (1992) and Nolle (1995). Comparable were the results in the studies of Avkiran (1997) and Sathye (2001) who both examined the Australian market. As far as the European markets are concerned, Hasan and Lozano-Vivas (1998), who used data from banks operating in Spain to obtain estimates of frontiers for local and foreign banks respectively, found that there was no any real difference in performance between those institutions. Berger et al. (2000) applied a similar methodology using both cost and profit frontiers to investigate the efficiency score of banks operating in US and four major European countries. In contrast to the US case, the results for the four EU countries, namely those of Germany, France, UK and Spain, indicated that, on average, local banks have a relevant cost advantage over their foreign rivals in UK Germany and France, while the opposite hold for those banks operating in US. In a relevant chapter, Kosmidou et al. (2004), by employing a multicriteria decision aid methodology, confirmed the previous findings of Berger et al. (2000) regarding the efficiency advantage of local banks in UK. The issue was further investigated by Kosmidou et al. (2006a). In this later chapter the relative advantage of local banks in the UK was attributed to specific financial performance measures.

In 2007, Pasiouras and Kosmidou estimated a linear regression equation for the period 1995 to 2001, examining a number of factors which are considered to influence European commercial banks' profitability. The authors concluded that in addition to internal parameters, there also some other important parameters that needs to be considered when evaluating banks' performance like the structure of the financial market and the major macroeconomic indicators (i.e. inflation, gross domestic product, etc.). Finally, in one of their most recent studies, Kosmidou and Zopounidis (2008) expanded their previous work by evaluating the performance and efficiency of the commercial and cooperative banks operating in Greece during the period 2003-2004. To perform such a multiple task, the authors applied the multicriteria PROMETHEE method on selected financial ratios to rank the sample banks according to their financial performance. The main advantage of this method compared to the previously mentioned DEA for the measurement of bank performance is that it is easier to implement, since DEA requires the same input and output measures for all banks before proceeding to any estimation. In addition, because the DEA frontier is not based on the whole sample, it is likely to be affected by extreme values as well as the market structure, which in turn can lead to wrong conclusions regarding the efficiency scores.

Taking into account the existing literature, this chapter aims to evaluate the performance of a representative sample of European commercial banks. For the purposes of this analysis, the multi-criteria PROMETHEE Method was implemented using a set of selected financial criteria derived from banks' financial statements. A presentation of the utilized methodology is provided in the following section.

Methodology: The Promethee II Multicriteria Approach

The PROMETHEE (Preference Ranking Organization Method for Enrichment Evaluation) belongs to the class of Multi-Criteria Decision Aid (MCDA) instruments. Several MCDA techniques have been developed over the years that deal with the ranking of numerous alternatives based on a variety of criteria. In other words, the MCDA allows for the selection of the best from the analyzed alternatives. Their development was actually the result of the practitioner's motivation to provide academics and researchers with improved decision making processes suitable for real-life multiple criteria decision situations by taking advantage of the recent evolutions in computer technology and the mathematical techniques involved (Wiecek et al., 2008). For the purposes of our analysis, following Kosmidou and Zopounidis (2008), we were based on one of the most recent MCDA techniques, the PROMETHEE II method. It is an outranking multi-criteria decision aid approach developed and presented for the first time by Brans (1982) at the University Laval, Quebec, Canada, during an organized conference on multi-criteria decision aid instruments by Nadeau and Landry. This method has attracted the increased attention of the researchers for practically complex problems and this can be easily illustrated by the growing records of conference presentations and academic chapters. As the time passed, a number of extensions have been suggested with the aim of assisting researchers in dealing with more complex problems. Indeed, PROMETHEE methodology has effectively been applied in a variety of areas such as Banking, Business and Financial Management, Chemistry, Energy resources, Health, Investments, Industrial Location, and other fields. As Brans and Mareschal (2005) have pointed out, the above technique owes its success mainly to its particular friendliness of use and to its' mathematical properties.

The PROMETHEE methodology gives the researcher the ability to solve a decision problem where a finite set of comparable alternatives is to be evaluated according to several and often opposing criteria. The implementation of the PROMETHEE method involves the construction of an evaluation table (Table 3), in which the alternatives are estimated on the preferred criteria and ranked from the best to the worst. The PROMETHEE methods are considered to provide solutions for multicriteria problems of the form (3.1) and their associated evaluation table.

Additional requirements for the application of PROMETHEE are the consideration of the relative significance of the selected criteria (i.e., the weights) and the information on the individually defined preference function of the decision-maker, regarding the comparison of the alternatives in terms of each single criterion.

The weights are typically arbitrary positive numbers, determined independently from the measurement units of the criteria. These numbers actually represent the relative significance of each criterion. The higher the value of the weight, the higher the significance of the relevant criterion and conversely. According to Macharis et al., (2004), the selection of the weights is of high importance in the case of multicriteria decision analysis, since it reflects the decision-makers' insights and priorities.

$$\textbf{Max } \{ \textbf{g}_1(\textbf{a}), \textbf{g}_2(\textbf{b}), ..., \textbf{g}_j(\textbf{a}), ..., \textbf{g}_k(\textbf{a})| \textbf{ a} \in \textbf{ A} \} | \qquad (3.1)$$

where:

A is a finite set of possible alternatives $\{a_1, a_2, ..., a_i, ..., a_n\}$ & $\{g_1(*), g_2(*), ..., g_j(*), ..., g_k(*)\}$ is a set of evaluation criteria.

Table 3. Evaluation Table

a	$g_1(*)$	$g_2(*)$	...	$g_j(*)$	...	$g_k(*)$
α_1	$g_1(\alpha_1)$	$g_2(\alpha_1)$	...	$g_j(a_1)$	...	$g_k(a_1)$
α_2	$g_1(\alpha_2)$	$g_2(\alpha_2)$	...	$g_j(a_2)$	...	$g_k(a_2)$
.	.	.	.	.	.	.
.	.	.	.	.	.	.
.	.	.	.	.	.	.
α_i	$g_1(\alpha_i)$	$g_2(\alpha_i)$	...	$g_j(a_i)$	...	$g_k(a_i)$
.	.	.	.	.	.	.
.	.	.	.	.	.	.
.	.	.	.	.	.	.
α_n	$g_1(\alpha_n)$	$g_2(\alpha_n)$	...	$g_j(a_n)$	...	$g_k(a_n)$

Source: Brans and Mareschal (2005) .

Due to its simplicity in formation and utilization, in contrast to other methodologies used in the assessment of banking performance, such as DEA, PROMMETHE allows for the performance estimation and ranking of alternatives (i.e commercial banks) contingent upon a finite number of criteria (i.e. financial ratios) without requiring the specification of alternatives' inputs and outputs. The preference structure of PROMETHEE is based on pair wise comparisons. This means that a separate preference function for each criterion must be defined for all pairs of alternatives, reflecting the degree of preference for an alternative *a* over *b*. Vincke and Brans (1985) suggested six specific types of preference functions, provided in the appendix section, from which the researcher can easily define its preference structure. No matter which is the preference function, the decision maker has to define the values of q, p and σ parameters. In contrast to q which is an indifference threshold that corresponds to the largest deviation, p is a strict preference threshold with the smallest deviation, capable of generating a full preference sufficiently for the decision maker. As far as the σ parameter is concerned it represents an intermediate value between q and p.

According to Brans et.al (1986), this preference degree for all couples of actions, can be represented by the preferred index of the following form:

$$\Pi(a, b) = \frac{\sum_{j=1}^{n} w_j P_j(a, b)}{\sum_{j=1}^{n} w_j}$$

Where:

w_j is the weight for each criterion

$P_j(a, b)$ expresses the degree at which bank *a* is preferred to bank *b*, when all the criteria are considered at once. Its value varies between 0 and 1.

A value equal to unity for the index will imply a strong preference of a bank **a** over **b**, while a zero value will imply a weak preference respectively.

aPb if : $\quad \varphi^+(a) > \varphi^+(b)$ and $\varphi^-(a) < \varphi^-(b)$ or
$\qquad\qquad \varphi^+(a) > \varphi^+(b)$ and $\varphi^-(a) = \varphi^-(b)$ or
$\qquad\qquad \varphi^+(a) = \varphi^+(b)$ and $\varphi^-(a) < \varphi^-(b)$.

From the preference functions described above, this chapter utilized the Gaussian form for all the selected criteria. This function requires only for the parameter σ to be specified and at the same time, due to the lack of discontinuities, it gives robust and stable results.

As for the ranking of alternative actions, two flows should be defined, the leaving and the entering flow, briefly described below:

$$\Phi^+(\alpha) = \sum_{b \in X} \pi\,(a,b)$$

$$\Phi^-(\alpha) = \sum_{b \in X} \pi\,(b,a)$$

Where:

X is the total of alternative solutions

The leaving flow $\varphi^+(a)$ expresses how an alternative **a** dominates all the other alternatives of X (the outranking character of **a**). On the other hand, the entering flow $\varphi^-(a)$ measures how an alternative **a** is surpassed by all the other alternatives of X (the outranked character of **a**). According to PROMETHEE I partial ranking an action a is favored over an action **b**, (**aPb**) if the leaving and entering flows of action **a** are greater and smaller respectively than those of action **b**:

In the case that the leaving and entering flows of two actions **a** and **b** are the same, the indifference situation can be written with the following expression (**aIb**):

aIb if : $\varphi^+(a) = \varphi^+(b)$ and $\varphi^-(a) = \varphi^-(b)$

There is also the possibility for two alternative actions to be incomparable, (**aRb**), if the entering flow of action **a** is worse than the corresponding flow of action b, while the opposite is implied by the leaving flow:

aRb if : $\varphi^+(a) > \varphi^+(b)$ and $\varphi^-(a) > \varphi^-(b)$ or
$\qquad\qquad \varphi^+(a) < \varphi^+(b)$ and $\varphi^-(a) < \varphi^-(b)$

In this chapter we utililized only the PROMETHEE II method which provides a complete ranking of the comparable alternatives from the best to the worst. In contrast to the partial ranking of PROMETHEE I, we used the net flows to provide a ranking of the sample banks in the country they operate and by extension in the broader context of the European Union. The net flow implied by $\Phi(a)$, which is the difference between the two flows, corresponds to a value function for which the higher the value the higher the attractiveness of alternative a. For each action $a \in X$ the net flow can be described as follows:

$$\Phi(a) = \Phi^+(a) - \Phi^-(a)$$

The outranking relations in PROMETHEE II method are such that:

$aP^{II}b$	if	$\Phi(a) > \Phi(b)$,
$aP^{II}b$	if	$\Phi(a) = \Phi(b)$

When $aP^{II}b$, alternative a is preferred over b. When $aI^{II}b$, the decision maker is indifferent between alternatives a and b. In contrast to PROMETHEE I, incomparabilities are now absent between the alternatives. As a result, the alternative with the higher net flow is identified as the one optimizing all the criteria.

DATA AND VARIABLES

The methodology described in the previous section was utilized in a sample of European banks. The data used cover the period from 2005 to 2009 and includes 8.100 observations from the consolidated financial statements of exactly 162 commercial banks operating in the 15 European Union countries. The choice was based on the total assets of banks reported on their balance sheets.

Table 4. Number of commercial banks by country

Country	Number of banks
Austria	8
Belgium	9
Denmark	14
Finland	5
France	17
Germany	13
Greece	13
Ireland	9
Italy	13
Luxembourg	6
Netherlands	12
Portugal	6
Spain	15
Sweden	4
UK	18
Total EU-15	162

All financial data of the selected commercial banks were obtained from the Bankscope Database of Bureau van Dijk's company. There are two main advantages for using Bankscope. Not only it contains important information for over 10,000 banks, which constitute a very large proportion of total assets in each country (over 90%), but also presents the financial data in standardized accounting and reporting formats. A complete list of the commercial banks for each country is provided in the appendix.

The criteria (variables) used in this chapter are based on key accounts reported in the annual financial statements of the banks - according to IFRS accounting standards - and include indices expressed in the form of financial ratios that investigate the most important aspects of a bank's performance and financial situation especially in the areas of asset quality, capital structure, cost structure, liquidity and profitability. Table 5 provides us with the 5-year average of the main accounts of commercial banks by country for the period 2005-2009, while Table 6 presents the 10 financial ratios that we have selected for the evaluation of commercial banks' performance.

Table 5. Five-year average of the main accounts of commercial banks in EU-15 (2005-2009)

Country	Equity	Assets	Deposits (mil €)	Loans	Pre-tax Income
Austria (8)	2217,0	38432,6	23437,3	20169,7	266,0
Belgium (9)	5269,7	149452,3	103722,0	60681,2	268,5
Denmark (14)	2038,9	54106,2	23745,7	34602,8	223,1
Finland (5)	3138,2	45380,4	23725,1	18176,7	384,8
France (17)	11491,5	342618,2	148035,9	115755,7	1302,4
Germany (13)	6976,7	250638,8	112216,0	71298,2	577,2
Greece (13)	1855,1	26082,9	20377,3	18167,0	258,3
Ireland (9)	3190,1	91862,7	57811,8	55299,9	19,8
Italy (13)	9968,3	142975,9	72373,0	86442,5	942,8
Luxembourg (6)	1792,9	32655,8	24492,6	11010,8	230,0
Netherlands (12)	4993,7	167618,0	105487,6	88300,1	56,2
Portugal (6)	1831,2	28673,7	17211,2	19615,7	205,2
Spain (15)	7274,3	124783,0	75807,8	80697,7	1420,3
Sweden (4)	3918,8	106701,5	57403,6	61741,6	697,5
UK (18)	12331,4	352503,4	189520,6	156757,1	1478,5
EU-15 Average	5399,0	138645,5	72899,9	62601,5	735,9

Source: Calculations based on Bankscope.

Asset quality, also known as portfolio quality, is considered by financial analysts to be a key indicator of an institution's financial viability. Undoubtedly, the loan portfolio still remains the major element of a financial institution's asset structure despite their efforts to increase their deposits base and the range of non-balance sheet business.

Since, there is always the risk of an unprecedented delay or even a default in the servicing of an asset, its quality is fully determined by the ability of a bank to collect it during and at maturity period. Two asset quality indicators were selected for this chapter in order to judge a bank's efficiency in conducting healthy loan agreements: the Provisions to Gross

Profit ratio and Provisions to Total Assets ratio. The higher the value of these ratios, the lower the quality of loans that appear on the assets side of the balance sheet and conversely.

The financial ratio Equity / Total Assets is employed to analyze a bank's capital adequacy. Capital Adequacy measures allow a bank to investigate whether the various risks that have been incurred as a course of business are able to threaten its solvency. For a financial institution to be well capitalized under the European banking regulations the value of this ratio should not fall below 4%, otherwise this would imply that a bank relies less on stockholders funds than on short and long term liabilities. In other words, this ratio can be seen as an indicator of efficiency and stability of the financial systems under examination.

Cost ratios provide an understanding of the costs the bank is incurring as a proportion of its operations. The Administrative cost ratio which is the Administrative costs divided by the Total Assets shows the ability of the management to run the financial institution's operations efficiently.

Table 6. Financial ratios for performance evaluation

Key Indices		Desirable Sign
	Profitability Ratios	
C1	Net Income before taxes / Equity	Maximize (+)
C2	Net Income before taxes / Total Assets	Maximize (+) [16]
C3	Net Income before taxes / (Loans + Securities)	Maximize (+)
C4	Total Earning Assets / Total Assets	Maximize (+) [17]
C5	Net Interest Revenue / Total Earning Assets	Maximize (+) [18]
	Leverage Ratios	
C6	Equity / Total Assets	Maximize (+) [19]
	Liquidity Ratios	
C7	Loans / Deposits	Minimize (-) [20]
	Cost Ratios	
C8	Administrative costs / Total Assets	Minimize (-)
	Assets Quality Ratios	
C9	Provisions / Total Assets	Minimize (-) [21]
C10	Provisions / Gross Profit	Minimize (-)

Liquidity refers to the speed at which an asset can be turned by a bank into cash quickly. The greater the difficulty in converting an asset into cash when most needed (illiquid asset) the higher the liquidity risk that a bank might incur. Liquidity can be evaluated using a variety of tools, but for the purposes of this analysis the Loans / Deposits ratio is employed, also known as LTD ratio.

---

[16] Kosmidou and Zopounidis (2008)
[17] Kosmidou and Zopounidis (2005)
[18] Higher margins and profitability are desirable as long as the asset quality is being maintained (Kosmidou et al., 2006)
[19] The higher this ratio the lower the solvency risk (Spathis et al., 2002)
[20] The lower the value the lower the liquidity risk for a bank (Kosmidou and Zopounidis, 2005)
[21] Lower values of this ratio are more desirable (Kosmidou et al., 2006)

Table 7. Ranking of commercial banks in EU15 based on 2009 Promethee scores (1-55)

	Country	2009		2008		2007		2006		2005	
		Score	Ranking	Score	Ranking	Score	Ranking	Score	Ranking	Score	Ranking
Europabank	BE	29,39	1	30,09	2	42,51	2	34,75	4	26,43	10
Delen	BE	26,63	2	22,65	5	40,73	3	33,70	5	30,86	4
March	ES	25,40	3	34,87	1	34,40	5	50,54	1	33,26	2
Caixa	PT	24,08	4	22,34	7	18,73	15	16,92	21	6,19	34
Degroof	LU	23,24	5	22,51	6	33,19	6	17,54	19	-6,67	123
Mendes	NL	19,96	6	0,14	90	-9,40	135	-8,48	135	-7,26	128
Svendborg	DK	19,53	7	24,50	4	35,49	4	36,09	3	32,11	3
Keytrade	BE	16,83	8	14,16	17	32,55	8	25,24	12	19,78	17
Pueyo	ES	14,57	9	21,81	8	16,62	17	8,68	35	7,34	32
NBG	GR	13,98	10	18,47	10	13,80	21	4,85	46	5,29	40
J. Van	BE	13,77	11	11,47	23	9,90	33	9,39	33	24,59	14
UniCredit	LU	12,23	12	5,65	48	-2,75	95	-1,45	72	-3,07	93
BKS	AT	12,03	13	13,39	22	3,15	61	-1,85	79	-5,17	111
EBN	ES	11,83	14	14,07	18	17,05	16	24,07	13	12,82	21
WINTER	AT	11,40	15	17,34	12	3,39	57	-1,71	76	-3,96	105
Fideuram	IT	10,91	16	19,38	9	28,44	10	20,21	16	30,79	5
BinckBank	NL	10,65	17	16,06	14	3,09	64	33,55	6	29,28	6
ING	BE	10,46	18	10,59	25	0,21	75	-0,08	60	0,78	65
Comdirect	DE	10,09	19	15,46	16	13,57	22	16,63	22	12,82	22
Bilbao	ES	9,52	20	8,43	33	5,35	45	4,90	45	5,34	39
Desio	IT	9,33	21	10,26	26	28,53	9	13,53	24	19,40	18
Rabobank	IE	9,32	22	9,69	27	-12,58	141	-5,70	103	-5,58	115
Mediolanum	IT	9,31	23	7,38	36	16,61	18	14,16	23	25,21	13
Sardegna	IT	9,30	24	13,60	21	10,00	32	-1,48	73	0,07	69
Alpha	GR	9,14	25	5,00	52	10,28	31	2,62	52	0,99	62
Trinkaus	DE	9,12	26	9,64	28	5,12	47	3,59	47	5,52	36
PRObank	GR	8,89	27	10,89	24	3,11	62	-1,41	71	-18,28	154
Sparekassen	DK	8,85	28	16,09	13	48,47	1	48,20	2	42,13	1
Personal Finance	FR	8,32	29	3,73	59	-7,31	127	-6,86	117	-2,80	90
Attica	GR	8,31	30	2,86	69	-12,57	140	-34,42	160	-39,53	162
DAB	DE	8,10	31	5,54	49	3,87	54	-4,59	93	-3,41	96

Table 7. Continued

	Country	2009		2008		2007		2006		2005	
		Score	Ranking	Score	Ranking	Score	Ranking	Score	Ranking	Score	Ranking
KBL	LU	8,04	32	-14,51	144	5,37	44	30,88	7	0,85	64
EFG	GR	7,79	33	4,87	53	4,54	50	1,01	59	1,88	58
Oberbank	AT	7,71	34	9,58	29	-4,72	111	-6,28	111	-7,30	129
Nord	FR	7,53	35	5,92	47	5,20	46	5,39	43	3,99	48
CREDEM	IT	7,52	36	3,56	63	3,79	55	7,89	37	10,33	26
Proton	GR	7,49	37	-13,00	143	3,11	63	11,67	29	27,17	8
Dexia	LU	7,30	38	2,66	70	5,72	42	8,01	36	0,46	67
Arab	GB	7,28	39	17,91	11	7,35	41	6,29	41	26,58	9
Deutsche	ES	7,17	40	1,04	85	-1,83	87	-1,73	77	-5,30	112
BTV	AT	7,14	41	8,58	32	-5,71	117	-6,71	115	-9,00	138
Chartered	GB	6,91	42	4,31	55	1,75	69	-3,44	86	1,03	59
Sydbank	DK	6,58	43	1,99	78	22,95	13	17,08	20	6,39	33
HSBC ME	GB	6,53	44	27,40	3	26,43	11	25,54	10	25,70	11
Santander	ES	6,49	45	3,28	64	-4,06	101	-5,61	102	-4,25	107
Abbey	GB	6,47	46	6,83	42	-3,44	98	-7,40	124	-1,06	77
FOREX	SE	6,36	47	-36,88	160	-2,15	92	-29,38	157	-11,55	144
Palatine	FR	6,22	48	-2,10	104	7,44	40	-0,20	63	-5,43	114
Oesterreichische	AT	6,20	49	-5,05	122	-5,76	118	-3,75	88	-3,78	102
Popular	ES	5,97	50	7,74	35	12,50	23	10,71	31	7,64	30
Marche	IT	5,90	51	2,62	71	-0,04	76	-5,89	106	-3,80	103
Jyske	DK	5,78	52	6,13	44	8,02	38	18,76	18	8,58	28
Itau	PT	5,76	53	5,14	51	20,44	14	28,49	9	20,98	16
Degroof	BE	5,55	54	15,71	15	32,80	7	22,87	14	14,72	20
Carige	IT	5,31	55	6,96	41	1,56	70	-7,41	125	-8,01	133

Table 8. Ranking of commercial banks in EU15 based on 2009 Promethee scores (56-110)

Country		2009		2008		2007		2006		2005	
		Score	Ranking	Score	Ranking	Score	Ranking	Score	Ranking	Score	Ranking
Millennium	GR	5,30	56	3,80	58	-4,18	104	-6,95	119	10,70	24
FCE	GB	5,20	57	4,37	54	2,05	67	2,09	54	5,00	41
BGL	LU	5,13	58	7,00	40	8,23	37	9,23	34	4,99	42
BAWAG	AT	4,89	59	-14,78	145	-48,43	160	-31,67	158	-35,80	160
Lyonnais	FR	4,83	60	6,13	45	-14,68	147	-5,16	98	-6,28	117
Volksbank	AT	4,79	61	3,68	60	-6,08	121	-9,76	141	-7,79	131
Nordea	FI	4,70	62	9,01	31	8,59	36	11,07	30	-1,34	79
CA Consumer	FR	4,64	63	-0,32	93	-2,56	94	-7,83	128	5,46	37
Sabadell	ES	4,63	64	-3,63	113	0,80	73	-11,60	150	-3,86	104
BES	PT	4,51	65	7,31	38	9,79	34	4,91	44	2,98	53
Co-operative	GB	4,51	66	1,05	84	-29,70	156	-2,50	83	-9,89	141
Credit Europe	NL	4,48	67	2,90	68	4,38	51	-5,07	96	3,20	51
Nordfyns	DK	4,46	68	-10,24	135	12,27	25	20,25	15	21,18	15
Norddeutsche	LU	4,38	69	4,17	57	-6,62	125	-7,95	130	-3,00	92
Espirito	PT	4,27	70	2,08	76	-0,87	82	-5,36	99	-10,70	142
BANESTO	ES	4,27	71	6,08	46	-0,83	81	-4,94	95	-2,69	89
Gallego,	ES	4,10	72	4,24	56	-15,33	149	-10,34	145	-14,60	151
UniCredit	DE	4,02	73	2,42	73	-0,65	79	-10,60	146	-32,37	158
Deutsche	IT	3,79	74	-0,57	95	2,01	68	2,04	55	4,91	45
Valencia	ES	3,59	75	5,29	50	-7,12	126	-4,20	92	-2,17	86
Bankinter	ES	3,41	76	3,64	62	2,17	66	-5,57	101	-3,76	101
Aland	FI	3,40	77	0,23	89	-0,54	78	-4,82	94	-4,68	108
UBA	AT	3,21	78	-1,38	99	3,92	53	12,70	27	-2,49	88
Sampo	FI	3,12	79	6,44	43	-1,96	88	1,45	56	4,93	44
HSBC	GB	3,03	80	1,47	80	-6,44	124	-5,78	104	-2,29	87
AIB	GB	2,85	81	7,01	39	13,91	20	12,06	28	15,42	19
Piraeus	GR	2,53	82	0,12	91	5,11	48	6,40	40	-1,93	85
Dexia	BE	2,25	83	1,09	83	-1,50	84	-0,94	69	-0,80	75

Table 8. Contineud

Country		2009		2008		2007		2006		2005	
		Score	Ranking	Score	Ranking	Score	Ranking	Score	Ranking	Score	Ranking
Guipuzcoano	ES	2,20	84	1,47	81	-12,73	142	-7,74	127	-3,60	98
HSBC	FR	2,16	85	3,13	66	-5,93	119	-7,32	122	2,00	57
Newedge	FR	2,03	86	8,07	34	11,06	29	-3,55	87	4,96	43
Scalbert	FR	1,99	87	2,07	77	-2,04	90	-16,56	152	-1,12	78
Kreditbank	DE	1,92	88	-1,34	98	9,29	35	-9,81	142	-1,03	76
SEB	DE	1,87	89	3,67	61	-10,58	138	-9,03	137	-13,27	149
Westminster	GB	1,59	90	2,99	67	3,61	56	2,26	53	7,34	31
Mutuel	FR	1,28	91	-6,25	124	-4,43	107	-3,80	89	-3,52	97
Handelsbanken	SE	1,26	92	2,60	72	-0,74	80	1,30	57	4,62	46
UniCredit	IT	1,04	93	3,15	65	-6,13	122	-5,47	100	-8,24	134
Spar Nord	DK	1,01	94	-1,11	96	7,72	39	13,21	26	2,30	55
LBB	DE	0,95	95	-4,39	117	-9,52	136	-4,12	91	-14,39	150
ING	NL	0,53	96	-1,52	101	-4,51	109	-1,71	75	0,85	63
Sanpaolo	IT	0,30	97	-3,12	110	-4,11	102	-1,81	78	0,64	66
Industriel	FR	0,23	98	-1,89	103	-1,44	83	-9,93	143	5,45	38
LeasePlan	NL	0,21	99	1,37	82	-1,98	89	-9,37	138	-0,04	70
Fédérative	FR	0,06	100	-6,70	125	-5,52	115	-2,64	85	-6,42	119
Pastor	ES	0,02	101	2,21	75	-4,31	106	-6,21	110	-7,40	130
CIC	FR	-0,21	102	-17,18	149	-8,64	133	-5,91	107	-11,96	146
Friesland	NL	-0,26	103	-4,86	120	3,20	59	2,73	51	-3,29	94
KBC	IE	-0,39	104	0,39	88	0,72	74	-0,64	65	1,02	60
BNP	FR	-0,67	105	-2,17	106	-5,47	114	-6,18	108	-5,35	113
Barclays	GB	-0,86	106	0,84	86	-3,22	96	-0,70	68	-0,53	72
Marfin	GR	-0,98	107	-2,74	109	3,27	58	-7,28	121	-4,93	110
UGF	IT	-1,24	108	-17,15	148	-7,41	128	-8,82	136	-28,49	157
Enskilda	SE	-1,37	109	0,75	87	-4,26	105	-0,25	64	-3,40	95
Millennium bcp	PT	-1,39	110	-2,12	105	-7,64	129	-1,89	80	0,15	68

Country		2009		2008		2007		2006		2005	
		Score	Ranking	Score	Ranking	Score	Ranking	Score	Ranking	Score	Ranking
Clydesdale	GB	-1,55	111	-1,71	102	-2,07	91	-0,64	66	-6,21	116
DVB	DE	-1,57	112	-0,34	94	-4,11	103	-8,04	132	-8,28	135
Nordea	DK	-1,74	113	2,27	74	-1,54	85	-0,19	62	-0,44	71
Postbank	DE	-1,86	114	-2,57	107	-4,72	110	-6,69	114	-3,64	99
Monte	IT	-2,26	115	-11,56	137	-9,17	134	-7,12	120	-9,08	139
Deutsche	DE	-2,54	116	-4,95	121	-8,51	132	-9,42	139	-6,70	124
Générale	FR	-2,64	117	-3,44	112	-17,95	150	-5,07	97	-1,66	81
Länsförsäkringar	SE	-2,87	118	-1,47	100	-13,78	144	-11,66	151	-11,93	145
Danske	DK	-2,96	119	-7,21	129	-3,77	99	-0,67	67	3,47	50
Pohjola	FI	-3,02	120	-5,26	123	-2,38	93	-7,83	129	-6,59	122
Aareal	DE	-3,99	121	-2,69	108	-6,17	123	-17,75	153	-39,15	161
Barclays	ES	-4,16	122	-4,26	115	-5,04	113	-9,73	140	-8,84	137
KBC	BE	-4,91	123	-1,30	97	5,57	43	6,72	39	5,79	35
Nykredit	DK	-5,50	124	-11,77	138	-3,34	97	-0,97	70	-1,86	84
Life	GB	-5,55	125	-4,21	114	-13,96	145	-7,68	126	-10,78	143
Commerzbank	DE	-5,73	126	-4,37	116	-7,70	130	-10,11	144	-7,87	132
Dexia	FR	-7,61	127	-18,66	150	-7,87	131	-6,53	113	-7,05	125
Depfa	IE	-7,70	128	-18,91	151	-14,79	148	-8,25	134	-1,38	80
Investec	GB	-7,75	129	-8,88	134	-3,97	100	7,30	38	3,00	52
Irish Life	IE	-8,04	130	-4,57	118	-14,07	146	-6,80	116	-3,73	100
BHF	DE	-8,30	131	13,93	19	3,16	60	-0,09	61	-0,72	74
SNS	NL	-8,52	132	-4,62	119	-11,35	139	-11,24	149	-6,39	118
Natixis	FR	-8,56	133	-7,87	131	-13,34	143	-7,96	131	-6,54	121
Agricole	FR	-10,29	134	-12,93	142	-34,03	159	-10,63	147	-7,21	127
Rabo	NL	-10,78	135	-12,21	140	11,99	26	-2,36	82	-12,69	148
Allied	IE	-11,07	136	1,95	79	10,92	30	13,22	25	7,83	29
ATE	GR	-11,15	137	-10,47	136	4,17	52	2,89	48	-6,54	120

Table 9. Continued

Country		2009		2008		2007		2006		2005	
		Score	Ranking	Score	Ranking	Score	Ranking	Score	Ranking	Score	Ranking
Nederlandse	NL	-11,16	138	-12,53	141	-23,21	153	-22,31	155	-23,03	156
NIBC	NL	-11,91	139	-6,81	127	-10,24	137	-5,82	105	-4,80	109
DiBa	DK	-13,50	140	-8,77	132	11,69	27	20,01	17	28,88	7
Evli	FI	-14,09	141	-8,85	133	-5,96	120	-26,73	156	-16,75	153
Ulster	IE	-14,35	142	0,05	92	2,24	65	2,80	49	2,96	54
Ireland	IE	-14,35	143	-16,19	146	11,30	28	2,78	50	3,91	49
RBS	NL	-14,88	144	-19,46	152	-24,81	154	-32,19	159	-1,82	83
Ulster	GB	-15,72	145	-7,23	130	1,15	71	-2,34	81	-0,71	73
General	GR	-15,94	146	-7,14	128	-33,46	158	-55,37	162	-33,76	159
Emporiki	GR	-16,39	147	-20,01	153	-29,14	155	-49,31	161	-11,97	147
BNP	BE	-16,43	148	-25,97	157	-20,50	151	-6,37	112	-8,53	136
Realkredit	DK	-16,52	149	-16,57	147	-21,17	152	-19,24	154	-20,22	155
Lloyds	GB	-17,17	150	-3,17	111	0,91	72	1,22	58	4,59	47
Artesia	NL	-18,00	151	9,41	30	-0,27	77	-6,18	109	2,19	56
Amagerbanken	DK	-18,02	152	-25,31	156	14,53	19	25,33	11	25,28	12
Royal	GB	-18,45	153	-6,77	126	-1,57	86	-2,58	84	-1,75	82
Northern Rock	GB	-20,51	154	-26,07	158	-32,09	157	-11,23	148	-3,98	106
Zurich	IE	-24,78	155	13,67	20	24,95	12	29,60	8	9,12	27
Scotland	GB	-25,18	156	-21,49	154	-5,66	116	-1,48	74	0,99	61
Italease	IT	-25,86	157	-53,02	161	-56,72	161	-6,90	118	-15,68	152
BPN SA	PT	-36,04	158	-62,63	162	-70,96	162	-8,15	133	-9,12	140
TT	GR	-37,04	159	-23,76	155	-4,85	112	-4,04	90	-2,94	91
DnB NORD	DK	-43,74	160	-11,84	139	-4,47	108	-7,32	123	-7,12	126
Bankaktieselskabet	DK	-45,80	161	-26,27	159	4,81	49	5,58	42	10,38	25
Anglo	IE	-54,60	162	7,32	37	12,49	24	9,77	32	12,25	23

Profitability ratios influence banks managers to make credit risk assessment decisions and strategic planning. The five ratios Net Income before taxes / Equity, Net Income before taxes / Total Assets, Net Income before taxes / (Loans + Securities), Total Earning Assets / Total Assets and Net Interest Revenue / Total Earning Assets, were selected as profitability measures for this analysis to indicate sufficiently a commercial bank's earning efficiency and overall performance. The Net Income before taxes to Equity ratio shows the bank's ability to generate profits with the amount of shareholders equity. The Net Income before taxes to Total Assets ratio indicates how profitable a financial institution is compared with its total assets. The Net Income before taxes to Loans & Securities ratios measures the proportion of revenues generated from securities and loans than that from other forms of assets. The ratio of Total Earning Assets to Total Assets shows the ability of the management in putting the bank assets to work. Finally, with the Net Interest Revenue to Total Earning Assets ratio, also known as Net Interest Margin (NIM), it is examined how wise the financial institutions have been in their investment decisions.

With the aid of the above ratios and the implementation of the multicriteria PROMETHEE method, this chapter attempted to evaluate the performance and efficiency of European commercial banks. The results are provided in the following section.

RESULTS

Taking into account 50 different scenarios of weights for each of the selected criteria at the same time, the PROMETHEE method was implemented using the Gaussian preference function for all financial criteria.

The aggregate tables below (Tables 7-9) provide the overall ranking of the examined European commercial banks in this chapter, for the period 2005 - 2009, according to the scores that they have achieved by the implementation of the PROMETHEE method.

Furthermore, we focus on the main characteristics depicted for banking sector in each country from the respective sample.

I. Austrian Banking Sector Characteristics

Looking at the results of the Austrian banking sector, we observe that Bank Winter & Co, last ranked in the 2nd position, has been relatively stable over the five year period; a performance which can be mainly attributed to its lower provisions for loan losses and the very strong figures in C4 ratio. Bank Winter & Co is followed by Oberbank and BTV for 2009 which have gained two and three places respectively since 2005. Similarly, despite the increase in its loan loss provisions, BKS has moved up to the 1st place recording the best scores in C2 and C4 ratios in relation to its competitors. Concerning the performance of the other banks, with the exception of UBA and Oesterreichische Kontrollbank, we notice no great changes. For example the 6th in order Bawag Psk Group was the only bank that remained almost unaffected by the financial turmoil. Relative stability was also evident in the case of Volksbank although it dropped from the 5th place in 2008 to the 7th in 2009 due to the decrease in its pre-tax income by 47.33%. On the other hand, Oesterreichische Kontrollbank saw a considerable decrease in its pre-tax income in 2008 and fell in the 7th position (4 places down in relation to 2005), while UBA's great fall over the entire period can be accredited to its poor performance in the majority of ratios compared to their rivals and especially to the large increase in its loan loss provisions (4 times higher than the 2007 level). However, for the full year 2009 Oesterreichische recorded the best performance in the Net Income before taxes to Equity ratio and improved its ranking by two places.

II. Belgium Banking Sector Characteristics

Taking into account the ranking in Belgium, it reveals a general stability in the performance of commercial banks with slight variations from year to year. It is noteworthy that BNP Paribas-Fortis Bank, the largest commercial bank in Belgium based on total assets, remained in the last position since 2005 due to its significantly low performance in the set of profitability ratios. Similarly, Banque Delen retained its 2nd position for the period 2006-2009 thanks to its strong performance in the C1 and C10 financial metrics. The 1st position went to Europabank presenting a clear advantage in the Net Interest Revenue to Total Earning Assets ratio. No significant change was observed for Keytrade Bank and J.Van Breda En Co who moved up from the 4th and 5th place in 2008 to the 3rd and 4th respectively in 2009. Among the strong points of Keytrade Bank we note the high profitability ratios all over the examined period, especially on the criterion Net Income before taxes / Equity, whereas the data show great stability in the majority of accounts for J.VAN. ING Belgium and Dexia also moved up from the 7th and 8th place in 2005 to the 5th and 7th respectively in 2009. However, the data reveal that this result is mainly due to the relatively lower performance of their rivals rather than to the improvement of their indices. Finally, Bank Degroof and KBC Bank were both ranked lower in 2009 revealing a large decrease in their pre-tax income (over 183% in the case of KBC Bank). Generally, the small commercial banks that operate in Belgium appear to have an advantage compared to larger institutions, presenting an overall performance that seems very impressive over the last few years despite the outburst of the financial crisis in late 2007.

III. Denmark Banking Sector Characteristics

Svendborg Sparekassen has topped the ranking results in Denmark for the last 2 years of our analysis. It was ranked first based on the criteria C2, C3 and C6, while Sparekassen Faaborg dropped to second place during the same period as a result of the decrease in its pre-tax income which negatively affected the majority of the profitability ratios. Sydbank, despite of the fact that the figures reveal considerable ups and downs over the period in analysis, improved its position in 2009 by two places, eventually ranking 3rd. However, this can be attributed to the relatively lower performance of its competitors since no improvement is evident to any of its financial indices. Jyske Bank gradually went up to third place in 2008 scoring the best performance in the Net Income before taxes / Equity ratio, but in 2009 it dropped again to the 4th place as, apart from the decrease in the bank's pre-tax income, there was a drastic increase in its provisions for loan losses which negatively affected the level of its assets quality.

In the 5th place we find Nordfyns Bank recovering after a significant drop in 2008 because of the losses in its pre-tax income. As for the other banks that were ranked in the last 7 places, DIBA Bank, Bankaktieselskabet Alm Brand Bank and Amagerbanken witnessed a significant drop to their ranking, falling from the 3rd, 6th and 4th position in 2005 to the 10th, 14th and 12th in 2009 respectively. The relevant figures reveal a considerable year by year decline in the pre-tax income for all three banks in addition to the increase in provisions. With the exception of Bank DnB NORD which retained its last position since 2005, all other banks were ranked higher in 2009 with Spar Nord Bank and Nordea Bank Danmark benefiting the most as they went up from the 10th and 11th to the 6th and 7th position respectively. However, in both cases this is due to the relatively low performance of its competitors since no improvement is evident to any of its financial indices. Danske Bank was ranked 8th, one position up in relation to 2005, while Nykredit Bank and Nykredit Realkredit gained 3 places ending up in the 9th and 11th position respectively for 2009. Despite its low ranking, Nykredit Bank seems to have the most impressive score on the criterion Administrative costs / Total Assets.

IV. Finnish Banking Sector Characteristics

The improvement in the ranking of Nordea Bank Finland from the 2th to the 1st position reflects the considerable increase the bank has experienced in its deposits during the last four years of our analysis positively affecting its liquidity levels. The pattern shows stability for Pohjola Bank and Evli as they both retained their 4th and 5th place correspondingly since 2005. In fact the majority of their financial indices appear to be slightly worse compared to those of their rivals all over the examined period. For the full year 2009 the Bank of Aland reveals a slight improvement in its deposits and pre-tax income and it was ranked 2nd. However, the opposite seems to hold for the 3rd position in order Sampo Bank which saw its pre-tax income to fall from 2005 to 2009 by 87.04%, in addition to dramatic increase in provisions for loan losses.

V. French Banking Sector Characteristics

With the exception of Credit Agricole and Natixis where there have been no great changes, the pattern shows great variation in the ranking results for the commercial banks in France over the period 2005-2009. In the 15th place we find Dexia Credit Local. It has reached its peak in 2006 with the 10th position but in the last two years the figures reveal the lowest score in the capital adequacy metric. Moreover, the pre-tax income of the bank decreased by more than 63% during the same period. Similarly Societe Generale, despite the decline in its liquidity, seems to have performed better in 2009 (14th place) compared to 2007 (17th place), but considerable worse than any other year. This is mainly due to the fluctuations observed in its pre-tax income during the period of the analysis. The same factor appears to be the major reason that BNP Paribas dropped from the 8th position in 2007 to the 13th in 2009. What is more, the bank increased not only its administrative expenses by almost 22% but also its provisions by more than 431% during the same period. Likewise, CIC fell in the 12th place in 2009, 4 places down than its 2006 ranking, while Banque Federative Du Credit

Mutuel dropped to the 11th place in 2009 after the considerable decrease in its pre-tax income in addition to the increase in provisions and administrative expenses. For the same reasons, Credit Industriel De I' Quest was ranked 6 places down than its 2007 ranking eventually ending up in the 10th place for 2009. Regarding the banks that were ranked in the first nine positions, Credit Mutuel, despite its rises and falls, finally retained the same place for both 2009 and 2005 recording average performance in the majority of ratios. Scalbert was ranked 8th due to the changes incurred in its pre-tax income and its provisions which have negatively affected the relevant ratios. The same also holds for Newedge Group, HSBC, CA Consumer Finance ranked in the 7th, 6th and 5th place respectively, whereas Le Crédit Lyonnais, regardless of its lower ranking in 2009 in relation to 2008, gradually moved up to the 4th position revealing that the majority of its accounts remained almost unaffected after the outburst of the financial turmoil. As for the 2009 top 3 banks - BNP Paribas, Personal Finance, Credit Du Nord and Banque Palatine - since no improvement is evident to any of its financial indices, their apparent higher ranking can be accredited to the relatively low performance of its competitors.

VI. German Banking Sector Characteristics

In the case of Germany, the bank that dominated the 1st position for the entire period was Comdirect Bank. Overall, the bank's profitability records based on the criteria Net Income before taxes / Total Assets and Net Income before taxes / (Loans + Securities) were well above the corresponding scores of the rival banks. No significant change was observed for HSBC Trinkaus & Burkhardt and in fact the main reason behind its slight fall in the 3rd place for 2008 was the increase in its pre-tax income in addition to decrease in its provisions which inevitably affected the correspondent ratios. DAB Bank seems that it gradually went up to the 3rd place since 2005 scoring the best performance in the C1 and C2 profitability ratios. An increasing trend is also evident for Unicredit, as it gained 8 places during the 5-year period. It is noteworthy that during 2009, Unicredit was ranked first based on the criterion Equity to Total Assets. Deutsche Kreditbank and SEB were ranked 5th and 6th respectively in 2009 despite the ups and downs up to 2008. In both cases, the rises and falls can be mainly attributed to the fluctuations in the banks' provisions and pre-tax income. In the 7th place we find LBB Holding AG which witnessed a considerable improvement in relation to 2008 due to the increase in its equity capital and its pre-tax income. Similarly, Aareal Bank has moved up from the 11th place in 2005 to the 8th in 2007 reporting higher records in almost all areas under examination. However, a decreasing trend is observed in the last two years following the outburst of the financial turmoil.

Taking a closer look in the bank's financial indicators the figures reveal that its provisions increased by 94.81% during 2009. Concerning the performance of DVB Bank, Postbank, Deutsce Bank, Commerzbank and LBB which were ranked in the 8th, 9th, 10th and 12th position respectively, the results reveal a decreasing trend, resulted mainly from the fall in their pre-tax income.

VII. Greek Banking Sector Characteristics

Based on the ranking of Greek commercial banks the following conclusions can be drawn with regard to 2009 order. To begin with, the National Bank of Greece and Alpha Bank were ranked in the first two positions followed by PRObank. The latter dropped to the 3rd position as it recorded lower performance in the provisions to gross profit ratio compared to Alpha Bank. In the 4th position we find Bank of Attica who seems to have been ranked higher in relation to previous years. However, this result came as a consequence of the relatively lower performance of the other banks rather than from an overall improvement on its own financial accounts. For instance, EFG Eurobank Ergasias seems to have significantly been affected by the consequences of the recent financial turmoil. It dropped from the 4th place in 2005 to the 5th in 2009 due to the large increase in its provisions for loan losses (over 280%). Proton Bank which was ranked 6th experienced an increase in its provisions by 117% between 2008 and 2009. The corresponding change for the 7th in order Millenium Bank was 46.06%. Pireaus Bank found in the 8th place, has witnessed considerable decrease in its pre-tax-income since 2007 and at the same time the provisions for loan losses increased by 342%. The same factors seem to be responsible for the lower ranking of Marfin Egnatia Bank during the last two years eventually ending up in the 9th place. On the other hand, concluding for the Greek banking sector, the ranking of ATE Bank presents rises and falls reaching its peak in 2006 (4th place). As for the last in ranking Emporiki bank, its poor performance can be attributed to the great losses in its pre-tax income and to the increase on non performing loans and provisions for loan losses. The 11th in order Geniki bank has reported great losses in its pre-tax-income since 2005 but the fact that they remain has effects that show through in more than one of the profitability measures. As for the last in ranking T Bank, the figures reveal that the bank has by far the highest administrative expenses as a percentage of total assets. It is noteworthy that Geniki Bank who recorded the second worst performance in the C7 ratio reported 57% better performance in this area compared to T Bank.

VIII. Irish Banking Sector Characteristics

Analyzing the performance of the Irish commercial banks, it can be easily seen why Depha Bank, the largest commercial bank in Ireland (based on total assets), was ranked in the last places over during the period 2005-2008. Up to 2006, the main reason behind its low ranking was the low liquidity levels. Apart from the liquidity problem, the bank saw its pre-tax income to decrease further in 2006, while in the next two years and especially in 2008 the losses in its income and the dramatic fall in its equity capital (99.76%) are considered to be the main reasons for the 9th position. However it went up to the 3rd place in 2009. Similarly, profitability issues and increased provisions for loan losses have negatively affected the overall performance of Zurich Bank and Bank of Ireland. As a result, Zurich Bank dropped to the 8th position in 2009, losing the 1st place that has retained up to 2008, while Bank of Ireland dropped from 3rd in 2007 to 7th in 2009. Ulster Bank Ireland Limited seems to have suffered from analogous issues in 2008, though it retained the same rank for the last two years in the 6th position. Allied Irish Bank showed a stable pattern all over the period with slight variations from year to year in the period between 2005 and 2009. It fell in the 5th position in 2009 due to the losses recorded in its pre-tax income in addition to the significant change in its loan loss provisions which increased by 4952% during the same period. On the other hand, great improvement is observed for Irish Life & Permanent Plc and Depfa Bank as they have moved up from the 8th and 9th place to the 4th and 3rd respectively. However the improvement seems to have come as a result of the relatively lower performance of its competitors rather than from a considerable boost in their accounts. Finally, in the first two places of our analysis for 2009 we find Rabobank Ireland and KBC Bank. Taking a closer look in the banks' financial indicators the figures reveal that they both have recorded great stability as far as their accounts are concerned after the 2007 incidents. It should be noted here that these two banks were the only ones that retained the positive signs in their pre-tax income.

IX. Italian Banking Sector Characteristics

The PROMETHEE method results for the Italian commercial banks indicate relevant stability with Banca Fideuram maintanining its ranking since 2005. This bank outweighed all other banks based on the criteria C1, C2, C3, C7, C9 and C10 all over the period in analysis. In addition, a number of banks, namely those of Mediolanum Gruppo Monte, CREDEM-Credito Emiliano, Banca Carige, and Banca Italease, retianed the same ranking since 2007 in the 3rd, 5th 7th and 13th place respectively. Mediolanum Gruppo Monte recorded the second best performance on the criterion Net Income before taxes / Equity, while CREDEM-Credito Emiliano Delle Marche performed better in the Total Earning Assets / Total Assets ratio. Banca Carige scored higher on the criterion Equity / Total Assets but performed moderate in the Net Income before taxes / Equity, Net Income before taxes / Total Assets and Net Income before taxes / (Loans + Securities) profitability ratios, whereas Banca Italease had the lowest performance in the C1, C2, C3, C4 profitability indicators as well as in the Loans / Deposits and Provisions / Total Assets ratio. As for the other banks, significant was the change for Intesa Sanpaolo and Deutsche Bank. The former dropped from the the 6th place in 2005 to the 10th in 2009 while the latter fell from the the 5th to the 8th place, revealing a lower liquidity level, reduced pre-tax profits and increased provisions especially during the last two years although no improvement was evident to any of its accounts. On the other hand less important were the variations from year to year for Banco Desio, UGF Banca Spa and Gruppo Monte which were ranked in the 2nd, 11th and 12th place respectively for 2009. Sardegna climbed to the 2nd place in 2008 but its lower pre-tax income combined with the increased provisions during 2009 led to the bank being ranked 4th. Banca delle Marche SpA improve its position by 2 places in 2009 moving up in the 6th, although no considerable improvement was observed to any of its accounts.

X. Luxembourg Banking Sector Characteristics

Among the analyzed commercial banks that operate in Luxembourg, Banque Degroof Luxembourg seems to have retained the same ranking since the outburst of the turbulence. Indeed the data show great stability regarding the banks' major accounts and exceptionally good performance in the profitability and liquidity ratios. UniCredit Luxembourg also improved its ranking by 2 places during the period 2008-2009. It is noteworthy that in 2009 the bank's pre-tax income increased by more than 154%, while its provisions for loan losses fell by 116.3%. On the other hand, KBL European Private Bankers is characterized by the most volatile behavior. For instance, it was ranked 2nd in 2005, 6st in 2008 and 3rd in 2009. The main reason for its dip in 2008 was the great losses in the pre-tax income. Indeed, the bank recorded the worst performance in the set of profitability metrics during that year. Variations in ranking are also observed in the case of Dexia Bank Internationale all over the examined period. For the full year 2008 the relevant figures reveal a substantial increase in the bank's provisions as well as a great fall in profits (over 84% in relation to 2007). However, the same factors in addition to the improved capital adequacy level seem to have adversely affected the overall performance of Dexia during 2009. On the contrary, the pattern has been consistently stable for Bgl Bnp Paribas with minor changes up until 2008. In 2009 it dropped to the 5th place although it recorded better figures in relation to 2008 as it did not manage to surpass its competitors. Relatively stable are also the results for ING with the exception of a dip in 2006 due to the increase in its provisions. For the two last years, ING was ranked in the 1st position as it recorded the best scores in the majority of financial ratios. Relatively stable are also the results for ING with the exception of a dip in 2006 due to the increase in its provisions. Relatively stable are also the results for Norddeutsche Landesbank Luxembourg with the exception of 2008 when it moved up to the 4th position. In 2009 it returned back to the last place. The main reason behind its fall was the increase in its provisions by 92.42% and the losses in its pre-tax income.

XI. Dutch Banking Sector Characteristics

Analyzing the performance of commercial banks in Netherlands, we conclude that only Leaseplan Corporation and ING retained the same position for 2009 in relation to 2005 despite the ups and downs during the five-year period. As for the other banks considerable changes were observed between 2005 and 2009 regarding their ranking. Bank Mendes was ranked 10th in 2005 but it gradually went up to the 1st place in 2009 while BinckBank and Credit Europe have lost one place and they were ranked in the 2nd and 3rd place respectively. Bank Mendes was ranked first based on the criteria C1, C3, C9 and C10. BinckBank recorded the best score in the Net Income before taxes / Total Assets ratio whereas Credit Europe reported the highest level of capital adequacy (C5). The 6th in order Friesland Bank improved its performance in 2009 but not in the 2006 levels when it was ranked 3rd. The decrease in its pre-tax income resulted in the lowest scores for the C1, C2 and C3 profitability measures. On the other hand, though SNS Bank is found in the 7th position for 2009 (3 places up in relation to 2007), no improvement was evident to any of its accounts, correctly suggesting that its competitors have actually gone worse. This seems to be true as Rabo Vastgoedgroep, which was ranked 8th in 2009, had the worst performance in the administrative expenses to total assets ratio.

In addition, liquidity issues were observed for the 9th in order Bank Nederlandse Gemeenten as indicated by the Loans / Deposits ratio. As for the lower three rankers, NIBC Bank has lost 2 places since 2005 and it was ranked 10th in 2009 due to its low profitability and the bad performance in the asset quality ratios. The great losses incurred in their pre-tax income have also negatively affected the overall performance of Artesia Bank and RBS ranked in the 11th and 12th position respectively in 2009. In the case of RBS we also note the high administrative expenses as a percentage of total assets.

XII. Portuguese Banking Sector Characteristics

Looking at the ranking of commercial banks in Portugal, we see a consistently stable performance for all banks between 2005 and 2009. Yet, despite the recent financial turmoil, Caixa bank was ranked 1st in 2009 as it continued to improve its profitability figures with the ratio Net Income before taxes to Equity standing at 22%, up from 20% in 2007. At the same time Banco Itau Europa has also moved up to the 2nd place thanks to its very good performance in the majority of financial indices compared with those of the other banks, whereas Bes Investimento dropped to the 3rd position due to the fact that the bank increased its provisions by 1455%, its gross loans by 21% and its administrative expenses by 49%.

Unavoidably all these changes have negatively affected the bank's financial performance in almost all areas of our analysis. Banco Espirito Santo seems to have improved its position from 6th in 2005 to 4th in 2009, thought the figures do not reveal any improvement in its accounts. However, a direct comparison with the figures of the other banks shows that on average has performed relatively better than its competitors. The same is also evident for Millenium Bcp-Banco Somercial Protugues which was ranked 5th in 2009. On the other hand BPN dropped to the last position in 2006 and remained at this place up until 2009. The main reason behind its low ranking was the large losses in its pre-tax income and equity capital which have negatively affected the profitability ratios and the level of its capital adequacy.

XIII. Swedish Banking Sector Characteristics

The ranking results for the Swedish banks reveal a quite stable pattern for Handelsbanken since it remained in the 1st position up to 2008. In 2008 it was ranked first based on all the criteria except for C5, C6 and C7. However, it dropped to the 2nd place in 2009 due to the decrease in its pre-tax income by 5% and the increase in provisions by 143%. Forex Bank was ranked 1st in 2009 scoring the best performance in the ratios Net Income before taxes / Equity, Net Income before taxes / Total Assets, Net Income before taxes / (Loans + Securities) and Net Interest Revenue / Total Earning Assets as well as in the C7 liquidity indicator. Enskilda has lost one place since its 2005 ranking. This is due to the fact that the bank increased its administrative expenses by more than 26% while its pre-tax income decreased by 72.5%, negatively affecting its profitability. At the same time the provisions for loan losses increased by more than 308% in just one year. Last ranked in the4th position, Lansforsakringar Bank reveals minor changes in its accounts and its ranking over the examined period. In 2009, it recorded the worst performance on the criteria Loans / Deposits and Provisions / Gross Profit.

XIV. Spanish Banking Sector Characteristics

The 1st position in the ranking of Spanish banks belongs to Banca March. No other bank was ranked in this place since 2005. This bank recorded the best scores in the ratios Net Income before taxes to Total Assets and Net Income before taxes to Loans. Banca Pueyo was ranked 2nd in 2009, as it did in 2008, achieving the highest performance in the Net Interest Revenue / Total Earning Assets ratio as well as in the C9 and C10 asset quality ratios. The 3rd and 4th place for the period 2005-2007 can be attributed to its slightly lower performance in the majority of financial metrics compared with those of EBN Banco and Banco Popular Espanol. The former dropped to the 3rd place since 2008, while Banco Popular Espanol was ranked 7th losing 3 places in relation to 2007. This is due to the increase in its provisions by 67.91% and the fact that it reported less pre-tax income by 44.81%. Similarly, Banco Bilbao Vizcaya Argentaria moved from the 5th place in 2007 to the 4th in 2008 although no improvement was observed to any of its accounts. However, it was ranked first on the criterion Net Income before taxes / Equity. Deutsche Bank reveals volatile ranking results with ups and downs during the 5-year period eventually ending up in the 5th place. In 2009 it recorded the best score in the Total Earning Assets / Total Assets ratio. Last ranked in the 6th place, Santander showed a relatively stable pattern regarding its accounts all over the period in analysis. However, regarding the banks that were ranked from the 7th to the 15th during 2009, significant changes are observed compared to what they have achieved in previous years. For instance, the high inconsistency in the profitability figures of Banco De Sabadell is reflected on its ranking results. Nevertheless, in 2009 Banco De Sabadell was the only bank that moved up 6 places as its pre-tax income increased by 119.89% and at the same time its provisions for loan losses decreased by more than 60% in relation to 2008. BANESTO was ranked 6th in 2008 but it dropped to the 9th position in 2009 due to the higher provisions and the fall in the profitability figures which negatively affected the bank's overall performance. Banco Gallego reached its peak in 2008 (8th) but it dropped to the 10th position in 2009 because of the increased provisions and the disproportionate increase in administrative expenses in relation to total assets. For the same reasons Banco De Valencia dropped from the 7th to the 11th position while Bankinter fall from 6th in 2007 to 12th in 2009. Banco Guipuzcoano was ranked 13th in 2009 recording the second worst performance in the Provisions / Gross Profit ratio. Similarly, Pastor and Barclays witnessed a great increase in their provisions during 2009. It is noteworthy that the latter reported the worst performance on the criteria Provisions / Gross Profit and the C1, C2 and C3 profitability ratios which highly contributed to the bank being ranked in the last position.

XV. British Banking Sector Characteristics

The most notable changes for the banks that were ranked in places 1 to 4 for 2009 are these of Standard Graphered Bank and HSBC ME. Standard Graphered Bank has gained 4 places in relation to 2008. The relevant figures showed a considerable improvement in the Equity to Total Assets Ratio. On the other hand, HSBC ME dropped from the 1st to the 3rd place in 2009, revealing a drastic decrease in its pre-tax income (over 94.08%). In the 6th position we find Co-Operative Bank, which has gradually moved up to the 6th place since its 2005 ranking. In the case of HSBC Bank, although no improvement was evident in almost all financial ratios, overall its indices seem to be better, in relation to the figures of its competitors, the years after the outburst of the financial cricis. Standard Life Bank has also moved up from the last place in 2005 to the 12th in 2009. The figures reveal an increase in pre-tax profits over 386% in relation to 2008. Significant was the drop for AIB and Westminster losing 5 and 2 places respectively compared to its 2008 ranking while minor was the change for Clydesdale since 2006 despite the great fall in profitability during 2009. Considerable ups and downs are observed during the five year period for the banks ranked in the 13th, 14th, 15th, 16th position for 2009. Investec and Ulster suffered mainly from the variability in their pre-tax income and provisions for loan losses whereas Lloyds and Royal also witnessed some high administrative expenses which unavoidably negatively affected their overall performance, especially during the last two years. Northern Rock, found in the 17th place, recorded great losses in its pre-tax income during the last two years. The bank also suffered from great liquidity issues as a result of the disproportionate increases in gross loans in relation to deposits. As for the last in ranking (18th) Bank of Scotland the figures show that apart from the losses in its pre-tax income during the last two years, the bank has also suffered from great asset quality issues as a result of the problems arisen in its loans portfolio.

CONCLUSION

In the most recent years, the rapid changes occurred in the macroeconomic and financial environment as a consequence of the negative impact of the financial turmoil has created new challenges to the EU banking sector. Under this context, the present chapter attempted to evaluate the financial performance of 162 commercial banks operating in the 15 European Union countries with the aid of the PROMETHEE II multicriteria decision aid methodology which was utilized in a specific set of internal bank specific characteristics, expressed in the form of financial ratios, that investigate a bank's efficiency in the areas of asset quality, capital structure, cost structure, liquidity and profitability.

The results indicate that the unfavorable macroeconomic and financial markets conditions negatively affected the overall financial performance of commercial banks in European Union countries. The EU banking sector witnessed a considerable decrease in profitability as a consequence of the rapid spread of the financial crisis of 2007 into a global economic shock. In spite of the differences observed across the national banking sectors, the further deterioration in the global economic conditions in 2008, severely depressed the pre-tax income of most European commercial banks, with many institutions reporting significant losses for the full year. The weakening asset quality of banks as indicated by the rapid increase in provisions for loan losses has also been a major contributor to the overall fall in profitability. Nevertheless, the net interest income as a share of total assets retained or even improved its relatively good levels in many European countries. The situation seems to have somewhat improved in 2009 thanks to a slight recovery in banks' profitability and in particular, to a strengthening of capital buffers to well above their pre-crisis levels. Nonetheless, there were a number of countries where banks recorded weak or even negative profitability against the background of a recessionary environment.

Alongside with the deterioration in profitability, the aggregate capital adequacy measure dropped considerably in 2008, despite the capital injections by some national governments and the systematic efforts by banks to raise capital internally. Moreover, the insufficient liquidity in funding their medium and long-term obligations remains a key challenge for many banks although it seems that this issue has been partly mitigated by the implementation of government guaranteed debt schemes in most EU countries. Therefore, there is no room for complacency and banks will need to take all the necessary actions to maintain adequate liquidity and capital adequacy against the threat of possible future shocks. At the same time, however, it is also important that the problems of those banks that remain reliant on government and central bank support facilities are dealt with comprehensively and decisively. In some cases, given the prospect of exit from government support measures, these institutions need to ensure their long-term viability through a fundamental restructuring of their business models and further deleveraging of their balance sheets.

Finally, the aggregate administrative costs as a proportion of total assets showed a considerable decrease. However it should be noted here that a further reduction in these costs is required in order for banks to retain and enhance their competitiveness under the new reformed financial conditions. It is highly expected that the intensification of consolidation in the EU banking sector will play a major role in the cost cutting strategies of European commercial banks.

The approach adopted in this chapter for the evaluation of bank performance can be quite useful not only to academic researchers but also to the banks' management team, regulatory authorities, financial analysts, and even to simple investors seeking into profitable reserves. Obviously, the bank-specific financial characteristics represent only a fraction of the numerous factors that one might consider for a more enhanced investigation. The performance of banks is also subject to other industry-specific and macroeconomic factors concerned with the country's economic and political environment (i.e. Gross Domestic Product and Inflation rate) and the structure of the financial market (i.e. market share, business cycle and stock market capitalization).

APPENDIX

Table A1. Abbreviations

EU-15	Austria, Belgium, Denmark, Finland, France, Germany, Greece, Ireland, Italy, Luxembourg, the Netherlands, Portugal, Spain, Sweden and the United Kingdom.
ATM	Automatic Teller Machine
CAR	Capital Adequacy Requirements
CR5	The five-firm concentration ratio for total assets
DEA	Data Envelope Approach
DFA	Distribution Free Approach
EFTPOS	Electronic Funds Transfer at the Point of Sale
EMU	Economic & Monetary Union
FDH	Free Disposal Hull
GDP	Gross Domestic Product (C + G + I + NX). "C" is equal to all private consumption, or consumer spending, in a nation's economy. "G" is the sum of government spending. "I" is the sum of all the country's businesses spending on capital "NX" is the nation's total net exports, calculated as total exports minus total imports. (NX = Exports -Imports)
IAS 39	International Accounting Standard (The objective of this Standard is to establish principles for recognising and measuring financial assets, financial liabilities and some contracts to buy or sell non-financial items)
IFRS	International Financial Reporting Standards
LTD	Loans to Deposits ratio
M&A	Mergers and Acquisitions

Table A1. Continued

MCDA	Multi-Criteria Decision Aid
NIM	Net Interest Margin (Net Interest Revenue / Total Earning Assets)
PROMETHHE	Preference Ranking Organization Method for Enrichment Evaluation
SFA	Stochastic Frontier Approach
TFA	Thick Frontier Approach

Table A2. Types of preference functions

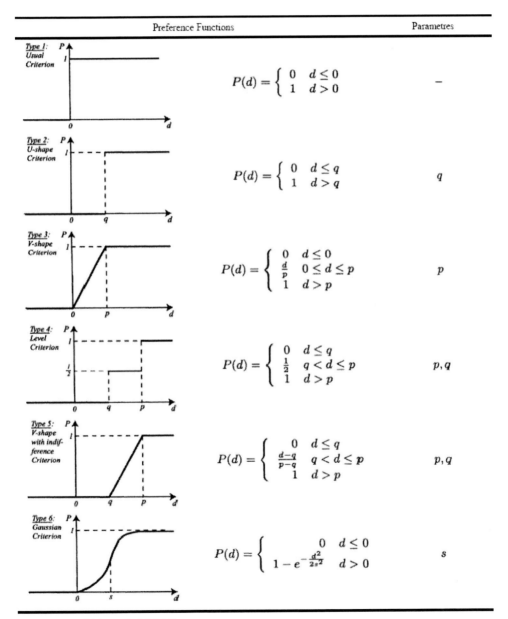

Source: Brans and Mareschal (2005).

Table A3. List of selected commercial banks by country and total assets

Country	Bank Name	Total Assets in mil € (2009)
AUSTRIA	BANK AUSTRIA - UNICREDIT BANK AUSTRIA AG	194.459,00
	BAWAG PSK GROUP	41.225,00
	OESTERREICHISCHE KONTROLLBANK AG	34.251,70
	OBERBANK AG	16.031,40
	VOLKSBANK INTERNATIONAL AG	13.863,10
	BTV	8.465,40
	BKS BANK AG	6.315,90
	BANK WITER & CO. AG	1.673,80
BELGIUM	BNP PARI BAS FORTIS BANK SA	435.038,00
	KBC BANK NV	281.614,00
	DEXIA BANK BELGIUM	253.770,70
	ING BELGIUM SA	153.586,90
	BANK DEGROOF NV SA	4.687,60
	J.VAN BREDA EN CO NV	3.025,60
	KEYTRADE BANK SA	1.643,40
	BANQUE DELEN NV	1.214,60
	EUROPABANK	913,00
DENMARK	DANSKE BANK A/S	414.411,80
	NYKREDIT REALKREDIT A/S	166.817,60
	NORDEA BANK DANMARK A/S	138.151,60
	JYSKE BANK A/S	30.038,70
	NYKREDIT BANK A/S	25.065,90
	SYDBANK A/S	21.108,10
	DnB NORD	10.021,80
	SPAR NORD BANK	8.630,60
	AMAGERBANKEN	4.499,00
	BANKAKTIESELSKABET ALM BRAND BANK	3.549,60
	SPAREKASSEN FAABORG A/S	1.064,40
	DIBA BANK A/S	945,90
	SVENDBORG SPAREKASSEN A/S	412,30
	SYDBANK A/S	268,20
FINLAND	NORDEA BANK FINLAND PLC	221.165,00
	POHJOLA PANKKI OYJ-POHJOLA BANK PLC	35.510,00
	SAMPO BANK PLC	24.867,90
	BANK OF ALAND PLO-ALANDSBANKEN ABP	3.379,00
	EVLI BANK PLC	690,80

Source: Bankscope.

Table A4. List of selected commercial banks by country and total assets

Country	Bank Name	Total Assets in mil € (2009)
FRANCE	BNP PARIBAS	2.057.698,00
	SOCIETE GENERALE	1.023.701,00
	CREDIT AGRICOLE CIB	712.432,00
	CREDIT MUTUEL	579.038,00
	NATIXIS	449.218,00
	BANQUE FEDERATIVE DU CREDIT MUTUEL	420.516,00
	DEXIA CREDIT LOCAL SA	360.265,00
	CREDIT INDUSTRIEL ET COMMERCIAL -CIC	235.597,00
	HSBC FRANCE	213.444,00
	LE CREDIT LYOANNAIS (LCL)	102.678,00
	BNP PARIBAS PERSONAL FINANCE	95.079,00
	CA CONSUMER FINANCE	57.321,40
	NEWEDGE GROUP	48.574,00
	CREDIT DU NORD	38.506,30
	CREDIT INDUSTRIEL DE I'QUEST-BANQUE CIO	18.113,10
	BANQUE SCALBERT DUPONT-CIN	17.108,00
	BANQUE PALATINE	10.371,80
GERMANY	DEUTSCH BANK AG	1.500.664,00
	COMMERZBANK AG	844.103,00
	UNICREDIT BANK AG	363.420,00
	DEUTSCHE POSTBANK AG	226.609,00
	LBB HOLDING AG - LANDESBANK BERLIN HOLDING AG	143.835,00
	SEB AG	52.813,20
	DEUTSCHE KREDITBANK AG (DKB)	51.841,60
	AAREAL BANK AG	39.569,00
	HSBC TRINKAUS & BURKHARDT AG	18.728,60
	BHF-BANK AG	18.698,00
	DVB BANK SE	17.268,60
	COMDIRECT BANK AG	9.785,20
	DAB Bank AG	3.120,60
GREECE	NATIONAL BANK OF GREECE SA	113.394,20
	EFG EUROBANK ERGASIAS SA	84.269,00
	ALPHA BANK SA	69.596,00
	PIRAEUS BANK SA	54.279,80
	AGRICULTURAL BANK OF GREECE	32.838,50
	EMPORIKI BANK OF GREECE SA	28.423,80
	MARFIN EGNATIA BANK SA	23.187,60
Country	Bank Name	Total Assets in mil € (2009)
	MILLENNIUM BANK SA	6.669,40
	ATTICA BANK SA	5.257,50
	GENERAL BANK OF GREECE SA	4.829,90
	PROBANK BANK SOCIÉTÉ ANONYME-PROBANK SA	3.729,50
	PROTON BANK S.A.	2.904,40
	T BANK S.A	2.427,90

Source: Bankscope.

Table A5. List of selected commercial banks by country and total assets

Country	Bank Name	Total Assets in mil € (2009)
IRELAND	DEPFA BANK PLC	212.578,00
	BANK OF IRELAND	181.106,00
	ALLIED IRISH BANKS PLC	174.314,00
	ANGLOIRISH BANK CORPORATION LIMITED	85.212,00
	IRISH LIFE & PERMANENT PLC	80.021,00
	ULSTER BANK IRELAND LIMITED	50.992,00
	KBC BANK IRELAND PLC	19.560,30
	RABOBANK IRELAND PLC	14.581,00
	ZURICH BANK	2.993,10
ITALY	UNICREDIT SPA	928.759,80
	INTESA SANPAOLO	624.844,00
	GRUPPO MONTE DEI PASCHI DI SIENA	224.815,00
	BANCA CARIGE SPA	36.299,40
	CREDEM CREDITO EMILIANO SPA	26.439,00
	DEUTSCHE BANK SPA	26.200,70
	BANCA DELLE MARCHE SPA	19.605,60
	BANCA ITALEASE SPA	17.056,20
	BANCO DI SARDEGNA SPA	13.630,00
	UGF BANCA SPA	11.308,10
	BANCA FIDEURAM SPA	10.323,30
	BANCA MEDIOLANUM SPA	8.843,70
	BANCO DESIO - BANCO DI DESIO E DELLA BRIANZA SPA	8.308,70
LUXEMBOURG	DEXIA BANK INTERNATIONALE 'a LUXEMBOURG SA	51.296,60
	BGL BNP PARIBAS	43.238,50
	UNICREDIT LUXEMBOURG SA	30.567,30
	NORDDEUTSCHE LANDESBANK LUXEMBOURG SA	23.716,80
Country	Bank Name	Total Assets in mil € (2009)
	KBL EUROPEAN PRIVATE BANKERS	13.907,00
	BANQUE DEGROOF LUXEMBOURG SA	2.076,30
NETHERLANS	ING BANK NV	882.119,00
	RBS HOLDINGS NV	469.345,00
	BANK NEDRLANDSE GEMEENTEN NV, BNG	104.496,00
	SNS BANK NV	80.289,00
	NIBC BANK NV	29.189,00
	RABO VASTGOEDGROEP-REAL ESTATE GROUP	22.395,40
	LEASEPLAN CORPORATION NV	17.126,20
	FRIESLAND BANK NV	11.009,50
	CREDIT EUROPE BANK NV	9.955,60
	BANK MENDES GANS NV	3.920,60
	BINCKBANK NV	2.930,00
	GE ARTESIA BANK	2.563,60

Source: Bankscope.

Measurement of Commercial Banks Performance in EU Countries

Table A6. List of selected commercial banks by country and total assets

Country	Bank Name	Total Assets in mil € (2009)
PORTUGAL	MILLENIUM BCP-BANCO SOMERCIAL PROTUGUES SA	95.550,40
	BANCO ESPIRITO SANTO SA	82.297,20
	BPN SA	7.510,60
	BES INVESTIMENTO SA	5.877,50
	BANCO ITAU EUROPA SA	5.055,40
	CAIXA BANCO DE INVESTIMENTO SA	1.930,50
SPAIN	SANTANDER SA	1.110.529,50
	BANCO BILBAO VIZCAYA ARGENTARIA SA	535.065,00
	BANCO POPULAR ESPANOL SA	129.290,10
	BANCO ESPANOL DE CREDITO SA, BANESTO	126.220,60
	BANCO DE SABADELL SA	82.822,90
	BANKINTER SA	54.467,50
	BARCLAYS	35.239,20
	BANCO PASTOR SA	32.325,20
	BANCO DE VALENCIA	22.830,20
	DEUTSCHE BANK SAE	16.089,70
	BANCA MARCH SA	12.531,70
	BANCO GUIPUZCOANO SA	10.344,90
	Bank Name	Total Assets in mil € (2009)
	CALLEGO SA	4.254,90
	BANCA PUEYO SA	940,10
	EBN BANCO-EBN BANCO DE NEGOCIOS SA	696,20
SWEDEN	SKANDINAVISKA ENSKILDA BANKEN AC	225.149,90
	SVENSKA HANDELSBANKEN	207.067,00
	LANSFORSAKRINGAR BANK AB	12.807,00
	FOREX BANK AB	367,10
UK	BARCLAYS BANK PLC	1.550.413,60
	ROYAL BANK OF SCOTLAND PLC	1.498.513,50
	HSBC BANK PLC	845.304,00
	BANK OF SCOTLAND PLC	743.471,10
	LIOYDS TSB BANK PLC	644.133,90
	NATIONAL WESTMINSTER BANK PLC - NATWEST	394.282,20
	ABBEY NATIONAL TREASURY SERVICES PLC	317.970,40
	STANDARD CHARTERED BANK	302.945,30
	NORTHERN ROCK PLC	98.304,70
	ULSTER BANK LIMITED	69.419,40
	CO-OPERATIVE BANK PLC	51.846,60
	CLYDESDALE BANK PLC	46.623,20
	AIB GROUP (UK) PLC	34.302,20
	HSBC BANK MIDDLE EAST	27.187,70
	INVESTEC BANK PLC	19.085,80
	FCE BANK PLC	18.220,70
	STANDARD LIFE BANK PLC	10.590,10
	BRITISH ARAB COMMERCIAL BANK PLC	3.712,80

Source: Bankscope.

REFERENCES

Abreu, M. and Mendes, V. (2001) Commercial bank interest margins and profitability: evidence from some EU countries. In: Chapter presented at the Proceedings of the Pan-European Conference Jointly Organized by the IEFS-UK & University of Macedonia Economic & Social Sciences. Thessaloniki, Greece, 17–20 May 2001.

Altunbas, Y. and Molyneux P. (1996) Cost economies in EU banking systems. *Journal of Business and Economics,* 48, 217-230.

Altunbas, Y., Gardener, E., Molyneux P. and Moore, B. (2001) Efficiency in European Banking. *European Economic Review,* 45, 1931–1955.

Arshadi, N. and Lawrence, E. C. (1987) An empirical investigation of new bank performance. *Journal of Banking and Finance,* 11, 33-48.

Avkiran, N. K. (1997) Performance of foreign banks in Australia. Australian Bank, 111 (6), 222–224.

Baele, L. M., Ferrando, A., Hordahl, P., Krylova, E. and Monnet, C. (2004) Measuring financial integration in the euro area. ECB occasional chapter no. 14.

Basel Committee on Banking Supervision (2003) The New Basel Capital Accord, Bank for International Settlements.

Basel Committee on Banking Supervision (2005) An Explanatory note on the Basel II IRD Risk Weight Functions, Bank for International Settlements.

Berg, S. A., Førsund, F. R., and Jansen, E. (1992) Malmquist indices of productivity growth during the deregulation of Norwegian banking 1980–89. *Scandinavian Journal of Economics,* 94, 211–228.

Berg, S. A., Forsund, F. R., Hjalmarsson, L. and Suominen, M. (1993) Bank efficiency in the Nordic countries. *Journal of Banking and Finance,* 17, 371–388.

Berger, A. and DeYoung, R. (1997) Problem loans and cost efficiency in commercial banks. *Journal of Banking and Finance,* 21 (6), 849–870.

Berger, A. and Humphrey, D. (1997) Efficiency of financial institutions: International survey and directions for further research. *European Journal of Operation Research,* 98, 175–212.

Berger, A. and Mester, L. (1997) Inside the black box: What explains differences in the efficiencies of financial institutions. *Journal of Banking and Finance,* 21, 895–947.

Berger, A., DeYoung, R., Genay, H. and Udell, G. (2000) Globalization of financial institutions: Evidence from cross-border banking performance. In: Litan, R. E. and Santomero, A. M. (eds.) *Bookings-Wharton Chapters on Financial Services. Brookings Institution Press,* Washington, DC, pp. 23–158.

Berger, A. N., DeYoung, R. and Udell, G. (2001) Efficiency barriers to the consolidation of the European financial services industry. *European Financial Management* 7, 117–130.

Berger, A. N., Dai, Q., Ongena, S., and Smith, D. (2003) To what extent will the banking system become globalized? A chapter of bank nationality and reach in 20 European countries. *Journal of Banking and Finance,* 27, 383–415.

Bikker, J. (2002) Efficiency and cost differences across countries in a Unified European banking market. DNB Staff Reports, Netherlands Bank. Report number: 87.

Brans, J.P., 1982. Lingenierie de la decision. Elaboration dinstruments daide a la decision. Methode PROMETHEE. In: Nadeau, R. and Landry, M. (eds.), Laide a la Decision:

Nature, Instrument s et Perspectives Davenir. Presses de Universite Laval, Qu ebec, Canada, pp. 183–214.

Brans, J. P., and Vincke, Ph. (1985) A preference Ranking Organization Method (The PROMETHEE Method for multiple criteria decision-making). *Management Science*, 31 (6), 647-656.

Brans, J. P., Vincke, Ph. and Mareschal, B., (1986) How to select and how to rank projects: The PROMETHEE method. *European Journal of Operational Research,* 24 (2), 228-238.

Brans, J. P. and Mareschal, B., (2005) In: Figueira, J., Greco, S., Ehrgott, M. (eds.), Multiple Criteria Decision Analysis: State of the Art Surveys. *Springer Science + Business Media, Inc.*, pp. 163–196.

Buch, C. M., and Heinrich, R. P. (2002) Financial Integration in Europe and Banking Sector Performance. Kie Institute of World Economics, Mimeo.

Cappiello, L., Hordahl, P., Kadareja, A. and Manganelli, S. (2006) The impact of the euro on financial markets. ECB working chapter no. 598.

Casu, B., and Molyneux, P. (2003) A comparative chapter of efficiency in European banking. *Applied Economics,* 35, 1865–1876.

Cavallo, L., and Rossi, S. P. S. (2002) Do environmental variables affect the performance and technical efficiency of the European banking systems? A parametric analysis using the stochastic frontier approach. *European Journal of Finance*, 8, 123–146.

Chang, C. E., Hasan, I., and Hunter, W. C. (1998) Efficiency of multinational banks: an empirical investigation. *Applied Financial Economics,* 8 (6), 689-696.

Claessens, S., Glaessner, T., Kliengebiel Daniela (2002) Electronic finance: A new approach to financial sector development. World Bank Discussion Chapter no. 431. Washington, D.C.

European Central Bank (2005a) *EU Banking Structures.* ECB, Frankfurt.

European Central Bank (2005b) Consolidation and diversification in the Euro area banking sector. *ECB Monthly Bulletin,* May, 79–87.

European Central Bank (2010) Structural indicators for the EU banking sector. ECB, Frankfurt.

Dietsch, M. and Lozano-Vivas, A. (2000) How the environment determines banking efficiency: a comparison between French and Spanish industries. *Journal of Banking and Finance,* 24, 985–1004.

Dietsch, M. and Weil, L. (1998) Banking efficiency and European integration: productivity, cost and profit approaches. In: Proceedings of the 21st Colloquium of the Societe Universitaire Europeene de Recherches Financieres. Frankfurt, Germany, 15–17 October 1998.

Field, K. (1990) Production Efficiency of British Building Societies. *Applied Economics*, 22 (3), 415–426.

Gilligann, T., Smirlock, M. and Marshall W, (1984) Scale and scope economies in the multi-product banking firm. *Journal of Monetary Economics,* 13, 393-405.

Goddard, J., Molyneux, P. and Wilson, J. O. S. (2004) The profitability of European banks: A cross-sectional and dynamic panel analysis. *Manchester School,* 72 (3), 363–381.

Goddard, J., Molyneux, P., Wilson, J. O. S., and Tavakoli, M. (2007) European banking: An overview. *Journal of Banking & Finance,* 31 (7), 1911-35.

Hartmann, P., Maddaloni, A. and Manganelli, S. (2003) The euro area financial system: Structure, integration and policy. *Oxford Review of Economic Policy,* 19, 180–213.

Hasan, I. and Hunter, W. C. (1996) Efficiency of Japanese multinational banks in the United States. In: Chen, A. H. (ed.) *Research in Finance*. vol. 14. London, JAI Press, pp. 157–173.

Hasan, I. and Lozano-Vivas, A. (1998) Foreign banks, production technology, and efficiency: Spanish experience. Working Chapter presented at the Georgia Productivity Workshop III, Athens, Georgia.

Humphrey, D. (1992) Flow versus stock indicators in bank output: Effects on productivity and scale economy measurement. *Journal of Financial Services Research*, 6, 115–135.

Humphrey, D., Willesson, M., Bergendahl, G. and Lindblom, T. (2006) Benefits from a changing payment technology in European banking. *Journal of Banking and Finance*, 30, 1631–1652.

Hunter, W. C., Timme, S. G. and Yang, W. K. (1990) An examination of cost subadditivity and multiproduct production in large U.S. commercial banks. *Journal of Money, Credit and Banking*, 22, 504-525.

Kosmidou, K., Pasiouras, F., Doumpos, M. and Zopounidis, C. (2004) Foreign versus domestic banks' performance in the UK: a multi-criteria approach. *Computational Management Science*, 1 (3–4), 329–343.

Kosmidou, K., Pasiouras, F., Doumpos, M. and Zopounidis, C. (2006a) A multivariate analysis of the financial characteristics of foreign and domestic banks in the UK. Omega, 34 (2), 189–195.

Kosmidou, K. and Zopounidis, C. (2005) Evaluating the performance of the Greek banking system. *Opertational Research: An International Journal*, 5 (2), 319-326.

Kosmidou, K. and Zopounidis, C. (2008) Predicting US commercial bank failures via a multicriteria approach. *International Journal of Risk Assessment and Management*, Vol. 9, Nos. 1-2, pp. 26-43.

Kosmidou, K. and Zopounidis, C. (2008) Measurement of bank performance in Greece. *South-Eastern Europe Journal of Economics*, 1, 79-95.

Laeven, L. and Levine, R. (2007). Is there a diversification discount in financial conglomerates? *Journal of Financial Economics*, 85, 331-367

Lang, G. and Welzel, P. (1996) Efficiency and technical progress in banking: Empirical results for a panel of German banks. *Journal of Banking and Finance*, 20, 1003–1023.

Lawrence, C. (1989) Banking costs, generalised functional forms, and estimation of economies of scale and scope. *Journal of Money, Credit and Banking*, 21, 368–379.

Lensink, R. and Hermes, N. (2004) The short term effects of foreign bank entry on domestic bank behaviour: does economic development matter. *Journal of Banking and Finance*, 28, 553–568.

Lozano-Vivas, A. (1997) Profit efficiency for Spanish savings banks. *European Journal of Operational Research*, 98, 381–394.

Macharis, C., Springael, J., De Brucker, K. and Verbeke, A. (2004) PROMETHEE and AHP: The design of operational synergies in multicriteria analysis. Strengthening PROMETHEE with ideas of AHP. *European Journal of Operational Research*, 153, 307–317.

Mahajan, A., Rangan, N. and Zardkoohi, A. (1996) Cost structures in multinational and domestic banking. *Journal of Banking and Finance*, 20, 283–306.

Maudos, J., Pastor, J.M., Perez, F. and Quesada, J. (2002) Cost and profit efficiency in European banks. *Journal of International Financial Markets, Institutions & Money,* 12, 33–58.

Maudos, J., Fernandez de Guevara, J. (2004) Factors explaining the interest margin in the banking sectors of the European Union. *Journal of Banking and Finance,* 28, 2259–2281.

McAllister, P.H. and McManus, D. (1993) Resolving the scale efficiency puzzle in banking. *Journal of Banking and Finance,* 17 (2–3), 389–406.

Mester, A. (1996) A chapter of bank efficiency taking in to account risk preferences. *Journal of Banking and Finance,* 20 (6), 1025–1045.

Miller, S. and Noulas, A. (1996) The technical efficiency of large banks production. *Journal of Banking & Finance,* 20, 3, 495-509.

Molyneux, P. and Thorton, J. (1992) Determinants of European bank profitability: a note. *Journal of Banking and Finance,* 16 (6), 1173–1178.

Molyneux, P. and Wilson, J. (2007) Developments in European banking. *Journal of banking and Finance,* 31 (7), 1907-1910.

Morttinen, L., Poloni, P., Sandars, P. and Vesala, J. (2005) Analysing banking sector conditions: How to use macroprudential indicators. ECB occasional chapter no. 26.

Murray, J. D. and White R. W. (1983) Economies of scale and economies of scope in multiproduct financial institutions: A chapter of British Columbia Credit Unions. *Journal of Finance,* 38, 887-902.

Nolle, D.E. (1995) Foreign bank operations in the United States: cause for concern? In: Gray, H.P. and Richard, R.C. (eds.) International finance in the new world order. London, Pergamon, pp. 269–291.

Pasiouras, F. and Kosmidou, K. (2007) Factors influencing the profitability of domestic and foreign commercial banks in the European Union. *Research in International Business and Finance,* 21, 222–237.

Pastor, J., Perez, F. and Quesada, J. (1997) Efficiency analysis in banking firms: an international comparison. *European Journal of Operational Research,* 98 (2), 395–407.

Rangan, N., Grabowski, R., Aly, H. and Pasurka, C. (1988) The technical efficiency of US banks. *Economic Letters,* 28, 169–175.

Rangan, N., Grabowski, R. Pasurka, C. and Aly, H. (1990) Technical scale and allocative efficiencies in US banking: An empirical investigation. *Review of Economics and Statistics,* 52, 211–218.

Rao, A. (2005) Cost frontier efficiency and risk–return analysis in an emerging market. *International Review of Financial Analysis,* 14 (3), 283–303.

Revell, J. (1980) Costs and margins in banking: An international survey. Paris, OECD.

Sathye, M. (2001) X-efficiency in Australian banking: an empirical investigation. *Journal of Banking and Finance,* 25, 613–630.

Schure, P., Wagenvoort, R., and O'Brien, D. (2004) The efficiency and the conduct of European banks: Developments after 1992. *Review of Financial Economics,* 13, 371–396.

Seth, R. (1992) Profitability of foreign banks in the US. Federal Reserve Bank of New York Research Chapter.

Shaffer, S. and David, E. (1991) Economies of superscale in commercial banking. *Applied Economics,* 23, 283–293.

Spathis, Ch., Kosmidou, K. and Doumpos, M. (2002) Assessing profitability factors in the Greek banking system: A multicriteria methodology. *International Transactions in Operational Research,* 9, 517-530.

Staikouras, Ch. and Wood, G. (2003) The determinants of bank profitability in Europe. In: Chapter presented at the Proceedings of the European *Applied Business Research Conference.* Venice, Italy, 9–13 June 2003.

Staikouras, Ch., Mamatzakis, M. and Koutsomanoli-Filippaki, A. (2008) An empirical investigation of operating performance in the new European banking landscape. *Global Finance Journal,* 19 (1), 32-45.

Vincke, J. P. and Brans, Ph. (1985) A preference ranking organization method. The PROMETHEE method for MCDM. *Management Science,* 31, 641–656.

Wiecek, M. M., Ehrgott, M., Fadel, G. and Figueira, J.R. (2008) Editorial: Multiple criteria decision making for engineering. *Omega,* 36, 337–339.

In: Financial Services: Efficiency and Risk Management
Editors: M. D. Fethi, C. Gaganis et al.

ISBN: 978-1-62100-560-5
© 2012 Nova Science Publishers, Inc.

Chapter 5

MARKET CRASHES AND BASEL REGULATIONS. THE CASE OF DEVELOPED, EMERGING AND FRONTIER STOCK MARKETS

*Adrián F. Rossignolo**
University of Leicester, United Kingdom

ABSTRACT

Following the subprime crisis of 2007-2008 which uncovered shortfalls in capital levels of most financial institutions, the Basel Committee on Banking Supervision decided to strengthen current regulations contained in Basel II. While maintaining the Internal Models Approach based on VaR, a stressed VaR calculated over highly strung periods is to be added to present directives to compute the new Minimum Capital Requirements. However, as the Basel Committee on Banking Supervision refrained from demanding a particular VaR technique, the adoption of the appropriate specification remains a subject of paramount importance as it determines the financial condition of the firm in the event of abrupt market swings. In this chapter I explore the performance of several models to compute Minimum Capital Requirements in the context of Developed, Emerging and Frontier stock markets within the current Basel II and the future Basel III capital structures. Considering the evidence gathered, two major contributions arise: a) Heavy-tailed distributions –specifically those belonging to the Extreme Value family– emerge as the most accurate technique to model market risks, hence preventing huge capital deficits under Basel II regulations; b) The application of such methods could allow slight modifications to the present mandate and either avoid the stressed VaR factor or at least reduce its weight, thus mitigating its huge impact regarding the enhancement of the capital base. Therefore, I suggest that the inclusion of Extreme Value distributions in VaR models in the respective supervisory accords should reduce the costs associated with the development of accurate schemes and foster healthier financial structures.

---

* Tel.: 0054 11 4503 3632. E-mail: afr5@le.ac.uk

1. INTRODUCTION

In the wake of the subprime crisis that unravelled in 2008 the Basel Committee on Banking Supervision (BCBS) launched a series of proposals intended to reduce the probability of capital shortfalls in banks. These initiatives, contained in two documents, Revisions to the Basel II Market Risk Framework (BCBS (2009)) and Strengthening the Resilience of the Banking Sector (BCBS (2009)), aim at enhancing the capital base that institutions ought to set aside against trading book losses.

Regulations stated in Basel II Capital Accord (2004) -which were established in the Amendment to the Basel Capital Accord to Incorporate Market Risks (1996)- featured a certain leeway by allowing banks to select an appropriate risk management model to calculate the Value-at-Risk (VaR) based Minimum Capital Requirements (MCR) subject to several quantitative and qualitative requirements. Even though this approach is bound to be broadly conserved in the aforementioned scheme, it has suffered further toughening via the introduction of the Stressed-VaR (sVaR) to be added to the previous MCR to constitute the new MCR.

It is acknowledged that while these innovations represent a healthy concern on the part of the supervisors in order to avoid a repetition of banking crashes which effects undoubtedly spill over the rest of the economy, several important facts are worth of being pointed out. In line with the argument posed by Danielsson, Hartmann and de Vries (1998) when discussing Basel II directives, I remark that the proposed Basel framework will act as a deterrent for the adoption of more accurate or precise VaR specifications. Additionally, this chapter supplies evidence that the adoption of methodologies focusing on the extreme variations of the distribution of returns could have avoided or mitigated the extent of the financial collapse for a range of Developed, Emerging and Frontier markets. Another contribution states that although in many respects Basel II needs to be revised, the implementation of schemes grounded on Extreme Value Theory (EVT) even within the current framework would have provided banks with enough capital cushion to endure the crisis. Finally, I venture beyond to suggest that Basel III regulations should contemplate either the specific inclusion of some kind of heavy-tailed models (ideally those based on EVT) or, at least, allow the recalibration of security factors to take into account the quality of the technique applied. Therefore, those representations featuring a good track record in crisis times ought not to be penalised in the same fashion that the schemes with a deficient behaviour, hence providing the necessary motivation to develop sound and accurate VaR models.

The chapter unfolds as follows. BCBS directives to calculate current and next MCR are sketched in the second section; the third one briefly introduces the VaR models whereas the fourth one presents the data and methodology. Parts five and six perform the empirical analyses. Finally, Section 7 reflects on the results.

2. BASEL COMMITTEE DIRECTIVES

2.1. The 2004 Basel II Capital Accord

The Basel I Capital Accord of 1988 constituted the first approach to acknowledge the need for an agreement to strengthen the international banking system, simultaneously removing the competitive inequality springing from diverse capital requirements. It established a minimum uniform coefficient –the Cooke proportion- equivalent to 8% to be applied to the risk-weighted portfolio. This precarious measure evolved in response to the financial catastrophes of the 1990s (Jorion (1996)) and in 1996 the Committee issued the Market Risk Amendment designed to tackle a wider variety of risks other than credit risk (FX, equity, interest rate, commodity and derivatives). The key contribution of this document was the introduction of internal VaR models to act as a basis to quantify market risk capital requirements, i.e., banks were free to adopt their own risk schemes subject to strict qualitative and quantitative standards (BCBS (2004)): the treatment that Basel II Capital Accord dispenses to market risks pursues a more risk-oriented strategy.

Risk-based capital charges are obtained from:

$$MCR_{t+1} = \max \left(\frac{m_c}{60} \sum_{i=1}^{60} VaR(99\%)_{t-i+1} \; ; VaR(99\%)_t \right) \tag{1}$$

i.e., the maximum between the previous day's VaR and the average of the last 60 daily VaRs increased by the multiplier[22] $m_c = 3(1+k)$ where $k \in [0; 1]$ according to the result of Backtesting. BCBS demands VaR estimation to observe the following quantitative requirements:

a) Daily-basis estimation;
b) Confidence level α set at 99%;
c) One-year minimum sample extension with quarterly or more frequent updates;
d) No specific models prescribed: banks free to adopt their own schemes;
e) Regular Backtesting and Stress Testing programme for validation purposes[23].

The factor m_c entails several considerations. Although its derivation would appear as an example of political compromise, Stahl (1997) produces a theoretical justification based on the Chebishev inequality valid for any statistical distribution, by means of which the multiplication factor is bound to lie in the range [3; 4]. Danielsson, Hartmann and de Vries (1998) emphasise that the conservatism attached to m_c compensates those specification errors that may arise from the application of imprecise models or inaccurate distributions. Consequently, no reward is granted from the usage of sharp models as the basic factor "3" is homogeneously applied to every representation.

---

[22] m_c will be, at minimum, 3.
[23] The focus of the present chapter is restricted to Backtesting (BCBS (1996, 2004, 2009)). Christoffersen (2003) or Dowd (2005) cater for basic concepts and extensive treatment of stress testing.

The quality of the risk measurement specification ends up determined by the value of the scaling factor k in [1] and evaluated through Backtesting, which simply involves a comparison between the VaR forecast with the actual portfolio losses both calibrated to a one-day holding period. This proof denotes an effort to discover whether the model is capable of capturing the trading volatility by counting the number of times that VaR is exceeded by real losses in approximately 250 trading days (excessions, exceptions or violations). The reference to ascertain k and its impact on the bank's scheme is contained in BCBS's Three-Zone approach:

Table 1. Basel II Three-Zone Approach

Zone	Definition	Number of exceptions	Value of k	Observations
Green	No evidence of inaccurate model	0 - 4	0,00	No capital surcharge Model approved
Yellow	Results uncertain and compatible with either precise (bad luck) or inaccurate model	5 6 7 8 9	0,40 0,50 0,65 0,75 0,85	Suggestion of inaccuracy as exceptions increase Model scrutinised
Red	Presumption of inaccurate model	10 or more	1,00	Model invalidated

Notes:
(1): Values correspond to a forecast period of 250 independent observations. For other quantities the Table should be reworked.
(2): Probabilities obtained using a Bernoulli distribution with probability of success 99%.
(3) The Yellow Zone begins at that number of exceptions where the probability of obtaining at a maximum that quantity equals or exceeds 95%.
(4): The Red Zone starts where the probability of obtaining that quantity or fewer violations is at least 99.99%.

2.2. The Revision of MCR Calculation

Lehman Brothers' bankruptcy in September 2008 sparked abnormal losses of such an extent that financial institutions found their capital buffers hugely insufficient to cover those deficits. Even acknowledging the unprecedented nature of those market swings, BCBS (2009) implicitly blamed the framework established in the 1996 Amendment for failing to grasp extreme movements and put forward an initiative to strengthen the MCR contained in Basel II. However, the proposals stopped short of pinpointing that perhaps the capital levels delivered by the scheme in [1] could render acceptable values provided the correct assumptions to elaborate it were taken. In particular, the FSA identified that, besides the deficiencies of VaR as a risk measure[24]: "Short-term observation periods plus assumption of

---

[24] Acerbi and Tasche (2002) and Artzner et al (1999) provide an excellent review of the inconsistencies and limitations of VaR as a risk measure and suggest the application of coherent metrics like Expected Shortfall (ES) or Tail Conditional Expectation (TCE).

Normal distribution can lead to large underestimation of probability of extreme losses" (FSA, (2009:23))[25].

The new approach conserves in general lines the current VaR setting (cVaR) nevertheless adding a new element termed Stressed VaR (sVaR); its calculation complies with the same guidelines though the dataset must belong to a "continuous 12-month period of significant financial stress..." (BCBS (2009:14)), i.e., when market movements would have inflicted great losses on financial positions.

The stricter daily capital demands reflect in sVaR added to cVaR:

$$MCR_{t+1} = \max\left(\frac{m_c}{60}\sum_{i=1}^{60} cVaR(99\%)_{t-i+1} \; ; cVaR(99\%)_t \right) + \max\left(\frac{m_s}{60}\sum_{i=1}^{60} sVaR(99\%)_{t-i+1} \; ; sVaR(99\%)_t \right) \quad (2)$$

where:

- $cVaR(99\%)_t$: 99% cVaR for day t;
- m_c : multiplier for cVaR (Section 3.1);
- $sVaR(99\%)_t$: 99% sVaR for day t;
- m_s : multiplier for sVaR

with $m_s = 3(1+k)$ and k arises from Backtesting results for cVaR (not for sVaR). As $k \in [0; 1]$ institutions are encouraged to develop precise VaR models in order to keep $k \approx 0$ and avoid penalties to establish MCR.

3. VALUE-AT-RISK (VaR) SPECIFICATIONS

The present section synthetically defines the representations to model the dynamics of the negative returns (i.e., losses) of the individual portfolios comprising each of the stock market indices, in accordance with the scheme proposed by Christoffersen and Gonçalves (2007):

$$r_{t+1} = \sigma_{t+1} z_{t+1} \qquad \text{for } t = 0, 1, ..., T\text{-}1 \qquad (3)$$

where r_{t+1} states losses and σ_{t+1} represents the forecast for $t+1$ of the volatility dynamics using the information available up to time t and $z_{t+1} \sim F(0;1)$.

At a given point of time, VaR_{t+1} describes the risk in the tails of the conditional distribution of losses over a one-day horizon expressing the maximum loss in the value of exposures due to adverse market movements that will not be exceeded within a pre-specified coverage probability α if portfolios are held static during a certain period of time t, thus $Pr(r_{t+1} < VaR_{t+1}) = \alpha$. It could be characterised as:

---

[25] FSA makes a point about the procyclicality that emerges using observation periods as short as one year: falls in confidence raise volatilities which vanish liquidity and further increase volatility. (FSA (2009)).

$$VaR(\alpha)_{t+1} = \sigma_{t+1} \, F^{-1}(\alpha)$$

(4),

and $F^{-1}(\alpha)$ denotes the inverse of the cumulative density function of the distribution of the standardised losses $z_{t+1} = r_{t+1}/\sigma_{t+1}$ (i.e., the α-quantile of F).

Six models are applied and its results compared in light of BCBS's mandates.

3.1. Historical Simulation (HS)

This simple, intuitive and easy to explain non-parametric technique calculates VaR employing the appropriate quantile of a window of past sample returns:

$$VaR(\alpha)_{t+1} = Q_\alpha \left(r_t \, ; r_{t-1} \, ; \ldots ; r_{t-n+1} \right)$$

(5)

Despite reducing the dimensionality to univariate category, it carries a host of limitations. Manganelli and Engle (2004) and Dowd (2005) emphasise the reliance on a particular data set, the equal weighting structure, the extrapolation of the sample distribution and the problems with the length of the sample period.

3.2. Filtered Historical Simulation (FHS)

It represents a significant improvement over HS that combines a model-based variance with a data-based conditional quantile. It demands fitting some representation (e.g., GARCH) to the sample return data that accommodates the empirical patterns to obtain a string of volatility forecasts useful to generate a set of iid standardised returns. Hence,

$$VaR(\alpha)_{t+1} = \sigma_{t+1} \, F^{-1}(\alpha)$$

(6),

where σ_{t+1} originates from the conditional volatility model and $F^{-1}(\alpha)$ belongs to the empirical distribution of standardised residuals. Although FHS takes into account the changing market conditions by blending conditional volatility modelling with the empirical distribution (Dowd (2005)), Pritsker (2001) affirms that FHS VaR is still unable to capture extreme events.

3.3. Conditional Volatility

The time-varying variance schemes have been designed to acknowledge the stylised facts present in financial time series, like autocorrelation of squared returns and volatility clustering (Christoffersen (2003), McNeil, Frey and Embrechts (2005)). Postulating the dependence of current volatility on past volatilities and returns, they appear capable of tracing the volatility clouding effect and the non-normality of returns. Pursuing practical motivations, only GARCH (General Autoregressive Conditional Heteroskedasticity) restrained to first-order lags will be employed:

3.3.1. GARCH

Introduced by Bollerslev (1986) and Taylor (1986), GARCH equations are expressed:

$$r_{t+1} = \sigma_{t+1} z_{t+1} \qquad \text{(coinciding with equation [3])}$$

$$\sigma_{t+1}^2 = w + \alpha r_t^2 + \beta \sigma_t^2 \tag{7}$$

with $z_{t+1} \sim$ iid $F(0;1)$ and $w > 0$; $\alpha, \beta \geq 0$; $\alpha + \beta < 1$

In addition to seizing the volatility clustering effect (though in a symmetric fashion), the conditional variance is treated as a persistent phenomenon by means of the parameter β: a high β (persistence) means that volatility takes a long time to fade after a crisis episode, whereas a high α (error) indicates promptness to react to market movements. GARCH power might also be enhanced by affixing other distribution rather than the Normal for the standardised returns, in order to reflect the departure from Gaussianity. This chapter will feature the heavy-tailed t besides the typical GARCH-Normal setting:

$$VaR(\alpha)_{t+1} = \sigma_{t+1} \Phi^{-1}(\alpha) \tag{8}$$

$$VaR(\alpha)_{t+1} = \sigma_{t+1} \sqrt{(d-2)d^{-1}} \, t_d^{-1}(\alpha) \tag{9}$$

where σ_{t+1} represents the volatility forecast derived from GARCH model and $\Phi^{-1}(\alpha)$ and $t^{-1}(\alpha)$ the inverse of the cumulative normal and t distributions respectively with d degrees of freedom.

There is a vast amount of evidence in the literature body indicating that GARCH(1;1) models appear to work reasonably well for a variety of financial assets, particularly with frequencies equal or higher than daily ones (Alexander (2008) and Andersen and Bollerslev (1998)).

3.4. Extreme Value Theory (EVT)

EVT embodies an alternative to former specifications as it stresses the tails of the series allowing right and left ends to be modelled separately and, most importantly, recognising the heavy-tailed nature of empirical distributions. On the grounds of efficiency and pragmatism, the chapter will develop within the Peaks-Over-Threshold (POT) variant disregarding the Block Maxima Method (BMM) (Coles (2001)). It is recommended that for an in-depth theoretical development the reader should refer to Embrechts, Klüppelberg and Mikosch (1997), McNeil, Frey and Embrechts (2005), or Reiss and Thomas (2007).

According to the scheme posed by McNeil and Frey (2000) and McNeil, Frey and Embrechts (2005) based on the QML approach, the tail of the implied residuals $z_{t+1} = r_{t+1} / \sigma_{t+1}$ of the GARCH-Normal standardisation is sufficiently approximated by a heavy-tailed distribution. This distribution is the two-parameter Generalised Pareto Distribution (GPD) $G_{\xi,\sigma}(y)$, fitted for all the excesses y above a certain threshold u. Therefore,

$$G_{\xi,\sigma}(y) = \begin{cases} 1 - \left(1 + \xi\, y/\sigma\right)^{-1/\xi} & \text{if } \xi \neq 0 \\[2ex] 1 - \exp\left(- y/\sigma\right) & \text{if } \xi = 0 \end{cases}$$

(10)

ξ represents the tail index parameter and σ denotes a scale parameter as u increases, where $\sigma > 0$, and $x \geq 0$ when $\xi \geq 0$ and $0 \leq y \leq -\sigma / \xi$ when $\xi < 0$. For finance exercises $\xi > 0$ ought to be verified, then $G_{\xi,\sigma}(y)$ becomes the classic Pareto or Fréchet distribution picturing heavy tails. Reiss and Thomas (2007) remark that GPD precision could be enhanced affixing a location parameter μ, effectively making $G_{\xi,\sigma}(y - \mu)$.

Given the absence of an optimal method to select the threshold u (Christoffersen (2003)), the technique described in Reiss and Thomas (2007) based on the analysis of the sample Mean Excess Function (MEF), QQ plots, sample Kernel Density and sample Quantile Function is applied. Afterwards, the GPD parameters ξ, σ and μ are estimated via the Method of Moments (MM) (Reiss and Thomas (2007)). Algebraic operations make the POT-quantile (McNeil, Frey and Embrechts (2005), McNeil and Saladin (1997)) read:

$$G^{-1}(\alpha) = u + \hat{\sigma}\, \hat{\xi}^{-1}\left[\left(\frac{1-\alpha}{w\,/n}\right)^{-\hat{\xi}} - 1\right]$$

(11)

where w represents the number of observations above the threshold u and the rest of the symbols conserve their meaning. The final VaR expression then becomes: $VaR(\alpha)_{t+1} = \sigma_{t+1}G^{-1}(\alpha)$ [12], σ_{t+1} being the volatility forecast derived from GARCH-Normal model and $G^{-1}(\alpha)$ representing the inverse of the cumulative density function of the GPD distribution (α-quantile of G).

4. DATA AND METHODOLOGY

4.1. Data

Daily data series to be applied belong to fifteen stock markets, divided in five Developed (UK, France, Germany, Spain and Switzerland), six Emerging (Brazil, Hungary, India, Czech Republic, Indonesia and Malaysia) and four Frontier (Argentina, Lithuania, Tunisia and Croatia). The usage of an ample span of markets across the three categories would in principle strengthen the conclusions and generalise the implications to be drawn. The summary statistics pictured in Table 2 coincide with the general patterns pointed out in the literature: the time series of raw returns are driftless (thus backing the exclusion of the constant in [3] and [7]) and seem to exhibit significant leptokurtosis. According to the kurtosis statistic the additional probability mass present in the tail areas appears high which, coupled with the skewness, results in striking differences between both ends of the distribution. Jarque-Bera coefficients alongside the empirical percentiles overcoming the theoretical Gaussian ones confirm the significant departure from normality. Finally, the evidence for every market corroborates the appreciable heteroskedasticity: slight or virtually no autocorrelation at the linear level ($Q(20)$) and very high values for squared returns ($Q^2(20)$), thus paving the way for models acknowledging clusters in volatility.

4.2. Methodology

The idea underlying the chapter consists in following BCBS framework as closely as possible: VaR estimations are anchored at α=99% with a daily horizon (t=1); however, the ten-day holding period rule will purposefully be left aside due to the inconsistencies of the square-root-of-time rule (Danielsson and Zigrand (2005)) and to forestall the possibility of masking the inaccuracy of the models by increasing insufficient daily VaR using extrinsic multiples.

The following parameters apply to VaR representations: HS is calculated using a rolling window of 1000 days; FHS, like conditional volatility schemes derive from GARCH-Normal and GARCH-t models estimated via ML; and EVT VaR is achieved via POT (Section 3.4.) after pre-whitening the raw data with QML GARCH-Normal.

The accuracy of VaR models is gauged employing Backtesting, in accordance with the stipulations laid out in BCBS (2004) synthesised in Section 2.1., whereas the calculation of the sVaR gets carried out adhering to the instructions stated in BCBS (2009) explained in Section 2.2. The terms of heavy losses for the indices selected are exhibited in Table 3.

5. BASEL II FRAMEWORK. VaR OUTCOMES, BACKTESTING AND BANK CAPITAL

5.1. VaR Outcomes. Backtesting

The outcomes depicted in Table 4 and Table 5 reflect the extent of the inaccuracy of the empirical and normality assumptions. At the required 99% level HS grossly underestimates VaR, falling in the Red Zone for every market (except Indonesia). FHS delivers some improvements particularly in Emerging markets (at best 8 or 9 exceptions recorded), but despite the progresses chiefly due to GARCH pre-whitening (no significant distinction between the Normal and t filters) it is unable to escape the Red or high-Yellow Zones.

As predicted, VaR values increase employing conditional volatility GARCH, consequently reducing the number of excessions. In particular, the leptokurtic t distribution achieves remarkable results in France, Germany, Spain, India, Malaysia and Croatia. The advantages of heavy-tailed distributions become noticeable as the difference in performance between GARCH-Normal and GARCH-t is assessed, given that an analogous specification assuming different distributions for the standardised residuals provokes a sizeable distance in terms of the increase in the multiplication factor k (GARCH-Normal demands for extra capital to be constituted in every market to the point of invalidation in Indonesia, Lithuania and Croatia). However, although GARCH-t setting represents a huge leap forward, it does not completely prevent shareholders from supporting the bank with additional capital in nine out of fifteen exposures (except France, Germany, Spain, India and Croatia).

Table 2. Stylised facts about asset return series

Market	Developed Markets					Emerging Markets						Frontier Markets			
Country	UK	France	Germany	Spain	Switzerland	Brazil	Hungary	India	Czech Rep	Indonesia	Malaysia	Argentina	Lithuania	Tunisia	Croatia
Index	Ftse100	CAC	DAX	IGBM	SMI	Bovespa	Cetop20	Sensex	Px	JKSE	KLSE	Merval	OMX	Tunindex	Crobex
Period	03/04/1984	02/03/1990	27/11/1990	03/02/1984	12/11/1990	02/01/2000	31/01/2002	02/07/1997	01/01/1995	04/01/2000	04/01/1999	08/10/1996	04/01/2000	02/01/1998	01/01/1999
	31/12/2007	31/12/2007	31/12/2007	31/12/2007	31/12/2007	31/12/2007	31/12/2007	31/12/2007	31/12/2007	31/12/2007	31/12/2007	31/12/2007	31/12/2007	31/12/2007	31/12/2007
Observations	5999	4499	4310	6238	4059	1975	1493	2600	3243	1926	2216	2777	2039	2496	2248
Mean	0.0003	0.0002	0.0004	0.0005	0.0005	0.0007	0.0008	0.0006	0.0004	0.0007	0.0004	0.0005	0.0008	0.0004	0.0009
Max return	0.0760	0.0700	0.0755	0.0694	0.0746	0.0734	0.0403	0.0859	0.0705	0.0673	0.0585	0.1612	0.0458	0.0304	0.1270
Min return	-0.1303	-0.0768	-0.0987	-0.0973	-0.0838	-0.0754	-0.0555	-0.1181	-0.0708	-0.1093	-0.0634	-0.1476	-0.1022	-0.0212	-0.0903
Std. Dev.	0.0102	0.0131	0.0138	0.0113	0.0112	0.0182	0.0123	0.0160	0.0119	0.0139	0.0105	0.0222	0.0091	0.0044	0.0143
Skewness	-0.5375	-0.1203	-0.2148	-0.3468	-0.2150	-0.2133	-0.4552	-0.3349	-0.2874	-0.7150	-0.2374	-0.1658	-0.7228	0.4005	0.2877
Kurtosis	10.7803	5.8589	6.8178	8.0763	7.8805	3.7063	4.6069	6.3967	5.6649	7.6493	8.5065	8.6906	13.5985	6.2037	12.9352
Jarque-Bera	15390.55	1538.17	2645.33	6800.54	4104.48	55.53	209.23	1291.99	1005.66	1904.67	2901.29	3743.38	9698.40	1128.21	9215.90
	(0.00)	(0.00)	(0.00)	(0.00)	(0.00)	(0.00)	(0.00)	(0.00)	(0.00)	(0.00)	(0.00)	(0.00)	(0.00)	(0.00)	(0.00)
q(0.0001)	-0.0905	-0.0763	-0.0848	-0.0903	-0.0733	-0.0744	-0.0552	-0.1069	-0.0677	-0.1033	-0.0632	-0.1464	-0.0904	-0.0204	-0.0899
q(0.01)	-0.0286	-0.0361	-0.0396	-0.0315	-0.0328	-0.0451	-0.0371	-0.0441	-0.0333	-0.0398	-0.0310	-0.0664	-0.0256	-0.0107	-0.0399
q(0.025)	-0.0202	-0.0272	-0.0284	-0.0231	-0.0233	-0.0374	-0.0262	-0.0346	-0.0257	-0.0287	-0.0198	-0.0449	-0.0173	-0.0082	-0.0272
q(0.05)	-0.0156	-0.0210	-0.0224	-0.0173	-0.0171	-0.0309	-0.0191	-0.0248	-0.0271	-0.0218	-0.0144	-0.0344	-0.0134	-0.0055	-0.0199
q(0.10)	-0.0113	-0.0146	-0.0151	-0.0120	-0.0119	-0.0222	-0.0138	-0.0184	-0.0132	-0.0150	-0.0098	-0.0231	-0.0087	-0.0045	-0.0124
q(0.90)	0.0113	0.0146	0.0153	0.0130	0.0125	0.0221	0.0156	0.0182	0.0140	0.0160	0.0116	0.0226	0.0107	0.0055	0.0145
q(0.95)	0.0150	0.0202	0.0213	0.0180	0.0172	0.0291	0.0201	0.0251	0.0154	0.0217	0.0160	0.0337	0.0148	0.0076	0.0216
q(0.375)	0.0197	0.0255	0.0273	0.0229	0.0218	0.0343	0.0232	0.0310	0.0235	0.0274	0.0225	0.0449	0.0184	0.0099	0.0305
q(0.99)	0.0264	0.0345	0.0366	0.0302	0.0281	0.0441	0.0314	0.0375	0.0296	0.0338	0.0308	0.0616	0.0267	0.0130	0.0445
q(0.9999)	0.0658	0.0693	0.0744	0.0658	0.0707	0.0713	0.0403	0.0842	0.0665	0.0646	0.0582	0.1514	0.0457	0.0290	0.1241
Q(20)	76.30	46.45	45.78	133.04	58.01	30.35	23.39	74.81	81.50	42.24	107.96	40.72	114.54	601.49	17.18
	(0.00)	(0.00)	(0.00)	(0.00)	(0.00)	(0.06)	(0.10)	(0.00)	(0.00)	(0.00)	(0.00)	(0.00)	(0.00)	(0.00)	(0.64)
$Q^2(20)$	3463.40	3179.80	4107.70	2868.10	3146.10	164.23	270.88	616.75	1100.10	154.49	656.12	1475.90	30.63	1618.70	431.97
	(0.00)	(0.00)	(0.00)	(0.00)	(0.00)	(0.00)	(0.00)	(0.00)	(0.00)	(0.00)	(0.00)	(0.00)	(0.06)	(0.00)	(0.00)

Note: p-values between parentheses.

Table 3. Stressed VaR (sVaR). Periods of heavy losses

Country	Index	Period		Loss posted
		From	To	(annual)
UK	FTSE100	02/04/2002	31/03/2003	35.43%
France	CAC40	02/04/2002	31/03/2003	56.31%
Germany	DAX	02/04/2002	31/03/2003	77.36%
Spain	IGBM	01/10/2000	30/09/2001	37.65%
Switzerland	SMI	02/04/2002	31/03/2003	47.82%
Brazil	BOVESPA	25/10/2000	28/09/2001	39.32%
Hungary	CETOP20	01/03/2001	28/03/2002	17.03%
India	SENSEX	01/10/2000	30/09/2001	39.17%
Czech Rep	PX	01/09/2000	31/08/2001	41.87%
Indonesia	JKSE	01/04/2000	31/03/2001	42.02%
Malaysia	KLSE	01/06/2000	31/05/2001	45.96%
Argentina	MERVAL	01/10/1997	31/10/1998	86.36%
Lithuania	OMX	01/09/2000	31/08/2001	29.39%
Tunisia	TUNINDEX	01/03/2002	28/02/2003	20.08%
Croatia	CROBEX	01/04/2002	31/03/2003	19.73%

Note: Panels separate market categories: Developed, Emerging and Frontier.

Table 4. Backtesting - Quantity and proportion of exceptions in forecast period

Model / Index	Expected Number	Historical Simulation	FHS		Conditional Volatility		EVT
			GARCH-N	GARCH-t	GARCH-N	GARCH-t	
Developed markets							
UK	3	20	9	9	8	8	2
	1%	7.91%	3.56%	3.56%	3.16%	3.16%	0.79%
France	3	20	11	10	5	3	1
	1%	7.84%	4.31%	3.92%	1.96%	1.18%	0.39%
Germany	3	20	15	13	6	4	3
	1%	7.84%	5.88%	5.10%	2.35%	1.57%	1.18%
Spain	3	20	11	8	7	3	2
	1%	7.63%	4.20%	3.05%	2.67%	1.15%	0.76%
Switzerland	3	18	16	14	7	6	2
	1%	7.14%	6.35%	5.56%	2.78%	2.38%	0.79%
Emerging markets							
Brazil	2	16	9	8	8	6	2
	1%	6.43%	3.61%	3.21%	3.21%	2.41%	0.80%
Hungary	3	15	8	9	7	5	4
	1%	5.98%	3.19%	3.59%	2.79%	1.99%	1.59%
India	2	14	9	9	8	3	3
	1%	5.74%	3.69%	3.69%	3.28%	1.23%	1.23%
Czech Rep.	3	16	10	9	6	5	0
	1%	6.35%	3.97%	3.57%	2.38%	1.98%	0.00%
Indonesia	2	9	18	15	13	7	1
	1%	3.72%	7.44%	6.20%	5.37%	2.89%	0.41%
Malaysia	2	10	8	10	6	4	1
	1%	4.05%	3.24%	4.05%	2.43%	1.62%	0.40%
Frontier markets							
Argentina	2	17	13	13	6	5	1
	1%	6.85%	5.24%	5.24%	2.42%	2.02%	0.40%
Lithuania	2	17	26	29	16	8	0
	1%	10.70%	11.93%	12.35%	3.29%	7.41%	0.00%
Tunisia	2	16	17	17	8	6	1
	1%	6.50%	6.91%	6.91%	3.25%	2.44%	0.41%
Croatia	2	19	11	26	11	4	0
	1%	7.63%	4.42%	10.44%	4.42%	1.61%	0.00%

Note: Quantity of excessions and proportion of excessions pictured in first and second lines of the respective market.

150 Adrián F. Rossignolo

The evidence gathered, exhibited in Table 5, situates EVT as the best performer, as it does not require a supplementary capital buffer in any market, appreciation conveyed by the highest VaR for every Developed, Emerging and Frontier index among those schemes avoiding the Red Zone and consequent reestimation. Furthermore, as Brooks, Clare and Persand (2000) affirm, its levels cannot be regarded as excessive or insufficient as the proportion of excessions remains close to the stipulated value: only Germany (1.18%), Hungary (1.59%) and India (1.23%) exceed the standard 1% demanded (Table 4).

Table 5. Backtesting - The Three Zone Approach – Increase in scaling factor k

Model / Index	Historical Simulation	FHS		Conditional Volatility		EVT
		GARCH-N	GARCH-t	GARCH-N	GARCH-t	
Developed markets						
UK	1.00	0.85	0.85	0.75	0.75	0.00
	Red	Yellow	Yellow	Yellow	Yellow	Green
France	1.00	1.00	1.00	0.40	0.00	0.00
	Red	Red	Red	Yellow	Green	Green
Germany	1.00	1.00	1.00	0.50	0.00	0.00
	Red	Red	Red	Yellow	Green	Green
Spain	1.00	1.00	0.75	0.65	0.00	0.00
	Red	Red	Yellow	Yellow	Green	Green
Switzerland	1.00	1.00	1.00	0.65	0.50	0.00
	Red	Red	Red	Yellow	Yellow	Green
Emerging markets						
Brazil	1.00	0.85	0.75	0.75	0.50	0.00
	Red	Yellow	Yellow	Yellow	Yellow	Green
Hungary	1.00	0.75	0.85	0.65	0.40	0.00
	Red	Yellow	Yellow	Yellow	Yellow	Green
India	1.00	0.85	0.85	0.75	0.00	0.00
	Red	Yellow	Yellow	Yellow	Green	Green
Czech Rep.	1.00	1.00	0.85	0.50	0.40	0.00
	Red	Red	Yellow	Yellow	Yellow	Green
Indonesia	0.85	1.00	1.00	1.00	0.65	0.00
	Yellow	Red	Red	Red	Yellow	Green
Malaysia	1.00	0.75	1.00	0.50	0.00	0.00
	Red	Yellow	Red	Yellow	Green	Green
Frontier markets						
Argentina	1.00	1.00	1.00	0.50	0.40	0.00
	Red	Red	Red	Yellow	Yellow	Green
Lithuania	1.00	1.00	1.00	1.00	0.75	0.00
	Red	Red	Red	Red	Yellow	Green
Tunisia	1.00	1.00	1.00	0.75	0.50	0.00
	Red	Red	Red	Yellow	Yellow	Green
Croatia	1.00	1.00	1.00	1.00	0.00	0.00
	Red	Red	Red	Red	Green	Green

Note: Increase in scaling factor k pictured in second row of respective stock exchange.

5.2. Bank Capital

Capital charges as of 01-Jan-09 displayed in Table 6 logically ground on VaR performance and Backtesting, which determines the value of the add-on factor k. Among those models avoiding the Red Zone -excluding France, Indonesia, Malaysia and Croatia where EVT delivers the highest capital buffer- the performance is largely explained by the poor accomplishments in Backtesting, for all specifications belong to the Yellow Zone in the three categories. Moreover, the unreliability of those schemes would surely concern both shareholders and regulators given the fact that the extra capital ranges from 75% to 85% in Emerging markets -where the plight appears exceptionally grave-; 50% to 75% in Developed markets and 40% to 75% in Frontier class. The failure of HS and FHS and the peripheral situation of GARCH-Normal to establish capital coverage undoubtedly confirm that true exposures are underestimated in crunch times.

As a result of the satisfactory accomplishments in Backtesting, the most consistent capital charges across Developed, Emerging and Frontier markets appear to be delivered by heavy-tailed distributions, although GARCH-t would in most examples match EVT levels at the expense of surcharges (UK, Switzerland, Brazil, Hungary, Czech Republic, Indonesia, Argentina, Lithuania and Tunisia, where it would face close inspection on the part of the authorities). One of the major concerns about the EVT-VaR residing in the high amount of regulatory capital could well be averted as they do not (except Malaysia) significantly exceed the quantities provided by the second-best model (GARCH-t) and still deliver the smallest values in seven markets (UK, Switzerland, Brazil, Hungary, Czech Republic, Argentina and Lithuania) with the Green Zone bonus, thus avoiding periodic revisions demanded by the Yellow Zone (Table 6).

6. THE REVISION TO BASEL II MARKET RISK FRAMEWORK

6.1. The Stressed VaR (sVaR)

The guidelines to calculate sVaR (BCBS (2009)) coincide with those envisaged for the base VaR in Basel II, albeit the dataset ought to belong to a 12-month continuous term wreaking havoc on the financial position of the bank (Section 2.2.). Values pictured in Table 7 show that, excluding the schemes that failed Backtesting in Table 3 (marked in bold letters), techniques recognising the fat tailed nature of empirical distributions deliver the highest values (EVT and GARCH-t respectively). However, understandably the rest of the models match and overcome them once the inaccuracy penalties are applied: HS in Indonesia (85%), GARCH-t in UK (75%), Switzerland (50%) and Argentina (40%), GARCH-Normal in Germany (50%), Spain (65%), Brazil (75%), India (75%) and Tunisia (75%) and FHS GARCH-t in Hungary (85%) and Czech Republic (85%), hence casting doubts on their trustworthiness again (Table 8).

While the panorama is more evenly spread among all the techniques, it is noteworthy that EVT gives the lowest amount of capital from sVaR in six markets belonging to the three categories (UK, Switzerland, Brazil, Hungary, Czech Republic and Argentina) and stays close to the bottom for the rest of the exposures, performance attributable to the outstanding Backtesting results. Where the total capital charge (Table 9) to be calculated (current levels and planned increase due to sVaR), the heavy-tailed representations would claim the top spot in eight markets (5 EVT and 3 GARCH-t) and in 14 out of 15 markets deliver the smallest capital buffer (6 EVT and 8 GARCH-t), considering that EVT values, unlike GARCH-t, are not tinged with suspicion as its VaRs always fall into the Green Zone.

Table 6. Minimum Capital Requirements VaR MCR(VaR) – Current Directives

Market / Model	UK	France	Germany	Spain	Switzerland	Brazil	Hungary	India	Czech Rep	Indonesia	Malaysia	Argentina	Lithuania	Tunisia	Croatia
Hist. Simul.	25.75%	22.63%	26.80%	25.05%	18.78%	36.04%	33.14%	30.07%	32.50%	28.26%	18.35%	29.58%	21.04%	8.22%	33.56%
FHS GARCH-N	41.34%	17.07%	44.84%	42.50%	33.27%	51.52%	49.36%	41.35%	56.54%	32.28%	17.02%	20.71%	18.00%	8.81%	29.41%
FHS GARCH-t	42.88%	17.58%	48.14%	39.52%	37.89%	50.78%	52.41%	41.76%	55.80%	37.26%	18.36%	20.89%	18.61%	8.89%	20.97%
GARCH-N	41.55%	13.30%	36.86%	36.73%	32.35%	51.59%	45.48%	42.92%	48.69%	33.64%	15.33%	19.05%	22.57%	11.03%	29.05%
GARCH-t	43.99%	10.04%	28.11%	27.33%	34.71%	47.23%	41.42%	27.45%	51.58%	36.67%	11.34%	20.06%	27.26%	10.13%	18.62%
EVT	34.75%	16.46%	30.54%	31.13%	27.23%	41.80%	39.08%	28.56%	42.36%	36.95%	28.49%	17.50%	26.94%	10.83%	25.57%

Note: Values in bold letters indicate specifications belonging to the Red Zone to be eventually excluded by regulators.

Table 7. The stressed VaR (sVaR) proposal - sVaR values

Market / Model	UK	France	Germany	Spain	Switzerland	Brazil	Hungary	India	Czech Rep	Indonesia	Malaysia	Argentina	Lithuania	Tunisia	Croatia
Hist. Simul.	3.78%	4.56%	5.36%	3.70%	4.51%	5.21%	3.61%	5.34%	3.54%	4.39%	4.54%	6.63%	1.95%	1.14%	5.12%
FHS GARCH-N	4.71%	5.94%	6.69%	4.80%	4.37%	6.09%	2.29%	5.46%	2.27%	2.85%	2.39%	9.14%	3.20%	0.49%	2.46%
FHS GARCH-t	4.81%	5.95%	6.81%	4.95%	4.75%	6.02%	2.34%	5.49%	2.25%	3.42%	2.16%	9.73%	3.35%	0.49%	2.01%
GARCH-N	5.31%	6.53%	7.24%	5.11%	5.04%	6.22%	2.27%	6.27%	2.68%	3.38%	2.54%	9.86%	4.54%	0.72%	2.45%
GARCH-t	5.52%	6.89%	8.15%	6.22%	5.79%	6.46%	2.48%	7.01%	2.95%	4.17%	2.78%	11.30%	6.04%	0.76%	3.23%
EVT	7.77%	11.36%	9.11%	7.15%	6.91%	8.82%	3.22%	7.31%	3.49%	6.46%	7.12%	13.33%	10.63%	1.24%	4.33%

Note: Values in bold letters indicate specifications belonging to the Red Zone to be eventually excluded by regulators.

Table 8. Minimum Capital Requirements sVaR: MCR(sVaR) - Proposed Directives

Market / Model	UK	France	Germany	Spain	Switzerland	Brazil	Hungary	India	Czech Rep	Indonesia	Malaysia	Argentina	Lithuania	Tunisia	Croatia
Hist. Simul.	22.28%	27.38%	31.80%	21.03%	26.91%	29.14%	22.98%	29.54%	21.16%	24.42%	25.82%	36.36%	11.86%	6.94%	30.95%
FHS GARCH-N	17.96%	23.38%	31.84%	18.96%	21.79%	21.03%	14.56%	16.30%	17.42%	18.21%	16.66%	45.07%	8.71%	4.01%	15.23%
FHS GARCH-t	18.29%	23.74%	32.67%	15.68%	23.09%	19.79%	15.62%	16.20%	16.09%	20.33%	18.55%	46.23%	7.88%	4.01%	12.73%
GARCH-N	19.27%	18.07%	25.81%	16.65%	19.70%	21.11%	13.42%	17.77%	15.48%	21.32%	15.62%	35.27%	12.41%	5.15%	15.14%
GARCH-t	20.10%	13.78%	19.53%	11.90%	19.94%	18.72%	12.34%	11.20%	15.09%	20.06%	11.92%	35.24%	12.49%	4.67%	10.39%
EVT	16.11%	22.37%	21.66%	14.11%	16.36%	17.10%	11.53%	11.88%	13.47%	20.39%	28.47%	33.50%	14.81%	5.06%	13.54%

Note: Values in bold letters indicate specifications belonging to the Red Zone to be eventually excluded by regulators.

Table 9. Total Minimum Capital Requirements MCR = MCR(VaR) + MCR(sVaR)

Market / Model	UK	France	Germany	Spain	Switzerland	Brazil	Hungary	India	Czech Rep	Indonesa	Malaysia	Argentina	Lithuania	Tunisia	Croatia
Hist. Simul.	48.08%	49.61%	58.60%	46.08%	50.03%	65.19%	53.10%	59.61%	53.65%	52.70%	44.17%	65.94%	32.89%	15.16%	54.51%
FHS GARCH-N	56.30%	40.46%	76.67%	61.40%	55.06%	72.65%	53.92%	57.55%	75.95%	50.49%	33.70%	65.79%	26.71%	12.82%	44.63%
FHS GARCH-t	61.17%	41.10%	80.82%	55.10%	50.98%	70.55%	58.03%	57.96%	71.89%	57.55%	37.01%	67.12%	26.60%	12.89%	33.70%
GARCH-N	60.82%	31.37%	52.69%	53.37%	52.55%	72.70%	56.88%	60.89%	54.18%	58.96%	31.65%	55.32%	34.99%	15.18%	44.19%
GARCH-t	64.05%	23.77%	47.64%	39.25%	54.65%	65.98%	53.77%	36.98%	57.86%	56.72%	22.76%	58.30%	39.75%	14.79%	28.41%
EVT	50.86%	36.93%	52.60%	45.24%	49.65%	56.92%	50.60%	40.39%	55.83%	57.35%	56.96%	51.11%	41.75%	15.89%	39.53%

Note: Values in bold letters indicate specifications belonging to the Red Zone to be eventually excluded by regulators.

6.2. The Effect of Basel III Regulations on MCR: A Sensitivity Analysis

Stemming from the results in Sections 5 and 6.1, the next exercise evaluates the impact of new directives to strengthen banks' capital levels applying EVT, the sharpest model.

Considering Basel II directives in [1], EVT appears to provide enough protection against a violent adverse market swing, as deficits higher than twice the maximum loss of the forecast period could be matched by the current capital buffers (saving France 1.74 and Argentina 1.36) (Table 10-Column 1). These values translate into substantial maximum daily losses in the order of 28%, 36% and 20% (average values) for Developed, Emerging and Frontier markets respectively, with significant peaks of 35% in UK, 42% in Brazil and 27% in Lithuania (Table 10-Column 2).

The introduction of sVaR as in [2] would achieve its objectives by driving the total coverage to more than four times the maximum loss recorded in 2008 turmoil in the three groups (Table 11-Column 1), figures that mean more than 50% average increase (Table 11-Column 2) regarding the current directives (the maximum daily loss covers amounts to 53%, 59% and 51% of the portfolio value in Germany, Brazil and Argentina[26] in Table 11-Column 3). Though the virulence of future shocks should never be underestimated, it appears that the intended mandate demand abnormally high MCR in light of the shortfalls recorded in times of past crises, thus foreseeing an excessive penalty by putting aside unproductive funds which could otherwise be directed to credit purposes.

There is a strong inkling that Basel III provisions conceived to toughen the capital base in a substantial quantity -particularly considering the m_s factor featured in [2]- could discourage companies to develop sound models and enforce their motivation to resort to inaccurate ones. In this vein, a sensitivity analysis concerning different scenarios for the values of m_c and m_s is impact on MCR[27] is carried out and exhibited in Tables 12, 13 and 14 from where some interesting implications could be drawn. Initially, given that domestic supervisors rule on the base period to calculate sVaR, they could simultaneously manage the level of the multiplier m_s to be applied to their respective markets, for the evidence collected suggest that it could comfortably be set below the uniform value of 3 and still provide considerable coverage. For instance, if m_s were set at 1.5, 0.5 or even 0 (Table 13-Columns 1-6), the MCR would shield more than 4.20 (Developed markets), 3.50 (Emerging) and 3.25 (Frontier) times the greatest loss in the forecast period, representing daily shortfalls in the region of 36%, 42% and 27% respectively (all average values)[28]. However, even though the former figures increase the current capital base more than 33%, 17% and 36% (Developed, Emerging and Frontier positions respectively) (Table 14-Columns 1, 3 and 5), they relieve the pressure that sVaR would exert on shareholders as the amounts would record decreases of more than 19%, 15% and 14% (Developed, Emerging and Frontier exposures) (Table 14-Columns 2, 4 and 6)[29].

---

[26] The new regulations bring about an increase in the minimum capital requirements of 136% in Germany, 100% in Malaysia and 190% in Argentina, for example.

[27] MCR equal the maximum daily loss, as capital levels are built to match shortfalls in portfolios.

[28] The maximum and minimum values for each category are still huge in comparison with deficits posted in each category. For Developed: UK 42% and France 27%; for Emerging: Brazil 51% and Malaysia 36% and for Frontier: Lithuania 38% and Tunisia 12%.

[29] Although Argentina observes an increase in MCR of 1% if m_c=3 and m_s=0.5.

Market Crashes and Basel Regulations

Table 10. Current MCR Loss Coverage - Maximum Daily Loss

Market	Loss Coverage [1]	Maximum daily loss [2]
UK	3.75	34.75%
France	1.74	16.46%
Germany	4.16	30.94%
Spain	3.22	31.13%
Switzerland	3.37	27.29%
Avg. Devel.	3.25	28.11%
Brazil	3.46	41.80%
Hungary	3.03	39.08%
India	2.46	28.56%
Czech Rep	2.62	42.36%
Indonesia	3.37	36.96%
Malaysia	2.85	28.49%
Avg. Emerg.	2.97	36.21%
Argentina	1.36	17.60%
Lithuania	3.82	26.94%
Tunisia	2.16	10.83%
Croatia	2.41	25.97%
Avg. Frontier	2.44	20.33%

Note: Loss Coverage = MCR(VaR) / Maximum Loss Forecast Period.

Table 11. Proposed MCR Loss CoverageMaimum daily loss-Variation over Current MCR

Market / Index	Loss Coverage [1]	Variation over present MCR [2]	MCR = Maximum daily loss [3]	Var. over present Max. daily loss
UK	5.49	46.37%	50.86%	46.37%
France	4.10	135.86%	38.83%	135.86%
Germany	7.08	69.99%	52.60%	69.99%
Spain	4.67	45.32%	45.24%	45.32%
Switzerland	5.38	59.96%	43.65%	59.96%
Avg. Devel.	5.34	71.50%	46.23%	71.50%
Brazil	4.87	40.92%	58.90%	40.92%
Hungary	3.93	29.50%	50.60%	29.50%
India	3.48	41.40%	40.39%	41.40%
Czech Rep	3.45	31.80%	55.83%	31.80%
Indonesia	5.24	55.16%	57.35%	55.16%
Malaysia	5.71	99.94%	56.96%	99.94%
Avg. Emerg.	4.44	49.79%	53.34%	49.79%
Argentina	3.95	190.37%	51.11%	190.37%
Lithuania	5.93	54.99%	41.75%	54.99%
Tunisia	3.17	46.70%	15.89%	46.70%
Croatia	3.67	52.12%	39.50%	52.12%
Avg. Frontier	4.18	86.05%	37.06%	86.05%

Note: Loss Coverage = MCR(sVaR) / Maximum Loss Forecast Period.

Table 12. Sensitivity Analysis - Total MCR with varying scaling factors m_c and m_s

Case N°	mc - ms	UK	France	Germany	Spain	Switzerland	Brazil	Hungary	India	Czech Rep	Indonesia	Malaysia	Argentina	Lithuania	Tunisia	Croatia
1	mc=3	34,75%	16,46%	30,94%	31,13%	27,29%	41,80%	39,08%	28,56%	42,36%	36,96%	28,49%	17,60%	26,34%	10,83%	25,97%
2	mc=3/ms=0	42,51%	27,82%	40,06%	38,28%	34,19%	50,31%	42,30%	35,87%	45,85%	43,42%	35,61%	30,99%	37,76%	12,07%	30,35%
3	mc=3/ms=0.5	42,51%	27,82%	40,06%	38,28%	34,19%	50,61%	42,30%	35,87%	45,85%	43,42%	35,61%	30,99%	37,76%	12,07%	30,35%
4	mc=3/ms=1	42,51%	27,82%	40,06%	38,28%	34,19%	50,61%	42,92%	35,87%	46,85%	43,76%	37,98%	30,99%	37,76%	12,51%	30,43%
5	mc=3/ms=1.5	42,80%	27,82%	41,77%	38,28%	35,47%	50,61%	44,84%	35,87%	49,09%	47,16%	42,72%	34,35%	37,76%	13,36%	32,74%
6	mc=3/ms=2	45,49%	31,37%	45,38%	40,53%	38,19%	53,20%	46,76%	36,45%	51,34%	50,55%	47,47%	39,94%	37,76%	14,20%	34,99%
7	mc=3/ms=2.5	48,17%	35,10%	48,99%	42,88%	40,92%	56,05%	48,68%	38,42%	53,58%	53,95%	52,21%	45,52%	39,28%	15,04%	37,25%
8	mc=3/ms=3	50,86%	38,83%	52,60%	45,24%	43,65%	58,90%	50,60%	40,39%	55,83%	57,35%	56,96%	51,11%	41,75%	15,89%	39,50%
9	mc=3.5	40,54%	19,21%	36,10%	36,32%	31,83%	48,76%	45,59%	33,32%	49,42%	43,12%	33,24%	20,53%	31,43%	12,70%	30,30%
10	mc=3.5/ms=0	48,30%	30,56%	45,21%	43,47%	38,74%	57,58%	48,81%	40,63%	52,91%	49,58%	40,35%	33,92%	42,25%	13,88%	34,68%
11	mc=3.5/ms=0.5	48,30%	30,56%	45,21%	43,47%	38,74%	57,58%	48,81%	40,63%	52,91%	49,58%	40,35%	33,92%	42,25%	13,88%	34,68%
12	mc=3.5/ms=1	48,30%	30,56%	45,21%	43,47%	38,74%	57,58%	49,43%	40,63%	53,91%	49,92%	42,73%	33,92%	42,25%	14,32%	34,81%
13	mc=3.5/ms=1.5	48,59%	30,56%	46,93%	43,47%	40,01%	57,58%	51,35%	40,63%	56,15%	53,32%	47,47%	37,29%	42,25%	15,16%	37,06%
14	mc=3.5/ms=2	51,28%	34,12%	50,54%	45,72%	42,74%	60,16%	53,27%	41,21%	58,40%	56,71%	52,22%	42,87%	42,25%	16,01%	39,32%
15	mc=3.5/ms=2.5	53,97%	37,84%	54,15%	48,07%	45,47%	63,01%	55,20%	43,18%	60,64%	60,11%	56,96%	48,45%	43,77%	16,85%	41,58%
16	mc=3.5/ms=3	56,65%	41,57%	57,76%	50,42%	48,19%	65,86%	57,12%	45,15%	62,89%	63,51%	61,71%	54,04%	46,24%	17,69%	43,83%
17	mc=4	46,33%	21,95%	41,26%	41,50%	36,38%	55,73%	52,10%	38,09%	56,48%	49,28%	37,98%	23,47%	35,31%	14,44%	34,63%
18	mc=4/ms=0	46,33%	21,95%	41,26%	41,50%	36,38%	64,54%	55,32%	45,39%	59,97%	55,75%	45,10%	36,86%	46,74%	15,68%	39,01%
19	mc=4/ms=0.5	54,09%	33,30%	50,37%	48,66%	43,29%	64,54%	55,32%	45,39%	59,97%	55,75%	45,10%	36,86%	46,74%	15,68%	39,01%
20	mc=4/ms=1	54,09%	33,30%	50,37%	48,66%	43,29%	64,54%	55,94%	45,39%	60,97%	56,09%	47,47%	36,86%	46,74%	16,12%	39,14%
21	mc=4/ms=1.5	54,39%	33,30%	52,09%	48,66%	44,56%	64,54%	57,87%	45,39%	63,21%	59,48%	52,22%	40,22%	46,74%	16,97%	41,39%
22	mc=4/ms=2	57,07%	36,86%	55,70%	50,91%	47,29%	67,13%	59,79%	45,97%	65,46%	62,87%	56,97%	45,80%	46,74%	17,81%	43,65%
23	mc=4/ms=2.5	59,76%	40,59%	59,30%	53,26%	50,01%	69,98%	61,71%	47,94%	67,70%	66,27%	61,71%	51,39%	48,26%	18,65%	45,90%
24	mc=4/ms=3	62,44%	44,31%	62,91%	55,61%	52,74%	72,83%	63,63%	49,91%	69,94%	69,67%	66,46%	56,97%	50,73%	19,50%	48,16%
25	mc=4.5	52,12%	24,69%	46,41%	46,69%	40,93%	62,39%	58,61%	42,85%	63,54%	55,44%	42,73%	26,40%	40,40%	16,24%	38,95%
26	mc=4.5/ms=0	59,89%	36,05%	55,53%	53,84%	47,83%	71,51%	61,83%	50,15%	67,03%	61,91%	49,85%	39,79%	51,23%	17,49%	43,33%
27	mc=4.5/ms=0.5	59,89%	36,05%	55,53%	53,84%	47,83%	71,51%	61,83%	50,15%	67,03%	61,91%	49,85%	39,79%	51,23%	17,49%	43,33%
28	mc=4.5/ms=1	59,89%	36,05%	55,53%	53,84%	47,83%	71,51%	62,46%	50,15%	68,03%	62,24%	52,22%	39,79%	51,23%	17,93%	43,47%
29	mc=4.5/ms=1.5	60,18%	36,05%	57,24%	53,84%	49,11%	71,51%	64,38%	50,15%	70,27%	65,64%	56,97%	43,15%	51,23%	18,77%	45,72%
30	mc=4.5/ms=2	62,86%	39,60%	60,85%	56,10%	51,84%	74,09%	66,30%	50,73%	72,52%	69,03%	61,71%	48,74%	51,23%	19,61%	47,98%
31	mc=4.5/ms=2.5	65,55%	43,33%	64,46%	58,45%	54,56%	76,94%	68,22%	52,70%	74,76%	72,43%	66,46%	54,32%	52,75%	20,46%	50,23%
32	mc=4.5/ms=3	68,23%	47,06%	68,07%	60,80%	57,29%	79,79%	70,14%	54,67%	77,00%	75,83%	71,20%	59,91%	55,22%	21,30%	52,49%
33	mc=5	57,91%	27,44%	51,57%	51,88%	45,48%	69,36%	65,13%	47,61%	70,66%	61,60%	47,48%	29,33%	44,89%	18,05%	43,28%
34	mc=5/ms=0	65,68%	38,79%	60,68%	59,03%	52,38%	78,48%	68,35%	54,91%	74,09%	68,07%	54,60%	42,72%	55,72%	19,29%	47,66%
35	mc=5/ms=0.5	65,68%	38,79%	60,68%	59,03%	52,38%	78,48%	68,35%	54,91%	74,09%	68,07%	54,60%	42,72%	55,72%	19,29%	47,66%
36	mc=5/ms=1	65,68%	38,79%	60,68%	59,03%	52,38%	78,48%	68,97%	54,91%	75,09%	68,40%	56,97%	42,72%	55,72%	19,73%	47,79%
37	mc=5/ms=1.5	65,97%	38,79%	62,40%	59,03%	53,66%	78,48%	70,89%	54,91%	77,33%	71,80%	61,72%	46,09%	55,72%	20,58%	50,05%
38	mc=5/ms=2	68,65%	42,35%	66,01%	61,29%	56,38%	81,06%	72,81%	55,49%	79,57%	75,19%	66,46%	51,67%	55,72%	21,42%	52,30%
39	mc=5/ms=2.5	71,34%	46,07%	69,62%	63,64%	59,11%	83,91%	74,73%	57,46%	81,82%	78,59%	71,21%	57,25%	57,24%	22,26%	54,56%
40	mc=5/ms=3	74,02%	49,80%	73,23%	65,99%	61,84%	86,76%	76,65%	59,43%	84,06%	81,99%	75,95%	62,84%	59,71%	23,11%	56,82%

Notes: Cases 1, 3, 4, 5, 8, 9 and 17 are highlighted in bold letters as referenced in the main text.

Case 1: Current Basel II directives (no sVaR).

Case 8: Proposed Basel mandate (2009).

Cases 3, 4 and 5: Lessened ms values: 1.5, 1 and 0.5.

Cases 9 and 17: Augmented mc values: 3.5 and 4, no sVaR computed.

Table 13. Sensitivity analysis – Selected examples. Loss Coverage and Maximum daily loss

Market Index	EVT mc=3/ms=1.5		EVT mc=3/ms=1		EVT mc=3/ms=0.5		EVT mc=3.5		EVT mc=4	
	Loss Coverage	MCR = Maximum daily loss	Loss Coverage	MCR = Maximum daily loss	Loss Coverage	MCR = Maximum daily loss	Loss Coverage	MCR = Maximum daily loss	Loss Coverage	MCR = Maximum daily loss
	[1]	[2]	[3]	[4]	[5]	[6]	[7]	[8]	[9]	[10]
UK	4.62	42.80%	4.59	42.51%	4.59	42.51%	4.38	40.54%	5.00	46.33%
France	2.94	27.82%	2.94	27.82%	2.94	27.82%	2.03	19.21%	2.32	21.95%
Germany	5.62	41.77%	5.39	40.06%	5.39	40.06%	4.86	36.10%	5.55	41.26%
Spain	3.95	38.28%	3.95	38.28%	3.95	38.28%	3.75	36.32%	4.29	41.50%
Switzerland	4.37	35.47%	4.22	34.19%	4.22	34.19%	3.93	31.83%	4.49	36.38%
Avg. Devel.	4.30	37.23%	4.22	36.57%	4.22	36.57%	3.79	32.80%	4.33	37.48%
Brazil	4.18	50.61%	4.18	50.61%	4.18	50.61%	4.03	48.76%	4.61	55.73%
Hungary	3.48	44.84%	3.33	42.92%	3.28	42.30%	3.54	45.59%	4.04	52.10%
India	3.09	35.87%	3.09	35.87%	3.09	35.87%	2.87	33.32%	3.28	38.09%
Czech Rep	3.03	49.09%	2.89	46.85%	2.83	45.85%	3.05	49.42%	3.49	56.48%
Indonesia	4.30	47.16%	3.99	43.76%	3.96	43.42%	3.94	43.12%	4.50	49.28%
Malaysia	4.28	42.72%	3.81	37.98%	3.57	35.61%	3.33	33.24%	3.81	37.98%
Avg. Emerg.	3.73	45.05%	3.55	43.00%	3.49	42.28%	3.46	42.24%	3.95	48.28%
Argentina	2.65	34.35%	2.39	30.99%	2.39	30.99%	1.59	20.53%	1.81	23.47%
Lithuania	5.36	37.76%	5.36	37.76%	5.36	37.76%	4.46	31.43%	5.10	35.91%
Tunisia	2.67	13.36%	2.50	12.51%	2.41	12.07%	2.52	12.63%	2.89	14.44%
Croatia	3.04	32.74%	2.83	30.48%	2.82	30.35%	2.81	30.30%	3.22	34.63%
Avg. Frontier	3.43	29.55%	3.27	27.94%	3.25	27.79%	2.85	23.72%	3.25	27.11%

Loss Coverage [1],[3],[5] = MCR(sVaR) / Maximum Loss Forecast Period
Loss Coverage [7],[9] = MCR(VaR) / Maximum Loss Forecast Period.

Table 14. Sensitivity analysis: Selected examples–Variation over Current and Proposed directives

| Market Index | EVT mc=3/ms=1.5 Variation over | | EVT mc=3/ms=1 Variation over | | EVT mc=3/ms=0.5 Variation over | | EVT mc=3.5 Variation over | | EVT mc=4 Variation over | |
	Current Directives [1]	Proposed Directives [2]	Current Directives [3]	Proposed Directives [4]	Current Directives [5]	Proposed Directives [6]	Current Directives [7]	Proposed Directives [8]	Current Directives [9]	Proposed Directives [10]
UK	23.19%	-15.84%	22.35%	-16.41%	22.35%	-16.41%	16.67%	-20.30%	33.33%	-8.91%
France	68.98%	-28.36%	68.98%	-28.36%	68.98%	-28.36%	16.67%	-50.54%	33.33%	-43.47%
Germany	35.00%	-20.59%	29.45%	-23.85%	29.45%	-23.85%	16.67%	-31.37%	33.33%	-21.57%
Spain	22.98%	-15.38%	22.98%	-15.38%	22.98%	-15.38%	16.67%	-19.72%	33.33%	-8.25%
Switzerland	29.98%	-18.74%	25.31%	-21.66%	25.31%	-21.66%	16.67%	-27.07%	33.33%	-16.65%
Avg. Devel.	36.03%	-19.78%	33.81%	-21.13%	33.81%	-21.13%	16.67%	-29.80%	33.33%	-19.77%
Brazil	21.10%	-14.07%	21.10%	-14.07%	21.10%	-14.07%	16.67%	-17.21%	33.33%	-5.38%
Hungary	14.75%	-11.39%	9.83%	-15.19%	8.24%	-16.42%	16.67%	-9.91%	33.33%	2.96%
India	25.59%	-11.18%	25.59%	-11.18%	25.59%	-11.18%	16.67%	-17.49%	33.33%	-5.70%
Czech Rep	15.90%	-12.06%	10.60%	-16.08%	8.24%	-17.87%	16.67%	-11.48%	33.33%	1.17%
Indonesia	27.58%	-17.78%	18.39%	-23.70%	17.49%	-24.28%	16.67%	-24.81%	33.33%	-14.07%
Malaysia	49.97%	-24.99%	33.31%	-33.32%	24.98%	-37.49%	16.67%	-41.65%	33.33%	-33.31%
Avg. Emerg.	25.81%	-15.25%	19.80%	-18.92%	17.61%	-20.22%	16.67%	-20.42%	33.33%	-9.06%
Argentina	95.18%	-32.78%	76.07%	-39.36%	76.07%	1.00%	16.67%	-59.82%	33.33%	-54.08%
Lithuania	40.20%	-9.55%	40.20%	-9.55%	40.20%	-9.55%	16.67%	-24.73%	33.33%	-13.97%
Tunisia	23.35%	-15.92%	15.57%	-21.22%	11.48%	-24.01%	16.67%	-20.47%	33.33%	-9.11%
Croatia	26.06%	-17.13%	17.37%	-22.84%	16.87%	-23.17%	16.67%	-23.31%	33.33%	-12.35%
Avg. Frontier	46.20%	-18.84%	37.30%	-23.24%	36.15%	-13.93%	16.67%	-32.08%	33.33%	-22.38%

Loss Coverage [1],[3],[5] = MCR(sVaR) / Maximum Loss Forecast Period
Loss Coverage [7],[9] = MCR(VaR) / Maximum Loss Forecast Period.

In the second place, BCBS could also reinforce the capital base by increasing the base multiplication factor m_c, simultaneously suspending the sVaR scheme. A further look at Table 13-Columns 7-10 indicates that, augmenting m_c to 3.5 or 4[30] (phasing out m_s) would supply banks with enough reserves for losses in the interval [3.79-4.33], [3.46-3.95] and [2.85-3.25] (Developed, Emerging and Frontier markets respectively) times the heaviest shortfall in the forecast year 2008, representing an average maximum daily deficit of more than 32%, 42% and 23%[31]. MCR set in this fashion hint at the advantages of working with heavy tailed distributions like Generalised Pareto that resemble the empirical behaviour of data series as they would dodge the constitution of excessive capital cushions via formulas like [2] designed to underpin deficient models.

Finally, the adoption of an EVT-like scheme may grant national authorities with enough flexibility to determine the level of the m_s factor in accordance with the characteristics of the country concerned: for instance, authorities in Argentina might deem that m_c=4, delivering a Loss Coverage of 1.81 (Table 13-Column 9) is insufficient to meet potential losses and demand the combination m_c=3 m_s=0.5, hence pushing up the ratio to 2.39; on the other hand, Lithuanian regulators could decree the demise of sVaR scheme, resort to m_c=3.5 and brace banks for likely daily losses of 31% (Table 13-Column 8).

7. CONCLUSION

It is widespread knowledge that the empirical distribution of financial asset returns portrays leptokurtic characteristics, where the tails of the distribution appear fatter than predicted by the Gaussian distribution. The immediate action for risk managers to take seems, then, the implementation of VaR schemes which closely replicate the observed patterns. In this sense, HS and FHS confirm the snags widely documented in the literature –chiefly the high reliance on the sample period- and the normal distribution fails to grasp violent swings in the event of turmoil, both schemes severely underestimating VaR. The evidence collected through a variety of Developed, Emerging and Frontier stock markets show that models based on Extreme Value Distributions –or on the t distribution to a lesser extent- would prove vital at the time of determining Minimum Capital Requirements demanded by the Basel Committee on Banking Supervision.

Important repercussions derive from the evaluation of Basel regulations as they seem to encourage the operation of inaccurate models and dissuade sharper ones like EVT. Danielsson, Hartmann and de Vries (1998) state that some provisions contained in Basel II – namely the 10-day holding period, the square-root-of-time rule and the size of the fixed multiplication factor- have introduced unnecessary conservative elements that have hitherto kept HS, FHS and normal specifications alive, eventually hampering the development of more useful models like the ones aforementioned.

---

[30] Given that k=0 for EVT models in all markets, mc=3(1+k)=3 or the corresponding figure employed in the sensitivity analysis. Analogously, ms=3(1+k)=3 or the respective constant stated. The former reflection applies to Table 11.

[31] It is noteworthy that Hungary and Czech Republic report an enhancement of their capital base of 3% and 1% if mc=4 in relation to the proposed directives (Table 14-Column 10); these exceptions nevertheless do not invalidate the proofs gathered.

For every position analysed the intended sVaR modification that applies a base multiple $m_s=3$ in addition to the current MCR appears somewhat excessive and freezes funds unproductively. Provided an accurate and reliable model featuring EVT were employed, the values of m_c and m_s could be dissociated and set independently at the discretion of national supervisors in view of the particulars of each market: this chapter sheds some light to consider that BCBS may have acted excessively prudently. Two alternative suggestions are instead proposed: the first one would involve working out a combination between present MCR and a lighter m_s value, whereas the second one might scrap the sVaR scheme and increase the base multiplication factor m_c to some value between 3 and 4, for instance. This last possibility coincides with the Japanese viewpoint regarding the modification to Basel II.

Although the BCBS remains genuinely concerned about the health of the financial system, the direction of the reforms again penalises banks developing accurate models and prevents them from enjoying the advantages of precise VaR configurations. It is shown for a wide range of markets that EVT techniques provide extensive coverage, avert procyclicality avoiding the constitution of superfluous capital buffers and allow the institutions to match huge future losses without incurring in high development costs to estimate sVaR. Therefore, in a few words, they prove effective for risk managers and conservative for authorities simultaneously.

REFERENCES

Acerbi, C., and Tasche, D., (2002), On the Coherence of Expected Shortfall, *Journal of Banking and Finance* 26, pp. 1487-1503.

Alexander, C., (2008), *Market Risk Analysis Volume II: Practical Financial Econometrics*, John Wiley & Sons Ltd., The Atrium, Southern Gate, Chichester, West Sussex, United Kingdom.

Andersen, T. G., and Bollerslev, T., (November 1988), Answering the Skeptics: Yes, Standard Volatility Models do Provide Accurate Forecasts, International Economic Review, Vol. 39, No. 4, Symposium on Forecasting and Empirical Methods in Macroeconomics and Finance, pp. 885-905.

Artzner, J., Delbaen, F., Eber, K., and Heath, D., (1999), Coherent Measures of Risk, *Mathematical Finance*, Vol. 9, No. 3, pp. 203-228.

BASEL COMMITTEE ON BANKING SUPERVISION, (1996), Amendment to the Capital Accord to Incorporate Market Risks, Bank for International Settlements, Basel, Switzerland.

BASEL COMMITTEE ON BANKING SUPERVISION, (June 2004), International Convergence of Capital Measurement and Capital Standards, Bank for International Settlements, Basel, Switzerland.

BASEL COMMITTEE ON BANKING SUPERVISION, (June 2006), International Convergence of Capital Measurement and Capital Standards. A Revised Framework. Comprehensive Version, Bank for International Settlements, Basel, Switzerland.

BASEL COMMITTEE ON BANKING SUPERVISION, (July 2009), Revisions to the Basel II market risk framework, Bank for International Settlements, Basel, Switzerland.

BASEL COMMITTEE ON BANKING SUPERVISION, (December 2009), Strengthening the resilience of the banking sector, Consultative Document issued for comment by 16 April 2010, Bank for International Settlements, Basel, Switzerland.

Bollerslev, T., (1986), Generalized Autoregressive Conditional Heteroskedasticity, *Journal of Econometrics*, 31, pp. 307-327.

Brooks, C., Clare, A. D., and Persand, G., (2000), An EVT Approach to Calculating Risk Capital Requirements, Discussion Papers in Finance 2000-2007, ISMA Centre, University of Reading, Reading, United Kingdom.

Christoffersen, P., (2003), *Elements of Financial Risk Management*, Academic Press, New York, United States.

Christoffersen, P, and Gonçalves, S., (2007), Estimation Risk in Financial Risk Management, in *The Value at Risk Reference, Key Issues in the Implementation of Market Risk*, Edited by Danielsson, J., Risk Books, London, United Kingdom, pp. 187-219.

Coles, S., (2001), *An Introduction to Statistical Modeling of Extreme Values*, Springer Series in Statistics, Springer-Verlag London Limited, Berlin, Germany.

Danielsson, J., Hartmann, P. and De Vries, C., (January 1998), The Cost of Conservatism: Extreme Returns, Value-at-Risk and the Basle 'Multiplication Factor', January 1998 issue of *RISK*.

Danielsson, J., and Zigrand, J. P., (July 2005), On time-scaling of risk and the square root-of-time rule, Department of Accounting and Finance and Financial Markets Group, London School of Economics, London, United Kingdom.

Dowd, K. (2005), *Measuring Market Risk*, Second Edition, Wiley series in Frontiers in Finance, John Wiley & Sons Ltd, Chichester, West Sussex, United Kingdom.

Embrechts, P., Klüppelberg, C., and Mikosch, T., (1997), *Modelling Extremal Events for Insurance and Finance*, Springer-Verlag, Berlin Heidelberg, Berlin, Germany.

FINANCIAL SERVICES AUTHORITY, (March 2009), The Turner Review: A regulatory response to the global banking crisis, Publication Reference 003289, The Financial Services Authority, London, United Kingdom, available at: http://www.fsa.gov.uk. (Accessed October 2009).

JAPANESE BANKERS ASSOCIATION, (March 2008), Comments on the Consultative Documents for "Revisions to the Basel II Market Risk Framework", etc. issued by the Basel Committee on Banking Supervision, available at http:/www.bis.org. (Accessed October 2009).

Jorion, P., (1996), *Value-at-Risk: The New Benchmark for Controlling Market Risk*, Irwin, Chicago, United States.

Manganelli, S., and Engle, R. F., (2004), A Comparison of Value-at-Risk Models in Finance, in *Risk Measures for the 21st Century*, in Szegö, G. (ed.), (2004), John Wiley & Sons, Chichester, West Sussex, United Kingdom.

Mcneil, A. J., FREY, R., and EMBRECHTS, P., (2005), *Quantitative Risk Management*, Princeton University Press, Princeton, New Jersey, United States.

Pritsker, M., (June 2001), The Hidden Dangers of Historical Simulation, Working Paper, Board of Governors of the Federal Reserve System and University of California at Berkeley, The Federal Reserve Board, Washington DC, United States.

Reiss, R.-D., and Thomas, M., (2007), *Statistical Analysis of Extreme Values with Applications to Insurance, Finance, Hydrology and Other Fields*, Birkhäuser Verlag, AG, Berlin, Germany.

Stahl, G., (1997), Three Cheers, *Risk*, 10, pp. 67-69.

Taylor, S., (1986), *Modeling Financial Time Series*, John Wiley & Sons, New York, United States.

In: Financial Services: Efficiency and Risk Management
Editors: M. D. Fethi, C. Gaganis et al.

ISBN: 978-1-62100-560-5
© 2012 Nova Science Publishers, Inc.

Chapter 6

AN ANALYSIS OF EUROPEAN CENTRAL COUNTERPARTY CLEARING

Alessandra Tanda[*]
Cattolica University; Largo Gemelli, 1; 20123 Milano; Italy

ABSTRACT

Central Counterparty Clearing (CCP Clearing) is a process by which a third party interposes itself in every trade, replacing the original counterparties, thereby concentrating and redistributing counterparty risk. The importance of CCP Clearing has been recognised by the literature and by the European regulator. The latter created some Study Groups to investigate the role of these institutions in the context of European market integration, to achieve greater efficiency and to ease cross-border transactions. A very important issue is represented by the costs of services provided by Central Counterparties to traders. In 2006 the major Stock Exchanges, Central Counterparties (CCPs) and Central Securities Depositories (CSDs) voluntary subscribed to the "Code of Conduct for Clearing and Settlement". The aim of the Code was to foster integration and efficiency of European equity markets by improving transparency of price lists, establishing access and interoperability conditions, unbundling services and implementing accounting separation.

Starting from the results of the European Commission on trading and post-trading costs the chapter focuses on prices charged by some European CCPs on the regulated equity markets. Part of the literature claims that the form of integration of trading and post-trading services providers can determine the level of prices. Therefore the chapter briefly describes the structures of the institutions operating along the value chain. The analysis of pricing highlights some discrepancies with part of the literature and it also shows how clearing fees have been reduced since the introduction of the Code of Conduct.

---

[*] Tel: 0039 347 4463 103; E-mail: alessandra.tanda@unicatt.it

1. INTRODUCTION

Central Counterparty Clearing (also known as CCP clearing) is a "process by which a third party interposes itself directly or indirectly, between the transaction counterparties in order to assume their rights and obligations, acting as direct or in direct buyer to every seller and the direct or in direct seller to every buyer" [CESAME, 2005c, p. 5]. In this way traders can transfer the counterparty and liquidity risk originated by the transaction to the Central Counterparty (CCP). The CCP does not remove the risk from the financial system, but it concentrates and redistributes it [Hills, B., et al., 1999; Ripatti, K., 2004]. The implementation of sound risks management procedures is therefore crucial. One of the main aims of a CCP should be to avoid the contagion effect: the default of a member should not affect other members. The importance of these systems is particularly evident in the case of financial crises because CCP can limit the domino effect and can help in overcoming information asymmetries.

Although the topic of CCPs has been widely explored, as confirmed by the availability of extensive literature, a range of unresolved issues remains. Among them, the relationship between the industry structure and the costs related to the CCP Clearing service. Most of the studies on this specific issue have been conducted by Study Groups formed under the European Commission, such as CESAME[32]. Another major contribution has been provided by the industry itself, with the publication of the European Code of Conduct for Clearing and Settlement[33] (hereafter, the Code). The document aims at establishing a strong European market, thereby offering traders an efficient and competitive environment. The Code collects the main principles regarding transparency, pricing conditions and services unbundling.

The benefits associated with the presence of a CCP in a trading system are translated into higher costs for the traders. This chapter analyses the pricing structure and fees charged by some European Central Counterparty Clearing Systems, in order to evaluate the relative costs from traders' perspective.

A non-econometric analysis of the pricing conditions is performed; the results underline some contradictions with part of the literature. The amount of fees charged to members of CCP systems on equity markets is computed. The analysis of pricing enables us also to see how the clearing fees have evolved from the end of 2008 through February 2010. In particular, a decrease in the clearing fees is observed, especially for those CCPs that were the most expensive at the end of 2008. Beside this, there has been a change in the pricing structures that have been substantially simplified. The results are in part consistent with what was reported in 2009 by the European Commission.

To the best of our knowledge, this is one of the few recent analysis on the structure and evolution of pricing of European CCPs.

The chapter is structured as follows: Section 2 and 3 present the role of CCPs in the markets and review the main findings of the literature; Section 4 describes the analysis; Section 5 concludes.

---

[32] Clearing and Settlement Advisory and Monitoring Export Group.

[33] European Code of Conduct for Clearing and Settlement was undersigned in November 2006 by FESE (Federation of European Securities Exchanges), EACH (Association of Central Counterparty Clearing Houses) and ECSDA (European Central Securities Depositories Association).

2. CENTRAL COUNTERPARTY CLEARING SYSTEMS

A CCP interposes itself in every transaction[34] executed on a given market[35]. The traders, in order to benefit from the CCP intervention, have to become *clearing members*, participating to the System guaranteed and managed by the CCP.

Three different types of membership exist: Individual Clearing Member (ICM), General Clearing Member (GCM) and Non Clearing Member (NCM). ICMs and GCMs have a direct relationship with the CCP and they are therefore usually addressed to as Direct Clearing Members. Non Clearing Members, on the contrary, do not trade directly with the CCP, but through a General Clearing Member (GCM). The main difference from the risk management point of view is that the counterparty risk of the NCM is assumed by the relative GCM and not by the CCP.

CCP risk management structure is based on three main levels: minimum requirements, margins and default fund.

The first level is represented by a number of capital, technological and organizational requirements that members have to fulfil. These requirements are usually more stringent for DCMs and are set to minimise the probability of default.

As standards are not sufficient to ensure the solvency of members, the CCP has to implement a second level of risk management, which is activated in the case of member's default. In order to cover possible losses in the event of default, CCP requests the clearing members to hold liquid funds, which comprise of margins and a default fund.

Margins are constituted by cash or highly liquid assets that members must hold at the CCP account. The CCP sets a minimum level of margin (initial margins) and then this level is adjusted every day (variation margins) or more than once in a day, in case of extreme market conditions (intra-day variation margins), according to the fluctuations in the value of the securities held by the member in its portfolio. This mechanism enables the CCP to face market risk only in the event of a member default and to limit the losses to the period of time from the default to the transfer or liquidation of a member's positions.

The default fund is an additional form of guarantee used when margins are not sufficient to cover the losses generated by the member's default. The funds deposited by each member are pooled into a single default fund[36].

The main benefit of a CCP is the concentration and redistribution of counterparty and liquidity risks in the trading system (among the others, see Koeppl, T.V., and Monnet, C., 2008). This enables the traders to transfer their counterparty and liquidity risk to a third party

---

[34] Interposition may occur through novation or open offer. The two modalities differ in the moment of the interposition. By novation, the original trade is replaced and split into two different contracts. With open offer, instead, the CCP intervenes as soon as the transaction is matched on the trading system. [Bliss, R., Papathanassiou, C,. 2006]

[35] The chapter will focus on regulated equity markets, but the main characteristics of CCP described here can be extended to other markets.

[36] A default procedure is activated if a member is unable to fulfil its obligations towards the CCP or in general, towards its counterparties. As soon as the member is declared in default, the CCP has to transfer or liquidate the positions held by the member. Should this default cause losses, margin and default fund are usually accessed by the CCP in the following order:

1. member's margin;
2. member's default fund contribution;
3. default fund;
4. other funds (including the CCP capital).

and to overcome information asymmetries [Giordano, F., 2002]. Another advantage of Central Counterparty Clearing systems is the netting of positions. Netting (contractual netting) allows a member to compensate its gross exposures towards all the other members, with just one net exposure towards the CCP. Netting can be also applied to the level of margins: the effect is usually a decrease in the amount of liquidity held by the member on the CCP account that translates into a saving of funds for the member. An additional potential benefit is given by anonymity of trades that might enable the non disclosure of trading strategies. Despite this, anonymity is not a necessary condition for the sound functioning of a CCP system.

The main criticism of CCP Clearing system is represented by the concentration of risk (for a review see Knot, R., and Mills, A., 2002). The risks are in fact centralized in the hands of the CCP and its default could have destabilizing consequences on the whole financial system, because of the interconnection of members. CCP risk management procedures should be extremely efficient and effective, in order to avoid a "domino effect" on the financial markets. Additionally, CCPs themselves have often been recognized as "too big to fail" institutions [Giordano, F., 2002]. As suggested by the literature, this could cause a moral hazard problem, which is in part mitigated by the fact that they are usually under the supervision of Financial Authorities.

3. THE INDUSTRY

In order to understand the structure of pricing applied by CCPs, it is necessary to describe the main features of the industry. It is usually claimed that industry characteristics can determine the organizational structure of a CCP in the market, the level of efficiency attainable and consequently the costs and the prices charged [Knieps, G., 2006].

3.1. A Potentially Competitive Market

CCPs operate both in trading and post-trading markets. They have a role in the trading process, by interposing themselves between the traders, and during the post-trading process, by clearing the positions and preparing the basis for the securities settlement. This section reviews the main contributions related to CCPs, which are generally focused on their activity on post-trading markets.

Post-trading markets are characterized by network externalities. The utility a member gains from belonging to a CCP Clearing system increases as the number of members of that system enlarges[37]: trading opportunities amplify and costs decrease [Baglioni, A., Hamaui, R., 2006]. Utility is maximized when all the clearing members subscribe to the same CCP. Users in fact tend to prefer systems with a high number of members and clearing various securities [CESAME, 2005a].

The presence of network externalities suggests that the industry will consolidate horizontally, with the creation of a unique CCP. Despite the benefits of a unique CCP, it must

---

[37] The main considerations expressed here are also valid for Central Securities Depositories (CSDs) and Clearing Houses. However the focus will be on institutions operating in the CCP clearing process.

be underlined that a single CCP would be exposed to a high level of different risks, and it could become source of systemic risk itself [BCE, 2001].

It has also been claimed that post-trading markets present the characteristics of a monopoly [European Financial Services Round Table, 2003] or a monopolistic bottleneck. A monopolistic bottleneck is characterized by two conditions: i) the facility is necessary to reach the customers, i.e. there are no active substitutes; ii) the facility cannot be duplicated easily and cheaply, i.e. there is no potential substitute available [Knieps, G., 2006].

Post-trading markets have some common characteristics with telecommunication markets. Knieps (2006) observes that post-trading markets are not a natural monopoly, neither can they be considered as monopolistic bottleneck facilities. The author claims that post-trading markets are not an essential facility, but a high value-added service, and if contrasted with the telecommunication markets, they are more similar to e-mails than to the physical network. Knieps (2006) concludes that "Clearing and settlement markets are characterized by active and potential competition" [Knieps, G., 2006, p. 59]. His analysis separates the activity of Central Counterparty from the clearing activity on post-trading markets. However, as CCPs intervene in both the trading and the post-trading phases, by clearing the positions of the traders, it would be difficult to separate the two activities. The potential of competition can therefore be extended also to CCP Clearing processes in their entirety.

It becomes clear, therefore, that CCP market can be a competitive market and that any CCP fulfilling the industry standard and regulatory requirements can potentially compete with other CCPs on their specific trading venue. The changes we have assisted to seem to support this idea, for there has been the adoption of some forms of competition in the European markets; for example, LCH. Clearnet SA and Cassa di Compensazione e Garanzia (CC&G) clear contracts on MTS Italy, and LCH.Clearnet Ltd and SIX x-clear both act as CCPs of London Stock Exchange (LSE) and SIX Swiss Exchange[38] markets.

If we analyze the shape characterizing the industry until a few years ago, CCPs were *defacto* monopolistic entities operating on one or more markets. The rationale was however not clear and it was not necessarily linked to the industry features [Padoa Schioppa, T., 2006]. A few alternative reasons can be easily identified.

First of all, the integration of European markets is a recent phenomenon and the historical evolution of isolated national markets justifies the existence of a single CCP. The introduction of Euro has enhanced the level of integration. Besides, the underlying market can have the possibility to impede competition by imposing the presence of a given CCP and CSD [European Commission, Competition DG, 2006]. For example, Borsa Italiana, in its Instructions clarifies that the CCP designed for the contracts traded on its Equity and Derivatives markets shall be CC&G[39]. The lack of competition could also derive from other motivations: a CCP must take into consideration the potential profits before entering as a competitor on a market. A trading system with low volumes and limited counter value may not be attractive from the CCP's point of view.

---

[38] The interoperability agreement was previously on SIX Europe market; the latter merged with the Swiss Exchange in the mid of 2009.

[39] Istruzioni al Regolamento dei Mercati organizzati e gestiti da Borsa Italiana S.p.A., art. IA.12.2.

3.2. Forms of Integration

This section describes the forms of integration between CCPs and the institutions operating in other trading and post-trading activities, i.e. Stock Exchanges or trading platforms and Central Securities Depositories (CSDs).

These institutions can pursue different forms of integration; the main forms are represented by vertical integration and horizontal integration.

A vertical integration occurs when "exclusive relationships between trading on one side and clearing and settlement systems on the other" exist [European Financial Services Round Table, 2003, p. 3]. These structures are also known as "vertical silo". One main advantage of vertical silos is the increase in efficiency along the value chain, through the sharing of information and the use of integrated standards that helps in reducing costs, limiting errors and accelerating execution. This kind of process is known as *Straight Through Processing* (STP) [Hirata de Carvalho, C., 2004; Ripatti, K., 2004]. However, this form of integration has the potential to influence competition: potential entrants are not allowed to enter the market because the trading system "protects" the monopoly of the relative CCP and CSD. CCPs in vertical silos might also charge higher fees, exploiting their market power. Additionally, these structures represent an obstacle to the industry consolidation and to the creation of the single CCP. The prevalence of the negative factors has led part of the literature and the industry to advocate the dismantling of vertical silos (for a broader discussion see Evanoff, D.D., et al, 2006). The hypothesis that vertical silos tend to charge higher prices has been in part refuted by the empirical evidence. As underlined by the European Commission in 2006, Borsa Italiana, despite being a vertical silo, presented the lowest trading and post-trading costs in the European Union [European Commission, Competition DG, 2006]. At the same time, another vertical silo, Deutsche Börse, charged fees that were among the highest. The relationship between structural form and prices charged is not therefore clear. It could be argued that vertical silos can prevent competition only if they are used for this purpose [Trichet J. C., 2006].

Horizontal integration is reached when firms operating on the same level of the value chain consolidate or adopt other forms of co-operation. This type of integration implies a high level of concentration and it can be achieved only through long structural changes. Some forms of cooperation (like the definition of common standards, use of same technological platforms, interoperability and access agreements) can help to ease these changes. An access represents a standard service that allows a CCP or any other organisation to access another CCP (or another organisation). Interoperability is, instead, an advanced form of relationships among organisations where these agree to establish customised solutions. This kind of agreement has the objective to enable the traders to choose their service provider [FESE, EACH, ECSDA, 2006; FESE, EACH, ECSDA, 2007]. Although a horizontal structure can benefit from economies of scale, it is also exposed to excessive concentration of risks and might escalate the weaknesses of having a single CCP.

The main issues related to the integration processes have been addressed by the European Commission and by the industry in a document, named "European Code of Conduct for Clearing and Settlement". The document also emphasises transparency that should help in comparing fee schedules, fostering competition and therefore lower prices, irrespective of the type of integration achieved. The content of the main contributions are summarised in Table 1.

Table 1. Working Groups toward integration

A number of Study Groups formed under the European Commission or by industry exponents have helped in isolating the main obstacles to integration and providing solutions and suggestion on how to overcome these obstacles.

a) The Giovannini Group on barriers to integration
The Giovannini Group was formed in 1996 to advise Commission on the barriers to integration. The Group produced two reports. The first one was published in 2001 and it underlines the main barriers to integration related to difficulties encountered to overcome national differences in the industry, in the legal and fiscal framework (in total 15) [The Giovannini Group, 2001]. The second report was published after two years and it highlights the possible steps forward and the strategies to destroy barriers which would affect the creation of an integrated and efficient market [The Giovannini Group, 2003]. After the publication of the two Reports by the Giovannini Group, the European Commission created three more groups with the goal to destroy barriers at the industry, legal and fiscal level, respectively represented by: i) Clearing and Settlement Advisory and Monitoring Experts' Group (briefly CESAME Group); ii) Legal Certainty Group (LCG); iii) Fiscal Compliance Experts' Group (FISCO).
The CESAME Group mandate expired in 2008 and the work of the Group was continued by CESAME II Group.

b) Recommendation for Central Counterparties
In 2004 a task force formed by the Committee on Payment and Settlement System (CPSS) and by the Technical Committee of the International Organisation of Securities Commissions (IOSCO) published the "Recommendation for Central Counterparties". The document listed a series of recommendation that a CCP should follow in order to manage risks in an effective way. The importance of the document lays not in the listing of a series of standards, but in providing an instrument to classify and judge CCPs' standards from an objective and uniform point of view.

c) The European Code of Conduct
The European Code of Conduct for Clearing and Settlement is a voluntary code published in 2006 from the cooperation among FESE (Federation of European Securities Exchanges), EACH (European Association of Central Counterparty Clearing) and ECSDA (European Central Securities Depositories Association). The Code is primarily addressed to firms which provide post-trading services: CCP Clearing services offered by CCP, Clearing Houses and CSDs; settlement and custody services offered by CSDs. The Code has been inspired by the idea that transparency is an essential requisite to foster integration on European markets and that a voluntary implementation of shared standards could improve the overall level of transparency. "The ultimate aim of the Code is to offer market participants the freedom to choose their preferred provider of services separately at each layer of the transaction chain and to make the concept of "cross-border" redundant for transactions between EU member states" [FESE, EACH, ECSDA, 2006, p. 1]. In the Code, the signatories committed themselves to adopt behaviour aimed at fostering "greater efficiency and integration in Europe. To this end, they will comply with the present Code of Conduct ("Code") as a voluntary self-commitment and will adhere to a number of principles on the provision of post-trading services for cash equities" [FESE, EACH, ECSDA, 2006, p. 1].

The three main areas of intervention of the Code of Conduct are the transparency of price lists; establishing access and interoperability conditions; unbundling services and implementing accounting separation. The implementation of the Code is valued by the MOG (Monitoring Group of the Code of Conduct on Clearing and Settlement) chaired by the European Commission.
[CPSS-IOSCO, 2004a; FESE, EACH, ECSDA, 2006; MOG, 2008.]

4. EUROPEAN CENTRAL COUNTERPARTY CLEARING: AN ANALYSIS

Various subjects operate in Europe in the CCP Clearing process. The number of members of the European Association of Central Counterparty Clearing (EACH) is 20[40]. All the members have to comply with a list of requirements related to risk management standards and operating procedures. Among these, the Rules have to be approved by the competent Supervisor Authority and the CCP should adhere to the Code of Conduct.

The analysis focuses on the following European CCPs:

- LCH.Clearnet SA;
- LCH.Clearnet Ltd;
- Eurex Clearing AG;
- Cassa di Compensazione e Garanzia SpA (CC&G);
- SIX x-clear.

With reference to the regulated equity markets cleared, LCH.Clearnet SA and LCH.Clearnet Ltd operate on Euronext, LSE and SIX Swiss Exchange. They are horizontally integrated under the holding company named LCH.Clearnet Group. Eurex Clearing AG is part of Eurex Group, jointly owned by Deutsche Börse AG and SIX Swiss Exchange AG. This makes it part of a vertical silo, because the market (Eurex Frankfurt) fully owns the Clearing House acting as CCP. Eurex Clearing clears the transactions matched on the Frankfurt Stock Exchange (FWB) and on the Irish Stock Exchange (ISE). CC&G belongs to Borsa Italiana Group that merged with London Stock Exchange Group in 2007. The CCP is thus part of a vertical integrated structure. SIX x-clear is a Swiss CCP that clears contracts on SIX Swiss Exchange and London Stock Exchange (LSE). The CCP has been included because despite being Swiss and therefore not subject to European Commission recommendation, it operates on London Stock Exchange and it is a signatory of the European Code of Conduct. It also acted on SIX Europe, a cross-border equity market that has recently become a segment of SIX Swiss Exchange[41]. This market is cleared in an interoperability agreement with LCH.Clearnet Ltd. The Swiss CCP is also part of a vertical silo, member of the SIX Group that owns and manages firms operating along the value chain, from trading to post-trading (clearing and settlement) services.

These CCPs have been chosen for the importance of the relative markets cleared and for their international relevance.

The main aim of the paper is to study the fees charged by these CCPs on equity regulated markets. For this reason, the functioning and the ownership structures are not discussed in detail. Table 2 below shows the brief summary to the CCP's structure.

---

[40] Number of members as at 15 May 2010.
[41] The Blue Chip Segment on SIX Swiss Exchange consists of the securities previously admitted to trading in the SWX Europe's UK Exchange and EU Regulated Market Segment.

Table 2.

	LCH.Clear net Ltd	LCH.Clear net SA	Eurex Clearing	CC&G	SIX x-clear
Structure	Horizontal	Horizontal	Vertical	Vertical	Vertical
Shareholders	Owned by LCH.Clear net Group. Capital held by the members.	Owned by LCH.Clear net Group. Capital held by the members	Owned by Eurex Group. Capital: 50% held by Deutsche Borse and 50% held by SIX Swiss Exchange	Owned by LSE Group	Owned by SIX Group. Capital held by some banks that are also members
Supervisory Authority	FSA	Commissio n Bancaire	Bundesanstal t für Finanzdienst - leistungsaufs icht (BaFin)	Banca d'Italia and Consob	Swiss Federal Banking Commissio n Swiss National Bank
Admission Requirements	Capital Organisatio nal Technical	Capital Organisatio nal Technical	Capital Organisation al Technical	Capital Organisatio nal Technical	Organisatio nal Technical
Margins (methodology)	Based on SPAN®	Based on SPAN®	RBM	TIMS MVP	VaR
Margins (eligible instruments)	Cash Liquid assets	Cash Liquid assets	Cash Liquid assets	Cash Liquid assets	Cash Liquid assets
Default Fund	Yes	Yes	Yes	Yes	Yes
Markets cleared	Equity Derivatives Bonds Energy	Equity Derivatives Bonds	Equity Derivatives Bonds Energy	Equity Derivatives Bonds Energy	Equity Derivatives Bonds
Compliant with the Code of Conduct[+]	Yes	Yes	Yes	Yes	Yes

[+] Compliance as reported on the EACH website (www.eachorg.eu).
Source: Our elaboration on the content of CCPs websites and EACH website.

4.1. Methodology

The analysis is based on the computation of the clearing fees paid by a member for a given number of transaction cleared by each CCP analysed. Some hypotheses have been formulated in order to simplify the analysis and to enhance comparability of the results.

Since the Code of Conduct applies only to equity markets[42], we study the fees charged on these instruments. This also enables greater comparability of the results.

Equity markets are here considered homogeneous: though the actual decision to trade on a given equity market might depend on the stocks traded, the analysis will assume that the member is indifferent to trading in any of the regulated equity markets cleared by a CCP. This might be a strong simplification, but it does not invalidate the analysis.

The main source of information for pricing schemes is represented by the price lists published by the CCPs on their websites, available respectively as at December 2008, end of January 2009 and 15th February 2010. The choice of dates is mainly arbitrary and in part depends on the release of new pricing lists by the CCPs.

The analysis considers membership fees and clearing fees, since these are observable and objective costs. The costs faced by clearing member are in fact various and can be direct or indirect and might not be fully observed. Direct costs constitute of clearing fees, membership fees, and costs related to the IT infrastructure, fail management and other services. Indirect costs relate mainly to back-office and middle-office arrangements, human resources training and compliance with the requirements.

In general, indirect costs and part of direct costs are not observable: fail management costs depend on the so-called failed positions and these cannot be estimated ex-ante (because they usually depend on market conditions or on other members' behaviour); in addition, IT infrastructures are not always mandatory and they are not always provided directly by the CCP.

The first cost for the trader considered in the analysis is the membership fee, which is a given amount of money that the member should pay *una tantum* and/or each year to keep its member status in the clearing system.

The other cost included is represented by clearing fees. Clearing fees are related to trading activity of the member and they are usually computed on the basis of volume and counter value of transactions.

Clearing fees and membership fees are usually related to the type of membership requested (GCM, ICM or NCM). The analysis assumes the member is an ICM and has been a member for more than one year.

These hypotheses enable us to avoid two complications. The amount of fees paid by General Clearing Members and Non Clearing Members depends on non observable factors. In fact, GCMs usually pay membership fees in relation to the number of NCMs; as the list of NCMs for each General Clearing Member is not always publicly available, it would not be possible to determine the amount of fees paid by GCMs and NCMs. In addition, sometimes GCMs pay membership fees for their Non Clearing Members and no information is available to determine whether the GCM gets a refund for that fee or not.

---

[42] The discussion is going on at industry and European Commission level, in order to extend the validity of the Code on the other markets.

The time hypothesis has been introduced because membership fees can be reduced if the membership is obtained during the year, and, in some cases, the fee paid for the first year can be different from the one paid for the succeeding years.

Since every CCP can use a different price scheme, different variables will be used in the computation. If a CCP operates in more than one market, and applies different pricing schemes to the markets cleared, we suppose the member trades alternatively on one market or on the other and the level of fees is computed for each market separately. Among the CCPs here examined, this applies only to LCH.Clearnet Ltd and Eurex Clearing.

In the analysis the fees are therefore estimated for the following institutions:

- LCH.Clearnet Ltd on LSE,
- LCH.Clearnet Ltd on SIX Swiss Exchange,
- LCH.Clearnet SA,
- Eurex Clearing on Irish Stock Exchange (ISE),
- Eurex Clearing on Frankfurt Stock Exchange (FWB),
- CC&G
- SIX x-clear.

Other additional hypotheses are as follows: discount schemes are not applied, prices are calculated without VAT, and transactions are all executed in Euro currency. If the price list uses a different currency, the exchange rate suggested by the CCP or, alternatively, the exchange rate available on the price list publishing date is used.

Clearing and membership fees are estimated for four types of users that have different characteristics in terms of volumes and counter value of trades completed in one year, as reported in Table 3. The definition of the four users derives from the document "Competition in EU securities trading and post-trading – Issues Paper" issued by the European Commission [European Commission, Competition DG, 2006].

Table 3. Users characteristics

	Typical User (User A)	Many trades but small (User B)	Many trades and big (User C)	Few trades and small (User D)
Number of trades	959,802	1,919,604	1,919,604	479,901
Average trade size (€)	45,810	22,905	91,619	22,905
Value of transactions (€)	43,968,222,829	43,968,222,829	175,872,891,318	10,922,055,707

Source: European Commission, Competition DG, 2006.

4.2. Level of Fees

The first results are presented in Table 4 and show the fees estimated on the basis of the price lists available as at the 15th February 2010. For each user the following indicators are computed:

- tCF: total clearing fees are obtained on the basis of the number of trades, on the average trade size and on the fees applied by each CCP.
- tCMF: total clearing and membership fees. The value is the result of the sum of the annual membership fee (if applicable) and the total clearing fees (tCF).
- aCF: average clearing fee, resulting from the ratio between the tCF and the number of trades.
- aCMF: average clearing and membership fee, resulting from the ratio between the tCMF and the number of trades. This ratio captures the relative impact of membership fees on the average clearing fee per trade.
- tCF on total value: total clearing fee on total value that shows the impact of clearing fees on the total counter value of the transactions.

User A (Table 4, panel A) pays on average a CF equal to 0.18 Euros. However, as suggested by the high standard deviation of the figure, there is a substantial difference among the values for each CCP. Eurex Clearing is the most expensive, charging an aCF greater than 0.50 Euros on FWB and of 0.20 on ISE, while all the other CCPs charge an average clearing fee lower than 0.20 Euros.

User B (Table 4, panel B) is a user that trades many contracts with small counter value. The average clearing fee is lower due to the limited activity and it is 0.14 Euros. For this user, Eurex Clearing is the CCP which still charges the highest prices.

The user with a high number of transactions and a high counter value (user C) pays on average 0.24 Euros as aCF. Eurex Clearing is still the most expensive, charging around 0.98 Euros as aCF. This is due to the fact that Eurex Clearing pricing structure takes into account the counter value of the trades, and therefore user C is penalized by this specific modality of computation (Panel C). In greater detail, Eurex Clearing applies a fixed fee per trade and a value-based fee, expressed as percentage of the counter value of transactions, with a cap.

User D trades few contracts with small counter value and pays on average a clearing fee equal to 0.16 Euros per trade. The most expensive CCP is once again Eurex Clearing AG, charging 0.29 Euros on Frankfurt Stock Exchange (FWB) and 0.20 on Irish Stock Exchange (ISE). The other CCPs all charge an aCF lower than the mean, i.e. 0.16 Euros.

The same considerations hold true if we consider the aCMF, taking into account the membership fee. The relative weight of the membership fee does not seem to affect substantially the average clearing fee for the users.

Overall, the most expensive CCP appears to be Eurex Clearing AG, as highlighted above, especially for the trades executed on the Frankfurt Stock Exchange (FWB). In contrast, the CCP charging the lowest prices seems to be LCH.Clearnet SA. All the other CCPs charge fees slightly higher than LCH.Clearnet SA, as shown in Figure 1.

Table 4. Clearing and Membership fees charged by CCPs as at 15th February 2010.

Panel A						Panel C					
User A						User C					
Number of trades	959,802.00					Number of trades	1,919,604.00				
Average trade size	45,810.00					Average trade size	91,619.00				
Average daily trades	3,763.93					Average daily trades	7,527.86				
	tCF	tCMF	aCF	aCMF	tCF on total value		tCF	tCMF	aCF	aCMF	tCF on total value
Lch.Ltd LSE UK	121,355.97	121,355.97	0.13	0.13	0.00	Lch.Ltd LSE UK	234,445.53	234,445.53	0.12	0.12	0.00
Lch.Ltd SIX	106,235.13	106,235.13	0.11	0.11	0.00	Lch.Ltd SIX	212,466.32	212,466.32	0.11	0.11	0.00
Lch.SA	71,985.00	86,985.00	0.08	0.09	0.00	Lch.SA	143,970.00	158,970.00	0.08	0.08	0.00
Eurex Ise	191,960.40	216,960.40	0.20	0.23	0.00	Eurex Ise	383,920.80	408,920.80	0.20	0.21	0.00
Eurex FWB	497,273.42	637,449.66	0.52	0.66	0.00	Eurex FWB	1,873,898.23	1,873,898.23	0.98	0.98	0.00
CC&G	143,970.30	151,470.30	0.15	0.16	0.00	CC&G	153,568.32	161,068.32	0.08	0.08	0.00
SIX	117,442.49	123,776.82	0.12	0.13	0.00	SIX	193,586.53	199,920.85	0.10	0.10	0.00
mean	178,603.24	206,319.04	0.19	0.21	0.00	mean	456,550.82	464,241.44	0.24	0.24	0.00
std dev.	134,457.18	180,192.19	0.14	0.19	0.00	std dev.	583,304.89	580,807.26	0.30	0.30	0.00

Table 4. Continued

Panel B						Panel D					
User B						User D					
Number of trades	1,919,604.00					Number of trades	479,901.00				
Average trade size	22,905.00					Average trade size	22,905.00				
Average daily trades	7,527.86					Average daily trades	1,881.96				
	tCF	tCMF	aCF	aCMF	tCF on total value		tCF	tCMF	aCF	aCMF	tCF on total value
Lch.Ltd LSE UK	234,445.53	234,445.53	0.12	0.12	0.00	Lch.Ltd LSE UK	64,814.42	64,814.42	0.14	0.14	0.00
Lch.Ltd SIX	212,466.32	212,466.32	0.11	0.11	0.00	Lch.Ltd SIX	53,117.57	53,117.57	0.11	0.11	0.00
Lch.SA	143,970.00	158,970.00	0.08	0.08	0.00	Lch.SA	35,974.00	39,474.00	0.08	0.08	0.00
Eurex Ise	383,920.80	408,920.80	0.20	0.21	0.00	Eurex Ise	95,980.20	120,980.20	0.20	0.25	0.00
Eurex FWB	554,861.54	810,214.02	0.29	0.42	0.00	Eurex FWB	138,715.38	163,715.38	0.29	0.34	0.00
CC&G	153,568.32	161,068.32	0.08	0.08	0.00	CC&G	71,985.15	79,485.15	0.15	0.17	0.00
SIX	193,586.53	199,920.85	0.10	0.10	0.00	SIX	66,464.71	72,799.03	0.14	0.15	0.00
mean	268,117.00	312,286.55	0.14	0.16	0.00	mean	75,293.06	84,912.25	0.16	0.18	0.00
std dev.	138,333.13	217,876.84	0.07	0.11	0.00	std dev.	30,907.17	39,940.08	0.06	0.08	0.00

In the Table: Lch.Ltd LSE UK: Lch Clearnet Ltd on London Stock Exchange UK; Lch.Ltd SIX: Lch Clearnet Ltd on SIX Swiss Exchange (former SIX Europe); Lch.SA: Lch Clearnet SA; Eurex Ise: Eurex Clearing AG only on Ise market; Eurex FWB: Eurex Clearing AG only on FWB market; CC&G: Cassa di Compensazione e Garanzia; SIX: SIX x-clear.

The Table shows the main characteristics of users' trading activity (number of trades, average trade size, average daily trades) and the fees computed on the basis of the price lists applied by each CCP. The variables computed are: total clearing fees (tCF); total clearing fees including the annual membership fee, if applicable (tCMF); average clearing fee (aCF); the average clearing and membership fee (aCMF); total clearing fee on total counter value (tCF on total value).

Source: our elaboration.

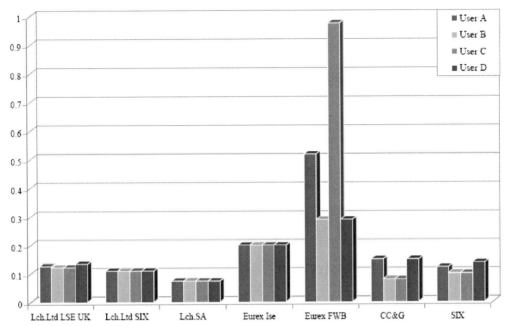

The Figure shows the Average Clearing Fee (aCF) paid by the different users, to the different CCPs considered in the analysis. Eurex Clearing AG charges a higher aCF for every user. The difference is particularly remarkable for the trades on FWB.
Source: our elaboration.

Figure 1. Average Clearing Fee (aCF) as at 15th February 2010.

The differences in the level of fees might originate from the different costs related to the trading systems that the CCPs guarantee.

At the time of writing, the lack of availability of data does not enable a deeper investigation on possible the causes of these differences, which might originate from the costs the CCPs has to face in guaranteeing a given trading system or from the level of efficiency; besides, accounting separation (see Table 2) has not been implemented at the time of writing. Further research is needed on this issue.

It is however possible to have a broader view on the fees applied by the CCPs, by analysing how these have evolved in the last years.

4.3. Evolution of Pricing

This section aims at providing a broader view on the evolution of fees from the end of 2008.

The results are presented only for the total average clearing fees (aCMF) charged to user A[43] (Figure 2). This indicator enables us to consider changes both in clearing fees and in membership fees for the period.

The dates used to compute the fees are December 2008, January 2009 and February 2010. From 2008 a substantial reduction in clearing fees can be observed, especially for

---

[43] The aCMF charged to all the users are collected in the Table A.1 in the Appendix.

LCH.Clearnet SA that has reduced its aCMF from about 0.65 Euros to 0.09 Euros within a year.

Some further simplifications are needed to estimate the clearing fees for LCH.Clearnet for December 2008 and January 2009 as the pricing scheme used by the CCP was different. Hence, the results could be influenced by these hypotheses; however the important decrease in the level of fees remains also with other specifications.

Furthermore the results are consistent with recent studies on clearing services commissioned by the European Commission, which register a reduction in overall prices of more than 60% from 2006 to 2008 [European Commission, Internal Market and Services DG, 2009].

From December 2008 to January 2009 Eurex Clearing fixed fee has been reduced from 0.30 Euros to 0.18 Euros per transaction. The same fee has been further reduced to 0.06 Euros in February 2010. The value-based fee was 0.0015% at the end of 2008 with a cap of 6 Euros per transaction, and it has been reduced to 0.0010% at the end of January 2009 with a cap of 3.80 Euros.

It can be concluded therefore, that since the Code of Conduct was published in 2006, clearing fees have diminished substantially. This could be a consequence of the improved level of efficiency, but also of the greater transparency and the increase in potential competition on markets which were previously characterised by a *de facto* monopoly.

In addition, apart from the reduction of prices, clearing fees structures have been simplified; simpler and immediate pricing models have been adopted.

SIX x-clear provides an interesting example in this sense. The amount of fees charged by Swiss CCP used to depend on various variables, such as the number of trades, the risk associated to the trader (evaluated through rating scores), the daily exposure and the type of instruments traded (individuated by ISIN codes). With this type of structure the *ex-ante* estimation of fees was particularly difficult. At the beginning of 2009, the CCP radically modified the pricing scheme, adopting a pricing structure based on members' monthly trading volume and rating. The explicit goal of the CCP was to facilitate the fees estimate for members and potential members [SIX x-clear, 2008c].

LCH.Clearnet SA also simplified the pricing scheme. Until the beginning of 2010 the member had to choose a band fee accordingly to its estimated trading volume. Fees were charged according to the band chosen[44]. However, starting from January 2010, the system was further amended and fees are now computed on the basis volume and the type of shares traded, differentiating between Blue Chips and other shares.

Many of the CCPs considered published an online calculator in order to help actual and potential members to estimate the level of clearing fees charged for a given volume and counter value of trades.

---

[44] In order to compute the clearing fees with this type of fee grid, we supposed every user was able to choose its band optimally, by correctly estimating its future trading volume.

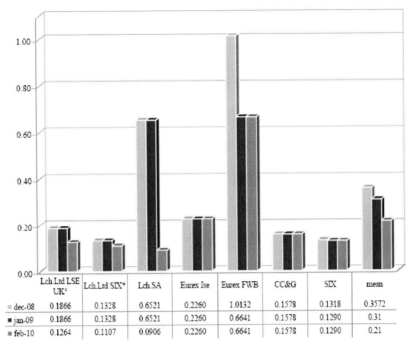

The Figure shows the level of the Average Clearing and Membership Fee (aCMF) as at end of December 2008, end of January 2009 and 15th February 2010.

°For December 2008 and January 2009, the fees attributable to Lch.Clearnet LSE UK were the ones applied to Lch.Clearnet Ltd on LSE and SIX, the latter only on UK&IRE markets

*For December 2008 and January 2009, the fees attributable to Lch.Clearnet Ltd SIX were the ones applied only on SIX Europe, the latter not including UK&IRE markets.

Source: our elaboration.

Figure 2. Evolution of Average Clearing and Membership Fee (aCMF) for User A.

4.4. Pricing and Industry Structure

From the above results and from the observation of CCP structures (Table 2) it can be concluded that no clear relationship seems to exist between the type of structure (vertical or horizontal) and level of fees charged.

CCPs in vertical silos examined here (CC&G, Eurex Clearing AG and SIX x-clear) present very variable clearing fees. This suggests that service providers in vertical silos are not always more expensive than other structures and they do not seem to take advantage of monopolistic power.

The only horizontal structure examined is LCH.Clearnet Group, holding company of LCH.Clearnet Ltd and LCH.Clearnet SA. Horizontal structures should be able to reach greater level of efficiency, exploit economies of scale and benefit from network externalities. Clearing fees charged by the two CCPs used to be very different in the past. LCH.Clearnet Ltd fees were cheaper than LCH.Clearnet SA at the end of 2008 and the beginning of 2009. At February 2010, however, we can see a convergence of the level of fees charged by the two CCPs.

Differences in clearing fees seem to be, therefore, more related to other factors than the type of structure in which the CCP operates. Higher fees could depend on higher costs for the CCP, originating from the trading platform that the CCP clears. As already pointed out, not all the CCPs here analysed clear in the same markets and the equity markets have different characteristics.

Likewise, the membership to a given CCP may not depend on the level of fees charged but on the trading strategy of the member. This chapter does not give criteria to choose among the CCPs, but tries to provide insight on the fees charged by the most relevant CCPs in Europe.

5. CONCLUSION

The chapter underlines some aspects of European Central Counterparty Clearing and its evolution in the last years, especially with respect to the pricing condition applied by some of the most relevant European CCPs.

The literature on the issue of Central Counterparty Clearing has been quite controversial. There has been however consensus in underlining the importance of the costs related to this service. Fees charged by CCPs can represent an important fraction of total costs paid overall by traders for trading and post-trading services [European Commission, Competition DG, 2006].

Part of the literature claims that the type of structure of the subjects providing services on trading and post-trading markets can influence the prices [Knieps, G., 2006].

The level of clearing fees charged by some CCPs is computed. The CCPs chosen for the analysis are the following: LCH.Clearnet Ltd, LCH.Clearnet SA, Eurex Clearing AG, CC&G and SIX x-clear. The results suggest that it is not possible to build a univocal qualitative relationship between the structure of the CCP and the level of fees charged.

CCPs in vertical silos are expected to charge higher fees. While this can be true for Eurex Clearing, two other CCPs part of vertical silos, CC&G and SIX x-clear, charge fees generally lower than the average.

The level of fees might likewise depend on many factors, related to the costs borne by the CCP or to the level of efficiency. The lack of reliable and complete data does not allow us to evaluate this issue in depth.

Pricing conditions from end of 2008 to the beginning of 2010 have been compared. The results show a general decrease in the level of clearing fees. Our results are consistent with the findings of the European Commission [European Commission, Competition DG, 2006; European Commission, Internal Market and Services DG, 2009].

It can be concluded, therefore, that the introduction of the Code of Conduct and the legislative provision in this direction (e.g. Mifid) might have caused a decrease in clearing fees. The implementation of common standards and more transparent pricing structures might have helped in comparability, which finally resulted in a consistent reduction in clearing fees.

We acknowledge that the reduction of prices could be also due to other factors. However, in some cases, there is an impressive drop in fees which could be hardly attributed only to increase in the level of efficiency.

APPENDIX

Table A.1. Evolution of average Clearing and Membership fee (aCMF).

Panel A				Panel C			
User A				User C			
Number of trades	959,802.00			Number of trades	1,919,604.00		
Average trade size	45,810.00			Average trade size	91,619.00		
Average daily trades	3,763.93			Average daily trades	7,527.86		
	dec-08	jan-09	feb-10		dec-08	jan-09	feb-10
Lch.Ltd LSE	0.19	0.19	0.13	Lch.Ltd LSE	0.19	0.19	0.12
UK°				UK°			
Lch.Ltd SIX*	0.13	0.13	0.11	Lch.Ltd SIX*	0.13	0.13	0.11
Lch.SA	0.65	0.65	0.09	Lch.SA	0.63	0.63	0.08
Eurex Ise	0.23	0.23	0.23	Eurex Ise	0.21	0.21	0.21
Eurex FWB	1.01	0.66	0.66	Eurex FWB	1.69	1.11	0.98
CC&G	0.16	0.16	0.16	CC&G	0.14	0.14	0.08
SIX	0.13	0.13	0.13	SIX	0.08	0.10	0.10
mean	0.36	0.31	0.21	mean	0.44	0.36	0.24
std. dev.	0.32	0.22	0.19	std. dev.	0.32	0.35	0.30

Panel B				Panel D			
User B				User D			
Number of trades	1,919,604.00			Number of trades	479,901.00		
Average trade size	22,905.00			Average trade size	22,905.00		
Average daily trades	7,527.86			Average daily trades	1,881.96		

Table A.1. Continued

	dec-08	jan-09	feb-10		dec-08	jan-09	feb-10
Lch.Ltd LSE	0.19	0.19	0.12	Lch.Ltd LSE	0.19	0.19	0.14
UK°				UK°			
Lch.Ltd SIX*	0.13	0.13	0.11	Lch.Ltd SIX*	0.13	0.13	0.11
Lch.SA	0.62	0.62	0.08	Lch.SA	0.70	0.70	0.08
Eurex Ise	0.21	0.21	0.21	Eurex Ise	0.25	0.25	0.25
Eurex FWB	0.66	0.42	0.42	Eurex FWB	0.70	0.46	0.34
CC&G	0.14	0.14	0.08	CC&G	0.17	0.17	0.17
SIX	0.08	0.10	0.10	SIX	0.23	0.15	0.15
mean	0.29	0.26	0.16	mean	0.34	0.29	0.18
std. dev.	0.32	0.18	0.11	std. dev.	0.32	0.20	0.08

Since December 2008 till February 2010 there has been a substantial reduction in aCMF for all users, on average. All CCPs have reduced their fees or kept them equal. The only exception is SIX x-clear for users B and C that used to pay 0.08 Euros as aCMF as at December 2008 and after the change in pricing paid 0.10 Euros. This might be due to simplification on the computation of aCMF for SIX x-clear and also to the change in the pricing structure. The fee is however lower than the mean

REFERENCES

Baglioni, A., Hamaui R. (2006). L'organizzazione industriale del post-trading. *Banca Impresa Società, vol. 25, f. 3,* pp. 407-424.

BCE. (2001). Eurosystem's policy line with regard to consolidation in central counterparty clearing. http://www.ecb.int/pub/pdf/other/centralcounterpartyclearingen.pdf

Bliss, R., Papathanassiou C. (2006). Derivatives clearing, central counterparties and novation: The economic implications. http://www.ecb.int/events/pdf/conferences/ccp/ BlissPapathanassiou_final.pdf

CC&G. (2008). Corrispettivi 2008. http://www.ccg.it/jportal/pcontroller/AllegatoHandler/ Corrispettivi%202008.pdf?lingua=1&allegato=65169&azioneprossima=21

CC&G. (2009). Fee schedule for the Central Counterparty guarantee system in force from 26 November 2009. http://www.ccg.it/jportal/pcontroller/AllegatoHandler/CC&G% 20pricing%20ITA%20con%20IDEX.pdf?lingua=2&allegato=81700&azioneprossima=21

CESAME. (2005a). Clearing and settlement impact assessment. http:// ec.europa.eu/internal_market/financial-markets/docs/clearing/draft/draft_en.pdf

CESAME. (2005b). Synthesis Report on the meeting held on 10 June 2005. http://ec.europa.eu/internal_market/financial-markets/docs/cesame/meetings/20050610-report_en.pdf

CESAME. (2005c). Commission Services Working Document on Definitions of Post-trading Activities. *Working document /MARKT/SLG/G2 (2005) D15283.* http://ec.europa.eu/ internal_market/financial-markets/docs/cesame/ec-docs/20051027_definitions1_en.pdf

CPSS-IOSCO: Commission on Payment and Settlement System (CPSS), Technical Committee of the International Organization of Securities Commission (IOSCO). (2004a). Recommendation for Central Counterparties.
http://www.bis.org/publ/cpss64.pdf?noframes=1

CPSS-IOSCO: Commission on Payment and Settlement System (CPSS), Technical Committee of the International Organization of Securities Commission (IOSCO). (2004b). Recommendation for Central Counterparties – Consultative Report.
http://www.bis.org/publ/cpss61.pdf

Eurex. (2006). Circular 255/06: Price list of Eurex Clearing AG: changes in relation to the implementation of "Code of Conduct". http://www.eurexchange.com/download /documents/circulars/cf2552006e.pdf

Eurex Clearing AG. (2006). Clearing Brochure.
http://www.eurexclearing.com/documents/publications/brochure_en.html

Eurex Clearing AG. (2008a). Clearing Conditions for Eurex Clearing AG. http://www. eurexclearing.com/download/documents/regulations/clearing_conditions/clearing_conditi ons_en.pdf

Eurex Clearing AG. (2008b). Pricing for Eurex Clearing AG. http://www. eurexclearing.com/download/documents/regulations/price_list/price_list_clearing_en.pdf

Eurex Clearing AG. (2010). Price list for Eurex Clearing AG. http://www. eurexchange.com/download/documents/regulations/price_list/price_list_clearing_en.pdf

European Commission, Competition DG. (2006). Competition in EU securities trading and post-trading – Issues Paper.
http://ec.europa.eu/competition/sectors/financial_services/securities_trading.pdf

European Commission, Internal Market and Services DG (and Financial Services Policy and Financial Markets, Financial markets infrastructure). (2007). Monitoring Implementation of the Code of Conduct for Clearing and Settlement. http://ec.europa.eu/ internal_market/financial-markets/docs/clearing/ecofin/20070228_ecofin_en.pdf

European Commission, Internal Market and Services DG. (2008). Improving the efficiency, integration and safety and soundness of cross border post-trading arrangements in Europe, Third Progress Report to Economic and Financial Affairs Council (ECOFIN). http://ec.europa.eu/internal_market/financial-markets/docs/clearing/ecofin/20080311_ecofin_en.pdf

European Commission, Internal Market and Services DG. (2009). The Code Of Conduct On Clearing And Settlement: Three Years Of Experience. http://ec.europa.eu/internal_ market/financial-markets/docs/code/2009-11-06-code-report-ecofin_en.pdf

European Financial Services Round Table. (2003). Securities clearing and settlement in Europe.
http://www.efr.be/members/upload/publications/63324clearing%20settlement.pdf

Evanoff, D.D., Russo, D., Steigerwald, R.S.. (2006). Policymakers, researchers and practitioners discuss the role of central counterparties, *Economic Perspective, 4Q/2006, vol. 30 num 4,* pp.2-21.
http://www.chicagofed.org/digital_assets/publications/economic_perspectives/2006/ep_4 qtr2006_part1_evanoff_etal.pdf

FESE, EACH, ECSDA. (2006). European Code of Conduct for Clearing and Settlement. http://ec.europa.eu/internal_market/financial-markets/docs/code/code_en.pdf

FESE, EACH, ECSDA. (2007). Access and Interoperability Guideline. http://ec.europa.eu/internal_market/financial-markets/docs/code/guideline_en.pdf

Giordano, F. (2002). Cross-Border trading in financial securities in Europe: the role of central counterparty, *ECMI Short paper n. 3*.

Hills, B., Rule, D., Parkinson, S. (1999). Central counterparty clearing houses and financial stability, *Financial Stability Review June 1999, Bank of England*, pp 122-133.

Hirata de Carvalho, C. (2004). Cross-Border Securities Clearing and Settlement Infrastructure in the European Union as a Prerequisite to Financial Markets Integration: Challenges and Perspective. *HWWA Discussion Paper 287*. http://ec.europa.eu/internal_market/financial-markets/docs/cesame/hwwa_discussion_paper_en.pdf

Knieps, G. (2006). Competition in the post-trade markets – A network economic analysis of the securities business. *Journal of Industry, Competition and Trade, Springer, vol. 6(1)*, pp 45-60.

Knott, R., Mills, A. (2002). Modelling risk in central counterparty clearing houses: a review. *Financial Stability Review, December 2002*, pp 162-174.

Koeppl, T.V., Monnet, C. (2008). Central Counterparties, *CFS Working Paper No. 2008/42*.

LCH.Clearnet Ltd. (2008a). EquityClear® Service Description. http://www.lchclearnet.com/Images/equityclear_service_description_v1.5_tcm6-46315.pdf

LCH.Clearnet Ltd. (2008b). General Regulation, Default Rules, Settlement Finality and Procedures (Clearing House procedures). http://www.lchclearnet.com/Images/rules_and_regulations_tcm6-43733.pdf

LCH.Clearnet Ltd. (2009). EquityClear® Fees from 1st July 2009. http://www.lchclearnet.com/Images/equityclear_fees_from_1st_July_2009_tcm6-49880.pdf

LCH.Clearnet SA. (2008). Clearing Rule Book. http://www.lchclearnet.com/Images/Clearing%20Rule%20Book%20updated%2026june%202008_tcm6-44081.pdf

LCH.Clearnet SA. (2010). LCH.Clearnet SA Fees CASH MARKETS. http://www.lchclearnet.com/Images/SA%20Fee%20grid%20-%20Cash%2020100201_tcm6-53376.pdf

London Stock Exchange (LSE). (2008). Service Description – competitive clearing. http://www.londonstockexchange.com/NR/rdonlyres/9339C609-E5E8-4C38-B4F4-A94E0467DAFC/0/CompetitiveClearingServiceDescriptionversion12.pdf

MOG: Monitoring Group of the Code of Conduct on Clearing and Settlement. (2008). ECSA feedback in relation to price transparency and comparability implementation. http://ec.europa.eu/internal_market/financial-markets/clearing/mog/20080409_ecsa_1_en.pdf

Padoa Schioppa, T. (2006). Central Counterparty: the role of multilateralism and monopoly. *Economic Perspective, Federal Reserve Bank of Chicago, vol. 30 num 4, Fourth Quarter 2006.* https://www.ecb.int/pub/pdf/other/rolecentralcounterparties200707en.pdf

Ripatti, K. (2004). Central counterparty clearing: constructing a framework for evaluation of risks and benefits. *Bank of Finland Research Discussion Paper No. 30/2004*. http://ssrn.com/abstract=787606

SIS Group. (2007). Annual Report 2007. http://www.ccp.sisclear.com/ccp/annualreport07.pdf

SIX x-clear. (2008a). Clearing Terms SIS x-clear AG for SIX Europe. http://www.ccp.sisclear.com/ccp/xclear-dienstleistung.pdf

SIX x-clear. (2008b). Explanation of clearing fee calculation. http://www.ccp.sisclear.com/ccp/fees-explanation-080201.pdf

SIX x-clear. (2008c). New pricing model as of 1 January 2009 http://www.ccp.sisclear.com/ccp/fees-ccp-081204-letter-new-price-model.pdf

SIX x-clear. (2008d). Pricing SIS x-clear (CCP). http://www.ccp.sisclear.com/ccp/fees-ccp-081101.pdf

The Giovannini Group. (2001). Cross-border Clearing and Settlement Arrangements in the European Union. http://ec.europa.eu/internal_market/financial-markets/docs/clearing/first_giovannini_report_en.pdf

The Giovannini Group. (2003). Second Report on EU Clearing and Settlement Arrangements. http://ec.europa.eu/internal_market/financial-markets/docs/clearing/second_giovannini_report_en.pdf

Trichet, J.C. (2006). Issues related to central counterparty clearing. *Speech delivered in occasion of the Joint European Central Bank - Federal Reserve Bank of Chicago conference.* http://www.ecb.int/press/key/date/2006/html/sp060404.en.html

- www.borsaitaliana.it
- www.ccg.it
- www.ccp.sisclear.com
- www.eachorg.eu
- www.eurexclearing.com
- www.lchclearnet.com
- www.londonstockexchange.com
- www.six-group.co

In: Financial Services: Efficiency and Risk Management
Editors: M. D. Fethi, C. Gaganis et al.

ISBN: 978-1-62100-560-5
© 2012 Nova Science Publishers, Inc.

Chapter 7

DO GREEK MUTUAL FUNDS INVESTING ABROAD OUTPERFORM?

Stephanos Papadamou and Konstantina Kiriazi
Department of Economics, University of Thessaly, Volos, Hellas.

ABSTRACT

By investigating Greek Mutual funds investing abroad for the period 2002 to 2008, this chapter tries to shed light on the home bias puzzle from a small country concentrated fund industry. By calculating traditional measures of performance and following rolling regression technique the paper provides evidence that Greek fund managers investing abroad do not outperform the market and do not present any timing skills. In order to achieve better performance than their benchmark they choose to follow different asset allocation as it is implied by our analysis.

JEL Codes: G1, G2
Keywords: Mutual Funds, Investment Performance

INTRODUCTION

Institutional investors, notably professional managers, have played an immensely important role in the stock market development of a country and consequently on its economic development. Their behavior has significant implications also for market efficiency.

In the mutual fund literature, while there are plenty of studies investigating the performance of fund managers in their local market there is a lack of systematic research on their trading behavior across borders and the informativeness of their cross-border trading activity in securities markets. Thus, the goal of this chapter is to address these critical issues in a small country with low capitalized stock market and with low level of trading activity.

Theoretical models of cross-border equity flows (Griffin, et al., 2004; Brennan et al., 2005) show that investors trade differently in foreign and domestic markets. These models argue that investors have more information about their own local stocks than do foreign investors, or that they have less information about foreign stocks than do foreign investors.

Researchers have proposed several explanations for the fact that investors prefer investing in local equity markets than abroad (the well known home country bias). Adler and Dumas (1983) and Cooper and Kaplanis (1994), for example, suggest that this bias arises because home assets provide better hedges against country specific risks. Graham et al. (2005) suggest that investors are willing to invest in foreign securities only after they fill competent about the benefits and risks involved in these investments. Lastly, Kilka and Weber (2000) and Strong and Xu (2003) provide a behavioral explanation for the home country bias: this bias arises because investors tend to be more optimistic towards home markets than towards international markets.

On the other hand, there are reasons to expect that institutional investors might follow similar trading strategies in their cross-border equity investments. Institutions are perceived to be sophisticated and resourceful (Shukla and Van Inwegen, 1995; Grinblatt and Keloharju, 2000) and would more likely to adopt the same investment strategies as they diversify into different markets. Based on data from single countries, empirical studies show substantial evidence that sophisticated institutional investors exhibit momentum behavior in the U.S. (for example, Grinblatt, et al., 1995) Korea (Choe et al. , 1999), and Finland (Grinblatt and Keloharju, 2000).

In Greece, after the significant increase of the stock market during 1999 a significant downward trend follows and lasts for almost four years until the end of 2003. Investors not convinced about the Greek stock market tried to find different types of investments that give them the opportunity to invest abroad. The fund industry in Greece following this trend created equity fund portfolios that invest in USA, Europe or Worldwide. Therefore Greece is an interesting case study of a small equity fund industry that after a significant bubble and its burst, mutual funds that invest abroad became an alternative type of investment for Greek investors. The main question that arises is whether Greek fund managers by presenting timing skills can achieve persistent performance abroad.

MUTUAL FUNDS AND MARKET EFFICIENCY IMPLICATIONS

In the beginning of the sixties a debate started about the asset pricing formulation. The main research question developed was whether stock prices are independent or not, the well known random walk hypothesis. If stock prices follow a random walk then historical information cannot be used for making money in a systematic way. Therefore academic community by trying to explain stock prices behaviour developed the theory of Market Efficiency. According to Fama (1965) a market can be characterized as efficient if all the available information is fully reflected in stock prices. Stock prices have the 'fair value' or the divergence from this value is due to transaction costs therefore abnormal returns cannot be achieved.

Similarly, Jensen (1968) argued that market efficiency should be tested in a specific set of information used. Risk adjusted return measures net from transaction costs should be used according to Jensen. In other words the marginal cost of obtaining information is equal to the marginal benefit from using it. The stock market prices in each time are based on two information sets. The first one is the information or data set available to investors and the other is their preferences. If we assume time constant investors' preferences and that investors react only to the new available information, we can summarize the implication of market efficiency as follows.

First, the observed market prices are equilibrium prices or in a statistical meaning they are unbiased estimators of equilibrium prices. Second, the observed market prices reflect every time all the available information. Finally, the prices that presents the above two characteristics will follow a random walk (Thomadakis et al., 2006).

Following works by Fama (1970, 1976) and Jensen (1968) we can identify three forms of market efficiency. Under weak market efficiency historical information cannot be used to achieve abnormal returns. Under semi-strong market efficiency any published information cannot also help us to achieve systematic profit. There is no time lag in reflection of information in prices. Under strong market efficiency neither public nor private information can lead to statistical significant profits.

Market efficiency over the last years have be criticised mainly by market analysts and some academics. They argued that some investor can beat the market due to asymmetric information. To beat the market in some cases or for a while does not mean that systematically beat the market and does not provide evidence against market efficiency. However, even in the case that you achieve a better performance than the market, after a while the ability of forecasting will be available in a wider set of investor and therefore this advantage disappears. Another view is that smart money coexists with noise traders. Finally, another important point that should be mentioned is that market efficiency is tested jointly with an asset pricing model. Therefore the assumption of the asset pricing model is crucial about the formulation of risk and consequently the final result about market efficiency or not.

The market efficiency in its strong form implies that no one can achieve abnormal returns by using public and private information. There have been a series of studies providing evidence concerning strong market efficiency by investigating the performance of mutual fund managers (see among many Sharpe, 1966; Ippolito, 1989; Elton et al 1993). This type of investments is selected mainly due to the fact that institutional investors might be closer to the source of information concerning fundamental values of companies. If these fund managers can achieve high performance this implies that some investors can use private information to make money.

However an interesting research question in the mutual fund literature is whether fund managers in a small country, like Greece, in a period that follows the burst of the local stock market bubble, can achieve significant performance by investing abroad. Do they mimic investment style of broader benchmark indices? Do they present any timing skills? These are some other interesting research questions investigated in this chapter.

The answer to these research questions can provide significant implications for the market efficiency in this market. Before getting further it is crucial to report what implies market efficiency. If one market can be characterized as efficient this implies that:

- The marginal benefit from analysts is zero.
- Investors that follow famous investment strategies cannot achieve systematically high performance.
- The benefits from fundamental analysis are offset from the cost of collecting fundamental data.

- A passive management strategy with high level of diversification across assets and small number of transactions is the dominant and the most performed strategy.
- Prices can diverge from equilibrium but these divergences are random.
- The fact that a fund manager can have a better performance for a time period than the market can be explained by lack.
- Portfolio management is important even in the case of market efficiency because there should covers the risk profile of each investor.

LITERATURE REVIEW

One of the first important studies concerning mutual fund performance is conducted by Sharpe (1966) who investigated the risk adjusted performance of 34 mutual funds over the period 1954-1963. In his study Sharpe, found that 19 of 34 funds presented higher performance compared to the market portfolio. However, when considering transaction costs only 11 out of 34, remain with higher performance to the benchmark. He argues that stock market is efficient but fund managers that correctly price risks can beat the market by diversify their portfolio.

Another important study is published by Jensen (1968) that investigates 115 mutual funds for the period 1945 to 1964. His empirical findings indicate that only 43 out of 115 presented high risk adjusted returns. By looking the returns of mutual funds on average are lower than the market returns even if their betas are higher than one. Overall Jensen argues for random walk and against market efficiency.

The empirical studies by Henriksson (1984), Chang and Lewellen (1984) covering the seventies found that net returns of funds before load fees are in capital market line. This implies that fund managers have private information that can help them to trade off their fees, but not to achieve better performance than the market.

Few years later Ippolito (1989) by studying 143 mutual funds for the period 1965-1984 found that fund alphas are positive even after considering transaction costs. The study of Elton, et al. (1993) comes to explain Ippolito's findings. They argued that portfolios with low correlation to S&P 500 should be considered differently. When this is taken into account Ippolito findings change and are in accordance with previous literature. They provide evidence for passive management. Funds charging high level of fees do not beat the market.

Evidence for market efficiency is also provided by Malkiel (1995) and by Carhart (1997) that suggest avoid funds with persistent low past performance. Additionally funds with previous positive performance do not indicate a persistent performance through time.

Daniel et al. (1997) by setting funds to different categories based among others on their characteristics like capitalization and book-to-market value, found that abnormal returns were absent. Changing investment style can help improve their performance in some cases however there is no clear evidence of timing skills for fund managers.

Papadamou and Siriopoulos (2004) by investigating 19 European equity funds investing in USA, provide evidence against active management and style drift. The most valuable investment style is those that focus mainly on diversification benefits.

The main findings of these studies provide evidence for market efficiency. Therefore fund managers face an increase level of competition in such environment. However, there is a number of studies providing evince against market efficiency.

Among others Jaffe (1974) argued that inside information can lead to abnormal returns and regulation concerning inside information cannot make a lot in USA. Ambachtsheer (1974) in his study examines whether fund managers can forecast stock prices movements. If fund managers do not have this ability to forecast then the correlation between fund performance and their forecast should be low. His findings indicate a low but non zero correlation (0,16) implying a weak forecasting performance can lead to abnormal returns.

We should mention at this point that previous literature provides evidence for market efficiency in seventies and after nineties. During eighties the significant increase of institutional investors, like mutual and pension funds in line with the significant increase of technology that help information to be available very quickly lead to instability of financial markets. However after the end of eighties mimicking behavior reduce the possibility of having consistent abnormal returns.

In case of Greece, there have been a series of studies focusing on fund performance but none of these investigated the ability of Greek fund managers investing abroad to achieve consistent performance. A similar study investigating the performance of American Fund managers investing in Europe is done by Papadamou and Siriopoulos (2004).This study investigates α and b for funds by allowing time variation of these parameters and taking into account any timing skills presented on fund managers.

Among previous studies that have been focused on the Greek Mutual Fund market, Babalos, et al. (2008) investigate the ex-post verification problem for equity funds investing locally. The probability of having persistent performance in Greek funds during the period 1998-2004 can be explained by modeling correctly risk. Under taking into account and correctly modeling risk persistent positive returns can be presented only for a short period before 2001 (Babalos et al., 2007).The opening of the small Greek capital market to foreign investors can explain a significant part of this finding.

Babalos et al. (2009) found that the Greek equity funds' performance is negatively related to their expenses, while investors' flows are not directly affected by expenses. Furthermore, the funds affiliated with one of the three dominant domestic banking groups achieve higher performance and attract higher net flows in comparison to their competitors in a small emerging market with an oligopolistic, bank-dominated financial system.

Moreover, Philippas (1999) by investigating equity funds investing locally reveal any ability of the Greek managers to time the market correctly or select undervalued securities. In contrary, five out of nineteen mutual funds present a negative statistical significant coefficient of market timing.

Finally, concerning bond funds in Greece the results are quite similar to Greek equity funds, in the study of Dritsakis et al. (2006). In this case also the fund cannot achieve abnormal returns compared to their benchmarks. Moreover in the case that management fees are taking into account the funds underperforms the benchmark.

DATA AND METHODOLOGY

The Greek Mutual Fund Market

The entrance of mutual funds in the Greek Capital Market has been allowed by a law in 1970. However the first fund is created by the Greek Commercial bank two years later. One year later, National Bank of Greece and "Interamerican" an insurance company also created their mutual funds and these were the only active funds in the Greek market until 1989. After the liberalization of the Greek capital markets in the end of eighties, the growth of the mutual fund industry in Greece was rapid. Therefore even if in the year 1990 only seven mutual funds existed in the Greek market in the end of 2005 this number was 258.

In the year 1999 there have been a significant increase in Greek Stock market mainly explained by the low interest rate environment due to the Greece entrance to common currency. A huge level of liquidity is directed toward Athens stock exchange in a low interest rate environment. However, the increase in the Greek stock market lasts for almost six months and after that period a downward trend lasts for many years.

Figure 1 provides useful information concerning share of asset values by type of fund. The money market funds investing in Greece attracts the majority of Greek Funds. Especially after the significant drop of the Greek stock market from 2000 to the end of 2003, indicating investors' preferences over short term liquid assets. However over the more recent years there is a clear trend for investing abroad mainly in money market funds but also on equity funds. Greek equity funds investing locally seem to exhibit low variation for the period 2002 to 2008.

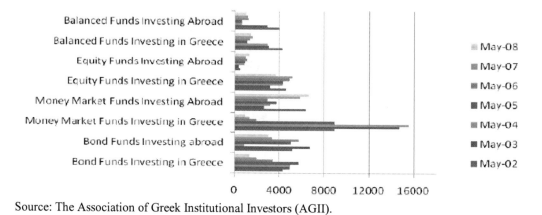

Source: The Association of Greek Institutional Investors (AGII).

Figure 1. Net asset values (in million Euros) by type of funds in the Greek Market.

The significant increase of the bond fund market during the period 2002-2003 has been explained by the significant drop of the stock market for all these years. Since 2003 an upward trend is also present in the equity fund market. However this time equity mutual funds investing abroad came to capture the need for investing outside the volatile Greek market.

This study investigates the mutual funds in Greek market that invest abroad. More specifically they invest in Europe, USA and all over the world. The following table presents sample of funds investigated. Eleven funds are investigated. Four of them invest in Europe, three in USA and four globally. The relevant weekly data for theses funds are collected from the Association of Greek Institutional Investors (AGII).

As benchmark indices are used the TMI for Europe, the S&P500 for USA and GLOBAL1800 for funds investing worldwide. Theses indices are collected from www.stoxx.com. The STOXX Europe Total Market Index (TMI) covers 95% of the free market capitalization of 18 European countries (Austria, Belgium, Denmark, Finland, France, Germany, Greece, Iceland, Ireland, Italy, Luxembourg, Holland, Norway, Portugal, Spain, Sweden, Switzerland and United Kingdom).

Table 1. Greek Mutual Funds Investing Abroad

Fund Title	Asset Management Company
Global	
ALLIANZ A/K MILLENIUM	ALLIANZ AEΔAK
ING A/K GLOBAL	ING AEΔAK
MARFIN GLOBAL	MARFIN GLOBAL ASSET MANAGEMENT CO.
DILOS	NATIONAL BANK ASSET MANAGEMENT CO.
Europe	
ALPHA EUROPE	ALPHA ASSET MANAGEMENT
HSBC PANEUROPEAN	HSBC ASSET MANAGEMENT CO.
INTERAMERICAN NEW EUROPE	EFG ASSET MANAGEMENT CO.
DILOS	NATIONAL BANK ASSET MANAGEMENT CO.
America	
ALPHA US	ALPHA ASSET MANAGEMENT CO.
ATE US	ATE ASSET MANAGEMENT CO.
MILLENNIUM AMERICA US	MILLENNIUM ASSET MANAGEMENT CO.

The STOXX Global 1800 Index includes 1800 stocks and covers mainly developed stock markets (600 European stocks, 600 American stocks and 600 Asian stocks). Returns are calculated in a weekly basis. As a risk free rate is used the Euribor for funds investing in Europe. While the effective federal fund rate for funds investing in USA. These data are collected from the IFS database provided by the IMF.

METHODOLOGY

The research methodology consists of two main parts. In the first part descriptive statistics can help reader to classify funds. Traditional measures of investment performance are used to classify funds. Risk adjusted measures of performance that are based on Capital Asset Pricing Model (CAPM) are calculated (Jensen alpha, Sharpe and Treynor ratios).

On the one hand, Sharpe ratio use standard deviation of returns as measure of total risk in order to calculate risk adjusted excess returns (Sharpe, 1966). Excess returns are calculated if we subtract risk free interest rate (RFR) from fund returns.

$$S_p = \frac{R_p - RFR}{\sigma_p} \qquad (1)$$

On the other hand, Treynor (1965) by assuming diversifying funds uses beta as a measure of systematic risk.

$$T_p = \frac{R_p - RFR}{\beta_p} \qquad (2)$$

Treynor ratio measures the ability of a fund manager to achieve better returns by selectivity skills compared to another manager with a similar level of systematic risk. Sharpe ratio measures can also be used to compare different fund managers but indicates also if fund manager can diversify effectively its portfolio. In this study Sharpe and Treynor indices are calculated for the whole period but also in a yearly basis in order to investigate their stability over time. Then Jensen alpha is calculated by estimating the following regression:

$$R_{p,t} - RFR_t = a_p + \beta_p \times (R_{M,t} - RFR_t) \qquad (3)$$

After having estimated the coefficients α_p and β_p then their time stability is investigated by adopting a rolling regression technique. For the linear regression model, rolling analysis may be used to assess the stability of the model's parameters and to provide a simple "poor man's" time varying parameter model. For a specific time window n < T, the rolling linear regression model may be expressed as:

$$y_t(n) = x_t(n) \cdot b_t(n) + e_t(n), \text{ t=n,.....,T} \qquad (4)$$

Where $y_t(n)$ is a (n×1) vector of observations, $x_t(n)$ is an (n×k) matrix of the explanatory variables, $b_t(n)$ is a (k×1) vector of parameters of interest and $e_t(n)$ is the (n×1) residual vector. The n observations in $y_t(n)$ and $x_t(n)$ are the n most recent values from times t-n+1 to t.

In the third step of our methodology, any timing skills presented in Greek fund managers investing abroad, are detected. The traditional measures of performance evaluate the selectivity skills of fund managers. However, as the risk premium of the market is time varying some of the fund managers change their asset allocation. In order to investigate whether a fund manager presents timing skills, Treynor and Mazuy (1966) developed the Quadratic Model. If fund managers have timing skills, this means that they increase their beta when the market follows an increasing trend and they reduce it when there is a downward trend. This can be easily achieved by changing the asset allocation across different type of assets or in each specific asset category by changing from offensive to defensive assets. This model is constructed in order to capture any possible non-linear relationship between fund returns and benchmark returns.

In line with the quadratic model of Treynor and Mazuy (1966), we estimated the following regression in order to investigate any timing skills presented in Greek fund managers that invest abroad.

$$R_{it} - RFR_t = a_i + \beta_i \times (R_{Mt} - RFR_t) + \gamma_i \times (R_{Mt} - RFR_t)^2 + \varepsilon_{it} \quad (5)$$

Where R_{it}, and R_{Mt} the weekly returns for the i fund and the market portfolio respectively. RFR is the risk free rate. The a_i, estimator represents the asset selection ability of the fund manager, the β_i measures the systematic risk of mutual fund and the γ_i indicates any timing skill present on the fund manager. The lack of statistical importance of γ estimator implies naturally lack of corresponding skill of the fund manager. The residual term ε_{it} measures the non-explanatory share of returns and has expected return zero. Next figure shows graphically a fund manager that presents timing skills.

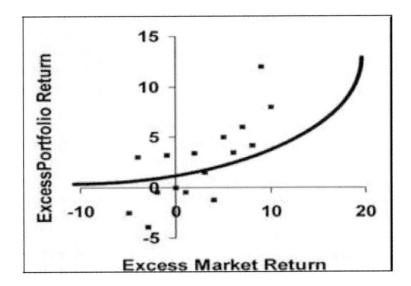

Figure 2. Timing Skill present based on Treynor & Mazuy 'Quadratic Model'.

When $\gamma_i >$ is positive and statistical significant the fund manager can be implied to have a timing skill. This means that they are placed temporally suitably in the market, by regulating beta factor depending on the changes that expect to happen in the market. When they expect increasing market yields they change their asset allocation by increasing the percentage of assets in their funds with more systematic risk. On the contrary, when the market yields are expected to decrease, the share of low risk assets is increased in their portfolios.

EMPIRICAL RESULTS

As mentioned in the methodology part, Sharpe and Treynor ratios are calculated for each fund for the whole sample period and presented in the following table 2. According to Sharpe and Treynor ratios, only three out of eleven funds outperform the benchmark. Another important point is that none of these funds invests in USA, two in Europe and one has a global investment strategy. By looking betas only four funds present values more than 0.80 and none of these funds invests in USA. Concerning alpha Jensen coefficient only Allianz and Hsbc funds outperform benchmark with statistical significance.

Table 2. Traditional Performance measures for the whole sample period

Mutual Funds	Sharpe Ratio	Treynor Ratio	Alpha coefficient	Beta coefficient
Global Benchmark	-0,0628	-0,0015	-	-
Allianz	0,0247	0,0008	0,0029 (2,94)***	0,7591 (11,71)***
Ing	-0,0668	-0,0017	0,0001 (0,11)	0,9155 (52,00)***
Dilos	-0,0657	-0,0025	0,0006 (1,75)	0,4588 (19,87)***
Marfin	-0,0688	-0,0019	-0,0005 (-1,12)	0,8805 (30,79)***
European Benchmark	-0,0461	-0,0013	-	-
Alpha	-0,0490	-0,0014	-0,0001 (-0,76)	0,9208 (157,41)***
Interam	0,0115	0,0004	0,0016 (1,09)	0,9200 (8,46)***
Dilos	-0,0646	-0,0028	0,0005 (1,32)	0,4812 (14,09)***
Hsbc	-0,0099	-0,0003	0,0008 (2,52)***	0,7508 (43,82)***
USA Benchmark	-0,0387	-0,0009	-	-
Alpha	-0,0957	-0,0039	-0,0017 (-1,67)	0,6479 (11,06)***
Millennium	-0,0601	-0,0024	-0,0005 (-0,89)	0,4622 (7,83)***
Ate	-0,0727	-0,0032	-0,0007 (-0,91)	0,4254 (10,64)***

Note: Numbers in parentheses are t-statistics,
*** indicates statistical significance at 99% level of significance.

In the next step of our empirical investigation Sharpe ratio and Treynor ratio are calculated on a yearly basis in order to investigate any time varying effect for the period from 2002 to 2008. By looking Sharpe ratios in figure 3a, the funds present a quite similar behavior, with the lower values occurred on funds investing in USA. Among funds that invest worldwide only Allianz fund outperforms persistently the market. While Dilos and Marfin funds achieve better performance compared to the benchmark only occasionally. Concerning funds investing in Europe few funds outperform the benchmark but for a short period. Exception being the Interamerican fund which underperforms the market only in 2005. The Hsbc, Dilos and Alpha funds present high performance mainly only during the recent period. By looking funds investing in USA none of these funds presents persistence in outperforming the market. The Terynor ratios confirm all the above in figure 3b.

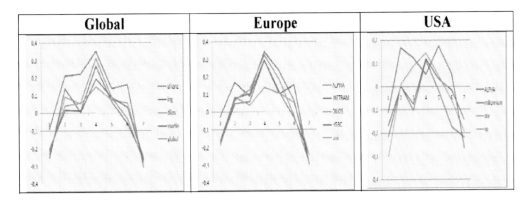

Figure 3a. Sharpe ratio per year.

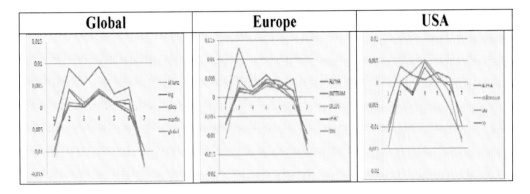

Figure 3b. Treynor ratio per year.

In the next step of our methodology time constancy of the alpha and beta coefficient is investigated. Equation 3 is estimated in a fixed three years rolling window. The estimates are presented graphically in figures 4a,b,c. As can be easily seen there is evidence of time varying coefficients. Only Allianz and Hsbc funds achieved a positive and statistical significant alpha and not for the whole period examined. For Allianz the positive performance achieved over the first period of investigation where its beta was small. Similarly Hsbc fund that invests in European stock markets outperformed over the second period where its beta was small. This implies that their asset allocation diverges from their benchmark in order to outperform.

The beta coefficients is time varying with ING and Marfin funds to present the higher degree of instability. It seems that fund managers follow several strategies in order to outperform the market but their results are poor by looking the alpha coefficients.

For the funds investing in Europe, Alpha fund underperforms the market over the first period that presents also high beta. Generally speaking lowering their betas coexists with improving performance. In this type of funds the betas are closer to one compared to the funds investing in USA or worldwide.

Finally by looking funds investing in USA, they present the worst performance but in theses cases also the fund manager improvement in performance coexist with lower betas. Moreover in contrast with the funds investing in Europe or Worldwide, theses funds present betas with significant variety. After 2004 their betas can be characterized by a greater degree of stability.

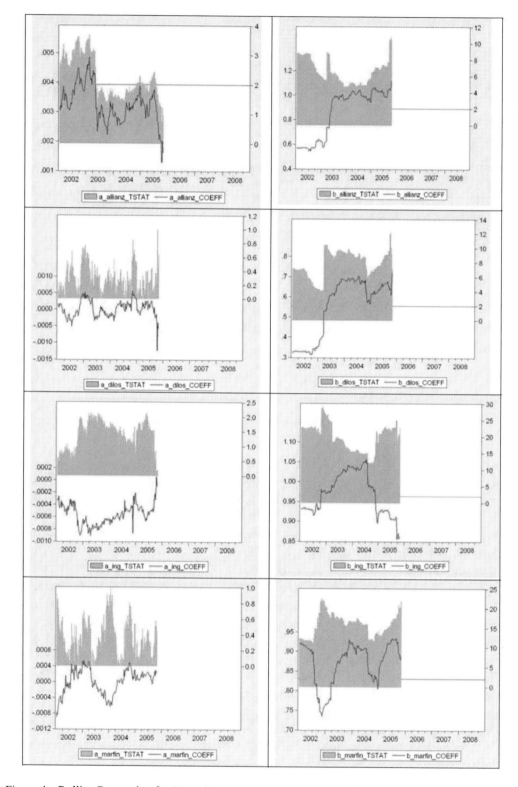

Figure 4a. Rolling Regression for Mutual Funds Investing Worldwide Global Market.

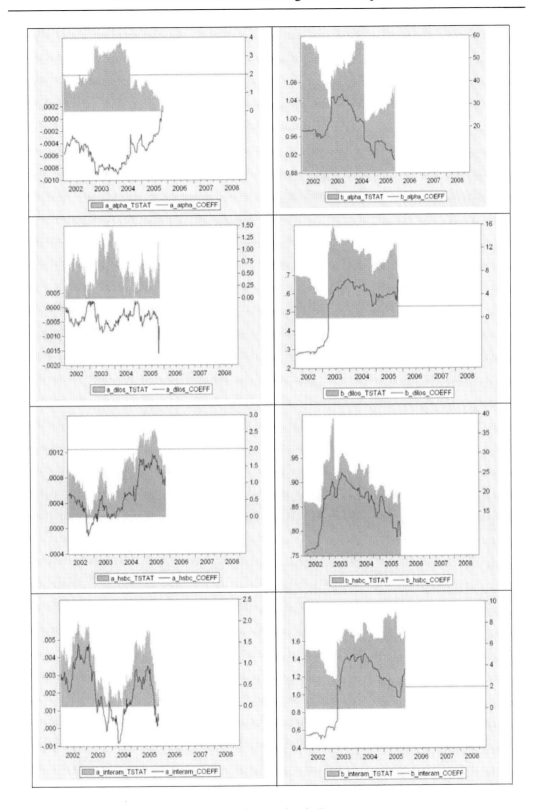

Figure 4b. Rolling Regression for Mutual Funds Investing in Europe.

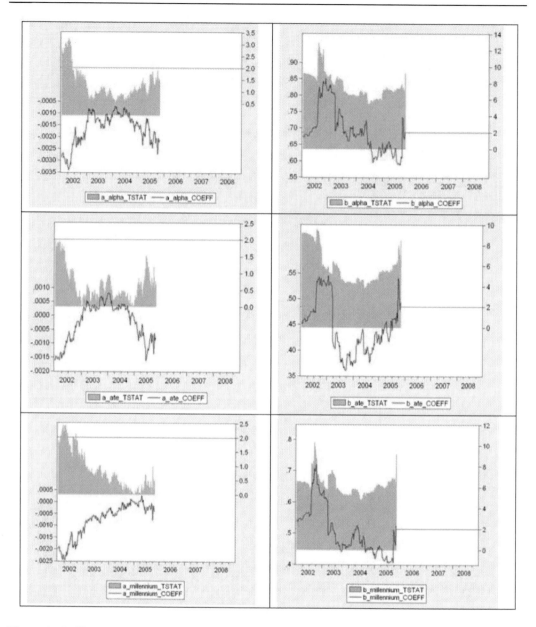

Figure 4c. Rolling Regression investing in USA.

In the final part of the empirical section the results from estimating equation five about timing skills are presented in table 3. The γ coefficient is positive in 5 out of 11 cases, however it is not statistically significant. Therefore fund managers even if they change asset allocation as can be implied by the time varying betas they cannot achieve better performance and they do not have any timing skills. Moreover in some cases the γ coefficients are negative and statistically significant implying that the fund managers, especially in funds investing worldwide, reduce their systematic risk when the market is in an upward trend.

Table 3. Coefficient for Timing Skills presence

Mutual Funds	γ coefficient (Timing Skill)	Mutual Funds	γ coefficient (Timing Skill)	Mutual Funds	γ coefficient (Timing Skill)
Global		*Europe*		*America*	
Allianz	-3,1799	Alpha	0,2579	Alpha	0,0408
	(-5,42)***		(-1.77)		(0,04)
Ing	0,4983	Interam	-4,7687	Millennium	0,6062
	(-1,74)		(-4.17)***		(0,66)
Dilos	-1,5460	Dilos	-0,6401	Ate	0,2633
	(-3,44)***		(-1,18)		(0,45)
Marfin	-0,2766	Hsbc	-0,1271		
	(-0,48)		(-0,29)		

CONCLUSIONS

Given that previous literature concerning mutual funds and market efficiency is focused on USA and other developed markets, our study shed light on fund managers behaviour from a small country that invest abroad. A significant downtrend for many years in the Greek market made investments abroad attractive for Greek investors. Therefore there has been a significant development on mutual fund industry concerning funds investing abroad. However the performance of such type of funds was not persistent.

Our study by investigating Greek fund managers investing abroad concludes the following. First the fund managers failed to beat the market even if there were some occasions of abnormal returns. These limited cases of abnormal returns are missing from funds investing in the USA. Second, there was evidence of time varying betas, implying that managers follow different strategies in order to achieve high performance. Moreover, over the recent years there is a convergence in betas for funds investing worldwide and across Europe. This finding implies that given their poor performance fund managers over the recent years try to mimic benchmark behaviour. On the contrary the betas in funds investing in USA are low especially in period of increasing performance. Third, by combining alpha and beta behaviour we can say that high performance in Europe and worldwide coexist with low levels of betas. Finally there is evidence of no timing skills across fund managers providing evidence against market efficiency in its strong form assuming that fund managers have access to public and private information.

REFERENCES

Adler, M., and Dumas, B., (1983) "International portfolio choice and corporate finance: a synthesis," *Journal of Finance,* 38(3), 925-984.

Ambachtsheer, K. P., (1974) "Profit potential in an "almost efficient" market" *The Journal of Portfolio Management*, Fall, 84-87.

Babalos, V. Kostakis, A., and Philippas, N., (2007) "Spurious results in testing mutual fund performance persistence: evidence from the Greek market," *Applied Financial Economics Letters*, 3(2), 103-108.

Babalos, V., Caporale, G.M., Kostakis A., and Philippas N., (2008) "Testing for persistence in mutual fund performance and the ex-post verification problem: evidence from the Greek market," *European Journal of Finance*, 14(8), 735-753.

Babalos, V., Kostakis, A. and Philippas, N., (2009) "Managing mutual funds or managing expense ratios? Evidence from the Greek fund industry," *Journal of Multinational Financial Management*, 19(4), 256-272.

Brennan, M. J., Cao, H.H., Strong, N., and Xu X., (2005) "The dynamics of international equity market expectations," *Journal of Financial Economics,* 77, 257–288.

Caporale, G.M., Philippas, N., and Pittis, N., (2004) "Feedbacks between mutual fund flows and security returns: evidence from the Greek capital market," Applied Financial Economics, 14(14), 981-989.

Carhart, M.M., (1997) "On Persistence in Mutual Fund Performance," *The Journal of Finance,* 52(1), 57-82

Chang, E.C., Lewellen, W.G., (1984) "Market Timing and Mutual Fund Investment Performance" *The Journal of Business*, 57(1), 57-72

Choe, H., Kho, B-C., and Stulz, R., (1999) "Do foreign investors destabilize stock markets? The Korean experience in 1997," *Journal of Financial Economics*, 54, 227-264.

Cooper, I., and Kaplanis, E., (1994) "Home Bias in Equity Portfolios, Inflation Hedging, and International Capital Market Equilibrium," *Review of Financial Studies,* 7, 45-60.

Daniel, K., Grinblatt, M., Titman, S., Wermers, R., (1997) "Measuring Mutual Fund Performance with Characteristic-Based Benchmarks," *The Journal of Finance*, 52(3), 1035-1058.

Dritsakis, N., Grose, C., Kalyvas, L., (2006) "Performance aspects of Greek bond mutual funds," *International Review of Financial Analysis*, 15(2), 189-202.

Elton, E. J., Gruber, M. J., Das, S., Hlavka, M., (1993) "Efficiency with Costly Information: A Reinterpretation of Evidence from Managed Portfolios," *The Review of Financial Studies*, 6(1), 1-22.

Fama, E (1965) "Random Walks In Stock Market Prices", *Financial Analysts Journal*, 21 (5), 55–59.

Fama, E., (1970) "Efficient Capital Markets: A Review of Theory and Empirical Work," *The Journal of Finance*, 25 (2), 383-417.

Fama, E., (1976) "Efficient Capital Markets: Reply," *The Journal of Finance*, 31(1), 143-145.

Graham, J.R., Harvey, C.R., and Huang, H., (2005) "Investor Competence, Trading Frequency, and Home Bias," NBER Working Paper No. W11426.

Griffin, J.M., Nardari, F. and Stulz R.M., (2004) "Are daily cross-border equity flows pushed or pulled?", *Review of Economics and Statistics,* 86, 641–657.

Grinblatt, M., and Keloharju, M., (2000) "The investment behavior and performance of various investor types: A study of Finland's unique data set", *Journal of Financial Economics* 55, 43-67.

Grinblatt, M., Titman, S. and Wermers, R., (1995) "Momentum investment strategies, portfolio performance, and herding: A study of mutual fund behavior," *American Economic Review,* 85, 1088-1105.

Henriksson, R. D., (1984) "Market Timing and Mutual Fund Performance: An Empirical Investigation," *The Journal of Business*, 57(1), 73-96.

Ippolito, R.A., (1989) "Efficiency With Costly Information: A Study of Mutual Fund Performance, 1965-1984," *The Quarterly Journal of Economics*, 104(1), 1-23.

Jaffe, J.F., (1974) "Special Information and Insider Trading", *The Journal of Business*, 47(3), 410-428.

Jensen, M. C., (1968) "The Performance of Mutual Funds in the Period 1945-1964" *The Journal of Finance*, 23(2), 389-416.

Kilka, M., and Weber, M., (2000) "Home Bias in International Stock Return Expectations," *The Journal of Psychology and Financial Markets,* 1(3/4), 176-192.

Malkiel, B.G., (1995) "Returns from Investing in Equity Mutual Funds 1971 to 1991," *The Journal of Finance*, 50(2), 549-572.

Papadamou, S., and Siriopoulos, C., (2004) "American Equity Mutual Funds in European Markets: Hot Hands Phenomenon and Style Analysis," *International Journal of Finance and Economics*, 9(2), 85–97.

Philippas, N., (1999) "Are Greek Mutual Fund Managers Market Timers?," *European Research Studies Journal*, II(1-4), pages 33-42.

Sharpe, W. F. (1966): "Mutual Fund Performance" *The Journal of Business*, 39(1), 119-138.

Shukla, R. K., and Van Inwegen, G.B., (1995) "Do locals perform better than foreigners?: An analysis of UK and US mutual fund managers", *Journal of Economics and Business* 47, 241-254.

Siriopoulos, C. (1999) *International Capital Markets Volume I, Theory and Analysis*, Ed. Anikoula, Thessaloniki, (In Greek).

Strong, N., and Xu, X., (2003) "Understanding the Equity Home Bias: Evidence from Survey Data", *Review of Economics and Statistics*, 85(2), 307-312.

Thomadakis S., Ksanthakis M. (2006) *Money and Capital Markets, Banking Science Theory and Practice*, Greek Banking Association, Ed. Stamoulis, Athens, (In Greek).

In: Financial Services: Efficiency and Risk Management
Editors: M. D. Fethi, C. Gaganis et al.

ISBN: 978-1-62100-560-5
© 2012 Nova Science Publishers, Inc.

Chapter 8

ACCOUNTING CHOICE THEORY: DERIVATIVES FAIR VALUE IN BANKS IN BRAZIL

Bruna Perlingeiro Iannazzo[1*], Luiz Nelson Guedes de Carvalho[2*], Gerlando Augusto S. Franco de Lima[3*] and Iran Siqueira Lima[4*]

[1] Masters Degree Student (2007-2009) Department of Accounting and Actuarial Sciences
University of Sao Paulo
Av. Prof. Luciano Gualberto,
908 – FEA 3 – Cidade Universitária,
05508-900 São Paulo/SP Brazil.

[2] Professor Department of Accounting and Actuarial Sciences
University of Sao Paulo
Av. Prof. Luciano Gualberto, 908 – FEA 3 – Cidade Universitária,
05508-900 São Paulo/SP Brazil.

[3] Professor Department of Accounting and Actuarial Sciences
University of Sao Paulo
Av. Prof. Luciano Gualberto, 908 – FEA 3 – Cidade Universitária,
05508-900 São Paulo/SP Brazil.

[4] Professor Department of Accounting and Actuarial Sciences
University of Sao Paulo
Av. Prof. Luciano Gualberto, 908 – FEA 3 – Cidade Universitária,
05508-900 São Paulo/SP Brazil.

Abstract

The purpose is to verify whether there are Earnings Management practices (regarding Accounting Choices) resulting from the impact of accounting for derivatives in Bank institutions available in Brazil under Brazil's Central Bank supervision. One of the innovations presented is that in addition to the use of all Banks on the specified date, which consists of a census, those practices have their focus on Accounting Choice Theory. The approach of the paper is an empirical-analytical one, and its general hypothesis is that there is no Earnings Management for all considered institutions. Additionally, the method considers the panel data analysis and regressions with dummy variables. The classification for the use of these variables includes: size of the Banks; origin; differed levels of Corporate Governance; and accompaniment by analysts. The data range from 2002 to 2008, for 158 Banks, with 1044 observations. In the models, the evidence points out that it was not possible to identify Earnings Management through Accounting Choices. It means that empirical evidence was not found in the Banks in Brazil, regardless of the size, origin, differed levels of Corporate Governance and accompaniment by analysts using accounting for derivatives as a tool for Earnings Management.

Keywords: Bank Accounting; Financial Markets; Derivatives; Brazil

1. Introduction

The various number of derivatives used for hedging, speculation and arbitrage evolved considerably since the initial ones, much simpler, known as Plain Vanilla. Considering Banks, (such as: Barings, Bank Negara Tanah Melayu, Chemical Bank, Credit Lyonnais, Daiwa, Kidder Peabody, Marka and Fonte-Cindam (in Brazil), Midland Bank, National Westminster Bank, Société Générale and Sumitomo) among different disasters that occurred in recent years, these institutions were involved in corporate scandals, widely disclosed by the media and research. (GALDI; LOPES, 2007, p. 397; HULL, 2005, p. 528; POLICARPO JUNIOR, 2001; LOPES; LIMA, 2003, p. 5-6; VISCUSI; CHASSANY, 2008).

Due to that fact, the necessity for improvement has been recognized in the Transparency of Financial Statements; Harmonization of accounting standards and Accounting for derivatives, mainly by standard-setters – International Accounting Standards Board (IASB); Financial Accounting Standards Board (FASB) and government agencies (Brazilian Central Bank or *Banco Central do Brasil*/Bacen and Brazilian Securities and Exchange Commission/*Comissão de Valores Mobiliários*).

Because of this necessity for improvement, there has been a search for greater understanding of what is Earnings Management and what the boundaries are between what is or is not allowed by the Generally Accepted Accounting Principles (GAAP). Thus, trying to accomplish goals and certain interests, one may not accurately capture the accounting, financial-economic and tributary impacts of an organization.

Earnings Management is one of the components of the Accounting Choice Theory (ACT) and we focus on the options among alternative practices in the accounting for derivatives.

Practitioners and academics that deal with accounting might have a deficiency in the knowledge toward such subject, which includes derivatives and their accounting parts in the Financial Statements. So, it seems that this discipline has been supported (mainly) by disclosure of positions and effects in Foot Notes (lacking an accounting model that is universally consecrated and that serves as a benchmark).

In addition, it seems that the task of storing all the information of the market has been very difficult (due to either legal limits or GAAP), mainly with regard to the accounting for financial instruments in the Financial Statements. Another important feature is the metric. The criteria for assets and liabilities' measurement has always been surrounded by discussions and divergences. Lately, the target has been the Historical Cost (HC) and Fair Value (FV), which means that different choices exist for the same event, given different interests. Thus, subjectivity is part of the accounting process.

The importance of this topic represents the fact that from 2010 onwards, all companies listed on the stock exchange in Brazil will have to present their Financial Statements, according to IFRS (International Financial Reporting Standards) from IASB (as required by Instruction CVM 457, of 13th July 2007); Banks will also comply according to Bacen's Communication 14259 on March 10th, 2006.

Thus, the problem to be analysed is:

What are the factors that affect Accounting Choices, regarding Earnings Management, in accounting for derivatives in Banks in Brazil?

To answer this question, we use six models of Panel Data, in order to find out the extent to which derivatives and their accounting practices impact Banks, by considering ACT as a background. One of the purposes is to analyse whether, under Bacen's supervision, there is Earnings Management provided by the impact of accounting for derivatives in Banks in Brazil. To determine whether there is Earnings Management, we use size, origin, differenced levels of Corporate Governance (CG) and whether accompaniment by analysts have any influence.

This chapter is divided as follows: this first part, the introduction, that presents the issue to be studied and its importance; the second part, theoretical background, hypotheses and relevant remarks about Fair Value and accounting for derivatives in Brazil; the third part research design with specification of variables and econometric models detailed; forth, results and interpretations; fifth, conclusion.

2. Theoretical Background and Hypotheses

Fields et al. (2001, p. 256) define Accounting Choice (AC) as "any decision whose primary purpose is to influence (either in form or substance) the output of the accounting system in a particular way, including not only financial statements published in accordance with GAAP, but also tax returns and regulatory filings".

The authors discuss the subject, by building a delimitation of three proxies of influence:

i) agency costs are related to contractual issues, such as: managerial compensation and debt covenants (e.g. executives compensation and managerial opportunism to value maximization); ii) information asymmetries refer to the relationship between (better informed) managers and (less well informed) investors (e.g. asset pricing motivations, through accounting numbers and stocks price return, as well as capital cost and disclosure politics – the more companies disclose information, the lower their/third parties capital costs become), and iii) externalities are generally related to third party contractual and non-contractual relationships (*Ibid*, 2001).

The literature about AC has been criticizing managers that search for advantages toward the flexibility allowed by accounting standards, due to the possibility of earnings manipulation in situations where it is possible to use discretion (*Ibid*, 2001). The concept that fairly describes this issue, while choosing among different accounting policies is called Earnings Management (EM).

Schipper (1989, p. 92) defines that managing earnings is a purposeful intervention in the external financial reporting process, with the intent of obtaining some private gain. Healy and Wahlen (1999, p. 368) broaden the concept, by evidencing judgment on behalf of managers in elaborating financial statements:

> "Earnings management occurs when managers use judgment in financial reporting and in structuring transactions to alter financial reports to either mislead some stakeholders about the underlying economic performance of the company or to influence contractual outcomes that depend on reported accounting numbers" (HEALY; WAHLEN, 1999, p. 368).

In accordance with this definition, the importance of the role of CG in Financial Institutions is clear. Barton and Simko (2002 p. 24-25) explain that the balance sheet accumulates the effects of previous AC and the level of net assets partly reflects the extent of previous EM. Thus, considering that the more regulated sectors are (Banks) the less discretionary choices, so that CG in those sectors also act on their valuation, performance and behavior toward risk-taking (POLO, 2007, p. 2).

EM is part of ACT, motivations for manipulation are usually linked to capital markets; contracts (such as covenants); CEO compensation; loans and their conventions; regulation and political costs; in order to sustain performances that converge with the analysts expectations. Also, the separation of the property and control can introduce additional incentives for EM purposes and sustain non-optimal asset portfolios. (MARTINEZ, 2001, p. 38-9; GALAI *et al.*, 2003, p. 17).

Banks exercise CG in companies, as creditors, and their practices are crucial for the progress of the economy. In Brazil, the differenced levels of CG (Level 1, Level 2 and New Market, implemented in December 2000) are special segments of listing that were developed with the aim at providing a transaction environment, that could stimulate investors' interests and the value of the companies to increase (BM&FBOVESPA, 2009).

The CG in Banks of underdeveloped countries, such as Brazil, is particularly important for some reasons: i) Banks possess strong and dominant positions in financial systems, and are the core for economic growth; ii) Banks are typically the main financial source for companies, because in these economies, financial markets are generally underdeveloped (KING; LEVINE, 1993b; LEVINE, 1997, ARUN; TURNER, 2004); iii) They are the main depositaries for the national savings; iv) Recently, most of these economies entered in a liberalization process of their banking systems, through privatization and reduction of the role of economic regulation (ARUN; TURNER, 2004).

Given the previous details, the problem of CG tends to be worse in Banks, because, while information asymmetries (e.g. moral hazard and adverse selection) disturb all corporations, Banks are particularly opaque, so it is very difficult for stakeholders to try to monitor and valuate managers in these institutions. For that reason, the opacity of the banking industry, jointly with pervasive governmental regulations, limit CG and it becomes even more difficult for those in emergent economies (comparing to those in developed ones) (CAPRIO; LEVINE, 2002).

Thus, this peculiar nature requires stakeholders' protection, mainly depositaries against opportunistic banking management that can be held by accounting for derivatives through FV.

2.1. Fair value, Accounting for Derivatives in Brazil and its Relevant Features: A Remark

Goulart (2007, p. 106-7) states that among accounting for derivatives, opportunities for EM activities arise in the classification of operations, such as: hedge or speculation, market-to-market and effective realization (or undone). Relevant comments are with respect to the classification as: i) hedge can induce smooth results, and ii) market-to-market, opportunities increase in choices for measures that result in greater (smaller) amounts for assets (liabilities) favorably.

Moreover, when the market price is not available, it is necessary to estimate the Fair Value (FV), which involves subjectivity in the accounting for derivatives and enables EM.

According to IASB (2007, p. 1367) FV *"is the amount for which an asset could be exchanged, or a liability settled, between knowledgeable, willing parties in an arm's length transaction"*.

FV has been recurrent in the literature, as well as the discussion about the extension in which it can be considered an appropriate measure for different types of financial instruments. In Brazil, for example, the HC Accounting has been adopted. However, in 2001, an approach similar to the one used by the FASB 115 – *Accounting for Certain Investments in Debt and Equity Securities* (1993) –, that deals with FV measurement, was adopted by Bacen in the *Circular* 3.068/01.

In January 2002, the Bacen issued another normative – *Circular* 3082 – that incorporated recommendations of the IASB and the FASB standards. This was done, by undertaking the recognition of derivatives as assets and liabilities, and accordingly with FV, adopted as the market value measure, when available (BACEN, 2002).

Lopes and Martins (2007, p. 52-3) explain that the two main traditions: Civil and Common Laws are different views as a means of didactic aims, since it is not probable that just one of them can be found purely and solely in one country.

Italy, France, Germany, Portugal, Spain and other countries that used to be Iberian colonies (including Brazil) adopt Civil Law, so that the standards in these countries emanate from the law. In contrast, in the other regime (Common Law), that comprises the United States, Canada, Australia, New Zealand, Malaysia and the United Kingdom, the origin of regulation is basically linked to traditions and customs.

These authors point out that the accounting system suffers intense regulation in the former regime. In Brazil, the two main examples are: the Corporate Law 6404/76, which regulates the accounting for companies, traded in the Brazilian stock exchange, and Cosif, that is the accounting plan for the institutions in the National Financial System. Therefore, strong governmental presence in accounting.

As shown, the differences in both legal models influence, not only the accounting practices, but also CG in institutions in different countries. This is of extreme relevance, since the convergence into the IFRS in Brazil took place in 2010, and they are issued by Common Law countries (the UK and the US). Thus, this fact causes a concern, since Brazil tends to value the concept of HC; and Common Law's (the UK and the US), FV.

The former metric (HC) is more objective if compared to the latter (FV), because assertions can be done through verifying documents and it fits easier in Civil Law countries. While the latter needs estimation, it is the essence of the transaction over the accounting form. (LOPES; MARTINS, 2007, p. 53-4).

Consequently, FV adoption by the Bacen (especially with regard to the IFRS convergence in 2010) differs from the traditional approach of HC, as a parameter of measurement and that provides a foundation to the Corporate Law 6404/76. This fact will reflect (significantly) in the divergences upon the current accounting practices and in the effects that tend to influence the earnings and equity of entities.

Accordingly, the hypotheses, based on what is stated above and on the problem presented in the introduction are:

Methodological Hypothesis 1: There is no EM for all banking institutions operating in Brazil, under Bacen's supervision (data base on 12/1/2008). Even if there is no rejection of this hypothesis, the choice was to carry out the subsequent ones, with the aim at verifying the relationship among the variables in the factors (size, origin, differenced levels of CG and accompaniment by analysts);

Methodological Hypothesis 2: The size of the Bank does not influence EM practices;

Methodological Hypothesis 3: The origin of the Bank does not influence EM practices;

Methodological Hypothesis 4: The differenced levels of Corporate Governance do not influence EM practices;

Methodological Hypothesis 5: The accompaniment by analysts does not influence EM practices.

All of the hypotheses are presented in the negative form, because that would be the implied intuition of the expected result in each of them.

3. Research Design

We attempt to verify whether there is EM (through AC), provided by the impact of accounting for derivatives (in ACT approach) in Banks in Brazil, under Bancen's supervision.

The data are provided by derivatives' accounts in the population of Banks in December 2008. The approach of this chapter is empirical-analytical and according to Martins (2002, p. 34) are techniques of collection, treatment and data analysis, which are remarkably quantitative in practical studies and promote causal relations among variables.

The method performed is Panel Data Analysis. It has three common approaches: Pooling, Fixed and Random Effects. To decide between Fixed and Random Effects, it uses the Hausman Test (W Test), that tests whether the coefficients of the models are systematically different, regardless of the correlation between the non-observed and explaining variables.

For Random Effects and Pooling, we use the Breusch-Pagan Test (1980), which is a LM Test (Lagrange Multiplier Test) that verifies whether the variance of the non-observed effect is statistically different from zero, and if it is equal to zero the Pooling will be consistent and efficient.

In addition, the Baltagi and Li Test (1995) for idiosyncratic errors' serial autocorrelation of first order and Baltagi and Li Test (1991), that tests jointly whether the variance of the non-observed component is equal to zero and whether there is serial autocorrelation of first order in the residues. If the use of Pooling is not statistically rejected, we use this model, but if it is, it will be used the model of Panel Data, with Fixed or Random Effects.

We use 158 Banks for seven years, the period ranges from 2002 (beginning of the accounting standards for derivatives in Brazil) to 2008, and the institutions are the same in all of them, which means that there were not variations through time. Also, for each unit of cross-section there was the same number of time series, except for 23 Banks. Thus, the panel data is unbalanced.

3.1. Specification of Variables

The variables below are compounded by the accounts from the Accounting Plan (*Plano Contábil*) of Balance Sheet and Income Statement of the financial institutions, obtained through the Trimestral Financial Information (*Informações Financeiras Trimestrais* – IFT), that belongs to Bacen. The Banks under analysis are found in the appendix (Table 10).

$Rderiv_{it}$ = Derivatives' Result for Bank i in year t (account 10.1.1.10.10.16) – also known as ("Operations Income with Derivatves");

LL_{it} = Net Profit/Loss of the Bank i in the year t (account 10.0.0.00.00.00);

$LLantes_{it}$ = Net Profit/Loss excluding Rderivit for Bank i in year t;

Derivativos_AC_{it} = Derivatives' Balance in Short Term Assets for Bank i in year t (account 10.1.3.85.00.00);

Derivativos_RLP_{it} = Derivatives' Balance in Long Term Assets for Bank i in year t (account 10.2.3.85.00.00);

Derivativos_PC_{it} = Derivatives' Balance in Short Term Liabilities for Bank i in year t (account 40.1.9.87.00.00);

Derivativos_ELP_{it} = Derivatives' Balance in Long Term Liabilities for Bank i in year t (account 40.2.9.87.00.00);

$PosLiq_{it}$ = Derivatives' Net position (Asset - Liability) for Bank i in year t;

$AjFV_{it}$ = Equity balance (adjustments through fair value of Bonds available for sale and cash flow hedges) for Bank i in year t (account 40.6.7.00.00.00);

$RBIFin_{it}$ = Financial Intermediation Gross Result for Bank i in year t (account 10.1.1.10.00.00);

$RTVM_{it}$ = Operations Result (Bonds and Securities) for Bank i in year t (account 10.1.1.10.10.15);

$RCamb_{it}$ = Forex Operations Result for Bank i in year t (account 10.1.1.10.10.17);

$Ativo\_Total_{it}$ = Total Assets for Bank i in year t (account 10.0.0.00.00.00).

3.2. Econometric Models

Before carrying out the models for the tests, the values of the accounts (above specified) were transformed into scale, which means that all the variables were divided by the Total Assets of the period. This procedure is suggested by Brown, Lo, Lys (1999) to avoid the problem of the scale effect. Thus, when we reference (from here onwards) about any of the variables, it is understood that it is the account scaled by Total Assets of the Bank i in the year t.

Galdi and Pereira (2007, p. 13) analize the data to identify the relationship between the Rderiv and other accounts and positions of the Banks. For that, six models were developed:

Model 1 verifies whether the accounting for 'Derivatives' Result' fits in the concept of FV. The premise is that when there are negative results with derivatives, it will incite a consequent reduction of the Assets in derivatives or an increase in the account 'Derivatives' Balance for Liabilities' (either Short or Long Terms):

$$Rderiv_{it} = \beta_{0i} + \beta_1 DerivativoAC_{it} + \beta_2 DerivativoPC_{it} + \beta_3 DerivativoRLP_{it} + \beta_4 DerivativoELP_{it} + u_{it} \tag{1}$$

The next five hypotheses (after the verification of the use of the FV's concept in Model 1) aim at investigating the relationship between 'Derivatives' Result' and different variables (accounts) for EM:

Model 2 tests the relationship between 'Derivatives' Result' and Net Profit/Loss (excluding Rderiv). This enables the identification of the strategy of the hedge:

$$Rderiv_{it} = \beta_{0i} + \beta_1 LLantes_{it} + u_{it} \tag{2}$$

Model 3 tests whether 'Derivatives' Result' account of the Banks analyzed is influenced by 'Financial Intermediation Gross Result', which is composed of Result with Credit Operations, Leasing, Operations with Bonds, Securities and Forex:

$$Rderiv_{it} = \beta_{0i} + \beta_1 RBIFin_{it} + u_{it} \tag{3}$$

Model 4 analyses, exclusively, the relationship between 'Derivatives' Result' and 'Operations Result (Bonds and Securities)'. This model has greater possibility of non-observable and/or omitted variable effects:

$$Rderiv_{it} = \beta_{0i} + \beta_1 RTVM_{it} + u_{it} \tag{4}$$

Model 5 assesses the relationship between 'Derivatives' Result' and 'Forex Operations Result'. That enables the validation (or not) of the influence of the Profit/Loss in that account, therefore, presence/absence of EM:

$$Rderiv_{it} = \beta_{0i} + \beta_1 RCamb_{it} + u_{it} \tag{5}$$

Model 6 consists of the inclusion of more result variables, including 'Forex Operations Result', in order to analyze the impact on 'Derivatives' Result'. This is an attempt not to omit any variable, which would be more harmful than adding useless ones in the model:

$$Rderiv_{it} = \beta_{0i} + \beta_1 RBIFin_{it} + \beta_2 RTVM_{it} + \beta_3 RCamb_{it} + u_{it} \quad (6)$$

As shown, in all of the models, the account 'Rderiv$_{it}$' represents the dependent variable, and in essence is the market value of the derivatives. Each derivative has a peculiarity, but all of them follow the general rule below in Brazil:

Swap: Difference of curves (Asset and Liability) + market adjustment;
Forward: Difference between the forward value and the spot value (in the case of covered sale) + market adjustment;
Futures: Daily adjustments + market adjustment;
Options: Premium and exercise value (only in the maturity) + market adjustment.

The account 'Rderiv$_{it}$' is called "Operations Income with Derivatives" (7.1.5.80.00-9) – Cosif. The subtitles are:

Swap (7.1.5.80.11-9);
Swap – Held to Maturity Hedge (7.1.5.80.13-3);
Forward (7.1.5.80.21-2);
Forward – Held to Maturity Hedge (7.1.5.80.23-6);
Futures (7.1.5.80.31-5);
Futures – Held to Maturity Hedge (7.1.5.80.33-9);
Options – Shares (7.1.5.80.39-1);
Options – Financial Assets and Commodities (7.1.5.80.42-5);
Options – Held to Maturity Hedge (7.1.5.80.43-2);
Swap Intermediation (7.1.5.80.50-4);
Credit Derivatives (7.1.5.80.60-7);
Credit Derivatives – Held to Maturity Hedge (7.1.5.80.63-8);
Others (7.1.5.80.90-6).

The purpose of these accounts is to register the incomes in operations with derivatives, according to their category, including the adjustments at market value: credited by the value of the earned profits (received or not) and debited in the Balance Sheet, in order to determine the result.

The amount in 'Rderiv$_{it}$' account is not net of taxes. It is applied, for example, PIS, Cofins, CS and IR over the result and there are some peculiarities regarding the non-deductible sum. Therefore, the result accounts mentioned are used as a basis of calculation for the determination of the amounts.

In addition to the revenue account, there is the expense account (8.1.5.50.00), and the description is the same and is valid for all subaccounts.

4. Results and Interpretations

4.1. Preliminary View through Descriptive Statistics

Table 1 presents Descriptive Statistics (mean, median and standard deviation) of the accounts under analysis:

Table Descriptive Statistics

	Mean	Median	Standard Deviation	Observations
$AjFV_{it}$	0.002069	0.000000	0.030360	1044
$Derivativos\_AC_{it}$	0.013355	0.000010	0.037912	1044
$Derivativos\_ELP_{it}$	0.005622	0.000000	0.022608	1044
$Derivativos\_PC_{it}$	0.011687	0.000090	0.031379	1044
$Derivativos\_RLP_{it}$	0.005559	0.000000	0.021161	1044
LL_{it}	0.029519	0.022055	0.114087	1044
$LLantes_{it}$	0.014735	0.013285	0.115667	1044
$PosLiq_{it}$	0.001604	0.000000	0.030734	1044
$RBIFin_{it}$	**0.088854**	**0.066860**	0.123227	1044
$Rderiv_{it}$	**-0.000214**	**0.000000**	0.035827	1044
$RTVM_{it}$	**0.070806**	**0.051230**	0.124085	1044
$RCamb_{it}$	0.008118	0.000000	0.028804	1044

$Rderiv_{it}$'s mean and median are fairly reduced if compared to $RBIFin_{it}$ and $RTVM_{it}$. In order to basis the following tested hypotheses, the histograms of the three variables are analyzed ($LLantes_{it}$, LL_{it} and $Rderiv_{it}$ – Graphs 1, 2 and 3, respectively). This analysis does not represent a formal result, it helps to understand their behavior and to identify patterns to be empirically tested.

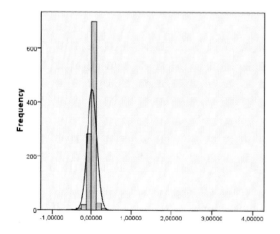

Statistics

$LLantes_{it}/AT$	
Mean	0.0147350
Median	0.0132849
Standard Dev.	0.1156665

Graph 1. Distribution of Net Profits of Banks in Brazil before the accounting for Derivatives' Result (divided by total assets).

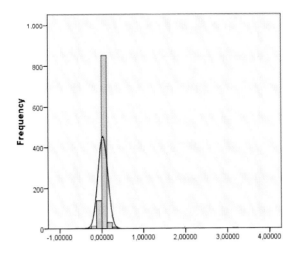

Statistics	
LL$_{it}$ (or Losses)/AT	
Mean	0.0295193
Median	0.0220556
Standard Dev.	0.1140864

Graph 2. Distribution of Net Profits of Banks in Brazil (divided by total assets).

It shows a high concentration of positive results and the visible leap in the number of Banks that present small losses to Banks that have small profits. We would expect this behavior to have been a smoother distribution in that area.

It shows that when considering Derivatives' Result, a greater number of Banks appear with positive results, and the contrary (negative results), in fewer Banks. Pointing out to the migration of these Banks, in order to obtain improved results.

It shows a high concentration in small positive results, surpassing the negative results. There are also some outliers if compared to the other two previous graphs, but with no relevance, since they represent a small number of Banks.

By comparing these results with the assets' size through the frequencies in the graph, we can state that ACs in Banks in Brazil are conservative, with regard to the use of financial instruments (derivatives), because the concentration surrounds zero.

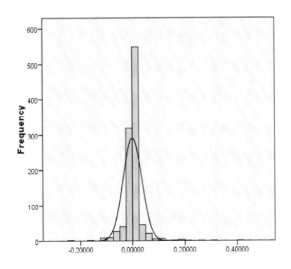

Statistics	
RDERIV$_{it}$/AT	
Mean	-0.0002138
Median	0.0000000
Standard Dev.	0.0358271

Graph 3. Distribution of Derivatives' Result of Banks in Brazil (divided by total assets).

4.2. Relationship among Variables

Before the analysis of the following tables (table 2 onwards), it is necessary to state that We aim at modeling or forecasting events; instead, it studies the relationship that exists among the variables presented (see 3.1 Specification of Variables). Thus, even if it was assessed, the level of significance expressed by p-value (0.05), was not relevant in terms of rejection of the variables (except for Chow, Hausman and Breusch-Pagan Tests). For the calculation of Fixed and Random Effects, both were employed only for the cross-sections, due to the number of Banks was greater than the time series (n>t).

Table 2 presents estimated coefficients by Pooling and the statistics for each model. Considering all the models together, there was a predominance of positive variables (except for liabilities), i.e., analyzing $Rcamb_{it}$ in the fifth model, for example, it is possible to state that for each increase in a thousand monetary units of Real (Brazilian Currency), $Rderiv_{it}$ suffers, on average, an increase of R\$ 0,076941.

The test below is used to illustrate possible breakup in a steady trend of a historical statistical series, consisting in the application of the F Test.

Table 2. Estimated Models – Pooling

		Coefficients	t-statistics	p-value
Model 1				
	Δ DerivativoAC$_{it}$	0.173422	2.321578	**0.0204**
	Δ DerivativoPC$_{it}$	-0.064599	-0.559552	0.5759
	Δ DerivativoRLP$_{it}$	0.439012	3.135807	**0.0018**
	Δ DerivativoELP$_{it}$	-0.301183	-2.962784	**0.0031**
	Constant	-0.002522	-2.549380	0.0109
Model 2				
	LLantes$_{it}$	0.025267	0.998541	0.3182
	Constant	-0.000586	-0.436868	0.6623
Model 3				
	RBIfin$_{it}$	0.031572	1.641505	0.1010
	Constant	-0.003019	-1.491058	0.1362
Model 4				
	RTVM$_{it}$	0.017783	0.847902	0.3967
	Constant	-0.001473	-0.854833	0.3928
Model 5				
	Rcamb$_{it}$	0.076941	1.934531	0.0533
	Constant	-0.000838	-0.753825	0.4511
Model 6				
	RBIfin$_{it}$	0.031214	1.771905	0.0767
	RTVM$_{it}$	0.000628	0.032022	0.9745
	Rcamb$_{it}$	0.076484	1.918112	0.0554
	Constant	-0.003653	-1.676603	0.0939

Accounting the Choice Theory

Table 3. Chow Tests (Pooling versus Fixed Effects)

	Effects Test	p-value
Model 1	Cross-section F	0.6671
	Cross-section Chi-square	0.3698
Model 2	Cross-section F	0.5698
	Cross-section Chi-square	0.2851
Model 3	Cross-section F	0.5500
	Cross-section Chi-square	0.2678
Model 4	Cross-section F	0.5551
	Cross-section Chi-square	0.2722
Model 5	Cross-section F	0.5292
	Cross-section Chi-square	0.2504
Model 6	Cross-section F	0.5809
	Cross-section Chi-square	0.2886

By not rejecting the null hypothesis (the intercept is the same for all cross-sections and, Pooling is preferred over Fixed Effect for all models), the following test carried out is the Breuch-Pagan, together with Baltagi and Li (1995) and Baltagi and Li (1991).

Table 4 assess whether the variance of the non-observable component is equal to zero, and whether there is serial autocorrelation of first order in the residues, respectively. The result of the test points out that in none of the models there was the rejection of the null hypothesis, and that the variance of the observable component is equal to zero.

The Breusch-Pagan test demonstrates that the variance of the residues that reflect individual differences is equal to zero, and the Pooling approach is the most suitable to be used, since the residues will not form any utility in the variables of the model.

Furthermore, the Baltagi and Li combined test for all models accept that the variance of the non-observable component equals zero, and at the same time it also accepts that there is no residual first order serial autocorrelation. Thus, the use of panel data with Pooling is recommended for all models, because it is not possible to ensure that the estimation of the other two approaches (Fixed and Random Effects) is consistent and efficient.

Table 4. Breusch-Pagan and Baltagi and Li (p-values)

	Breusch-Pagan two-tailed test	Baltagi e Li (1995)	Baltagi e Li (1991) combined
Model 1	0.5954	0.7310	0.8665
Model 2	0.9841	0.9030	0.9911
Model 3	0.9520	0.8765	0.9876
Model 4	0.9446	0.8726	0.9870
Model 5	0.9359	0.9862	0.9942
Model 6	0.9955	0.9162	0.9927

Table 5. Hausman Test

	p-value
Model 1	0.0000
Model 2	0.5896
Model 3	0.9194
Model 4	0.5658
Model 5	0.8927
Model 6	0.6712

The Hausman test on, Table 5, is merely illustrative, had the Chow test indicated Fixed Effect and not Pooling, it may have been used:

In accordance with the Hausman test, above, which tests whether the coefficients of Fixed and Random Effects are systematically different, only represented in Model 1, and could have rejected the null hypothesis. This means that, it would be considered that the estimators of Fixed and Random Effects are different. In contrast, in the other models, it does not cause the same effect and, and the correction model of the errors could have worked (Random Effect).

Before proceeding to the analysis for each model, it is necessary to mention that the coefficients of the constants are not examined, because they do not have further relevance. Therefore, the fact that all of them are negative, does not impact the results and final considerations.

Model 1: there is the (expected) relationship among the 'Derivatives' Result' and the variation of the Assets and Liabilities derivative's accounts. This means positive coefficients in the former, and negative in the latter (this occurs, due to the use of FV accounting for derivatives).

Coefficients b_1, b_3 and b_4 (Δ DerivativoAC$_{it}$, Δ DerivativoRLP$_{it}$ and Δ DerivativoELP$_{it}$, respectively) were significant (0.05), apart from b_2 (Δ DerivativoPC$_{it}$). This fact may have occurred since there was a reduced number of this sort of operation in the Banks analyzed.

Model 2, on the contrary to what would be intuitively economic, the relationship between 'Derivatives' Result' and Net Profit/Loss was inversely proportional to the greater the Rderiv$_{it}$, the smaller the LLantes$_{it}$. This points out to the existence of a direct relationship – positive coefficient 0.025267. However, this result does not have relevant impact on the model, since the coefficient was not significant.

The idea for this scenario is that Banks did not use derivatives with exclusive concern of protecting results (hedge), as stated by Galdi and Pereira in their model (2007), and possibly speculating in the market. In addition, there was the significance of coefficient b_1.

Model 3 presents a relationship that is not statistically significant between Rderiv$_{it}$ and RBIfin$_{it}$, so that the latter (independent variable) does not impact the former (dependent variable). In constrast, Perlingeiro *et al.* (2008), found the significance in the same model for a smaller sample and time series.

Model 4 considers Rderiv$_{it}$ with RTVM$_{it}$. Galdi and Pereira (2007) highlight that those securities are also valuated (Available for Sale, for example) by FV and one could expect a significant relationship among variables.

In contrast to the results found in Galdi and Pereira (2007), (negative coefficient in the majority of the cases), the coefficient was positive (0.017783). This may point out to possible speculation existance. In comparison to Galdi and Pereira (2007), we could indicate a greater development and sophistication reached by the Banks in Brazil if we compare to the beginning of derivatives' accounting standards in Brazil). This fact was corroborated by Perlingeiro *et al.* (2008).

Model 5 aims at verifying the behavior between $Rderiv_{it}$ and $Rcamb_{it}$. That account includes Forex transactions. The presence of floating rate confirms the search for security also provided by derivatives, such as operations with futures contracts of American dollar or swaps indexed to another currency, for example.

The result shows the existence of a direct relationship (positive coefficient b_1 0.076941) among the variables studied. This fact points out to purposes that are not likely to be only hedging activities, but also speculative. However, there is no significance for b_1 under 0.05.

Table 6. Panel Data Regressions with Dummy for Size – Attribute is Bank to be Large

		Coefficients	t-statistics	p-value
Model 1				
	Δ DerivativoAC$_{it}$	0.173589	2.316329	0.0207
	Δ DerivativoPC$_{it}$	-0.063326	-0.546821	0.5846
	Δ DerivativoRLP$_{it}$	0.442075	3.166353	0.0016
	Δ DerivativoELP$_{it}$	-0.302290	-2.957297	0.0032
	Dummy	**-0.001307**	**-0.646392**	**0.5182**
	Constant	-0.001869	-1.196374	0.2318
Model 2				
	LLantes$_{it}$	0.025387	1.002970	0.3161
	Dummy	**0.000673**	**0.306177**	**0.7595**
	Constant	-0.000938	-0.537184	0.5913
Model 3				
	RBIfin$_{it}$	0.033292	1.654215	0.0984
	Dummy	**0.002093**	**0.860725**	**0.3896**
	Constant	-0.004262	-1.538547	0.1242
Model 4				
	RTVM$_{it}$	0.018037	0.861311	0.3893
	Dummy	**0.000789**	**0.362287**	**0.7172**
	Constant	-0.001902	-0.946997	0.3439
Model 5				
	Rcamb$_{it}$	0.077766	1.947887	0.0517
	Dummy	**0.000724**	**0.326028**	**0.7445**
	Constant	-0.001222	-0.779164	0.4361
Model 6				
	RBIfin$_{it}$	0.033379	0.019057	0.0801
	RTVM$_{it}$	0.000255	0.019611	0.9896
	Rcamb$_{it}$	0.079321	0.040130	0.0483
	Dummy	**0.002402**	**0.002457**	**0.3285**
	Constant	-0.005093	-1.782065	0.0750

Model 6 presents the relationship among $Rderiv_{it}$ and independent variables $RBIfin_{it}$, $RTVM_{it}$ and $Rcamb_{it}$ (coefficients b_1, b_2 and b_3, respectively). All of them are not statistically significant under 0.05. Conversely, in their studies, Galdi and Pereira (2007) and Perlingeiro *et al.* (2008) found negative coefficient for $Rcamb_{it}$. This indicates that it is likely that institutions could have been taking hedge positions in Forex derivatives and losses occurred.

Regarding the size of the Banks, Table 6 presents the estimated coefficients by Panel Data regressions, in which the dummy variable represents the attribute of the Bank to be large. The statistics for each of the established models are:

This table shows that statistical significance occurred for the dummy. This means that the characteristic of the Bank's size, to be large, and possibly presents incidence of EM, is not part of the reality in Banks in Brazil.

Table 7. Panel Data Regressions with Dummy for Origin – Attribute is Bank to be Brazilian

		Coefficients	t-statistics	p-value
Model 1				
	Δ DerivativoAC$_{it}$	0.194155	2.571347	0.0103
	Δ DerivativoPC$_{it}$	-0.064911	-0.558518	0.5766
	Δ DerivativoRLP$_{it}$	0.462242	3.294547	0.0010
	Δ DerivativoELP$_{it}$	-0.310556	-3.026242	0.0025
	Dummy	**0.007191**	**2.787804**	**0.0054**
	Constant	-0.007790	-3.196171	0.0014
Model 2				
	LLantes$_{it}$	0.024822	0.982061	0.3263
	Dummy	**0.000802**	**0.284313**	**0.7762**
	Constant	-0.001128	-0.403797	0.6864
Model 3				
	RBIfin$_{it}$	0.031570	1.609685	0.1078
	Dummy	**0.00000219**	**0.000712**	**0.9994**
	Constant	-0.003020	-0.970529	0.3320
Model 4				
	RTVM$_{it}$	0.017568	0.836212	0.4032
	Dummy	**0.001470**	**0.485730**	**0.6273**
	Constant	-0.002463	-0.777492	0.4370
Model 5				
	Rcamb$_{it}$	0.084639	2.031905	0.0424
	Dummy	**0.002610**	**0.832665**	**0.4052**
	Constant	-0.002686	-0.886829	0.3754
Model 6				
	RBIfin$_{it}$	0.030382	1.710212	0.0875
	RTVM$_{it}$	0.000864	0.044127	0.9648
	Rcamb$_{it}$	0.079222	1.909666	0.0565
	Dummy	**0.000951**	**0.302904**	**0.7620**
	Constant	-0.004268	-1.278252	0.2014

In all of the models, except for the first one, the dummy was positive, and demonstrating that if the contrary was observed, i.e. 'being large' was a significant factor, it could occur greater incidence of positive results with EM practices.

Regarding the origin of the Banks and the level of EM, Table 7 presents the estimated coefficients by Panel Data regressions. In this scenario, the dummy represented to be a Brazilian Bank, and the statistics for each of the established models are:

This table shows that only the first Model presented statistical significance of the dummy. Thus, considering the other models jointly, the attribute of the Bank to be Brazilian and possibly presenting incidence of EM is not true for the Banks and the period analyzed.

In all models, the dummy was positive, demonstrating that if the contrary were to be observed: 'being Brazilian' was a significant issue, this could incur a greater number of positive results, due to EM practices.

Table 8. Panel Data Regressions with Dummy for Corporate Governance – Attribute is Bank to be in any of the Differenced Levels (Level 1, Level 2 or New Market)

		Coefficients	t-statistics	p-value
Model 1				
	Δ DerivativoAC$_{it}$	0.173225	2.316905	0.0207
	Δ DerivativoPC$_{it}$	-0.064607	-0.559453	0.5760
	Δ DerivativoRLP$_{it}$	0.439117	3.134543	0.0018
	Δ DerivativoELP$_{it}$	-0.301446	-2.960693	0.0031
	Dummy	**-0.000545**	**-0.288853**	**0.7728**
	Constant	-0.002471	-2.334180	0.0198
Model 2				
	LLantes$_{it}$	0.025303	1.001478	0.3168
	Dummy	**-0.001676**	**-0.819261**	**0.4128**
	Constant	-0.000441	-0.308124	0.7580
Model 3				
	RBIfin$_{it}$	0.031533	1.639122	0.1015
	Dummy	**-0.001419**	**-0.678128**	**0.4978**
	Constant	-0.002892	-1.385603	0.1662
Model 4				
	RTVM$_{it}$	0.017662	0.839822	0.4012
	Dummy	**-0.001257**	**-0.599784**	**0.5488**
	Constant	-0.001355	-0.749674	0.4536
Model 5				
	Rcamb$_{it}$	0.076698	1.928313	0.0541
	Dummy	**-0.001451**	**-0.704068**	**0.4815**
	Constant	-0.000710	-0.588961	0.5560
Model 6				
	RBIfin$_{it}$	0.031250	1.773906	0.0764
	RTVM$_{it}$	0.000489	0.024922	0.9801
	Rcamb$_{it}$	0.076313	1.913499	0.0560
	Dummy	**-0.001278**	**-0.614810**	**0.5388**
	Constant	-0.003533	-1.572253	0.1162

Regarding the different levels of CG in Banks, which distinguishes among those that are or are not placed on Level 1, 2 or New Market and EM practices, Table 8 presents the estimated coefficients by Panel Data regressions, in which the dummy variable represents the attribute of the Bank to adopt any of the three levels, and the statistics for each of the established models are:

Table 8 shows that in none of the models there was the statistical significance of the dummy variable, which means that, the attribute of the Bank to be in any of the three differenced levels of CG, and possibly present incidence of EM, does not make part of the reality in Banks under Bacen's supervision in Brazil.

Table 9. Panel Data Regressions with Dummy for Accompaniment by Analysts – Attribute is Bank to be Accompanied

		Coefficients	t-statistics	p-value
Model 1				
	Δ DerivativoAC$_{it}$	0.173497	2.319452	0.0206
	Δ DerivativoPC$_{it}$	-0.064586	-0.559225	0.5761
	Δ DerivativoRLP$_{it}$	0.438971	3.132717	0.0018
	Δ DerivativoELP$_{it}$	-0.301083	-2.955929	0.0032
	Dummy	**0.000178**	**0.105117**	**0.9163**
	Constant	-0.002542	-2.356088	0.0187
Model 2				
	LLantes$_{it}$	0.025280	0.999810	0.3176
	Dummy	**-0.000944**	**-0.508588**	**0.6111**
	Constant	-0.000485	-0.332789	0.7394
Model 3				
	RBIfin$_{it}$	0.031532	1.636770	0.1020
	Dummy	**-0.000436**	**-0.228349**	**0.8194**
	Constant	-0.002969	-1.396930	0.1627
Model 4				
	RTVM$_{it}$	0.017719	0.843097	0.3994
	Dummy	**-0.000586**	**-0.310035**	**0.7566**
	Constant	-0.001406	-0.769883	0.4415
Model 5				
	Rcamb$_{it}$	0.076720	1.928827	0.0540
	Dummy	**-0.000676**	**-0.362718**	**0.7169**
	Constant	-0.000764	-0.619551	0.5357
Model 6				
	RBIfin$_{it}$	0.031203	1.768858	0.0772
	RTVM$_{it}$	0.000611	0.031162	0.9751
	Rcamb$_{it}$	0.076419	1.916140	0.0556
	Dummy	**-0.000214**	**-0.112690**	**0.9103**
	Constant	-0.003627	-1.590354	0.1121

Accounting the Choice Theory

Table 10. Banks under Analysis: Data Base 2002-2008

BANCO A. J. RENNER S.A.	BANCO LEMON S.A.
BANCO ABC BRASIL S.A.	BANCO LUSO BRASILEIRO S.A.
BANCO ABN AMRO REAL S.A.	BANCO MATONE S.A.
BANCO ALFA S.A.	BANCO MÁXIMA S.A.
BANCO ALVORADA S.A.	BANCO MAXINVEST S.A.
BANCO ARBI S.A.	BANCO MERCANTIL DO BRASIL S.A.
BANCO AZTECA DO BRASIL S.A.	BANCO MERCEDES-BENZ DO BRASIL S.A.
BANCO BANERJ S.A.	BANCO MODAL S.A.
BANCO BANESTADO S.A.	BANCO MONEO S.A.
BANCO BANKPAR S.A.	BANCO MORADA S.A
BANCO BARCLAYS S.A.	BANCO MORGAN STANLEY S.A.
BANCO BBM S.A.	BANCO NOSSA CAIXA S.A.
BANCO BEG S.A.	BANCO OPPORTUNITY S.A.
BANCO BGN S.A.	BANCO OURINVEST S.A.
BANCO BM&F S.A.	BANCO PANAMERICANO S.A.
BANCO BMG S.A.	BANCO PAULISTA S.A.
BANCO BNP PARIBAS BRASIL S.A.	BANCO PECUNIA S.A.
BANCO BOAVISTA INTERATLANTICO S.A.	BANCO PINE S.A.
BANCO BONSUCESSO S.A.	BANCO PORTO SEGURO S.A.
BANCO BRADESCO BBI S.A.	BANCO POTTENCIAL S.A.
BANCO BRADESCO CARTÕES S.A.	BANCO PROSPER S.A.
BANCO BRADESCO S.A.	BANCO PSA FINANCE BRASIL S.A.
BANCO BRASCAN S.A.	BANCO RABOBANK INTERNATIONAL BRASIL S.A.
BANCO BRJ S.A.	BANCO RENDIMENTO S.A.
BANCO BVA S.A.	BANCO RIBEIRAO PRETO S.A.
BANCO CACIQUE S.A.	BANCO RODOBENS S.A.
BANCO CALYON BRASIL S.A.	BANCO RURAL MAIS S.A.
BANCO CAPITAL S.A.	BANCO RURAL S.A.
BANCO CARGILL S.A.	BANCO SAFRA S.A.
BANCO CARREFOUR S.A.	BANCO SANTANDER S.A.
BANCO CEDULA S.A.	BANCO SCHAHIN S.A.
BANCO CITIBANK S.A.	BANCO SEMEAR S.A.
BANCO CITICARD S.A.	BANCO SIMPLES S.A.
BANCO CLASSICO S.A.	BANCO SOCIETE GENERALE BRASIL S.A.
BANCO CNH CAPITAL S.A.	BANCO SOFISA S.A.
BANCO COMMERCIAL INVESTMENT TRUST DO BRASIL S.A.	BANCO SUMITOMO MITSUI BRASILEIRO S.A.
BANCO CR2 S.A.	BANCO TOYOTA DO BRASIL S.A.
BANCO CREDIBEL S.A.	BANCO TRIANGULO S.A.

Table 10. Continued

BANCO CREDIT SUISSE S.A.	BANCO TRICURY S.A.
BANCO CRUZEIRO DO SUL S.A.	BANCO UBS PACTUAL S.A.
BANCO DAYCOVAL S.A.	BANCO ÚNICO S.A.
BANCO DE LA NACION ARGENTINA	BANCO VOLKSWAGEN S.A.
BANCO DE LA PROVINCIA DE BUENOS AIRES	BANCO VOLVO BRASIL S.A.
BANCO DE LA REPUBLICA ORIENTAL DEL URUGUAY	BANCO VOTORANTIM S.A.
BANCO DE LAGE LANDEN BRASIL S.A.	BANCO VR S.A.
BANCO DE TOKYO-MITSUBISHI UFJ BRASIL S/A	BANCO WESTLB DO BRASIL S.A.
BANCO DIBENS S.A.	BANCO YAMAHA MOTOR DO BRASIL S.A.
BANCO FATOR S.A.	BANCOOB
BANCO FIAT S.A.	BANDEPE
BANCO FIBRA S.A.	BANESE S.A.
BANCO FICSA S.A.	BANESTES S.A.
BANCO FINASA BMC S.A.	BANIF S.A.
BANCO FININVEST S.A.	BANPARÁ S.A.
BANCO FORD S.A.	BANRISUL S.A.
BANCO GE CAPITAL S.A.	BANSICREDI S.A.
BANCO GERDAU S.A	BASA S.A.
BANCO GMAC S/A	BB BANCO POPULAR DO BRASIL S.A.
BANCO GUANABARA S.A.	BB S.A.
BANCO HONDA S.A.	BEP S.A.
BANCO IBI S.A.	BNB S.A.
BANCO IBM S.A.	BPN S.A.
BANCO INDUSTRIAL DO BRASIL S.A.	BRB S.A.
BANCO INDUSTRIAL E COMERCIAL S.A.	CEF
BANCO INDUSVAL S.A.	CITIBANK N.A.
BANCO INTERCAP S.A.	CONCÓRDIA BANCO S.A.
BANCO INTERMEDIUM S/A	DEUTSCHE BANK S.A.
BANCO INVESTCRED UNIBANCO S.A.	DRESDNER BANK BRASIL S.A.
BANCO ITAÚ BBA S.A.	GOLDMAN SACHS DO BRASIL S.A.
BANCO ITAÚ HOLDING FINANCEIRA S.A.	HIPERCARD S.A.
BANCO ITAÚ S.A.	HSBC BANK BRASIL S.A.
BANCO ITAUBANK S.A.	ING BANK N.V.
BANCO ITAUCARD S.A.	JBS BANCO S.A.
BANCO ITAUCRED FINANCIAMENTOS S.A.	JPMORGAN CHASE BANK, NATIONAL ASSOCIATION
BANCO ITAULEASING S.A.	NATIXIS BRASIL S.A.
BANCO J. SAFRA S.A.	NBC BANK BRASIL S. A.

BANCO J.P. MORGAN S.A.	PARANÁ BANCO S.A.
BANCO JOHN DEERE S.A.	SUDAMERIS S.A.
BANCO KDB DO BRASIL S.A.	UNIBANCO S.A.
BANCO KEB DO BRASIL S.A.	UNICARD S.A.

In all of the models, for the first time, the dummy variable was negative, pointing out that if the contrary was observed, which means that 'being in any of the three differenced levels of CG' was significant factor, it could occur greater incidence of negative results with EM practices. This scenario illustrates that CG can strengthen the idea of Banks tending to present smaller profits or smaller losses for stakeholders. Thus, confirming what was previously stated, with regard to the presentation of conservative results.

With respect to the accompaniment by analysts, the table below presents the estimated coefficients by Panel Data regressions, in which the dummy variable represents the attribute of the Bank to be accompanied by these professionals, and the statistics for each of the established models are:

In this case, the majority of dummies were equal to the previous Panel Data regression (Bank in any of the three Differenced Levels of CG) from Table 8, except for *Banestes* (which did not present attribute for Corporate Governance, but for accompaniment by analysts), *Unibanco* (*idem*) and *Itaú* (*idem*).

Table 9 shows that none of the models display a statistical significance of the dummy. This means that the Bank to be accompanied by analysts, and possibly present an incidence of EM, is not part of the Banks studied.

In all of the models, except for the first one, the dummy is negative, demonstrating that if the contrary was observed, 'being accompaniment by analysts' was a significant issue; it could incur a higher incidence of negative results with EM practices.

5. CONCLUSION

The aim was to assess the existence of EM, provided by the impact of accounting for derivatives in Banks in Brazil under Bacen's supervision (in 12/1/2008) with ACT as a background.

Empirical analysis answered the research problem presented in the introduction. Among the factors, we considered important issues for the Brazilian scenario, such as size, origin, differenced levels of CG and accompaniment by analysts. For the estimation of the models, the method in the research design was Panel Data techniques, as well as regression with dummy variables. This approach promoted the quantitative analysis of the economic relationships, gathering time-series and cross-sectional data in the same model.

The evidence points out to the absence of EM practices. This means that there is no empirical demonstration that Banks in Brazil, regardless of the size, origin, differenced levels of CG and accompaniment by analysts, use accounting for derivatives as a tool for EM.

Yet, as stated before, the aim of this chapter is not to employ modeling techniques or attempt to build any sort of forecast with the variables (accounts) presented, but to study the relationship among them. Thus, even if there is absence of statistical significance and lack of

EM practices, all of the proposed models were fully analyzed and indicated the respective relationships, even when there was (not) significance.

The component selected for the analysis of AC in the accounting for derivatives does not show models with any dummy statistically significant. Moreover, taking into account the four dummies selected, it is clear that if they had obtained statistical significance at 0.05, as in the first two cases (attributes: 'Large' and/or 'Brazilian'), there would have been a higher frequency of positive results in EM activities.

In order to broaden the scope, Fuji and Carvalho (2005) analyzed a specific account of expense (PCLD – *Provisão para Créditos de Liquidação Duvidosa*). In contrast, the authors found out a positive correlation between PCLD and earnings by the Banks. This finding suggests EM practices.

The *Instrução CVM n. 475/08* represents a conceptual basis that supplies guidance to the disclosure of the Demonstrative Sensitivity Analysis (*Quadro Demonstrativo de Análise de Sensibilidade*) in *Deliberação CVM n. 550/08* and the requirements for companies traded in the Brazilian stock exchange. It does this with the aim at the warranty of the presentation of information that allows users to assess (adequately) the risk profile inherent to the operations within the financial instruments (mainly derivatives). This is done through a qualitative analysis of the five largest Banks (*Banco Itaú S.A., Banco do Brasil S.A., Banco Bradesco S.A., Banco Santander Brasil S.A.* and *Caixa Econômica Federal*).

This scenario demonstrates that even if there is not a legal requirement for Banks, there is an incisive trend that these Financial Institutions are adhering to choices that improve disclosure information, which is demanded by different stakeholders (who are influenced by AC). This is also coherent with the good practices of CG by these institutions.

Thus, in agreement with above exposed and considering IFRS 7, the relevance becomes even more latent when considering the fact that since 2010 all of the Brazilian companies traded in the stock exchange are required to present their financial statements according to IFRS standards (*Instrução CVM n. 457/07*), and the same requirement is applicable to Banks since 2010 (*Comunicado Bacen 14.259/06*).

In summary, the limitations are recognized along with the importance of this subject for Banks under ACT. It is considered one of the most fecund fields not commonly explored in the Brazilian literature. The knowledge and research expansion are with great relevance, especially when accompanied by technical improvements in different branches of Accounting and Corporate Finance.

ACKNOWLEDGMENTS

Special thanks to Prof. Dr. Jose Elias Feres de Almeida, who provided priceless contributions toward the topic and Daniel Scott Iannazzo for revising the English translation.

REFERENCES

Arun, Thankom G.; Turner, John D. Corporate governance of banks in developing economies: concepts and issues. Corporate Governance: An International Review, vol. 12, n. 3, p. 371-377, 2004.

Baltagi, Badi H.; LI, Qi. A joint test for serial correlation and random individual effects. Statistics and Probability Letters, n. 11, p. 277-280, 1991.

_____. Testing AR(1) against MA(1) disturbances in an error component model. Journal of Econometrics, n. 68, p. 133-151, 1995.

Banco Central Do Brasil - Bacen. *Circular 3.068: Critérios para registro e avaliação contábil de Títulos e Valores Mobiliários*. Brasília: BACEN, 2001.

_____. *Circular 3.082: Critérios para registro e avaliação contábil de instrumentos financeiros derivativos*. Brasília: BACEN, 2002.

_____. *Comunicado 14.259: Procedimentos para a convergência das normas de contabilidade e auditoria aplicáveis às instituições financeiras e às demais instituições autorizadas a funcionar pelo BACEN com as normas internacionais promulgadas pelo IASB e pela International Federation of Accountants (IFAC)*. Brasília: BACEN, 2006. Available at: <https://www3.bcb.gov.br/normativo/detalharNormativo.do?N=106064950&method =detalharNormativo>. Access on: 09/07/2008.

_____. *Diagnóstico da convergência às normas internacionais* – IFRS 7 Financial Instruments: Disclosures. Brasília: BACEN, 2006. Available at: <http://www.bcb. gov.br/nor/convergencia/IFRS_7_Evidenciacao_de_Instrumentos_Financeiros.pdf>. Access on: 12/03/2009.

_____. *Informações Financeiras Trimestrais*. Brasília: BACEN, 2008. Available at: <http://www3.bcb.gov.br/iftimagem/>. Access on: 12/07/2008.

_____. *Os 50 maiores bancos brasileiros*. Brasília: BACEN, 2008. Available at: <http://www.bcb.gov.br/fis/TOP50/port/Top502007120P.asp>. Access on: 11/07/2008.

Barton, Jan; Simko, Paul J. The balance sheet as an earnings management constraint. The Accounting Review, vol.77, p. 1-27, 2002.

BOLSA DE VALORES, MERCADORIAS E FUTUROS - BM&FBOVESPA S.A.. *Governança Corporativa* – Bovespa Mais. Available at: <http://www.bovespa.com.br/ Empresas/NovoMercadoNiveis/BovespaMais.asp>. Access on: 30/04/2009.

Breusch, Trevor; PAGAN, Adrian Rodney. The Lagrange multiplier test and its applications to model specification in econometrics. Review of Economic Studies, n. 47, p. 239-253, 1980.

Brown, Stephen et al. Use of R^2 in accounting research: measuring changes in value relevance over the last four decades. Journal of Accounting and Economics, n. 28, p.83-115, 1999.

Caprio, Gerard, Levine, Ross. Corporate governance of banks: concepts and international observations. In: GLOBAL CORPORATE GOVERNANCE FORUM RESEARCH NETWORK MEETING, 2002. Washington, DC. Anais... Washington: World Bank Workshop, 2002.

COMISSÃO DE VALORES MOBILIÁRIOS - CVM. *Instrução n. 457: Dispõe sobre a elaboração e divulgação das demonstrações financeiras consolidadas, com base no padrão contábil internacional emitido pelo* International Accounting Standards Board – IASB, de 13 de julho de 2007.

_____. *Deliberação n. 550: Apresentação de informações sobre instrumentos financeiros derivativos em nota explicativa às Informações Trimestrais – ITR, de 17 de outubro de 2008.*

_____. *Instrução n. 475: Dispõe sobre a apresentação de informações sobre instrumentos financeiros, em nota explicativa específica, e sobre a divulgação do quadro demonstrativo de análise de sensibilidade, de 17 de dezembro de 2008.*

Fields, Thomas D. et al.. Empirical research on accounting choice. Journal of Accounting and Economics, vol. 31, issues 1-3, p. 255–307, 2001.

Fuji, Alessandra Hirano; Carvalho, Luiz Nelson Guedes de. Earnings management *no contexto bancário brasileiro.* In: CONGRESSO USP DE CONTROLADORIA E CONTABILIDADE, 5., 2005. São Paulo. Anais... São Paulo: USP, 2005.

Galai, Dan *et al.. Accounting values versus market values and earnings management in banks.* The Interdisciplinary Center, Herzliya. School of Business – The Hebrew University of Jerusalém, 2003.

Galdi, Fernando Caio; Pereira, Leonel Molero. Fair value *dos derivativos e gerenciamento de resultados nos bancos brasileiros: existe manipulação?* In: ENCONTRO BRASILEIRO DE FINANÇAS - SBFIN, 7., São Paulo, 2007. Anais... São Paulo: SBFIN, 2007.

_____; LOPES, Alexsandro Broedel. *Derivativos.* In: LIMA, I. S. et al. (Coord.) *Curso de Mercado Financeiro: Tópicos Especiais.* São Paulo: Atlas, 2007.

Goulart, André Moura Cintra. *Evidenciação contábil do risco de mercado por instituições financeiras no Brasil.* São Paulo, 2003. Dissertação (Mestrado) – Programa de Pós Graduação em Ciências Contábeis, Departamento de Contabilidade e Atuária, Faculdade de Economia, Administração e Contabilidade da Universidade de São Paulo.

_____. *Gerenciamento de resultados contábeis em instituições financeiras no Brasil.* São Paulo, 2007. Tese (Doutorado) – Programa de Pós Graduação em Ciências Contábeis, Departamento de Contabilidade e Atuária, Faculdade de Economia, Administração e Contabilidade da Universidade de São Paulo.

Healy, Paul M.; Wahlen, James M. A review of the earnings management literature and its implications for standard setting. Accounting Horizons, vol. 13, n. 4, 12/1999.

Hull, John C. *Fundamentos dos mercados futuros e de opções.* 4. ed. São Paulo: Bolsa de Mercadorias & Futuros, 2005.

International Accounting Standards Board - IASB. International Financial Reporting Standards (IFRSs) – International Accounting Standard (IAS) 32: Financial Instruments: Presentation, 2007.

_____. International Financial Reporting Standards (IFRSs) – International Accounting Standard (IAS) 39: Financial Instruments: Recognition and Measurement, 2007.

King, Robert G.; Levine, Ross. Finance and growth: Schumpeter might be right. The Quarterly Journal of Economics, vol. 108, n. 3, p. 717-737, 1993.

Levine, Ross. Financial development and economic growth: views and agenda. Journal of Economic Literature, 1997.

Lopes, Alexsandro Broedel; LIMA, Iran Siqueira. *Contabilidade e controle de operações com derivativos.* São Paulo: Pioneira Thomson Learning, 2003.

_____; MARTINS, Eliseu. *Teoria da contabilidade: uma nova abordagem.* São Paulo: Atlas, 2007.

Martinez, Antônio Lopo. *"Gerenciamento" dos resultados contábeis: estudo empírico das companhias abertas brasileiras.* São Paulo, 2001. Tese (Doutorado) – Programa de Pós Graduação em Ciências Contábeis, Departamento de Contabilidade e Atuária, Faculdade de Economia, Administração e Contabilidade da Universidade de São Paulo.

Martins, Gilberto de Andrade. *Manual para elaboração de monografias e dissertações.* São Paulo: 3. ed. São Paulo: Atlas, 2002.

Perlingeiro, Bruna et al. *Gerenciamento de resultados acerca da análise do impacto da contabilização de derivativos com base no fair value: evidência dos bancos brasileiros.* In: XII Congresso de Contabilidade e Auditoria, 12., 2008, Aveiro. Anais... Portugal, 2008.

Plano Contábil das Instituições do Sistema Financeiro Nacional - COSIF. *Conta 7.1.5.80.00-9 - Rendas em Operações com Derivativos.* Disponível em: <http://www.cosif.com.br/mostra.asp?arquivo=contas71580>. Access on: 10/05/2009.

Policarpo Junior. *As marcas do Marka: Escândalo do Marka assusta o governo, desencadeia um alarido – e já é reinvestigado.* Revista Veja, Edição 1 702, 30 de maio de 2001.

Polo, Andrea. Corporate governance of banks: the current state of the debate. Personal RePEc Archive (MPRA). Paper n. 2325, posted 7, 11/2007. Available at: < http://mpra.ub.uni-muenchen.de/2325/>. Access on: 13/05/2009.

Schipper, Katherine. Commentary on earnings management. Accounting Horizons, vol. 3, n. 4, 1989.

Viscusi, Gregory; Chassany, Anne-Sylvaine. Société Générale reports EU4.9 billion trading loss. Bloomberg, January, 24th, 2008. Available at: <http://www.bloomberg.com/apps/news?pid=20601087&sid=aTNMJaurCbB8&refer=home, Access on: 30/01/2009.

INDEX

A

access, ix, 28, 31, 163, 168, 169, 201

accessibility, 52

accounting, ix, 2, 10, 17, 18, 21, 24, 43, 87, 109, 163, 169, 177, 205, 206, 207, 208, 209, 210, 211, 212, 214, 218, 219, 225, 226, 227, 228

Accounting Choice Theory, vi, ix, 205, 206

accounting standards, 109, 206, 207, 211, 219

accurate models, 160

acquisitions, vii, 1, 6, 11, 26, 32, 33, 34, 35, 36, 37, 38, 39, 94, 96

ACs, 215

adjustment, 213

adverse effects, vii, 41, 58

agencies, 57, 206

agriculture, 68

algorithm, 56

allocative efficiency, 28

amortization, 27

anatomy, 36

antitrust, 18, 33

arbitrage, 206

Argentina, 146, 151, 154, 159

artificial intelligence, 45, 46, 61

assessment, 39, 106

asymmetric information, 189

asymmetry, 29

Austria, 25, 56, 95, 97, 98, 108, 109, 127, 193

authorities, 27, 96, 127, 151, 159, 160

authority, 30

B

balance of payments, 30

balance sheet, 43, 44, 49, 50, 61, 100, 102, 108, 109, 110, 127, 208, 227

bank capitalization, vii, 41, 51, 52, 55, 57, 58

bank efficiency, vii, 25, 34, 40, 41, 42, 58, 61, 103, 136

bank failure, 30

bank holding companies, 31, 39

bank mergers, vii, 1, 3, 4, 5, 6, 7, 8, 11, 13, 14, 16, 17, 18, 19, 20, 22, 23, 24, 25, 26, 27, 28, 32, 33, 34, 35, 36, 37, 39

Bank of England, 184

bank profits, 20

bankers, 37

banking back- office process, vii, 63

banking department, 74, 75, 81

banking industry, 1, 4, 14, 15, 20, 21, 32, 33, 34, 36, 38, 39, 62, 94, 96, 208

banking sector, vii, viii, 1, 4, 7, 14, 15, 17, 20, 28, 35, 42, 44, 45, 46, 49, 56, 57, 60, 61, 62, 93, 94, 95, 96, 97, 100, 102, 103, 117, 121, 126, 127, 134, 136, 160

Banking Supervision, viii, 30, 94, 133, 139, 140, 159, 161

bankruptcy, 142

bargaining, 10

232 Index

barriers, vii, 1, 7, 14, 15, 18, 19, 20, 26, 99, 133, 169
base, viii, 4, 5, 84, 95, 109, 139, 140, 151, 154, 159, 210, 227, 229
Basel Committee, viii, 30, 94, 133, 139, 140, 159, 161
Belgium, 95, 96, 97, 98, 108, 109, 118, 127, 193
benchmarking, 45, 46, 48, 91
benchmarks, 191
benefits, 5, 7, 12, 20, 21, 25, 26, 27, 102, 164, 166, 184, 188, 189, 190
bias, ix, 43, 187, 188
bond market, 39
bondholders, 22
bonds, 42, 71, 73, 74, 75, 79, 83, 85, 101
borrowers, 57
Brazil, vi, ix, 146, 151, 154, 205, 206, 207, 208, 209, 210, 211, 213, 214, 215, 219, 220, 222, 225
breakdown, 101
Britain, 101
building societies, 103
business cycle, 127
business model, 127
business processes, vii, 63, 64, 76
businesses, 43, 94, 127
buyer, 164
buyers, 11, 12

```
┌─────────────────────────────────┐
│                C                │
└─────────────────────────────────┘
```

capital adequacy, 28, 30, 99, 110, 119, 123, 124, 126
capital flows, 30
capital markets, 101, 192, 208
case studies, 39, 70
case study, 61, 70, 188
cash, 11, 12, 13, 21, 25, 26, 27, 71, 110, 165, 169, 211
cash flow, 11, 13, 21, 26, 211
casting, 151
catastrophes, 141
category a, 9, 154
category b, 194
CBS, 140

CCR, 66, 76, 82, 83
CEE, 11, 12
central bank, 127
Central Counterparty Clearing (CCP Clearing), ix, 163
Central Europe, 34
Central Securities Depositories (CSDs), ix, 163, 166, 168
challenges, 9, 25, 26, 74, 94, 100, 126
changing environment, 101
Chicago, 34, 39, 161, 184, 185
classification, ix, 46, 74, 206, 209
clients, 17, 43
cluster analysis, 44, 46, 56, 58, 61
clustering, 46, 56, 57, 91, 144, 145
clusters, 45, 46, 56, 57, 81, 147
collateral, 71
color, iv
commodity, 141
common law, 99
communication, 75
community, 32, 36, 188
comparative analysis, viii, 62, 93, 95
compensation, 6, 27, 28, 34, 39, 207, 208
compensation package, 6
competition, 2, 7, 11, 14, 18, 19, 42, 60, 94, 96, 99, 100, 102, 167, 168, 178, 183, 191
competitiveness, 45, 94, 95, 127
competitors, 18, 117, 118, 119, 120, 122, 123, 124, 125, 191
complexity, 66, 80
compliance, 172
complications, 172
computation, 172, 173, 174, 182
computer, 102, 105
computer technology, 105
conference, 105, 185
conflict, 14, 35
CONGRESS, iv
consensus, 22, 23, 180
consolidation, vii, 1, 2, 3, 4, 7, 8, 13, 15, 18, 20, 21, 23, 30, 33, 34, 36, 45, 96, 99, 100, 127, 133, 182
construction, 105
consulting, 45

consumers, 24, 36, 100

consumption, 127

controversial, 180

convergence, 30, 38, 179, 201, 209, 210

conviction, 23

cooperation, 168, 169

copyright, iv

Copyright, iv

corporate finance, 201

corporate scandals, 206

correlation, 52, 69, 77, 95, 102, 190, 191, 210, 227

correlation analysis, 95

correlations, 52

cost, viii, 5, 8, 9, 10, 13, 14, 15, 18, 20, 21, 22, 23, 24, 26, 28, 29, 32, 33, 35, 45, 46, 48, 49, 74, 89, 93, 94, 100, 102, 103, 104, 109, 110, 126, 127, 133, 134, 135, 172, 188, 189, 207

cost saving, 8, 15, 20, 22, 23, 28, 102, 103

cost structures, 46

covering, 16, 44, 49, 190

creditors, 208

crises, 42, 44, 45, 57, 60, 101, 154, 164

criticism, 166

Croatia, 146, 147, 150

CSD, 70, 167, 168

CT, 206

culture, 96

currency, 18, 42, 74, 75, 82, 83, 84, 85, 94, 173, 192, 219

current account, 210

customers, 8, 16, 49, 50, 52, 167

CV, 73

Czech Republic, 61, 146, 151, 159

D

damages, iv

data analysis, ix, 205, 210

Data Envelopment Analysis (DEA), vii, 41, 42, 44, 47, 57, 63, 64

data mining, 46

data set, 44, 46, 47, 49, 144, 189, 202

database, 3, 193

DEA, vii, 38, 41, 42, 44, 45, 46, 47, 48, 49, 50, 54, 57, 62, 63, 64, 65, 66, 68, 69, 72, 76, 77, 78, 82, 83, 88, 89, 90, 91, 103, 104, 106, 127

debts, 101

deconcentration, 96

decreasing returns, 48

deficiencies, 142

deficiency, 206

deficit, 159

DEL, 224

Denmark, 95, 96, 97, 98, 102, 108, 109, 118, 127, 193

Department of the Treasury, 31

dependent variable, 48, 52, 55, 68, 69, 83, 88, 213, 218

deposit accounts, 31

depository institutions, 31

deposits, 7, 36, 43, 44, 46, 49, 50, 52, 99, 102, 109, 119, 126

depression, 100

depth, 145, 180

deregulation, vii, 1, 4, 8, 11, 15, 21, 22, 45, 62, 94, 96, 99, 100, 133

derivatives, vii, ix, 15, 100, 101, 141, 205, 206, 207, 208, 209, 210, 211, 212, 213, 215, 218, 219, 220, 225, 226

destruction, 7, 9, 14, 24

developing countries, 11

deviation, 106

dimensionality, 46, 144

direct cost, 172

direct costs, 172

directives, viii, 99, 139, 140, 154, 156, 158, 159

disclosure, 18, 166, 206, 207, 226

discontinuity, 65

discrete variable, 67, 89

diseconomies of scale, 102

distribution, 80, 140, 141, 142, 143, 144, 145, 146, 147, 159, 215

divergence, 188

diversification, 4, 5, 7, 8, 9, 15, 16, 17, 18, 25, 26, 27, 28, 29, 36, 38, 96, 134, 135, 190

domestic markets, 80, 187

E

dominance, 20
draft, 182
drying, 101

earnings, vii, 207, 208, 210, 226, 227, 228, 229
Eastern Europe, 11, 25, 36, 135
ECOFIN, 183
Economic and Monetary Union, 96
economic crisis, 43, 100
economic development, 135, 187
economic downturn, 100
economic growth, 2, 94, 208, 228
economic integration, 2
economic performance, 208
economic progress, 11
economic relations, 225
economies of scale, 5, 7, 8, 13, 26, 102, 135, 168, 179
editors, iv
efficiency level, 8, 26, 27
elaboration, 171, 176, 177, 179
e-mail, 75, 167
emerging markets, 11, 29
empirical studies, 4, 188, 190
employees, 28, 45, 51, 52, 95
employment, 24, 96
employment growth, 96
EMS, 99
EMU, 26, 32, 96, 127
endorsements, 49
engineering, 137
environment, vii, viii, 2, 3, 15, 18, 42, 43, 67, 90, 93, 95, 100, 126, 127, 134, 164, 191, 192, 208
environmental characteristics, 91
environmental factors, vii, 8, 63, 66
environmental influences, 66
environmental variables, 48, 66, 134
equilibrium, 189, 190
equilibrium price, 189
equipment, 50
equities, 169

equity, ix, 22, 27, 30, 31, 52, 99, 101, 117, 120, 121, 124, 141, 163, 164, 165, 170, 172, 180, 187, 188, 190, 191, 192, 202, 210
equity market, ix, 163, 164, 165, 170, 172, 180, 188, 202
ester, 103
EU, v, viii, 1, 2, 3, 4, 9, 11, 15, 17, 18, 19, 20, 23, 24, 30, 32, 36, 37, 39, 62, 93, 95, 99, 103, 104, 108, 109, 126, 127, 133, 134, 169, 170, 173, 183, 185
Europe, vii, 1, 3, 7, 14, 15, 17, 18, 19, 20, 21, 22, 23, 24, 28, 29, 32, 34, 36, 37, 38, 39, 40, 103, 113, 123, 134, 137, 167, 169, 170, 176, 179, 180, 183, 184, 185, 188, 191, 192, 193, 196, 197, 199, 201
European Central Bank, 3, 4, 8, 20, 36, 134, 185
European Commercial banks, viii, 93
European Commission, ix, 3, 19, 20, 36, 163, 164, 167, 168, 169, 170, 172, 173, 178, 180, 183
European integration, 134
European market, ix, 3, 15, 25, 94, 96, 104, 163, 164, 167, 169
European Parliament, 19
European policy, 3
European Union, iv, viii, 1, 20, 37, 62, 75, 94, 95, 96, 107, 108, 126, 136, 168, 184, 185
evolution, 66, 67, 68, 164, 167, 177, 180
excess demand, 15
exchange rate, 43, 173
exclusion, 50, 84, 146
execution, 35, 70, 72, 168
exercise, 154, 208, 213
exploitation, 5, 94
exports, 127
exposure, 99, 166, 178
external financing, 13
externalities, 166, 179, 207

F

factor analysis, 46

faith, 31

fat, 151

FDIC, 31, 38

Federal Reserve, 31, 32, 33, 37, 38, 39, 40, 136, 161, 184, 185

Federal Reserve Board, 37, 39, 161

filters, 147

financial condition, viii, 127, 139

financial XE "financial" crisis, vii, viii, 42, 43, 93, 95, 101, 118, 126

financial data, 108

financial deepening, 49, 61

financial firms, 94

financial XE "financial" institutions, vii, viii, 15, 16, 18, 23, 24, 27, 33, 34, 38, 45, 48, 50, 61, 63, 94, 95, 96, 100, 103, 117, 133, 136, 139, 142, 211

financial intermediaries, 48

financial markets, viii, 32, 60, 61, 94, 96, 99, 102, 126, 134, 166, 191, 208

financial performance, 10, 33, 37, 46, 104, 124, 126

financial reports, 208

financial sector, 2, 14, 16, 17, 21, 32, 36, 42, 100, 101, 134

Financial Services Authority, 161

financial stability, 43, 61, 94, 184

financial system, viii, 14, 15, 21, 27, 42, 43, 93, 99, 102, 110, 134, 160, 164, 166, 191, 208

Finland, 96, 97, 98, 108, 109, 119, 127, 184, 188, 193, 202

firewalls, 31

firm size, 6, 24

fixed effects panel data regression, vii, 41

flexibility, 1, 5, 9, 159, 207

flight, 101

fluctuations, 119, 120, 165

force, 100, 169, 182

forecasting, 189, 191, 216

foreign banks, 11, 18, 24, 28, 32, 40, 45, 50, 52, 57, 61, 100, 104, 133, 136

foreign direct investment, 34

foreign exchange, 42, 50

formation, 30, 99, 106

foundations, 40

France, 20, 26, 96, 97, 98, 102, 104, 108, 109, 119, 127, 146, 147, 150, 154, 193, 209

freedom, 11, 18, 25, 145, 169

funding, 31, 126

funds, vii, ix, 15, 30, 31, 41, 42, 43, 44, 46, 50, 51, 52, 55, 56, 57, 58, 99, 100, 101, 110, 154, 159, 165, 166, 187, 188, 190, 191, 192, 193, 194, 195, 196, 197, 200, 201, 202

G

GDP, 11, 25, 127

GDP per capita, 11

Generally Accepted Accounting Principles, 206

Georgia, 135

Germany, 20, 25, 26, 56, 96, 97, 98, 102, 104, 108, 109, 120, 127, 134, 146, 147, 150, 151, 154, 161, 193, 209

Glass-Steagall Act, 18

globalization, 1, 8, 17, 34

governance, 27, 45, 227, 229

government intervention, 42, 43

government securities, 42

government spending, 127

governments, 95, 101, 126

Gramm-Leach-Bliley Act, 21

graph, 215

Great Britain, 100

Greece, 93, 96, 97, 98, 104, 108, 109, 121, 127, 133, 135, 188, 189, 191, 192, 193

Greek Mutual, v, ix, 187, 191, 192, 193, 203

gross domestic product, 104

Gross Domestic Product, 11, 127

grouping, 46

growth, 9, 11, 13, 22, 24, 25, 29, 42, 96, 100, 102, 192, 228

growth accounting, 102

growth rate, 11, 25, 42

guidance, 226

guidelines, 143, 151

H

health, 160
hedging, 206, 219
heteroskedasticity, 147
histogram, 214
history, 45
holding company, 32, 38, 170, 179
horizontal integration, 168
horizontal merger, 15
host, 3, 10, 20, 99, 144
House, 170, 184
human, 50, 172
human resources, 172
Hungary, 146, 150, 151, 159
Hunter, 94, 102, 104, 134, 135
hypothesis, ix, 5, 6, 7, 9, 11, 12, 13, 74, 75, 78, 84, 102, 168, 173, 188, 205, 210

I

Iceland, 193
identification, 88, 212
idiosyncratic, 210
illiquid asset, 110
IMF, 193
impact assessment, 182
imports, 127
improvements, 6, 9, 12, 18, 21, 22, 23, 24, 26, 43, 51, 103, 147, 226
in transition, 62
incidence, 220, 221, 222, 225
income, 13, 18, 22, 47, 49, 50, 52, 89, 94, 100, 102, 117, 118, 119, 120, 121, 122, 123, 124, 125, 126
increased competition, 7, 15, 26
increasing returns, 48, 103
independent variable, 42, 49, 51, 68, 77, 218, 220
India, 146, 147, 150, 151
individual differences, 217
individuals, 43, 50
Indonesia, 146, 147, 150, 151
industries, 12, 33, 37, 90, 134

industry, vii, ix, 1, 2, 4, 5, 6, 7, 8, 13, 16, 23, 29, 33, 34, 35, 36, 37, 38, 42, 45, 94, 100, 127, 133, 164, 166, 167, 168, 169, 172, 187, 188, 192, 201, 202
industry consolidation, 37, 168
inefficiency, 6, 51, 58, 65, 74, 75, 76, 88, 89, 103
inequality, 141
inflation, 43, 102, 104
information technology, 1, 94
infrastructure, 172, 183
injections, 101, 126
injury, iv
institutions, ix, 2, 3, 5, 7, 9, 11, 13, 15, 18, 20, 29, 30, 39, 40, 44, 94, 95, 96, 99, 100, 103, 104, 118, 126, 127, 140, 143, 160, 163, 166, 168, 173, 205, 206, 208, 209, 210, 211, 220, 226
integration, ix, 7, 19, 20, 26, 27, 28, 32, 33, 37, 94, 96, 100, 133, 134, 163, 167, 168, 169, 183
interbank deposits, 46, 49
interbank funds (ratio), vii, 41
interbank market, vii, 51, 101
interest margins, 64, 95, 101, 133
interest rates, 35, 42, 43, 45, 101
interference, 19
internal financing, 13
Internal Models Approach, viii, 139
international trade, 17, 83, 84, 85
internationalization, vii
interoperability, ix, 163, 167, 168, 169, 170
intervention, 72, 165, 169, 208
investment, 11, 17, 19, 26, 30, 42, 44, 50, 51, 58, 74, 75, 81, 83, 84, 85, 99, 100, 117, 188, 189, 190, 193, 196, 202
investment bank, 19, 74, 75, 81, 83, 84, 85, 100
investments, 13, 50, 55, 102, 188, 189, 201
investors, 28, 29, 48, 127, 187, 188, 189, 191, 192, 201, 202, 207, 208
Iran, vi, 205, 228
Ireland, 95, 97, 98, 100, 108, 109, 116, 121, 127, 193

issues, vii, 1, 3, 4, 14, 17, 23, 121, 123, 126, 164, 168, 187, 207, 225, 227, 228

Italy, 7, 26, 95, 97, 98, 102, 108, 109, 127, 137, 163, 167, 193, 209

iteration, 79, 80, 81, 82

J

justification, 141

K

Korea, 188

L

labour market, 20

landscape, 38, 137

language barrier, 8

laws, 17, 57

layoffs, 20

lead, 7, 8, 9, 12, 13, 15, 23, 27, 64, 69, 75, 100, 104, 142, 189, 191

legislation, 1, 15, 18, 99

lending, 31

letters of credit, 49, 50

liberalization, 11, 42, 43, 89, 96, 192, 208

LIFE, 131, 132

life cycle, 13

light, ix, 14, 51, 64, 143, 154, 160, 187, 201

linear programming, 67

liquid assets, 165, 192

liquidate, 100, 165

liquidity, vii, viii, 6, 12, 42, 44, 74, 93, 94, 101, 109, 110, 119, 121, 122, 123, 124, 126, 142, 164, 165, 192

liquidity ratio, 122

Lithuania, 146, 147, 151, 154

loan ratio, vii, 41, 42, 51, 52, 55, 56, 57, 58

loans, 15, 26, 43, 44, 45, 50, 51, 57, 58, 99, 102, 110, 117, 121, 124, 126, 133, 208

low risk, 195

lower prices, 94, 168

loyalty, 8

LTD, 110, 127

M

Macedonia, 133

macroeconomic environment, 43, 100

magnitude, 38, 77, 83, 84

majority, viii, 4, 11, 20, 25, 94, 95, 103, 118, 119, 120, 123, 124, 125, 192, 218, 225

Malaysia, 146, 147, 150, 151, 154, 209

Malmquist index, 45

man, 194

management, vii, 4, 5, 6, 7, 8, 9, 12, 13, 14, 16, 20, 24, 26, 27, 29, 34, 45, 50, 65, 66, 88, 89, 94, 100, 110, 117, 127, 164, 172, 190, 191, 208, 227, 228, 229

manipulation, 207, 208

manufacturing, 90

marginal costs, 23

marginal product, 65

market capitalization, 127, 193

market discipline, 99

market economy, 58

market share, 4, 11, 15, 17, 102, 127

market structure, 104

marketing, 5

masking, 147

mass, 146

matrix, 48, 49, 52, 194

matter, iv, 3, 61, 106, 135

measurement, vii, 49, 50, 63, 65, 71, 72, 94, 103, 104, 105, 135, 141, 206, 209, 210

measurements, 64

media, 206

median, 214

membership, 62, 165, 172, 173, 174, 176, 177, 180

mergers, iv, vii, 1, 2, 3, 4, 5, 6, 7, 8, 9, 10, 11, 12, 13, 14, 15, 16, 17, 18, 19, 20, 21, 22, 23, 24, 25, 26, 27, 28, 29, 32, 33, 34, 35, 36, 37, 38, 39, 40, 94, 96

methodology, viii, 9, 44, 46, 47, 49, 64, 93, 103, 104, 105, 108, 126, 137, 140, 171, 193, 194, 195, 197
Middle East, 61
migration, 215
Minimum Capital Requirements, viii, 139, 140, 152, 153, 159
missions, 101
misuse, 19
model specification, 227
modelling, 144
modifications, viii, 139
MOG, 169, 184
momentum, 188
monetary policy, 43
monetary union, 14
monopoly, 167, 168, 178, 184
Moon, 37
moral hazard, 52, 166, 208
Moscow, 61
motivation, 25, 42, 105, 140, 154
MTS, 167
multilateralism, 184
multiples, 147
multiplication, 141, 147, 159, 160
multiplier, 141, 143, 154, 227
multivariate analysis, 135

N

national borders, 2, 3
nationality, 133
negative effects, vii, 41
negative relation, 55, 84
negotiation, 12
net exports, 127
Netherlands, 95, 96, 97, 98, 108, 109, 123, 127, 133
neural network, 90
neutral, 25
New York, iv
New Zealand, 209
non-OECD, 49, 61
normal distribution, 159
North Africa, 61
North America, 33

Norway, 193
null, 217, 218
null hypothesis, 217, 218

O

obstacles, 20, 29, 30, 169
OECD, 17, 28, 36, 61, 136
opacity, 208
operating costs, 94, 100, 102
operations, 1, 5, 8, 10, 13, 17, 19, 20, 27, 44, 45, 52, 57, 71, 74, 100, 110, 136, 146, 209, 213, 219, 226
operations research, 45
opportunism, 207
opportunities, 7, 11, 13, 18, 45, 51, 94, 102, 166, 209
optimism, 7
ownership, 6, 10, 12, 20, 45, 52, 57, 61, 101, 170
ownership structure, 52, 170

P

parallel, 101
parameter estimation, 77
Pareto, 145, 146, 159
participants, 16, 96, 99, 169
peer group, 66
penalties, 143, 151
performance indicator, 26, 62
permission, iv
permit, 70
plants, 66
platform, 180
policy, 34, 43, 134, 182
policymakers, 101
politics, 207
poor performance, 10, 118, 121, 201
population, 80, 210
portfolio, 13, 38, 109, 126, 141, 154, 165, 190, 194, 195, 201, 202
Portugal, 62, 95, 97, 98, 108, 109, 124, 127, 193, 209, 229
positive correlation, 6, 226
positive relationship, 17, 52, 55

potential benefits, 8
pragmatism, 145
preparation, iv
present value, 21, 196
prestige, 6
price effect, 32
principles, 127, 164, 169
prior knowledge, 46
private banks, 50, 57
private information, 189, 190, 201
privatization, 11, 12, 208
probability, 17, 27, 75, 140, 142, 143, 146, 165, 191
product market, 16
production function, 65, 95, 102
production technology, 135
productive efficiency, 61, 89
productivity growth, 133
professionals, 225
profit, 5, 9, 11, 14, 18, 22, 23, 24, 26, 27, 28, 29, 32, 40, 45, 48, 51, 103, 104, 121, 134, 136, 189
profit margin, 14
profitability, vii, viii, 8, 9, 10, 16, 21, 22, 23, 24, 25, 26, 27, 38, 40, 41, 42, 52, 58, 60, 64, 93, 94, 100, 101, 104, 109, 110, 117, 118, 120, 121, 122, 123, 124, 125, 126, 133, 134, 136, 137
profitability ratios, 52, 118, 120, 122, 124, 125
protection, 17, 30, 99, 154, 208
public debt, 42
public schools, 68
public sector, 90
publishing, 173

Q

quality improvement, 26
quantification, 65

R

random walk, 188, 189, 190
reactions, 29
reality, 3, 70, 220, 222

reasoning, 11, 15
recognition, 30, 209
recommendations, iv, 209
recovery, 126
redistribution, 165
reform, 31
Reform, 31
reforms, 20, 160
regression, vii, ix, 41, 42, 44, 48, 49, 51, 52, 55, 57, 68, 69, 77, 78, 82, 83, 84, 85, 88, 104, 187, 194, 195, 225
regression equation, 104
regression line, 78, 88
regression model, 49, 68, 69, 77, 78, 88, 194
regulations, viii, 11, 17, 20, 30, 42, 99, 110, 139, 140, 154, 159, 183, 184, 208
regulatory requirements, 167
rejection, 84, 210, 216, 217
relative size, 10, 25, 27
relevance, 170, 209, 215, 218, 226, 227
reputation, 20, 43
requirements, 18, 28, 30, 31, 99, 105, 140, 141, 154, 165, 170, 172, 226
researchers, 11, 94, 101, 102, 105, 127, 183
reserves, 42, 100, 127, 159
residuals, 69, 144, 145, 147
residues, 210, 217
resilience, 160
resource management, 45
resources, 9, 30, 44, 50, 105
response, vii, 3, 19, 41, 141, 161
restrictions, 15, 18, 20, 29, 31, 42
restructuring, 13, 16, 42, 51, 96, 127
retail, 9, 19, 20, 35, 74, 75, 81, 84
returns to scale, 47, 48
revenue, 21, 23, 24, 25, 27, 28, 31, 35, 43, 46, 47, 213
rewards, 11
rights, iv, 164
risk, iv, vii, ix, 4, 5, 6, 8, 11, 16, 26, 27, 28, 29, 30, 31, 34, 36, 42, 75, 94, 99, 100, 101, 103, 109, 110, 117, 136, 140, 141, 142, 143, 159, 160, 161, 163, 164,

165, 166, 170, 178, 184, 189, 190, 191, 193, 194, 195, 200, 208, 226

risk assessment, 117

risk management, iv, vii, 140, 165, 166, 170

risk profile, 190, 226

risks, viii, 6, 15, 16, 42, 95, 110, 139, 141, 164, 165, 166, 167, 168, 169, 184, 188, 190

risk XE "risk" -taking, 208

robotics, 66

root, 147, 159, 161

rules, 30, 94, 99, 184

Russia, 61

S

safe haven, 101

safe havens, 101

safety, 27, 183

savings, 13, 20, 46, 62, 135, 208

savings banks, 46, 62, 135

scale economies, 5, 29, 33, 94, 102

scaling, 141, 150, 156, 161

school, 68

scope, 5, 8, 13, 15, 16, 17, 20, 24, 25, 26, 35, 69, 94, 102, 103, 134, 135, 136, 226

securities, vii, 2, 13, 15, 21, 24, 26, 30, 31, 32, 42, 44, 50, 63, 64, 69, 70, 71, 73, 74, 85, 88, 89, 91, 96, 101, 117, 165, 166, 170, 173, 183, 184, 187, 188, 191, 218

securities firms, 2, 24

securities settlement, vii, 63, 64, 69, 70, 71, 74, 88, 89, 166

security, 71, 140, 202, 219

selectivity, 194

self-confidence, 13

self-interest, 14

seller, 164

sensitivity, 154, 159

September 11, 100

service provider, 37, 168, 179

services, iv, vii, ix, 2, 5, 7, 8, 13, 15, 16, 19, 27, 30, 32, 33, 34, 64, 94, 96, 99,

100, 133, 163, 164, 169, 170, 172, 178, 180, 183

shape, 48, 167

shareholder value, 4, 6, 15, 18, 23, 24, 25, 26, 27, 28, 29

shareholders, 5, 6, 8, 12, 14, 16, 18, 20, 21, 22, 24, 25, 26, 27, 29, 35, 36, 38, 99, 117, 147, 150, 154

shock, 101, 126

shock waves, 101

shortfall, 159

showing, 18, 52, 57

significance level, 56, 84

signs, 122

single market, 17, 19, 34

skewness, 146

small firms, 2, 26

SNS, 115, 123, 131

software, 50, 51, 56

SP, 205

SPA, 131

Spain, 46, 62, 96, 97, 98, 100, 102, 104, 108, 109, 127, 146, 147, 151, 193, 209

specialization, 16, 38

specifications, 42, 44, 51, 140, 145, 150, 152, 153, 159, 178

speculation, 206, 209, 219

spending, 127

spillovers, 35

stability, viii, 46, 61, 93, 99, 110, 117, 118, 119, 122, 194, 197

stabilization, 43, 100

stakeholders, 208, 225, 226

standard deviation, 81, 82, 174, 193, 214

standardization, 70

state, 7, 11, 12, 18, 21, 28, 30, 31, 49, 50, 51, 52, 57, 69, 82, 99, 101, 159, 215, 216, 229

state borders, 7

state intervention, 101

states, 9, 30, 31, 69, 140, 143, 169, 209

statistics, 72, 73, 146, 193, 196, 216, 219, 220, 221, 222, 225

stock, viii, 2, 12, 20, 21, 24, 25, 27, 34, 60, 95, 100, 102, 127, 135, 139, 143,

146, 150, 159, 187, 188, 189, 190, 191, 192, 193, 197, 202, 207, 209, 226
stock exchange, 150, 192, 207, 209, 226
stock market development, 187
stock markets, viii, 2, 20, 25, 95, 139, 146, 159, 193, 197, 202
stock price, 188, 191
stockholders, 110
strategic planning, 117
stress, 141, 143
stress test, 141
stress testing, 141
stressed VaR, viii, 139, 152
structural changes, 168
structure, viii, 2, 33, 65, 67, 93, 100, 101, 102, 104, 106, 109, 126, 127, 144, 164, 165, 166, 168, 170, 174, 178, 179, 180, 182
structuring, 208
style, 189, 190
subjectivity, 207, 209
substitutes, 167
supervision, ix, 13, 18, 30, 39, 166, 205, 207, 210, 222, 225
supervisor, 20
supervisors, 99, 140, 154, 160
surplus, 32, 87
survival, 52
sustainable growth, 39
Sweden, 96, 97, 98, 108, 109, 127, 193
Switzerland, 17, 25, 146, 151, 160, 193
synthesis, 40, 201
systemic risk, 27, 29, 167

T

tactics, 24, 103
Taiwan, 62
takeover, 1, 5, 15, 24, 30, 33, 37
Tanzania, 1
target, 5, 6, 8, 9, 10, 11, 12, 13, 15, 17, 18, 21, 22, 25, 26, 27, 28, 29, 38, 206
taxation, 8
taxes, 110, 117, 118, 120, 122, 123, 124, 213

technical efficiency, 38, 48, 68, 69, 77, 90, 91, 95, 103, 134, 136
techniques, vii, 21, 24, 45, 61, 64, 65, 94, 104, 105, 151, 160, 210, 225
technological change, 94, 96
technological developments, 100
technologies, 20, 100
technology, 7, 28, 35, 50, 62, 66, 135, 191
telecommunications, 100
telephone, 30, 100
tension, 43
testing, 202
thrifts, 31
time deposits, 49
time frame, 45, 50, 56
time periods, 103
time series, 50, 144, 146, 211, 216, 218
total costs, 180
total factor productivity, 62
trade, ix, 69, 70, 71, 72, 73, 74, 75, 83, 85, 86, 88, 163, 165, 172, 173, 174, 175, 176, 181, 184, 187, 190
trade agreement, 71
trade-off, 88
trading partners, 75
traditions, 209
training, 46, 172
transaction costs, 188, 190
transaction value, 18
transactions, ix, 2, 3, 8, 10, 20, 24, 25, 38, 44, 50, 65, 70, 71, 72, 73, 74, 75, 77, 78, 80, 81, 82, 83, 84, 85, 89, 94, 163, 169, 170, 172, 173, 174, 190, 208, 219
transformation, 62, 68, 69
translation, 226
transmission, 94
transparency, ix, 96, 163, 164, 168, 169, 178, 184
transport, 30
Treasury, 31, 32
treatment, 87, 99, 141, 210
Treaty on European Union, 96
trustworthiness, 151
turbulence, 122
Turkey, vii, 41, 42, 43, 44, 45, 49, 51, 53, 56, 57, 58, 60, 61, 62

U

UK, 1, 20, 23, 25, 26, 93, 95, 96, 97, 98, 101, 102, 103, 104, 108, 109, 132, 133, 135, 146, 151, 154, 170, 175, 176, 179, 181, 182, 203, 209
underwriting, 31
unemployment rate, 102
uniform, 31, 141, 154, 169
unions, 68, 90, 94
unit cost, 23
United, 37, 39, 127, 135, 136, 139, 160, 161, 193, 209
United Kingdom, 127, 139, 160, 161, 193, 209
United States, 37, 39, 135, 136, 161, 209
urban, 28
US banking sector consolidation, vii, 1
USA, 46, 188, 190, 191, 192, 193, 196, 197, 200, 201

V

Valencia, 113, 125
validation, 69, 70, 71, 75, 84, 85, 141, 212
valuation, 2, 33, 34, 35, 36, 38, 208
Valuation, 40
variations, 16, 72, 118, 121, 122, 140, 211
VAT, 173
vector, 48, 66, 194

vein, 154
venue, 167
vertical integration, 13, 168
vertical merger, 16
visualization, 44, 46
volatility, 43, 142, 143, 144, 145, 146, 147
vulnerability, 42

W

wages, 49, 102
Washington, 62, 133, 134, 161, 227
wealth, iv, vii, 1, 4, 5, 11, 17, 24, 27, 29, 35, 36, 37, 38, 39, 40
wealth effects, 17, 37, 38
websites, 171, 172
well-being, 7
Western Europe, 11, 25
White Paper, 30, 99
wholesale, 20
withdrawal, 31
workers, 8
World Bank, 35, 134, 227
world order, 136
worldwide, 100, 101, 193, 196, 197, 200, 201

Y

yield, 15, 19, 51, 68, 88